Computers in Language Research 2

Trends in Linguistics

Studies and Monographs 19

Editor

Werner Winter

Mouton Publishers

Berlin · New York · Amsterdam

Computers in Language Research 2

Part I: Formalization in Literary and Discourse Analysis

Part II: Notating the Language of Music, and the (Pause) Rhythms of Speech

Edited by

Walter A. Sedelow, Jr.
Sally Yeates Sedelow

Mouton Publishers

Berlin · New York · Amsterdam

Sally Yeates Sedelow, Ph.D.
Professor of Computer Science and of Linguistics
The University of Kansas, Lawrence

Walter A. Sedelow, Jr., Ph.D.
Professor of Computer Science and of Sociology,
and in the Program for the History & Philosophy of Science,
The University of Kansas, Lawrence

Computers in Language Research: Formalization in Literary and Discourse Analysis and *Notating the Language of Music, and the (Pause) Rhythms of Speech* is the companion volume to *Computers in Language Research: Formal Methods*, Trends in Linguistics (Studies and Monographs), volume 5.

Library of Congress Cataloging in Publication Data

Computers in language research 2.

(Trends in linguistics. Studies and monographs; 19)

Includes bibliographies.

Contents: pt. 1. Formalization in literary and discourse analysis --pt. 2. Notating the language of music and the (pause) rhythms of speech.

1. Linguistics–Data processing. 2. Music–Data processing. 3. Formal languages. I. Sedelow, Walter A. II. Sedelow, Sally Yeates, 1931- . III. Title: Computers in language research two. IV. Series.

P98.C6129 1983 410'.28'5 83-011476
ISBN 90-279-3009-0

 Typesetting: Grestun Graphics, Abingdon. – Printing: Druckerei Hildebrand, Berlin. – Binding: Lüderitz & Bauer Buchgewerbe GmbH.

Printed in Germany.

Contents

Part I

Formalization in literary and discourse analysis

WALTER A. SEDELOW JR. and SALLY YEATES SEDELOW

Science and human language

1 Only a few centuries ago all but a very small fraction of the earth's population was engaged in the production and preparation of food. The implications of that fact have proved difficult to keep in mind as we seek to understand our current situation as to knowledge. One implication that bears on science in general and language research specifically is how extremely small is the amount of human energy that has been bound into the scientific study of language, and, against the species' life span, how extremely recent that effort is.

Human symbolic behavior may be the most complex sub-system in our world. In its totality and relationships – and in the comparative indivisibility of structure from function – it may in some respects exceed in complexity even the human central nervous system, out of which it pours in the process of CNS interactions with environment by way of input sensors and output effectors. A word of caution: one says it appears to be the most complex sub-system, since human knowing is itself a systemic process and the complexity of any specific reality domain is not a thing in itself and an a priori given, but rather is also a function of, inter alia, the notational system(s), and any paradigm, theory, or model using them, as well as the instrumentation employed. Complexity, too, is model-specific. Dramatic moments in the history of science are often occasions where a striking insight has occurred, such that what had been complex or even chaotic is successfully represented with radically greater simplicity. That is to say, major developments in science are characteristically symbolic events, and, more specifically, they are shifts toward greater brevity of expression either within or across notational systems. That could happen in symbolic behavior research – radically reducing one sense of the complexity of that phenomenal field.

It is proving to be extremely difficult for scientists to grasp as a matter of course how constructive, phenomenologically speaking, is the work of science. Dyadic, 'window-pane' images of the scientist cathecting with a reality under study have been so widely available and so strongly reinforced that the role of the symbolism he employs in constructing in some measure precisely the reality to be studied has been insufficiently attended to. As we consciously, explicitly, and formally examine that symbolism it, too, becomes an object of knowledge. When we more fully understand properties and implications of a given symbolism we tend to be emancipated from any uncritical and even compulsive use of it – from, that is, a byproduct of professional enculturation into the habits of an academic discipline, a discipline itself being very much a matter of dialect behavior.

How to get into focus properties of any system such that new powerful relationships are opened out is one of the most important and least understood facets of science. That is to say, a heuristics for new paradigm generation – a heuristics for, as it were, fomenting and formulating 'scientific revolutions' – is scarcely a subject of study, much less a well-understood phenomenon; even more directly to the point, the processes of 'discovery' within a paradigm are not an explicit part of a scientific education, even though in any discipline's professional imagery the establishing of powerful new relationships is a major goal.

The history of physics in the western world during the last dozen or so generations is marked by an unusual cumulativeness in the devising of such relationships. But scientists studying language have not been so fortunate; it should be emphasized, though, that the amount of attention given to each scientific field of study is sufficiently slight that we might well be surprised at how much we know in any of them, rather than unthinkingly uttering the stereotypic complaint about how little we know and the stereotypic putative solution of competition as a means to greater knowledge.

With language research we may suppose that the barriers to achieving success are the greater for the fact that one part of the means of study – that is, notation in use – is a facet of the order of reality under study: the language self-referencing problem. Contemporaneously, there is something of an analog to this situation in control theory, as attempts are made to apply it to computer-communications networks: unusually, the system to be controlled and the controlling system are identical. That fact poses fresh research problems, as the incompleteness problem has done for mathematical logic.

As suggested in the lead section ('Language and people, modelling and science') of *Computers in language research: Formal methods* (The Hague: Mouton, 1979) the symbolizing of symbolism is the most quintessentially human of our activities. The biological capability used for such activity being the most recently evolved among central nervous system structures, with it we may be closer than usual to stressing the limits of our capacities. Even so, that we are, except comparatively, anything like literally close to an anatomically and physiologically imposed limit is by no means clear; intuitively, one might even suppose we were closer to the limit in some athletic events, perhaps especially as to performance speeds. Only intra-societally and inter-societally widespread opportunities to engage in such activity, and heavy reinforcement for doing so, could reveal, by way of 'natural' experiment, whether we have major unused capacity in this area of the CNS. What we cannot take for granted is continuing progress in the use of any given human talent. Consider, for instance, that there are types and speeds of computation now regularly achieved by machine that there is no evidence for supposing the unaided human brain will ever be capable of.

Some artifactual forms seem at least for the visible future to have completed their evolution. Plate-mail armour would be a case in point. But where there is a continuing utility for an artifact, or artifactual class, we may expect it to continue to evolve; in a static environment it may continue to change until it approaches a limit, but so long as its environment changes there may be no limit. The environments of computers certainly continue to change. Hence, we may expect computers to do so, also especially since with computers there is a strong reflexive dynamic, a strong feed-forward and feed-back; that is, computers and software contribute to change in their own environments in ways which then induce still further changes in the computers and software themselves, and so on. Thus, when we speak about the computer, we are discussing unfinished business; and even though we may feel we can see some of its likely developments in the next decade or so, there could be surprises even within that time frame, much less beyond it. But even with their current characteristics it is very clear that computers are giving us an instrumentation for research on language which compares in impact with the telescope for celestial phenomena and with the microscope for seeing what is too fine for the unaided human eye. Just as without these devices what we know of phenomena of certain scales would be grossly reduced, so we may imagine in future generations the same will be said of what would be known about language without the computer. The telescope clearly was the driving engine of early modern astronomy. The computer may be seen, indeed, as driving much of the formalization which these volumes describe. And without formalization there can be no deep scientific results. Formalization makes possible efficacious critical feedback, as it also facilitates tight-coupled scientific collaboration. Thus it helps to make science cumulative and to accelerate cumulational processes.

If appropriate instrumentation is one prerequisite of successful science, notation and its use as a theory or model in some subset of its possible combinations is another. In the previous companion volume to this one (*Computers in language research: Formal methods*, The Hague: Mouton, 1979) Hedetniemi and Goodman have provided us with an introduction to one type of highly relevant notation. Bohnert and Backer have provided an introduction to another. Beyond that, they have given us an exemplification of its application to the analysis of language and intimations of the power of extending that application. In Benson's paper we see a very impressive demonstration of the utility of those notations as realized through a highly formal body of theory.

Further, that paper has the great advantage of carefully dissecting the anatomy of varied publications in a body of research literature and revealing comparabilities, cumulative effects, firm results, and, notably, important new problems, with the occasional suggestion as to a tack to take in moving toward solving these problems.

In the set of papers under discussion in this volume, we see a sample of preliminary results of this power of formalization. Since this introductory essay 'Science and human language' began by trying to communicate in the historical perspective of our species' evolution a sense of the amount of human information processing capability that has been brought to bear on all science as really small, and the fraction on a science of language as disproportionately smaller still, there will be no surprise, then, at this point in our discussion in the idea that the chapters which follow are, in a number of respects, truly pioneering.

2 Although the long tradition of text editing and the more recent tradition of text explication (e.g., the New Criticism) contribute to preparing us to look at the text as in itself an object of study, until recently there has been very little specifically scientific research with texts as the focal data. More especially, the statics and dynamics of relationship among textual elements have not been explored within the framework of a genuinely scientific paradigm – for against rigorous criteria of scientificity even contemporary structuralists and semioticists are essentially philosophical. But their endeavors are useful, and even more their orientation, for they may be seen as protoscientific – preparing at least younger minds for the precision and power of genuinely scientific understanding of texts, writing in general, and oral discourse as well.

Lest there be any misunderstanding as to the character and excitement of truly scientific analysis of language, allow us to quote from an article we have recently published in the *Journal of the History of the Behavioral Sciences* (1978):

> The broadest significance of what we have to say here is that, while (physical science) quantification subsumed and succeeded (positivistic) precision at the cultural center of science, quantification itself partly with the help of both the computer and computer science has been subsumed and succeeded at the core of science process by formalization. Similarly, prediction subsumed and succeeded description; and generation and control (formation and transformation) succeeded prediction as the most central proof of scientific knowledge.

In this series of volumes, *Computers in language research*, we are elaborating a new research paradigm – paradigm in the sense of a research 'matrix' as conceived by Thomas Kuhn in his *Structure of scientific revolutions* (2nd ed., 1970). In addition to exemplifying the process of paradigm formation, the work of these volumes – along with its entailment in the prior research of Walter Sedelow and Sally Yeates Sedelow, and the numerous other scholars and scientists whose studies contribute to making possible the paradigm – has generic significance for the paradigm-formation process, irrespective of the specific content or discipline(s) of any given paradigm. One source of this generic significance is located in the making explicit of the 'personal knowledge' (Michael Polanyi, *Personal knowledge*, 1958) component of any paradigm in the process of formally analyzing, and replicating if need be, its symbolic style/content, structure, and dynamics – as is now being made possible by computers and formalization in language research. There is an interesting and important parallel here to semiotics in that in a 'philosophical' and 'literary' (i.e., pre-scientific) way semiotics aspires to comprehensive generality of applicability, to being, that is, a fully general theory of signs, and employable in the explication of any use of any subset of them.

In some measure, no doubt as a consequence of his redaction of lectures of George Herbert Mead, Charles Morris (*pace* Charles Peirce) invented semiotics as socially-situated assertions. That is, if syntactic relations were to be understood intersymbolically, the semantics and, especially, the pragmatics of discourse were necessarily to be comprehended within a model of social relationships. Similarly now with reference to formalized and computational linguistics, including discourse analysis, and as indicated below in John Smith's discussion of sermon research, we are concerned to achieve rigor with reference to the modelling and synthesis of human language behavior both for the inherent importance of such knowledge and also for its criticality in later understanding its 'causes' and 'effects' neurologically and environmentally.

Owing, presumably in part at least, to the greater 'dignity', complexity, and stability of a literary text by comparison with, say, conversational discourse, some such texts have been more closely studied than have segments ('strings') of oral speech. Thus John Smith's study, 'Computer criticism', is consequential not only for its substantial contribution to our knowledge of what it is now possible to achieve in a formalized mode of analysis when applied to literature, but also for its prospective transfer value to the study of the more casual modes of writing as well as to the far greater volume of language which is educed only orally during interpersonal transactions. Interestingly enough – and helpfully – it is now still true that just as with pre-computer, pre-formalism more attention was (is) given to super-sentential structure in the study of literature than in other modes of verbal expression, the same pattern continues – in the sense that with literary texts both pre-computer formalists and computer formalists also devote more of their energies to supersentential structure. Per contra until recently modern linguists have tended to concentrate on (a) oral productions and, as to those, on (b) sentential and sub-sentential strings. Thus we may expect to find in the Smith paper, inter alia, technique, models, findings applicable to discourse analysis at large, as well as to – its announced 'target' of choice – the elucidation of pattern in literary work.

As has already been suggested earlier on in this chapter on science and human language, a critical condition that had to be met in order for our current state of the art in formalized analysis to be achieved was the practice of studying a text (or, in principle, any other verbal production, for that matter), as a thing in itself ('Ding an sich') and with its own history and mutations. In the medieval world, language was not yet manumitted from 'reflecting' an external reality (language as the correlated symbolism of nature); and in the early modern centuries (for some, still) language, emancipated from an analogality to Nature, had been instantaneously re-enslaved as a structural representation of that nebulous entity 'mind' (or, better, brain) – when, that is, it didn't suffer the (still common) worse fate of being symbolically confounded with the reality of brain behavior (as when we read of people's 'ideas' or 'thoughts' as the subject of discussion although in fact it is their words that are being construed). A subtler deprivation of freedom for language is to be found in 'correspondentialist' epistemologies, where the *petitio* of a confusion of language with something else (nature; mind) is avoided, but a (sometimes, oftentimes, usually unspecified) parallelism between language and some other order of reality is in effect taken for granted.

To the Formalists of an earlier day (as in Russia and Czechoslovakia) must go some of the credit for not only proclaiming but beginning to act on that great emancipation. Ironically, that school of scholars saw themselves not so much as scientists but as philosophical philologians or humanistic literary critics, the while attaining to one of the major conditions for scientificity, a sense of a separable object of study; today many linguists who, by contrast with those earlier Formalists, seek to present themselves to the world as scientists are, in this essential sense at least, less scientific, in that they are not experimental nor even neurally accurate in their postulations of parallelistic relationship between mind and language behavior. With John Smith let us, rather, when we study language, including its literary instances, study language – as a thing in itself, and without pseudo-philosophic and unnecessary assumptive entailments about either minds or nature.

Just as in the 'social sciences' non-scientists may by way of Functionalism talk or Social Systems talk provide for the possibility of an epistemological transition from empiricist crudities to an understanding of the role of controlling models (Frege) – as is perhaps beginning to happen in linguistics now in part through the agency of Firth/Halliday – so in the belle-lettristic realm the French explication de texte and the American New Criticism have helped to prepare the way for what is beyond them and for what is prospectively scientific – in their concentration on the text itself. But a failure to move on from that approach after several New Critical decades is now creating the opportunity for a critical regression. That is, instead of a clear move toward achieving the massive task, at least adumbrated by Charles Morris (pragmatics and semantics as well as syntactics) and others in the *Encyclopedia of Unified Science* set, of formally and in some sense comprehensively modelling the total ensemble (sources and consequences) within which symbols take their rise and have their meaning, the literary critics (who, after all, usually are not by education equipped for that task) either have remained fixated in the New Critical position (or in Structuralist or Semioticist embellishments of it) or have fallen back to neo-biographical or neo-social interpretational fantasies of a sort reminiscent of the years before the 1939-45 war, albeit enhanced by vast gains in the detail and imaginativeness of historical scholarship. Now we can only try to make it come to pass that the New Criticism serve as a prelude to the exact characterization of literary strings of symbols, with such precision of understanding of properties of the strings themselves as a needed condition for the exciting and powerful task of then emplacing the understanding of the statics and the dynamics of such strings within the more comprehensive ecologies of their origins in neural activity (itself to be understood in successively more encompassing environments: experiential, social/cultural, ecologic) and also in the reflexive or feed-back action of these environments upon those strings and their matrices of origin as functions of the resultant dynamics when those very strings are processed by the environment into which they are inserted (in-put).

Current rates of social/technological change alone, worldwide – apart from more critically system-situated dimensions and subsystems, such as, notably, population growth and expectation growth – assure us of the increasing need for science, if only (conservatively) for global systemic re-equilibration, (setting aside the far more onerous loading on the science machine implied by the progressive realization of ever higher expectations, of ever higher levels in 'the needs hierarchy'). Since all the major ethnicities and polyethnicities, and many of the lesser, are gravitating (though from different starting levels and at different rates – all however with powerful assists from symbol manipulation and communication high technologies) toward more 'totalitarian' forms of social organization, and since, also, for the short term and intermediate term at least, the required socially reactive science appears to be largely 'big science' (with the consequent implication of large funding), it is (only) from governance structures that the resources are likely to be forthcoming to support science on the scale required to provide any chance for quality of life stabilization (to express the work loading on science in the most minimalist way). But governors are showing – not at all surprisingly, however wrong-headedly and catastrophically – an increasingly 'fortress' and 'Titanic' mentality, precisely at that stage in the species' affairs when (did those governors but know it) the need for enrichment of that social compost out of which science grows has never been more needed, even against so modest a governors' goal as sufficient stabilization that they, or even their roles, may be preserved. But in the absence of sufficient systems understanding of our global predicament, it is not remarkable that the comprehension of comparative 'essentiality' of different functions is poor – and the less essential not sacrificed for the more (i.e., for science). But as it is, and especially in the United States, the fraction of human intelligence and energy being devoted to creating new scientific knowledge is not growing as our collective priorities would imply it should, and in some respects is even declining. Under those circumstances our one hope is that the way of doing scientific business may change: improve in efficiency by one or more orders of magnitude. Although externalist historians of science and sociologists of science to date have not been able to concentrate the necessary scholarly attention on understanding, comparatively, the critical infra-structures of science/society interfaces, we can see that, vis-à-vis general rates of cultural change, science seems (after allowing for continuing differentiation, changing standards of scientificness, bigger budgets, more professionalization, etc.) to have gone on in much the same general fashion since, roughly, 'the Age of Newton'. But that way of doing business will no longer suffice. Now we must move on to 'science of the 2nd order' – which can be done only by way of making a science out of the study of science, by way of a science of science.

Fascinatingly, it is precisely the effort to achieve a science of science which looks to afford the royalest road to a science of the humanities as well. And why not, since a science of science and a science of the humanities would be, each, but special cases of the knowledge generated by success with a general, comprehensive science of language behavior – language being defined in the encompassing, symbolic forms mode that we have consistently urged and sought to understand. Walter Sedelow's Verbal Measures Inventory was one of the steps in the direction of such a science; the developing of a Discourse Analysis paradigm is another; and now we also see more clearly the way to an understanding of Language Systemics. The studies in formalization for literary and discourse analysis presented here are other steps along the same road.

John Smith provides a clear demonstration of how, building on precomputer traditions of formalism, what we now can do with the aid of the computer is so substantially more than enhancing our established capacities for perception and recall that in a classic sort of way we have instrumentation which is providing the occasion for a paradigm shift – although, as is always in some degree the case, that paradigm shift is far from utterly discontinuous with antecedent intellectual activity. One of Smith's attractive contextual provisions for understanding 'computer criticism' is to show not only its consistency with movement away from the fantasms of authorial intention but also how it builds on the recognition that just as the literary work is a sequence of signs to be understood by increasingly formal transforms, so too, of course, for any work of criticism ostensibly 'about' a literary work. Instead of being 'evident' the relationship between the two must be first comprehended as entirely problematic, as a necessary prelude to creating ('understanding') that relationship as a function of the establishment of specific transformal patternings between the two: e.g., in what operationally specified ways may a criticism be comprehended as an encoding of the work under discussion? Against such criteria Semiotics is clearly apprehended as, professions to the contrary notwithstanding, insufficiently rigorous and operationalized, but of immense importance in a dialectical progression in which through sowing the seeds of disappointment in its devotees it prepares some of them, and their successors, for what is implied by geniune science.

It is interesting to observe that just as here we make the case for a comprehensive relevance for a fully scientific understanding of language, the French and American traditions of semiotics have made claims of comparable scope, whilst with rough simultaneity certain scientists and parascientists have begun to perceive the relevance of even literary criticism for the sciences themselves (and the scientifically aspirant social and behavioral studies as well). Stephen Jay Gould's recent *Ontogeny and phylogeny* (1977) can be seen as an extension of the tradition of Polanyi and Kuhn in its call to scientists to examine with hermeneutic care the sacred texts defining their respective paradigms – as for example with Darwin vis-à-vis much biology. The idea is, of course, that circumstances of composition (formation) produce certain implicit assumptions that, all unperceived, contribute to the vector defining the direction in which subsequent scientific work proceeds. It is argued, then, that these great texts need to be examined more carefully, and examined in dialectical context, in order more fully to open up the matrix of possibilities which a science may explore. A tradition of secular hermenueticism has also emerged with the less scientific and more philosophical work of sociologists, especially in Europe and in the tradition of the Frankfurt or Critical School.

So in this new hermeneutic effort we see a rather literary scrutiny of text for meanings beyond the most evident, and on behalf of better science; while, from the other direction, we see science – or, more precisely, its formal aspect – being brought into play in a fashion that bears on humanistic texts. And, also, philosophical formalism and scientific formalism both lay claims to comprehensiveness of applicability to symbolic materials. On behalf of that science of science effort which undertakes to model the languages of sciences by utilizing an ultimately computer-based discourse analysis, we urge the additional claim that it should contribute to making explicit the personal knowledge which is otherwise implicit, and in process also should render explicit the tacit content of dominating paradigms – thus rendering science more comprehensible and more rapidly improvable and more flexibly adaptive to its opportunities and challenges, as well as far more teachable, world-wide. One notices, then, that an entailment of this kind of effort is to break through the wall separating the phenomenological and the scientific – studying so carefully language behavior, including responses to any subset of it, as also to discover scientifically the structure and function of phenomenological responses. That is, science narrowly construed is also being brought to bear on attributions and other features of so-called subjectivity of response, on the dimensionalization and processuality of inner and conceptual spaces: Husserl and Hilbert reconciled.

This effort also requires us to pull together types of linguistic analysis currently not fully integrated, to undertake to make use of, for example, the derivations from the categorial logic and grammars of the '30's (Ajdukiewicz) along with the modal logics of more recent date (Hintikka; Burks), the current fuzziness logics (Zadeh), and, perhaps, most important of all – both for computer-based and pre-computer based formalization – the Montague grammars, which at the moment rightly command so much attention from formalists concerned to make progress with the study of natural language. The possibility not only of a breakthrough but of winning the war on this front makes us the more acutely conscious of just how important to the realization of production systems that would do much such natural language processing for unnumbered practical applications are mundane triumphs like optical character recognition systems (enabling us to break up the in-put bottleneck). And, far from the technological, far even from practical literary criticism, are the intimations of new insights into language which themselves may be formalized (if at all) only in a dimly foreseen future – such currently 'way out' insight into language and metaphor as are to be derived from, for example, Lacan and Ricoeur.

Every study of language – including of course its literary instantiations – may be perceived as a transform upon the strings under examination. That transform may be controlled and formal – mathematical -- or it may be worked not in accordance with any overt rules; and whether a ruleful process of transformation is devised ('discovered') a posteriori to cover the relationship of in-put (the string under study) to out-put (the strings that are 'the study') is a matter for research and intellectual invention/creativity. If, as we argue elsewhere, (the *Journal of the History of the Behavioral Sciences,* 1979), those transfer functions may be written much the more easily if connotation is factored out and science itself may then emerge as the equivalent of an abstract machine, it seems particularly likely that the symbol-string to symbol-string transforms which are linguistics and literary criticism will prove particularly tractable to such analysis. Relationalities are then operational in character. The selective transforms and the higher order transforms which, along with more direct and comprehensive transforms, John Smith discusses would then fall into place as but special cases in a more general process. Metaphors – such as geometric metaphors ('parrallel') and geologic metaphors ('strata') – now applied to such strings might be expected to then fade out of use, as containing too little information, or to be neologized as code for quite exact intersymbolic processes (of which result metaphors would seem to be archaic instances). Anthropomorphic metaphors – as of 'character' and (plot) 'action' – in discussing literary strings also might be expected to disappear as a function of their weakness in comparison with encodings (transforms) which dropped much less information. In general we would expect to see – a century hence? centuries hence? – metaphor as we know it disappear, or, at least, to reappear only within a context of explicit encoding, given their meaning within a model. So, too, of course, for metonymy.

The sentence had a beginning and for some uses it may well have an end – an end in historic time. The written sentence we can dimly see the emergence of; possibly even now we may be able to discern conditions of its passing (making way for more logical forms, even as – in economics and in many places else – mathematical expression in some measure has already replaced words). Folktales and other genres may also pass away, as a 'phase out' of an archaic orality. But at least until they do such efforts at supersentential grammar as Propp's and Todorov's will prove to be critically important as having gotten rolling the ball of formal understanding with reference to strings of story scale. When new verbal genres emerge, whether of sentence scale, or larger, they will contribute to the foundation of their own appropriate transformations. In proportion as such new forms do appear, they will help to make more flexible the whole process of genre formation and genre-transform formation. As that happens – and, again, the computer will be helpful in bringing it about – our successors may puzzle over the rigidity that kept even a pioneer like Barthes so closely tied to the categories derived from philological grammarians, rather than going for the far richer panoply of transforms made possibly by purely formalist analysis when aided by the computer.

One of the characteristics of science during the modern centuries has been the (differential) paradigm-boundedness of its practitioners. As increasing symbolic self-consciousness (as in the manner of Frege, or Whitehead and Russell, or Hilbert, or Einstein, or Gödel, et al.) and as the pragmatic force alluded to above of the need to go to a second order science in order to meet (under the condition of unduly restricted funds) the socially-induced requirement of substantially more science to maintain some minimum of social order, as, then, these two developments – the one more purely symbolic, the other more purely societal – impel us toward a science of science, one of the changes we may expect to see take place is the decay of paradigmatic or paradigm-bound scientific work. And in its place, greater flexibility, with each scientist or group creating their own models/paradigms as needed – and able to communicate with others in consequence of the greater explicitness (impersonal knowledge) brought about by formalization of procedure. As this intellectual system state-transition takes place it will do so in part owing to (both 'cause' and 'effect' in the older encoding) the availability of a Paradigm Smasher. One sign of the emergence of the Smasher is our Verbal Measures Inventory (*Bibliography for a science of language*, 1975) – an impersonal compendium of dimensionalities (variables and parameters), techniques, and findings in the measuring of language done to date. It is one of the ways in which we can 'place' in a matrix the (static) properties of language strings – such, of course, as those which define a traditional paradigm. But we are also on the verge of being able to do something about – to produce a 'calculus' for – the dynamics of language: Hintikka's *Game-theoretic semantics*, (1979) is one such start. The authors of this paper see their way into the solution of those problems by way of the development and application of various types of systems-theory (cybernetic) mathematics; but there is already available a prelude to that degree and power of formality in what John Smith discusses in this book as London School systemic grammars in the manner of M.A.K. Halliday out of J.R. Firth. Other indications of much more specific – and less comprehensive – lines of research to be followed in this activity are to be found in our two recent articles in the *Journal of the History of the Behavioral Sciences* (1978, 1979).

John Smith writes of Computer Criticism different from even recent structuralisms in that

> 'it demands formal rules for establishing strata, it suggests a greater number of strata relating to a greater range of textual features, but most important, all such strata are arbitrary.'

We speak above to the need for formalisms that would then go on from the analysis of the statics to the analysis of the dynamics, the systemic dynamics, of strings of arbitrary length – although, heuristically, it looks as though during the next decade or two the strings would be, by comparison with the work done to date, longer rather than shorter (if only because the current paradigm has made it impossible to understand what falls within its chosen scope by defining the lengths [sentences mostly] as so short as to rule out the possibility of ever discovering the larger strings within which are to be 'found' [transformed] the sources of much of the dynamism that governs their [micro-] structure). John Smith's own earlier work on Joyce's *Portrait of the artist* as well as his more recent work in homiletics give us a quick, and enjoyable, taste of the flavor of what is to follow when we begin to successfully present the dynamics of verbal systems. A hint of another kind as to what is involved in (time-dependent) verbal dynamics – in this instance with reference to extremely uncomplicated word 'choices' – is to be seen in the work of Bernard Cohen and Hans Lee (growing out of the Asch experiment literature). With the Lee - Cohen work, as also in our own paper (in *Computer applications in medical care; IEEE*, 1978) in which the Labov et al. *Therapeutic discourse* is used as a point of departure, the issue of the procedure for locating the boundaries of the string to be studied is a critical one. One could say, in fact, that the issue of 'frame' definition in current scientific literature emanating from computational linguistics is but a special case of the procedure and implications of boundary 'choice'. Good fortune in choosing the boundaries is a species of judgment in cutting a section out of a directed graph: poor cuts will almost necessitate non-success in getting at the dynamics (algebraic) of the topological system (machine). The tests here, as with all aspects of linguistic systemics (and linguistic science, and science), are wholly 'functional': what does one notation, or oral set of rules of usage, etc., enable one to do by comparison with the enablements apparently provided by alternatives?

It is a truism – and an attractive one – in science that one of the ways in which step-functional increments in achievement are realized in a research specialty is by discovering an isomorphism between some phase of what is being done in that specialty and what has already been accomplished – preferably very extensively – in another. Earlier on, for the analysis of business cycles and other socioeconomic phenomena, times series models were borrowed for use in the sciences of human behavior; much was achieved in part because, as with Fourier transforms, it was possible to borrow from techniques worked out still earlier for physical science applications (to the study of heat in the case of Fourier's method of analysis). Now Professor Smith demonstrates a further brilliant borrowing of that same formality: utilizing Fourier analysis for linearly tracking through a text properties of the lexical incidences. More than twenty years ago Walter Sedelow had proposed the application of Fourier transforms to historiography, but without specific reference to the stratum of lexical units and without demonstration. Not only does John Smith make clear – and with exceedingly vivid graphic accompaniment – a fresh way to utilize this method; but his earlier publication of results showing how striking effects in Joyce's *Portrait* were 'painted' deserves to be an exceedingly influential model for a new genre of critical explication. Professor Smith in proposing how to map out the networks of thematic associations also sketches out an application of graph theory – a mathematics presented in extenso in the Hedetniemi and Goodman capter of *Formal methods*, the volume antecedent to this book in the *Computers in language research* series. One of the intriguing and useful properties of this type of analysis is the way in which it simultaneously makes possible both a static and a dynamic understanding of a textual system: the synchronic and the diachronic are fused but separable, and an old antithesis on language research thereby is somewhat resolved.

The computer, and computer science and other foci of formalization, are contributing to major mutations in role characteristics for scientists, for humanists, even for artists, as well as for work force roles at large. At no time in the past has there been an opportunity for such an increase in the quality of scientific and humanistic studies. Professor Smith's work indicates quite remarkably how such a qualitative improvement is now possible in our understanding of a text as 'thing in itself,' and, what is more extraordinary, he goes on to initiate a demonstration of some ways in which exact delimitations of language string dynamics can be emplaced within a larger dynamism – in this case, the dynamism of audience response, as here exemplified with sermons.

As was also persuasively argued at the University of Pennsylvania conference on content analysis by Calvin Hall, it is a matter of importance to establish normalizations statistically in order to be able to locate critical stylistic differentiations that may account for differential audience effects; our Verbal Measures Inventory is probably the most extensive data base of work done to date that includes such statistical information, and Professor Smith points to the work of Lubomir Dolezel for an example of a model with which to place such stylistic traits. Such work contributes to the possibility of a science of the humanities, and, in providing for the possibility of reproducibility through formalization it goes beyond much previous sophisticated structuralism, such as that of Barthes. By contrast, the London School linguistics of Firth and Halliday do lend themselves quite clearly to a translation into a strictly scientific modality allowing for cumulative results; and, interestingly enough, Firth reached out beyond intersymbolic analysis to envision for linguistics interaction with academic psychology as well as psychiatry. One condition of success in such ventures is to be able to show a direct relationship back to the empirical data (which is the language string) with each (successively higher order; or alternative) transformation. Therein lies science.

3 In one way or another all theories, models, simulation vehicles, and the like are approximative. They also vary greatly in the extent to which they operate rulefully upon the phenomenal domain data of which they are encodings (transforms). All theories and models are constrained, as well as aided, in their types and degrees of effectiveness by the properties of the character set and rules of usage which constitute their notational system: by what as primitives goes into the makings of a model of a model, a model of a theory, etc. Under various rubrics, and as aspects of a science of symbolic behavior, the consequences of choosing any given notation system are now beginning to be a subject of study. Notation theory, iconics, knowledge representation theory, data structure and programming language theory are among the categoric terms used in part to encompass varied approaches to understanding the differential trade-offs that result from instantiating models and theories in

particular notational modes. Inasmuch as the computer requires considerable formality in its instructions and data, and since technical imagination is the only bound on its architecture and its component design, we are now in a situation where we are motivated to consider how to design languages vis-à-vis the sytems that process them; a generalization of the language design concept encourages us to think not only of how to design those languages (including analog, or graphics, languages) that are used at the interface of people with machines in such fashion that they relate attractively to human information processing requirements as well as to machine requirements/options, but also of how to design languages that are to be used by people in accord with our understanding of brain/nervous system functioning. There are strong pragmatic reasons for not flinching this task/opportunity: most problems and strengths in any given formulation ultimately turn out to be properties of the language of the formulation.

One question we repeatedly confront in work toward a science of language is how to model language, as well, of course, as what to model. Again, the results we get certainly will depend on the notation employed. On the assumption that one important notation for the future will be graph theoretic – important in part because its analogality affords a certain 'intuitive' comprehensibility and in part owing to its usefulness and established use in conveying contingent intrasystemic relationality, as in automata theorizing – *Computers in language research: Formal methods* includes an extensive, systematic introduction to it by Stephen Hedetniemi and Seymour Goodman. Also, in principle, all of the information in the graphs may be captured in an alternative, matrix notation, while in the Herbert Bohnert et al. chapter we have a logical notation for capturing language information. At the U.S.S.R. Academy of Sciences (Siberian Division) in Novosibirsk, Andrei Ershov, Alexander Nariyani and others are doing an extension of Jacob Schwartz' Set L set-theoretic language for use in modelling natural language behavior. There are the various logical notations suited to differing dimensions of language, such as modal logic notation for 'possible worlds', fuzzy logic notation for preliminary mentation and, among others, the especially promising notation of Richard Montague and his followers. Some scholars still use words in their research on language – in the extreme case (Kenneth Colby) minimizing the amount of theorizing/modelling, as well as using natural language for discussing natural language, on at least quasi-epistemological grounds. To latent issues implied in one's sense of what it is to be scientific in building a scientific understanding of language behavior we must now turn our attention, since the question of scientificity strongly conditions what is to be notated and how.

The scope and character of what is to be modelled within any notational system is by no means agreed upon by linguists, as is evident from the variety of approaches discussed by Yorick Wilks in his survey of the comparatively limited field of machine translation and the AI 'paradigm'. Reflection on the history and philosophies of science may suggest an underlying assumptional structure which, in a sense, could be one of the plural determinants of the variegation we behold in this research scene. That is, there is not a consensus as to what constitutes science, nor the highest scientific accomplishment; and, over the centuries, the meanings of 'science' in words and in actions have, to be sure, varied considerably. If – and not necessarily for the better, all told – there were more agreement now as to how to 'grade' scientific accomplishment, there might be more cumulativeness and speed of achievement in developing a science of language. In briefest form we would repeat:

'while (physical science) quantification subsumed and succeeded (positivistic) precision as at the cultural center of science, quantification itself *partly with the help both of the computer and of computer science* has been subsumed and succeeded at the core of science process by formalization. Similarly, prediction subsumed and succeeded description, and generation and control (formation and transformation), prediction as the most central proof of scientific knowledge.'

The Indo-European root from which 'science' derives signifies a cutting (as with scissors and schism), tearing, and, hence, metaphorically with reference to symbolic acts, a distinction. Originally empirical description – although, it must be stressed, description is one of the most important terms to render problematic if we are to learn how better to do things with words – with an admixture of primary process fantasizing (including magic), science was what we now self-consciously call ethnoscience: everyday knowledge (but also whatever hieratic statements the earliest professional symbolizers, priests, generated) expressed with varying degrees of precision.

On the current research scene the great advantage for the scientific study of language of the utilization of AI, or intelligent systems, approaches is that they necessarily entail the degree of explicitness and operationalization implied by the fact that they are to be implemented on the computer. Ambiguities of various sorts – such as the word-sense ambiguities, the case ambiguities, and the referential ambiguities cited by Wilks – cannot be dodged. The successful resolution of such problems as posed by these various types of ambiguity is signaled to us by the capacity of a system to successfully generate (by processes of formation and transformation) the very realities which they study. Wilks' study makes clear that, against that criterion, Chomskyan linguistics has not proved to have much scientific power, whatever other advantages it may have afforded in virtue of centering a great deal of attention on issues in the understanding of language. As we place in mental context the research that gives us our present capabilities both for machine translation and, more largely, for natural language computing, it is also worth noting that Bar Hillel in his criticism of the idea of machine translation not only set a standard which would rule out even the possibility of human translation from one language to another, but also seems to have neglected the fact that there is always some measure of 'friction' or 'noise' in any system.

Reflecting on Wilks' examination of language researches one might conclude that, at least as to those which he has studied, their generators might have profited from reflecting on the conditions of mature science as expressed in some such fashion as we have done earlier in this chapter. Wilks makes an argument for the minimization of criticism of accomplishment at this 'pre-scientific' stage of work, but it is at least arguable that the moral of the story is that more rather than less criticism has been needed and is needed now. In the preceding volume of this series, *Computers in language research: Formal methods*, Professor David Benson provided an effective critique of research at the intersection of formal language study and natural computing, indicating criteria which would give us a basis for evaluating accomplishment and dealing specifically with such types of projects as Wilks cites in his reference to Rulisson, Hewitt, Balzer, and others. From that same volume one may establish a sense of quality for the work of McCarthy and Hayes, as well as of Coles and Sandewall, as cited by Wilks, through a reflective reading of the chapter by Bohnert and Backer.

In his discussion of the work of Winograd, Wilks makes clear that Winograd was effectively and usefully influenced in a major way by the work of M.A.K. Halliday. In placing Winograd's work in perspective it may be helpful to appreciate how profoundly consistent with one of the major developments in the theory of method in modern physics, as exemplified by the operationalist orientation of Percy Bridgman even a half century ago, (*The logic of modern physics*, 1927), is the emphasis on 'meanings are procedures'. Winograd's work helped to make intelligent systems of greater linguistic significance, at the same time that it has contributed to making linguistic research more operationally meaningful. Other problems which Wilks feels need to be addressed, such as issues relating to the handling of anaphora, now are also being examined in the context provided by the emergence of discourse analysis.

Having earlier emphasized the importance of the work of Richard Montague for current developments in natural language computing, it may be mentioned here that the equivalence that Montague established between semantics and syntax would enable one through using an extended Montaguean grammar to obviate the necessity of the differentiation into the syntactic and the semantic which Winograd engaged in. We have also argued earlier on that in the absence of discourse analysis it has often been the case that problems were insoluble as a function of the fact that the systems within which sentences were embedded were well beyond the scale of the systems of verbal behavior to which linguists address themselves; some of the problems of ambiguity which occur in the exploratory work of Winograd may be eliminated as we build systems of more realistic scale, such as are needed in sustained discourse analysis. The further extension of Winogradean approaches implies, probably, the exploration of the formal equivalence between what Winograd has done and the augmented state transition network approach of William Woods. The graph theory exposition of Hedetniemi and Goodman in the volume on formal methods of this sub-series is a good source of understanding for the automata approach which Woods employed. One of the ways in which Woods and Winograd differ in emphasis is with reference to the exploration of the relationships among the symbols in a system or, alternatively, attention to the implications of those symbols and that system on a world beyond itself. Woods attends more to the former and Winograd, to the latter. The history of science, and more particularly the history of the formal sciences, would lead us to believe that we must rigorously attend to each of these two approaches – for on the one side we see the tradition of Poincaréan conventionalism that the elaboration of the symbol system without making it frequently 'touch down to reality' is critically consequential, while, on the other, we see that the elaboration of theory without reference to the ability to predict, much less to actually create, realities with those systems in control can lead to much bootless expenditure of effort. In this connection it also should be pointed out that the Chomskyan linguistics of recent years has been unfortunate in its minimization of the significance of performance testing, since, without such performance testing ultimately we do not have science but, rather, fantasizing. In the light provided by the history of AI research, though, it might be noted that contrariwise there are disadvantages to a premature concern for performance as a test while the scope of performance capability is so defined as to preclude the possibility of its generalization. To quote Wilks: '. . . *mere* performance based on ad hoc methods does not demonstrate understanding.'

The general issue in the philosophy of science having to do with what should be operationalized and how quickly operationalization tests should be introduced into a scientific enterprise and, in slightly old-fashioned terms, what is to be the role and character of theory in science, those issues are all raised again in effect by Winograd's preference for procedures over declarations. The computer scientist may see those issues in yet another light as he reflects on the advantages and disadvantages attendant upon fresh computation or retrieval for stored information, in instances where there is a choice to be made between those two stylistic elements in a program system.

The second generation systems, as Wilks calls them, show how a shift upward in the scale of realities dealt with has critically contributed to the growth of AI capability, as we have also noted to be the case with the shift upward in scale when linguistic and more particularly computational linguistics moved from the sentential and subsentential toward discourse, and at least to the supersentential. In a recent (1979) article by Brian Phillips in the *American*

Journal of Computational Linguistics we find an elaboration of techniques applicable to formally representing the content of the 'frames' of interest to Minsky utilizing a notation of the sort that Hedetniemi and Goodman prepare us for the employment of.

At the recent (Spring 1979) Rockefeller Foundation-supported conference 'Apollo Agonistes: The Humanities in a Computerized World', Monsignor Eammon O'Doherty, of University College Dublin, eloquently inveighed against the substitution of a Galilean universe for an Aristotelian. More specifically, he was expressing a profound concern for the abandonment of categories of intentionality and meaning from the scope of research on man, and the systematic substitution for them of operational tests, that is replicability tests. He advanced his case with primary reference to, as it happened, language research. The work of Kenneth Colby is a notable instance in point, in that in the effort to avoid 'fragility' he has developed in PARRY (the paranoid) a simulator of a partner to a conversation in which with his quite simple rules and a pattern matching scheme there is a plausible meaning of a Turing test without there being, in many specific conversational instances, any 'understanding' at all. PARRY impressively well meets the Turing test even when psychiatrists are a party to it. That achievement is the more impressive since at least in classical notions of what is to be theoretical, Colby's approach is the least theoretic that Wilks discusses.

The convergence of Wilks with Benson, when Wilks engages in a comparison of the different projects he has studied, is at least interesting – where Wilks tells us that it is the lack of theoretical precision which forestalls the making of precise relevant distinctions among the projects. Amidst the many telling observations made by Wilks in his analysis we are especially interested, in the light of our concern for the significance of the notational scheme which is used in analyzing language, that certainly Colby, and in some measure Charniak, favor the use of a language self-referentially in its own representation. It is also fascinating to meditate upon the apparent significance of the metaphors of 'surface' and 'depth' as governing perception in the study of language. It might appear that the tacit acceptance of that contrast between surface and depth has foreclosed realization that we may be able to effectively locate structure without the transformational implications of the concept of depth, as it has been used in the linguistics of the past twenty years.

A related issue along the same axis of particularism versus structuralism is to be found with reference to the characteristics of the 'real world' information that is utilized in making language analytic systems go. In the course of his discussion of Charniak's work, Wilks makes clear how important these issues are. He also brings forth into the explicit light of day the point of view with which we are associated, in representing all human enquiry as various forms of linguistic enterprise. Our position on that issue is expressed in more detail in such papers as 'History as language' (1968), 'Formalized historiography' (1978), and 'The history of science as discourse' (1979). There is a very interesting paradox implied by Wilks' argument that without his having an understanding of 'feelings' observers might think that an individual did not understand English; the paradox arises in, for example, a particular instance, that of Gerald Manley Hopkins, the eminent English poet, in that, according to the recent biography of him by Paddy Kitchen, Hopkins, who clearly was one of the best understanders and users of English in England, was also, simultaneously, clearly unable to use it in conventional ways when it came to taking into account such feelings knowledge as Wilks mentions. Kitchen has included entertaining exemplifying anecdotes.

Recent research about the changing character of 'interiorities' (mental words) may make us even more skeptical about assumptions as to mentation preceding action. Wilks' discussion of that issue of 'meaning' brings us around to problems posed by, among others, Husserl and to the issues raised by O'Doherty at the Albany conference in the spring of 1979. The situation is the more interesting for recent evidence that in the early middle ages there was very little in the way of the kind of interiority we take for granted.

Since, as the lawyers say, we clearly have an interest, it is probably not surprising that we take heart from Wilks' discussion with special reference to the importance to the development of computer-based analyses of general reference works for use in natural language processing – not only dictionaries, but thesauri and others – if we are to transcend the exceedingly ad hoc character of many such systems.

The emphasis that Wilks places on the argument of Hayes for set theoretic semantics (in a Tarskean sense) as a requirement for depth in the formal understanding of natural language is highly compatible with our conviction that there may be great latent importance in efforts to extend the Set L language of Jacob Schwartz to cope with natural language phenomena.

4 'Belief systems and language understanding' by Bertram Bruce, the fourth chapter in this volume, is an exceptionally clear and thoroughly worked out exemplification of a currently popular type of research in natural language computing. For Professor O'Doherty and others who are concerned about the extent to which the use of computers may substitute a more consistently 'Galilean' universe for the older 'Aristotelean' model, although there may be profound questions as to the significance of the implied 'understanding' of such an approach as Bruce here exemplifies, nonetheless it does constitute an effort to use the computer to cope explicitly with 'intentionality', as also with such associated constructs as 'belief' and 'meaning'. Bruce's exemplification of this approach can only sharply clarify some of the issues raised by Wilks in the chapter preceding it.

In larger and longer perspective it will be a matter of great interest to see whether this type of approach continues to be used, and used more effectively, or whether it comes to fade from the scene. This question is even an exciting one when understood as a special case of the question of how one is to determine when a new technology is inefficiently mimicking earlier technologies and when it is being used to exploit its own unique powers. In sum, the question might be 'Are these approaches *necessary* or *quaint*?'

Insofar as the process which Bruce so spectacularly crystallizes in his exposition leads to a decomposition and a making explicit of ways in which we are using language, one might argue that he has here a technique worthy of the aspirations of a Foucault. In those terms the question then becomes whether the making explicit of entailments of such language behaviors as we use proves to be a stage in a process leading to their extinction or, by contrast, whether it represents a stage in a process leading to their far more heightened use – by adding to human uses of them computer based utilizations. If the latter, we may feel that we are witnessing the emergence of an information system phenomenology.

One interesting technical implication of the Brucean approach for the use of computers in the study of natural language is in relationship to the development of ever more sophisticated forms of game-theoretic understanding as applied to exchanges of many sorts, including negotiations and bargains. One of the central issues in such current research has to do with the very question of credal regression, that is, beliefs about beliefs about beliefs. . . . It is an interesting fact – and paradox – that just as in conjunction with Wilks' analysis we had occasion to note how Gerard Manley Hopkins seemed simultaneously to be both exceptionally competent and incompetent as a user of language – here, with reference to Bruce's approach, we notice that professional specialists in the reading of strategists' intentions, namely generals, in U.S. staff schooling are regularly taught to avoid credal regression – and that in situations where the stakes might be about as high as they ever become.

It is sometimes argued that the work of the philosopher is to make evident the structure and the disarticulations among the terms used in a speech community. By that definition Bruce is a philosopher of high degree. The clarity of his exposition of some of our basic verbal habits is dazzling. One of its especially attractive features for those of us who are interested in psychiatry is its ready adaptability equally for the 'sane' and the 'non-sane' – in that his scheme allows for the representation of any kind of belief system, including such as any 'others' may regard as delusional.

In the context of the first and second volumes of this sub-series there also is a coming-full-circle character to what Bruce has done, in that the work of Fritz Heider on attribution theory which we pointed to with reference to its specific cognitive balance facet had a great deal to do with motivating the development of the very graph-theoretic notation which Hedetniemi and Goodman have presented in the first chapter of the first volume. And insofar as belief systems research is a product of the effort to look at multi-sentence productions, then too there is a linkage to issues in discourse analysis approaches which we have recently been discussing in this chapter. With reference to the central focus of his work, Bruce very explicitly indicates to us that there is a heavy reliance on 'a recognition of intentionality', and that central to the implications of that recognition in his work is Heider's concept of 'personal causation'.

In the use of the concept of intention there is that same notion of 'rationality' which Wilks has discussed with reference to, for example, the work of Schank. The implicit model – and not so implicit at that – is that thought precedes act. Whether that assumption will be progressively more heavily challenged remains to be seen. It is a traditional issue for the philosopher and currently one form of challenge is in Powers' book *Behavior, the control of perception* (1975). Whatever such challenges may prove to be in the future, at the present time those who are enthusiastic for Speech Act Theory in the tradition of Austin and Searle can only find Bruce's approach an attractive one. One of the fascinations that Bruce's approach affords is that he does make so very clear the constructed character of the whole process of motivation, or, more precisely, motivational imputation. We have come a long way since the time when motives were construed to be 'givens of nature'.

Bruce's emphasis upon the recursive character of belief provides one of the attractive points of entry into his discussion for such as have come to it out of an interest initially in the use of computers, rather than in the study of language by means of computing.

In his explicit utilization of the work of Colby with reference to the concept of credibility Bruce provides us with another strong link to the discussion of Wilks. Interesting vistas of research are opened up in this frame by the question of the extent to which belief depends upon shared uses of vocabularies and, more specifically, to what degree behavior labelled 'deviant' is behavior marked by lexical asymmetry.

With the rapid emergence of world-wide computer to computer communication networks, one of the interesting questions will be the extent to which the sorts of language uses which Bruce seeks here to explicate will appear to be a part of the solution or a part of the problem in the facilitation of more effective communication by individuals speaking across the boundaries from one language community to another.

It seems to us that, somewhat ironically, given the objective or purposes which Bruce would presumably attribute to his own work, it is not only good philosophizing but it is also excellent anthropology – more particularly a fine structure for handling ethno-methodological studies. Bruce's example of 'Joey' is an especially interesting one in that one wonders whether the utilization of intentionality language is, strictly speaking, redundant.

The clarity of each of the chapters in each of these volumes is a matter of great importance, given the uses to which they may be put. Bertrand Bruce's chapter is, in that way as well, a very fine conclusion to this second volume.

JOHN B. SMITH

Computer criticism*

1 Introduction

Computer applications for language and literature studies have generally fallen into two major groups: those concerned primarily with the production through textual manipulation of conventional aids for future research (dictionaries, concordances, etc.) and those in which the computer was used in the analysis of specific works of literature (thematic analyses, stylistic studies, etc.). The former group has, in general, been viewed as beneficial or, at least, inevitable; the products that have resulted have been familiar and their value apparent. The latter group of applications has presented certain problems. These studies have often been based on initial assumptions that are unfamiliar and developed through techniques that seem more mathematical than literary. (See Sedelow 1970, Widman 1971.) In such cases the critic has had to supply an intellectual context for his study, relating it to conventional critical approaches, or risk losing his reader. Preferable to statements of context on an ad hoc basis would be a general awareness, on the part of computer critic and general reader alike, of the assumptions and methods inherent in computer assisted studies of literature and the generic relation with major areas of conventional critical thought. Of greater consequence, however, would be the increased awareness of critics that this new critical methodology is available for use on a wide variety of problems. As late as 1973 Paul de Man wrote:

> 'It can legitimately be said . . . that, from a technical point of view, very little has happened in American criticism since the innovative work of New Criticism. There certainly have been numerous excellent books of criticism since, but in none of them have the techniques of description and interpretation evolved beyond the techniques of close reading established in the thirties and forties.' (De Man 1973: 27)

The computer, properly and sensitively applied, offers the literary critic a rich collection of new techniques; unfortunately, this new methodology has been overlooked, even by Structuralist critics such as de Man, largely because it has appeared in rather specialized journals not read by the profession at large, and not in the standard periodicals or full length works.

Computers in Language Research 2

In the remarks that follow, I shall try to speak to these needs by considering three aspects of computer studies of literature. First, I shall look exactly at some of what one does in using the computer to study language. Then, I shall try to identify a mode of criticism that arises from using the computer, which I term 'Computer Criticism'. Finally, I shall try to show that this mode of criticism, which appears rather foreign at first glance, is closely related to the major critical developments of this century and, in many respects, is a next logical step.

Let me confess at the outset that I am uncomfortable with the term, Computer Criticism, for it suggests that, somehow, it is the computer that does the criticism. Nothing could be further from the truth. A more accurate term might be 'applied semiological analysis', but this appelation is probably worse. The role of the computer is to gather the information the critic asks for, to display or present the information, or to apply some analytic model to the information. As with any mode of criticism, assimilation and interpretation takes place in the mind of the critic. One might argue that the computer is simply amplifying the critic's powers of perception and recall in concert with conventional perspectives. This is true, and what I have termed Computer Criticism could be viewed as a lateral extension of Formalism, New Criticism, Structuralism, etc. On the other hand, it is well known that occasionally a tool will emerge that proves to be of such seminal importance that it radically alters human culture and human self-concepts. (This process has been amply popularized by Marshall McLuhan, Arthur C. Clarke, Stanley Kubrick, and others.) The creative, sensitive, and extended use of the computer in pursuit of a fuller understanding of literature can lead to an intellectual perspective that is consistent with the main stream of critical thought but, nevertheless, different enough to warrant independent identification. Computer Criticism is, thus, parallel to recent schools of criticism but it is also an emerging school in its own right.

In attempting to document the relations between conventional criticism and Computer Criticism I shall concentrate most heavily on the material that I assume is least familiar to the reader; however, as I develop the assumptions and implications of this mode of inquiry, I shall relate them to assumptions and implications inherent in other perspectives. Because most readers are familiar with conventional criticism and because of the availability of numerous excellent surveys for those who are not, a summary of recent critical developments is not necessary; however, since my thesis is based on my particular view of those developments, I wish to pause momentarily to state that perspective.

In my view, the mainstream of twentieth century criticism has moved steadily, inexorably, toward greater formality and toward the notion of a 'science' or 'sciences' of criticism (these assertions are probably two sides of the same coin). In this country, this movement begins, at least in earnest, with the New Critics and their attempts to break criticism out of the philological mold, to remove the encumbrance of authorial intention (an epistemic impossibility), and to center the critical response on the language of the work itself. Similar intentions lie behind the earlier Russian Formalists. Concentrating more on linguistics, rather than on diction or rhetoric, they sought to distinguish the language of literature, viewed as coherent systems of linguistic traits, from other language/mental activities. They were most successful in their thematic studies (such as Propp) where their analyses really began after language per se was left behind and they were able to deal semiotically with the structure of symbols/categories derived from language. A necessary step toward formality is the awareness of the relativity of models or critical perspectives; this important step in the progression toward greater formality was provided by, among others, the Chicago Aristotelian critics. Stressing the necessity for critical pluralism, they liberated the work of literature from the critical statement just as the New Critics had liberated it from the author. More recently, formalism has moved one step further in the Structuralists' view of the literary work, itself, as a semiotic structure. The full implications of regarding the literary work as a sequence of signs, as a material object, that is 'waiting' to be characterized by external models or systems have yet to be realized. Inherent is the possibility for defining content by formal rules of association, contiguity, and syntax; inherent is the possibility of defining esthetic response by similar formal rules.

The potential of structuralist thought has not been realized, in my opinion, for two reasons. First, in spite of statements that structuralism is really only a method, it is not methodical enough; structuralists have never codified a set of methods or techniques that is adequate and general enough to accommodate close, sophisticated analyses of a variety of specific literary works. Second, and understandably because of their linear descent from de Saussure, their concept of structure has been overwhelmed by the notion of linguistic structure. There is no reason to believe, and in fact numerous reasons to believe otherwise, that segments larger than the sentence are structured in a form similar to the stuctures within a sentence. The next logical step in this progression toward greater formality would be a mode of criticism based on a coherent set of techniques that includes linguistic models but that goes beyond to include any concept of structure that is potentially useful for characterizing linear sequences of signs.

The progression toward the concept of a science of criticism is probably another manifestation of the movement toward greater formalism. The New Critics, while often using 'the scientist' as a whipping boy in their efforts to distinguish the rich, connotative language of poetry from merely descriptive language, nevertheless, endorse a mode of criticism that would be more precise, systematic, structural, i.e., 'scientific'. The Russian Formalists were more direct: as William Harkins has observed, they quite consciously saw themselves as 'trying to create a literary science' (Harkins 1951: 184). While not calling criticism a 'science' per se, Northrop Frye has forcefully described the scientific aspects of contemporary inquiry:

> It seems absurd to say there *may* be a scientific element in criticism when there are dozens of learned journals based on the assumption that there is, and hundreds of scholars engaged in a scientific procedure related to literary criticism. Evidence is examined scientifically, texts are edited scientifically. Prosody is scientific in structure; so is phonetics; so is philology. Either literary criticism is scientific, or all these highly trained and intelligent scholars are wasting their time on some pseudo-science like phrenology. (1957: 8)

Similarly, Robert Scholes has identified the 'scientific' aspect of criticism with the 'cumulative' aspect of scholarship (1974: 77), a practice prescribed by McKerrow in 1952 and now expected by virtually every serious journal. A final, and perhaps extreme, view of a science of criticism is that of Roland Barthes stated in 1967: 'Science versus literature'. Barthes not only identifies a scientific mode of criticism present in French Structuralist/Semiological Criticism, but asserts that the emerging field of semiology will constitute a 'meta-language' (by which he means a meta-science involving both perspective and method) that will eventually include and absorb the sciences proper.

This brief overview of the structuralist/formalist tradition and the related movement toward a science of criticism has omitted reference to social, psychological, and phenomenological criticisms. There have, of course, already been partial attempts to bring Marxist and Freudian criticism into the domain of structuralism. It is my personal belief that this trend is likely to increase and that social and psychological approaches will make substantial, permanent impact only to the extent that they can be incorporated into a formal consideration of the text itself. As for phenomenological approaches, I see them as the 'loyal opposition', the inevitable and opposite reaction to this very strong main current of thought.

In the remarks that follow, I shall try to infer through a consideration of specific analyses the intellectual perspective termed Computer Criticism and to link this perspective at key points with the formalist/structuralist tradition. For the reader unfamiliar with the computer, however, I shall look first at what is actually done in exposing a literary text to a computer before considering the more general implications of these applications.

2 Textual processing

In principle, a computer is a very simple machine. It is a symbol manipulator that can recognize 256 codes or characters.[1] These codes, which are thought of as being ordered from zero to 225, can stand for numbers, letters of the alphabet, or practically anything that one wishes to associate with them. They may be considered separately, as is usually the case for language processing, but they can be considered in groups in order that numbers larger than 255 can be represented or texts with more than 256 characters (texts with a variety of fonts) can be represented. The second major point to remember is that computers operate sequentially: they can look at two characters, compare them to see if they are equal, see if one is higher or lower than the other in alphabetic sequence, or move them from one place to another. For numbers, the computer does the same things but it may also add them, subtract them, multiply them, divide them, etc. Using these basic operations one can describe procedures that can be applied to a text to do something useful and, eventually, to do something interesting.

Before such a procedure can be applied to a text, however, the text must be presented to the computer in a form that it can recognize; unfortunately this is normally not in the form of a physical book. Usually the text must be typed onto cards or, preferably, typed directly into the computer memory using a keyboard terminal. Both keypunches and keyboard terminals have a (virtually) standard typewriter keyboard; in fact, several popular terminals employ the IBM Selectric typewriter mechanism. When a key is struck on a keypunch, it prints the character on the top of the card but also punches a series of holes that the computer can interpret as one of its group of 256 characters. Similarly, the terminal types or displays the character but instead of punching holes it sends via a regular telephone line a Morse code-like representation of the character that is received and kept by the computer until it is told what to do.

Texts are normally typed virtually as they appear in the printed book: one textual line per card or one textual line per terminal line. To facilitate later processing or to represent characters in the text that do not appear on the keyboard, one may employ special typing conventions; for example, one may wish to mark italics by placing, say, a pound sign (£) immediately before or after the word to inform the computer that this word is of different font and to mark it accordingly. With most textual material and with many sets of conventions, the encoded text can be read both by the computer and by the human being without great difficulty.

After the text has been encoded it must be 'read' by the computer. For cards, this is done by a card reader, a device that examines each column of each card, in order, to determine which of the 256 characters is represented. For texts typed directly into the computer through a terminal, this is done through a statement which is typed on the terminal but which the computer recognizes as a command rather than as more text. To read the text and to process it, the computer requires a detailed sequence of instructions or program; this can be written by the analyst but there are an increasing number of such programs available. These may be stored in the computer's program library and simply called by the analyst when required.

As far as the computer is concerned, the text will appear as one long sequence of characters, starting with the first, continuing from card to card or line to line, to the last. It is usually preferable to segment the text into recognizable units: words, sentences, paragraphs, etc. Each segment, however, must be described to the computer in terms that it can 'understand'; for example, a word might be described to the computer as a sequence of non-blank characters bounded on the left and right by blanks. The situation can get a bit more complicated for abbreviations, words before commas, the last word in the sentence, etc.; but by careful planning and through a set of encoding conventions that anticipates such difficulties, the computer can be trained to recognize a word within the stream of characters. Similarly, it may be given a set of instructions or rules to recognize sentences, paragraphs, chapters, etc.

Once the appropriate unit is recognized, it may be moved out of the flow of characters and placed somewhere else where it is more accessible. For example, it may be placed in a list of words, one per line, where each word may be dealt with as a single item. After the entire text has been processed and all words extracted, one word in the list could be compared with the word below it in the list. If the lower word is higher in alphebetic sequence, the computer could then exchange the two words. Repeating this operation over and over, the computer could eventually arrange the entire list into descending alphabetic sequence. It would then be quite easy to derive a dictionary for the text being processed as well as the frequency of occurrence for each word.

If two texts were processed, one placed in one list and the other in a second list, the computer could be used to collate the two. That is, it could be instructed to compare the first word in each list. If they are identical, it would go to the next word in each list and repeat the process. If they are not identical it could then move down one list until the words match or if that doesn't work move down the second list. In some cases the comparison can be a bit tricky requiring a jump ahead and comparisons both backwards and forwards within both lists, but the computer is far more accurate than the human eye, particularly for texts representing different type settings.

If the computer is instructed to recognize not just words but also sentences, the words may be placed in one list and the entire sentence for each word placed in a second wider, but corresponding, list. When the list of words is rearranged alphabetically, the corresponding sentences may also be rearranged. In this manner the computer can be used to construct a concordance providing full sentence context. The entire concordance could be printed by the computer, or it could be instructed to print a selected concordance for only a specific set of words supplied. It could even be instructed to print a concordance for only those sentences in which particular combinations of words appear.

In practice, these techniques are often expanded or modified for efficiency and to accommodate large texts. However, these brief examples will give the reader unfamiliar with computers a sense of how they operate and how they can be used to process a text. The 'products' that resulted were all familiar critical apparatus: a dictionary, a collated text, a concordance. In the remarks that follow, where I shall be dealing with computer materials that may be less familiar, I shall not burden the reader with discussion of *how* the particular aid was produced; I shall concentrate more on describing the product itself, the assumptions that have led to it, and its implications for literary research and critical perspective.

3.1 Computer criticism: Materialist view of a text

It is well known that the act of reading includes a number of assumptions and a number of mental actions that are normally unconscious. We can, but seldom do, distinguish between the concept of a character and its shape or form; we are even less likely to examine (consciously) the physical aspects of the character: the ink that is used to form it, the paper on which it is printed, etc. Instead, we normally deal with the character – or, more often, aggregates of characters – on the level of meaning. We see configurations of characters and we think word, phrase, or concept. The important point, however, is that if pushed not only can we distinguish between signifier and signified, we can move in the opposite direction and distinguish between physical medium and signifier.

These strata do not exist for the computer. Its total 'awareness' resides in its ability to distinguish among a small (256) set of states or sequential combinations of states. The only physical dimension of these states is the electrical impulses that constitute them. All other 'awareness' is relational: one state 'higher' or 'lower' than another (A higher than B in alphabetic sequence).

Because the computer is a sequential processor of symbols, there is a notion of linearity and segmentation inherent in its design. The concept of linearity is fundamental to the 'stream' of characters that it receives from outside – through the card reader or terminal. Any concept of segmentation based on the length of the card or the length of the terminal line is physical and, hence, lost when the text is considered in its encoded, symbolic form. The fundamental segment is, of course, the character. Since each character is represented by one of 256 states there is no variable spacing: all characters occupy equal space in the sequence and all are segmented from one another. Segmentation, then, in the linguistic sense must be defined for the computer formally and functionally: the sequence of non-blank characters between blanks, or some equivalent definition. If these segments, words in this case, are moved to a list where each slot is of equal width, then this transformed version of the text becomes a text of equally spaced segments analogous to the character-level defined text. Thus, the items in the list, words, become the fundamental units or states and are usually dealt with by the computer as 'wholes'; and the text considered as a sequence of words emerges with the same material characteristics as the text viewed as a sequence of characters.

The notion of signified is, therefore, missing from the text considered as a sequence of words just as it is missing from the text considered as a sequence of characters. When the computer 'reads' a text, the three levels – the physical, the signifier, and the signified – collapse into the single stratum of the signifier: the sequence of characters or internal states of the computer. The process is necessarily and formally reductive but perhaps not as limiting as it may first appear. While the computer can deal only with *encoded* material, there is no reason that physical as well as semantic characteristics cannot be encoded into parallel symbol sequences. That is, characteristics such as physical segmentation (page, line, position within line), font, etc. can be encoded as separate sequences of symbols parallel to the actual textual characters. Similarly, semantic relations such as synonymity, oppositeness, etc., can be encoded in another symbol sequence (or if necessary, several such sequences), and the text 'viewed' by the computer as three or more parallel symbol sequences; unlike the human being, however, the computer cannot infer any relation or order among these separate sequences unless that relation is supplied, directly or indirectly, by the researcher. So considered, a text becomes for the computer a material, linear sequence or sequences of symbols (Fig. 1).

This stratified view of a text is dependent on the notion of category. At the physical level, the researcher might establish categories denoting italics, bold face, etc. and encode this information by appropriate symbols in a sequence parallel to the main stream of characters. One could consider the stream of characters that constitute the text a category system as well: that is, a set of 256 categories into which the characters of the physical text are mapped. Since this correspondence is usually straight-forward, one is seldom even conscious of the categorical aspect. Much more important is the concept of category at the level of the signified. Since the computer can deal only with formal relations among characters, words, or other segments, the researcher must provide all concepts of 'meaning'; this is usually done through a system or systems of categories.

Since the computer can produce a dictionary, we may assume that the researcher has at his disposal an alphabetized list of the words that occur in the text under consideration. One concept of category is equivalent to

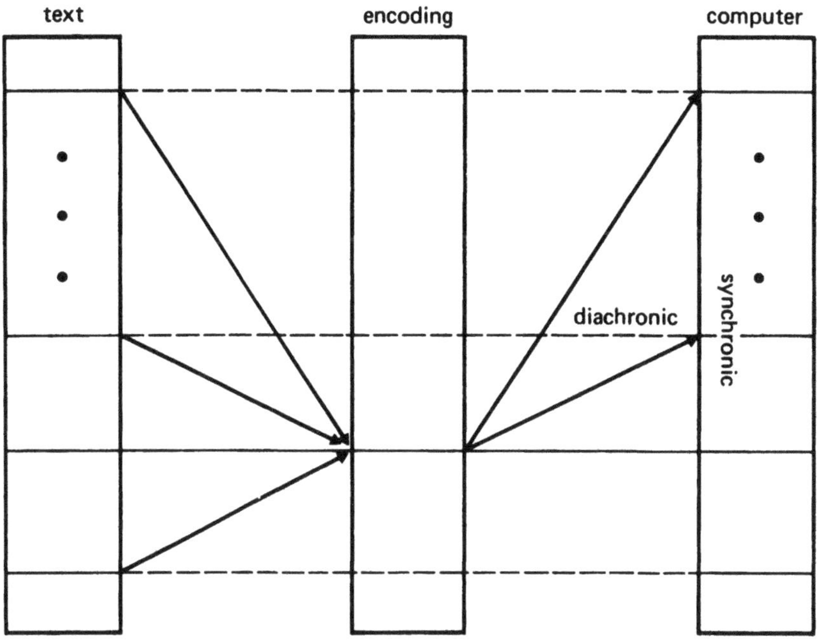

Figure 1. Computer 'view' of a text

dividing or partitioning the dictionary. That is, the researcher might read down the dictionary and divide the vocabulary into words that suggest sensory impressions (images) or words that carry content (as opposed to some list of functors), or any other grouping appropriate for the study. The computer, in its capacity as symbol manipulator, could then be instructed to consider only that category or collection of words and ignore the rest. Similarly, the researcher may wish to designate a number of categories, as appropriate for a thematic analysis, in which the vocabulary of the text is divided into a number of separate categories. For example, he may select for the theme, *fire*, the words *burn, burned, burning, fire, heat, hot*; and for *water: damp, water, watery, wet*, etc. It is this information, encoded as some set of symbols such that the appropriate symbol is associated with the corresponding word in the textual sequence, that would constitute one of the signified strata. A broader study might deal with all content words but ignore, in its semantic emphasis, syntactic variability indicated by suffix. An appropriate category system for such an analysis, instead of having twenty or thirty categories, could employ several thousand with each category standing only for a single root-group (*hope, hoped, hoping*, etc.) and containing only a half-dozen or so members. From the standpoint of the computer, it makes no difference whether the vocabulary is divided into two categories, thirty categories, or several thousand, nor does the rationale behind the particular categorization scheme matter: all such relations can be handled analogously.

This notion of category, dependent on the concept of a dictionary, alone, is not sufficient for many studies. For example, the configuration of characters, *r o s e*, may signify a flower, as appropriate for an imagery study; but it may also describe an action – *he rose from his chair*. Here context must be taken into consideration. Since the computer can produce a concordance, we may assume the researcher has at his disposal a concordance as well as a dictionary. Consequently, the concept of category can be refined to include linear, diachronic relations as well as dictionary-based, synchronic relations defined for every occurrence of a given configuration of characters. Since the computer, through its ability as symbol manipulator, can be instructed to regard a number of different words as equivalent, the category of linear configuration of words can be extended to include linear configurations of word categories: that is, instances involving a paradigm-like configuration where members of the paradigm may be any specific word within a category. One of the earlier content analysis program, The General Inquirer, formally defined content as precisely this: the logical configuration of conceptual categories of words (see Stone 1966). In retrospect, we have seen that the text can be formally segmented in a step by step manner such that each higher segment is defined in terms of units at the next lower level, ranging from the character to the entire work considered as a whole and by extension to the corpus. For each level of segmentation, parallel strata of symbols representing both physical as well as conceptual aspects of the text may be established. These may refer directly back to the textual sequence, itself, and are hence parallel to one another, but they may also be established hierarchically by referring directly to some secondary stratum (category of categories, categories of syntactic forms, etc.). Concepts of form, structure, and meaning relate to patterns along, across, and among these various strata. Below I shall describe some of the formal models that are available for characterizing such relations, but first I shall pause to relate these basic concepts of textual materiality and interpretive categorical strata to similar concepts within several recent conventional critical perspectives.

3.2 Conventional criticism: Materialist view of a text

The concepts of the autonomy of art, the materiality of the text, and the primacy of category to define and characterize form are all central for Russian

Formalism as well as its second generation in Prague. As Victor Erlich has observed, the autonomy of art for the Formalists ranges 'from the autonomy of the individual poetic word *vis-à-vis* its object to the autonomy of the literary work of art with regard to reality' (1955: 177). At the level of word or figure, the observance of *ostranenie* or 'making strange' was an attempt to liberate the word from fixed connotations so that its full richness could be seen (Erlich 1955: see especially his discussion of Skaftymov in Chapter 10). At the other extreme, Skaftymov demonstrated that character in a narrative, the action in the plot, and, indeed, the philosophic dimensions of the fictive universe must be considered first as components organized within an autonomous esthetic structure before substantive extrapolation can be attempted (Erlich 1955: 176–177).

The concept of category, also, is both pervasive and varied in its manifestation. To reveal the universal narrative structure of a collection of fairy tales, Vladimir Propp (1968) reduced the texts of a collection of some 479 tales to sequences of basic actions or 'functions'. Since Propp's 'function' represents an action described in the narrative, it is analogous to the category of logical configurations of dictionary groupings discussed above; Propp's familiar symbolic representation of thematic structure could be viewed as a sequence of symbols parallel to the textual sequence, analogous to one of the semantic strata inherent in Computer Criticism (Propp 1968, especially Chapter 2). A. A. Reformatsky is one step closer to the 'bootstrap' hierarchical relations of Computer Criticism's category strata. He distinguishes among 'themes', 'the simplist static unit of plot construction', 'motif', a set (usually two) of themes joined by a verb, and 'plot theme', units composed of combinations of themes and motifs (1973: 88–89). Because Reformatsky is primarily interested in narrative sequence, he often collapses these logically distinct categorical strata into a single symbol sequence in order to represent narrative structure. More important, particularly in later structuralist thought, is the concept of metonymy. In distinguishing between figures of speech natural for poetry and those natural for prose, Roman Jakobson (1936) distinguishes between the relation of comparison inherent in metaphor and logically contiguous substitution inherent in metonymy. The latter, of course, when considered methodologically, is clearly an example of semantic category: the collection of textual items used individually to stand for the set.[2]

More familiar, but less directly related, is American New Criticism. The concept of a materialistic text is apparent in Ransom's ontological concern for the 'poem as object', a predominantly holistic perspective in which sound and meaning must be joined phenomenologically by the critic (Ransom 1940). Ransom's perspective is made much more concrete and applicable in Wellek and Warren's delineation of perceptual strata. They divide the text into: (1) the sound stratum; (2) the units of meaning; (3) stylistic devices such as image and metaphor; (4) the fictive world of the poem; and (5) the metaphysical dimensions of that world (Wellek - Warren 1956: 157). While their delineation of strata has been useful for students of literature, their emphasis is historical and comparative rather than methodological. In fact, it is one of the great ironies that the New Critics, while never establishing a general methodology, produced an unusual amount of perceptive and helpful criticism through the extraordinary talents of its major practitioners. Perhaps the closest approximation to a New Critical methodology is Caroline Spurgeon's earlier categorization and tabulation of Shakespeare's images (1958), although her biographical extrapolations were, of course, contrary to New Critical principles.

More directly related to Computer Criticism's assumptions of a material text and the notion of categorical strata is French Structuralist Criticism, perhaps best summarized in Roland Barthes' 'The Structuralist activity' (1972). Most Structuralists claim at least all of the arts as their domains while their near kind, the Semiologists, claim all knowledge; consequently, when Barthes addresses first the ontological nature of the object of scrutiny and, next, its dissociation into parts from which collections (paradigms) are formed, he does so for areas other than literature:

> The goal of all structuralist activity, whether reflexive or poetic, is to reconstruct an 'object' in such a way as to manifest thereby the rules of functioning (the 'functions') of this object. . . .
>
> The structuralist activity involves two typical operations: dissection and articulation. To dissect the first object, the one which is given to the simulacrum-activity, is to find in it certain mobile fragments whose differential situation engenders a certain meaning; the fragment has no meaning in itself, but it is nonetheless such that the slightest variation wrought in its configuration produces a change in the whole; a *square* by Mondrian, a *series* of Pousseur, a versicle of Butor's *Mobile*, the 'mytheme' in Levi-Strauss, the phoneme in the work of the phonologist, the 'theme' in certain literary criticism -- all these units . . . have no significant existence except by their frontiers: those that separate them from other actual units of the discourse . . . and also which distinguish them from other virtual units, with which they form a certain class (which linguistics calls a *paradigm*); this notion of paradigm is essential, apparently, if we are to understand the structuralist vision: the paradigm is a group or reservoir – as limited as possible – of objects . . .; what characterizes the paradigmatic object is that it is, vis-à-vis other objects of its class in a certain relation of affinity and dissimilarity. . . . The dissection operation thus produces an initial dispersed state of the simulacrum, but the units of the structure are not at all anarchic: before being distributed and fixed in the continuity of the composition, each one forms with its own virtual group or reservoir an intelligent organism, subject to a sovereign motor principle: that of the least difference. (Barthes 1972: 214, 216–217)

Illustrative of Barthes' view of the text as 'mobile fragments' and his insistence on the primacy of category (paradigm) for critical analysis is Tzvetan Todorov's *Grammaire du Decameron* in which he proposes a specific instance (Grammar of Narrative) of a universal grammar appropriate for all conceptualization.

Similar to Propp's study of Russian folk tales, Todorov's study is a highly abstract study of narrative sequence after it has been reduced to several strata of categories. He first distinguishes among textual segments: stories, sequence (a complete 'little tale'), propositions (basic narrative sentence), and parts of speech. He next reduces all actions to the verb categories and all attributes to the other categories. He then proposes a transformational grammar of narrative to accomodate the individual tales. Both the statement of principle as well as the illustrative example emphasize a critical perspective based on a segmented text of functional units that may be grouped in various ways in order to define relational patterns. Computer Criticism shares this perspective but, of course, is more inclusive; that is, it demands neither Barthes' concept of the smallest possible set or Todorov's specific categories. Even greater flexibility is present in its liberation from linguistic concepts of structure – virtually a universal assumption of French Structuralism.

The formalist group closest to Computer Criticism is the London School, centered around J.R. Firth but most thoroughly and articulately developed by M.A.K. Halliday. Earlier, we saw that the computer 'considers' a character as one of 256 distinguishable states ordered sequentially; analogously, it is convenient to consider a text as a seqence of equally spaced character patterns or words. Firth and Halliday use the concept of 'exponent' both to define the substantive within a categorical stratum and to connect the various strata. Halliday, who borrows the concept from Firth, states the relation as follows:

> Exponence is the scale which relates the categories of the theory, which are categories of the highest degree of abstraction, to the data . . . . Each category can be linked *directly* by exponence to the formal item. This has then to be related, in turn, to the substance . . . . When grammar reaches the formal item, either it has said all there is formally to be said about it or it hands it over to lexis. (1961: 270–271)

'Lexis', for Halliday, is the 'set' of substantives that occupy the places in the sequence of categorical units within a stratum; at the lowest, or most delicate level, this consists of the orthographic or phonemic symbols. Larger units – words, phrases, syntactic patterns, etc. – are produced by formal patterns of textual co-occurrences, called 'collocations', which may be ennumerated to form sets. There is, thus, a direct correspondence between the Firth/Halliday notion of 'sets' and the Computer Criticism concept of 'states' that constitute textual items; both share the view that subsequent categorical strata can be formed by formal delineation of patterns within a lower level; finally, both establish correspondences between strata, one by the concept of exponency, the other through the concept of location and direct co-occurrence. This and other similarities will be explored further in the discussion of the concept of structure below.

This brief, but I hope not too distorted, comparison illustrates the close compatibility between several recent structuralist schools and Computer Criticism. All contain the basic premise that the text exists as an object in its own right and all approach the text by establishing with varying degrees of formality strata through which the critic views the text. Computer Criticism differs in that it demands formal rules for establishing strata, it suggests a greater number of strata relating to a greater range of textual features, but most important, all such strata are arbitrary and can be established in response to a wide range of specific critical intents. By contrast, the conventional perspectives discussed assign strata a fixed definition (syntactic, thematic, etc.) with prescriptive structural frameworks. Conceptually, then, the specific aspects of textual materiality and interpretive categorical stratification of these examples can be viewed as special cases of the more general concepts found in Computer Criticism.

4.1 Computer criticism: Concepts of structure

A functional concept of form or structure emerges from the functional notions of sequence and category. Inherent in the sequence of signifiers is a concept of form based on contiguity or transition: one item is followed by another item, followed by another item, etc. Between the level of signifier and all other levels there exists an inherent, diachronic relation; symbols occur in the same slot in the text as the signifier whether that signifier is a textual segment or a segment within some higher categorical stratum. All other concepts of form are relations that work in a state of tension with these fundamental relations: that is, structures that associate in some meaningful way items that are not adjacent or parallel.

The domain or textual segment for which structural relations are sought is most important. If the segment is the sentence, then structure becomes essentially linguistic (for example, syntax is a system that associates in a meaningful way sometimes noncontiguous words on the basis of grammatical categories). If the segment is the paragraph, the concept of structure would be that of discourse analysis. For an entire text, a description of the structure and its rules and dynamics could be seen as interpretive criticism; for the canon of the author, the endeavor can be seen to resemble Frye's concept of contextual criticism.

By viewing the text as a functional, materialist sequence of symbols, the critic is free to employ linguistic models where they are appropriate but he is also entitled to employ any model that fits this view of a text and which is potentially useful. I shall try to locate some of the domains in which descriptive models may function and some of the specific, non-linguistic models that can be employed. To give this discussion an illustrative content, I shall discuss these models as they could be used for a thematic analysis, where theme means a collection or metonymic category of words that suggest the same basic concept (such as the collection of words related to *fire* and *water* mentioned above).[3] Other definitions of 'theme' as well as other critical foci can, of course, be accommodated under the general notion of category.

The concept of category 'exists' conceptually on the level of the signified regardless of whether it is encoded as a sequence of symbols parallel to the textual sequence of signifiers or represented in some other way.[4] Mere designation of the theme or category, as was seen in Spurgeon's study of Shakespeare, draws the critic's attention to the functional equivalence of the words or units of the category. It also suggests the further possibility of describing the form or 'behavior' of the theme over the entire text. That is, we may count the number of times the category appears and by comparing this value with similar totals for other thematic groups gain some partial insight into its relative prevalence and, perhaps, importance. If the text is segmented on the physical level into units of equal length (say, 500 words) and subtotals for each such unit computed, the resulting values may be used to produce a distribution of the theme over the text (see Figure 2: a distribution of the theme, *fire*, for Joyce's *A portrait of the artist as a young man*). In such a drawing we may not only confirm critical impressions of thematic density, we may see exactly the proportional concentration in one section of the text compared with another.

While a distribution of a theme can be regarded as a structual description of that theme, Computer Criticism can go one step further and employ models that characterize that distribution. That is, the critic may not only display the actual distribution, but uncover the underlying form or dynamics of that distribution and compare it with similar analyzed distributions. By regarding the diachronic sequence of words as analogous to the unitary progression of time, the critic may employ a variety of analytic models, known collectively as Time Series Analysis, to characterize the distribution. One such model is Fourier Analysis.

To apply Fourier Analysis to the distribution of a category or theme, the critic must view the distribution as analogous to a wave over time, such as a graph of a sound wave over some period of time. If the sound wave has definite maximum and minimum frequencies, as would a sound wave carried over a telephone, it is a remarkable mathematical fact that no matter how irregular the wave appears, it can be reproduced by combining a definite number of flowing, perfectly regular (sine and cosine) waves of different frequencies and amplitudes/heights. By picking only the highest, most important waves, adding them together, and ignoring the rest, one can produce a 'smoothed' transformation of the original distribution in which the form and

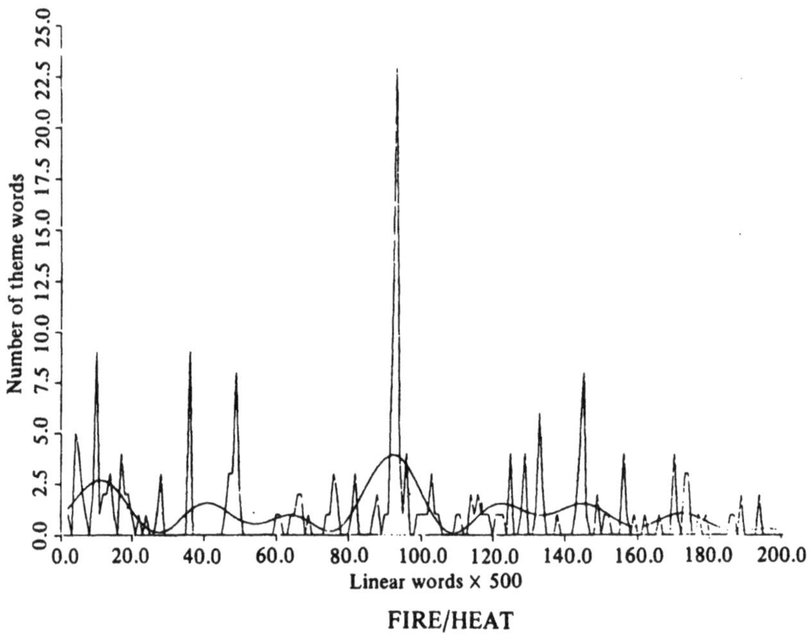

Figure 2. Distribution of *fire*

major dynamics of the theme are readily apparent. Further, a distribution of the amplitudes (actually, a function of the amplitudes) of the smooth waves can be regarded as a formal description of the complexity of the theme; a thematic distribution with only eight important terms or rhythms might be considered less 'complex' than a distribution with sixteen. Thus, the critic may use the computer to draw attention to the variety of words connoting a theme, to compute its frequency of occurrence, to display its form or behavior over an entire text, and to characterize that form. The techiques described could also be employed to consider a variety of themes and the resulting materials used for comparative purposes. Other techniques more directly suited for considering thematic comparisons and interactions, however, will be discussed below.

The concept of distribution is a diachronic concept of structure that parallels the three levels – physical segmentation, sequence of signifiers, sequential categories of significants – described earlier; a different concept of form or structure is the collection of synchronic relations among a number of such distributions and, further, changes in the pattern of such interrelations over the text. Synchronic patterns of interrelation are, essentially, patterns of co-occurrence. For example, in Joyce's *Portrait*, a great deal is revealed about Stephen by the combination of themes and images that flow through his mind. In Chapter 1, he seldom recalls the pleasant and secure hearth fire of home without recalling the dreadful fall into the cold waters of the ditch; other combinations abound. While techniques for determining synchronic patterns of interrelations will reveal thematic groups that tend to cluster, of even greater interest are techniques for revealing the progression of such interactions through the text. Returning to *Portrait*, the strong interaction between fire and water imagery disappears and is replaced by other strong associations. In fact, the entire development of Stephen's personality can be traced by first establishing the dominant patterns of association or co-occurrence for a section of text and then observing the shifts that take place at epiphanal moments.

A number of models are available for determining such patterns of co-occurrence: one I have found particularly useful is factor analysis or, more specifically, Principal Component Analysis. To use it, in the context cited above, the critic would determine a section of text – possibly the entire text – in which he feels that thematic interaction is relatively consistent. By next dividing that portion of the text into small, uniform physical units (perhaps 100 words) and by computing distributions on the basis of those units for all themes or categories to be considered, he may use factor analysis to determine specific clusters or groups of themes that consistently occur close to one another. With this information he may return to his concordance or to the text to explore the specific thematic significance suggested by these patterns of inter-relation.

To trace the developing network of associations among themes, I shall describe two approaches. The first, employing a device known as the state diagram, is rather simple to apply; the second, known by the acronym, CGAMS, at present requires rather specialized computing equipment but is more powerful. State diagrams are widely used in Automata Theory to designate the particular configurations or states of a theoretical computing machine, the history of the 'machine,' or the permissible transitions from state to state. This is done by representing the states as a set of points and the transitions by lines or arrows between the points. The technique can be used to reveal the developing structure or network of thematic associations by representing each theme by a point and indicating the associative relations between themes as lines joining the appropriate points/themes. More specifically, one could have the computer mark each theme or, perhaps, cluster of a theme (a cluster could be a section of text in which, say, three words in the same theme occur within 100 words of one another).

The progression from theme to theme or from cluster to cluster can be traced by drawing and numbering the lines from appropriate point to appropriate point. Close thematic interaction will be revealed in points close to one another in the diagram and by those having a number of lines joining them. An example of a thematic network of this sort is shown in figures 3 and 4,

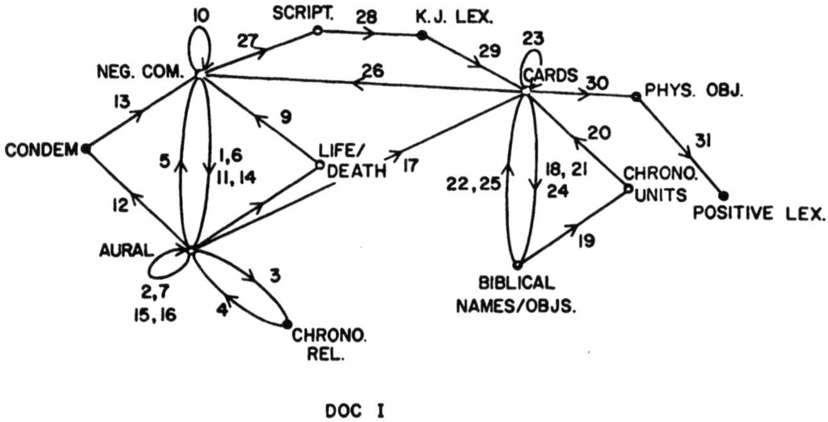

Figure 3. Thematic structure of DOC I

representing two versions of the same basic text, in this case, a folk sermon.[5] While the diagram itself represents a synchronic structure for the entire text, the diachronic progression from theme to theme can be traced: locate START; find the path marked 1, move to the next point or theme; find the path marked 2; move to the next theme; etc. Used singly, diagrams of individual texts reveal the specific thematic structure of that text; diagrams for several texts can be used in combination for comparative purposes to approach questions such as thematic complexity and the relation of thematic structure to other aspects of the work.[6]

When the critic wishes to explore the dynamics of thematic interaction over a long text, the computational system, CGAMS, may be more appropriate (Smith 1974). CGAMS, while most useful for deriving a macroscopic representation of thematic relations, may also be used for close inspection of specific thematic relations within a small textual segment. The system produces a pictorial representation of the relations between a selected set of themes on a T.V.-like screen (see figure 5). The basic picture resembles an aerial view of a mountain range in which there is a peak for each theme. The height of a peak represents the relative prevalence of that theme for the section of text under consideration. The horizontal distance between peaks represents the proportional diachronic distances in the text between those two themes relative to similar distances for all other theme pairs. The slope of the facet between two themes/peaks indicates whether the two themes tend to be a stable distance from one another (for example, nearly always ten or twelve words apart) resulting in a sharp, abrupt facet, or whether the distances vary considerably (sometimes two or three words apart; sometimes twenty or thirty words apart) resulting in a sloping facet. The perspective on the 'mountain

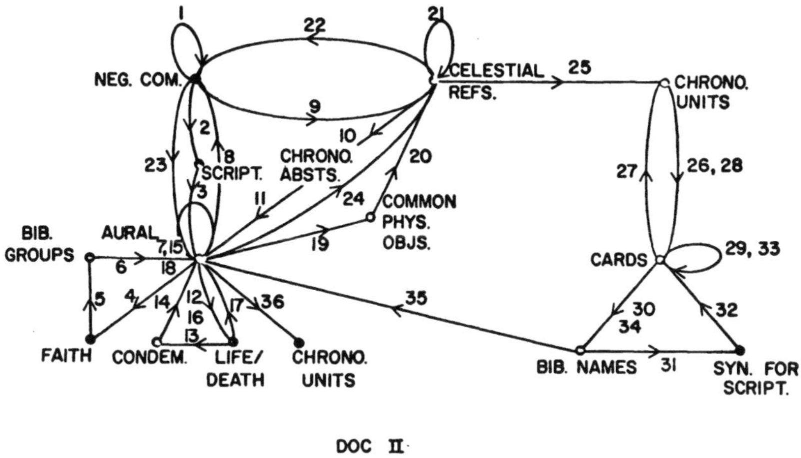

Figure 4. Thematic structure of DOC II

range' may be changed by turning dials so that the critic can zoom up and look down on it from above, move down and look at it from ground level, or assume any other position he wishes. By producing an entire picture for, say, the first 1000 words of the text, another, cumulative, picture for the first 2000 words, another for the first 3000, etc. through the entire text one can note in the progression of pictures the way in which themes grow and shift in relation to one another over the diachronic course of the work.

The basic view of the peaks resembles a fishnet laid over mounds of sand; to gain a closer, more detailed perspective of the exact pattern of thematic interaction for a section of text, the researcher may remove the 'fishnet' and examine the specific information on which the picture is based. Thus, CGAMS can portray the structural dynamics for selected themes from a micro-perspective as well as a macro-perspective.

An example of a CGAMS application may be helpful. I have argued elsewhere (Smith 1972) that in Joyce's *Portrait* the personality of Stephen remains constant between moments of epiphanal transition (the pandybat episode, the encounter with the prostitute, the confession, the encounter on the beach, etc.). At these moments of epiphany, however, what exactly changes is the pattern of associations among images manifest in changes in the pattern of proximity of images in the text. CGAMS is helpful for tracing the nature of those shifts for major thematic groups of images; figure 4, as noted, is a representation of some half dozen thematic groups for the first chapter. The careful reader will, of course, notice certain shifts in proximity and association, but CGAMS marks the exact place where shifts occur, reveals the precise nature of the shift relative to other thematic relations, indicates the relative

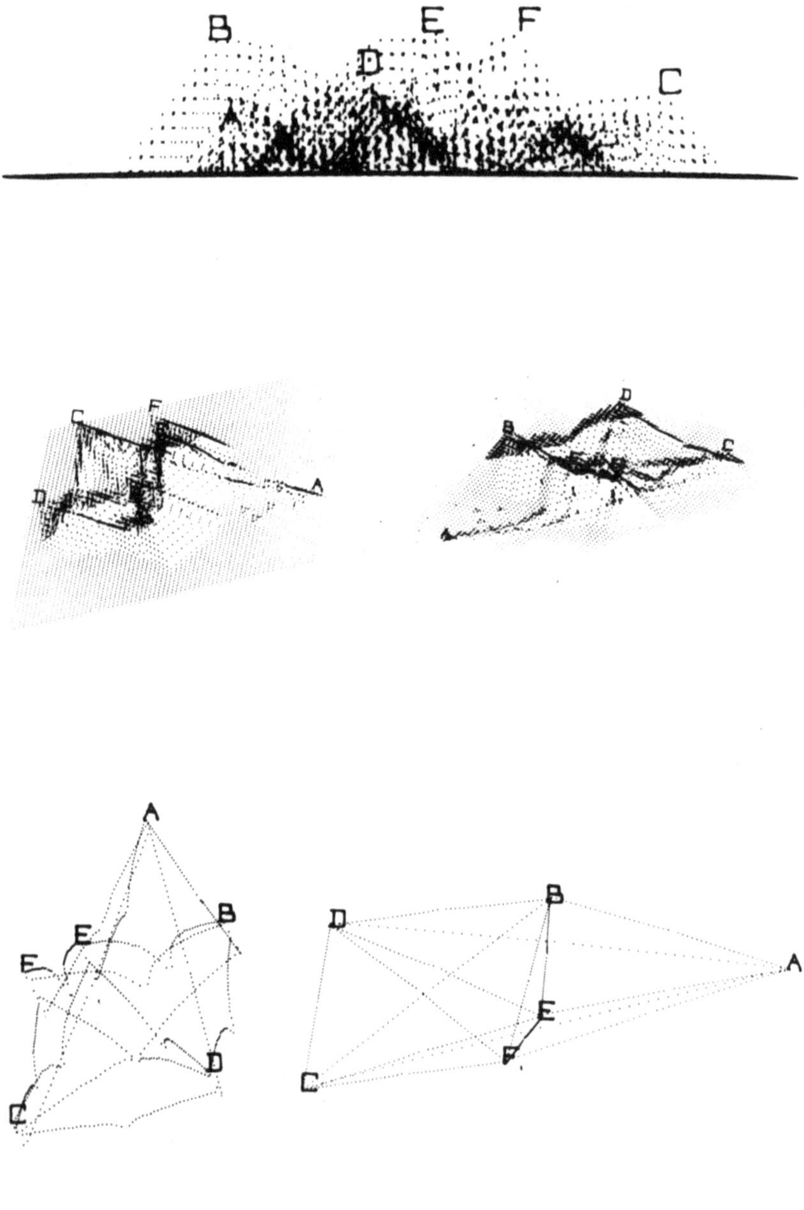

Figure 5. CGAMS images, from varying perspectives

importance of the shift, but most importantly, produces an actual visual representation that can be used for demonstration or for comparison with similar representations of thematic activity in other textual sections.

Diachronic distributions, Fourier Analysis, Principal Component Analysis, state diagrams, and CGAMS are a few of the models that may be used to explore thematic structure and relations. All, except the state diagram, were models appropriate for examining an entire text, such as a novel. There are numerous other concepts of structure useful for such textual segments; similarly, there are other models appropriate for other segments: the word, the sentence, the paragraph, etc. This brief selection of examples, hopefully, will give the reader a glimpse of the range of potential critical approaches that can be derived from the materialistic view of a text and the other assumptions and implications discussed above.

4.2 Conventional criticism: Concepts of structure

Most of the formalist schools of criticism discussed above have also used a stratified view of the text as the basis of their concept of form or structure. Summarizing the theoretical assumptions of the Russian Formalist, Tzvetan Todorov observes (1973: 11): 'The concept of form produces and is then fused with the concept of function. Analysis of form . . . leads to the identification of its function, i.e., the relation between its various components. Its components . . . are connected by algebraic signs of co-relation and integration . . .: horizontal relations of distribution and vertical relations of integration.' The concept of vertical strata is most strongly associated with Shklovsky's metaphor of 'staircase' construction. Without explicitly identifying the nature of individual stratificational levels, Shklovsky asserts that a considerable part of the esthetic effect of a literary work is produced by the artful juxtaposition of episodes and other narrative features in varying contexts. Erlich comments on Shklovsky's concept of staircase structure (1955: 212): 'The principle of juxtaposition, Shklovsky asserted, is especially pertinent to the short story, the most 'artful' fictional genre. In short stories and novelettes the esthetic effect rests more often than not upon deliberate exploitation of various types of contrasts and incongruity. These range from a 'realization' of a pun in terms of narrative structure through a motif of misunderstanding to that of a collision between two codes of morals.' While Shklovsky's staircase structure necessarily embodies a horizontal narrative medium, it emphasizes the effect of modulated vertical tensions and attractions among the various denotative and connotative strata parallel to the text.

An *Opojaz* structural notion emphasizing the horizontal dimension of a text was that of retardation. Closely related to the factors producing staircase structure, retardation is the effect of delay in the narrative of episodic development relative to time or what might be expected if one simply stated the sequence of narrative events without digression, supplementation, or embellishment. By noting the relation between suspense and retardation, the Formalists suggest the possibility of developing a formal explanation of esthetic response or behavior; unfortunately, they did not pursue this lead to its logical conclusion.

Integration of vertical and horizontal concepts of structure was also foreseen by the Russian Formalists, but the development of specific methods or models for achieving this was, again, only partially realized. As already noted, A.A. Reformatsky established several distinct strata of categories, denoting theme, motif, etc., parallel to the textual sequence. Propp went one step further by formulating comparable symbol sequences for a number of narratives and then deducing the inclusive underlying structure shared by all such sequences under omission or simple transformation. The concept of structure in both, however, is the unidimensional projection of strata into a single sequence of symbols. Pattern or form must be inferred through observation of repeated sequences of symbols or symbol groups.

The Russian Formalists' concept of structure was extended by the Prague Structuralists in two important respects. With their emphasis on esthetic theory and esthetic response, they made important contributions toward establishing normative patterns; second, they were able to define more clearly the functional strata operating in a literary work and to demonstrate the value of this perspective by actually tracing structural patterns within and across the various strata.

The relation between normative expectation and variation is most thoroughly developed by Jan Mukařovský in considering the relation between standard language and poetic language.

> The function of poetic language consists in the maximum of foregrounding of the utterance. Foregrounding is the opposite of automatization. . . . The standard language in its purest form, as the language of science . . . , avoids foregrounding. . . . In poetic language foregrounding achieves maximum intensity to the extent of pushing communication into the background as the objective of expression and of being used for its own sake; it is not used in the service of communication but in order to place in the foreground the act of expression, the act of speech itself. (1964: 19)

Mukařovský goes on to suggest that since non-normative language can only be perceived against a background of standard language, the esthetic effect of poetic language is determined in large part by patterns of transition between the two:

> Foregrounding arises from the fact that a given component in some way . . . deviates

from correct usage. . . . The simultaneous foregrounding of all components is therefore unthinkable. (1964: 65)

Having observed that the transition from esthetically indifferent speech to esthetically colored speech can occur quite rapidly, often in the same sentence, Mukařovský concludes that the structure of such transitions and juxtapositions constitutes the esthetic structure of the work:

The work of poetry forms a complex, yet unified, esthetic structure into which enters as constituents all of its components, foregrounding or not, as well as their interrelationships. . . . The predominancy of the esthetic function in poetic language, by contrast with communication speech, thus consists in the esthetic relevance of the utterance as a whole. (1964: 65)

To become a practical method of analysis, this view must be supported by a description of normative language. A functional model for normative stylistic traits has recently been described by Lubomir Doležel, a member of the Prague School now at the University of Toronto. Doležel proposes that the investigator begin with a large collection of statistical measures for a text. Among these, he can determine empirically those that represent objective factors of language in general and, hence, remain constant throughout all texts (distributions of graphemes and phonemes), those that vary widely in all texts and, thus, represent subjective factors (distributions of specific content words), and, finally, those that range within certain limits over a number of texts and, hence, represent context sensitive or 'subjective-objective' characteristics (sentence and word length distributions). Under this taxonomy, Doležel proposes that we may determine empirically not only normative values for a variety of statistical measures but an adequate set of distinctive features for characterizing a spectrum of styles over a variety of authors and subjects. While Doležel does not specifically say so, it is clear that the computer affords the only practical way to apply his model to a text of any substantial length. To the best of my knowledge, this had not been attempted.

The second major contribution by the Prague Structuralists in the continuing development of a stratified concept of structure is contained in the rather recent and controversial paper by Jakobson and Levi-Strauss. While numerous structuralists, we have seen, have indicated the possibility of analyzing literary works formally in terms of complex relations within and among a number of linguistic strata, Jakobson and Levi-Strauss (1973) have demonstrated the validity of this view by exhaustively examining a sonnet by Baudelaire. Beginning with the rhyme scheme, they go on to factor out the phonic, syntactic, and semantic levels, and the patterns and relation within each. However, it is in the complex relations across these strata that the poem presents the most difficulty; all are drawn into a coherent organization within the interpretive domain as they contribute to a highly generalized theme of dialectic tension and resolution.

The notion of structure most prevalent in American New Criticism is that of organic unity, relating part to whole, defined primarily in terms of metrical relations and image patterns. Caroline Spurgeon's classification and cataloging of Shakespeare's imagery has already been mentioned; the concept of structure, however, contained in that work is that of category and frequency. By classifying images and then counting the members of the various classes present in each play, she draws our attention to the tone-setting, often substantive, backdrop of verbal figures. Questions concerning combinations and patterns among categories, not her concern, were raised by later New Critics, such as Cleanth Brooks. In his discussion of imagery in *Macbeth*, he concentrates on two predominant patterns: images of clothes and concealment and images denoting babes. He goes beyond Spurgeon's method, however, by showing that it is the interaction of these two groups that underscores and comments upon the major action and theme of the play. Macbeth's ill fitting garments, like adult clothes on a child, make him ridiculous in his present cricumstances; the naked babe, paradoxically, suggests the strength of historical continuity that eventually crushes Macbeth's vain hopes. While it is the interweaving of these two image groups that results in the complex, multi-faceted semantic structure that attracts the critics' attention, the concept of structure involved is still that of 'organic form' suggested by combination and juxtaposition.

In theory, however, the New Critics do move a bit closer to a formal definition of structure. Wellek and Warren, describing the levels of existence of a text, present an interpretive stratification somewhat similar to that described above. They note some eight interpretive dimensions (1956: 157): (1) the sound stratum, euphony, rhythm, and meter; (2) the units of meaning which determine linguistic and stylistic structure; (3) image and metaphor; (4) mythic level of poetic symbols; (5) the fictive world; (6) the system of genres inherent in literature; (7) the evaluative domain; and (8) the historical context of the work. Within each stratum, they discuss the historical background of critical concern and often suggest approaches that could lead to methodological formality. For example, in discussing the level of euphony, rhythm, and meter, they note Tomashevsky's statistical methods as well as other acoustic approaches; in their discussion of stylistics they, similarly, note the possibility of a stylistics based on normative values and a set of distinctive features; but in their attempt to be suggestive rather than critically dogmatic, they stop short of advocating any specific methodology beyond recognition of these factored strata. Structure remains a metaphoric concept suggested by 'orchestration' or 'organic form'.

Within French Structuralist criticism there has been extremely wide variability concerning the concept of structure. For Barthes, structure means primarily patterns of recurrence and association:

Once the units are posited, structural man must discover in them or establish for them certain rules of association. . . . What we discover in every work of structural enterprise is the submission to regular constraints whose formalism . . . is much less important than their stability; for what is happening . . . is a kind of battle against chance; this is why the constraint of recurrence of the units has an almost demiurgic value: it is the regular return of the unit and of the association of units that the work appears constructed . . . . Form, it has been said, is what keeps the contiguity of units from appearing as a pure effect of chance. (1972: 217)

The best known application of Barthes' concept of structure is his study, *S/Z*. Barthes divides a short story by Balzac, entitled *Sarrisine*, into some 561 textual segments or 'lexies' each of which represents Barthes' judgment of the smallest portion of the narrative that carries 'meaning'. He then factors this 'meaning' into five vertical planes or 'codes' parallel to the horizontal sequence of lexies. Each code represents a fundamental relation between the narrator, the subject matter of the text, and reality. The first code identified is the code of action, including all physical gestures, movements, etc. Above that is the hermeneutic code or code of questions, motives, and puzzles. Next is the cultural code which includes the common information of the culture as well as its stock expressions and clichés. The fourth code is the connotative structure established within the context of the work, while the last code, the symbolic, is the interpretive dimension in which the major theme of the work is cast. Barthes' method of application for this unusual stratified structural model is to work his way through the story, lexis by lexis, commenting on the portion of his experience as a highly informed reader drawn into focus by the various codes. The result is a brilliant but highly idiosyncratic reading. Associations and patterns of repetition are observed and discussed but are limited to the patterns Barthes happens to notice through his polarized critical apparatus. There is no attempt at formality or reproduceability.

Todorov's analysis of structure in the *Decameron* (1969) includes a concept of structure that is essentially that of the transformation: individual tales are shown to be derivable from a general, paradigmatic form. Todorov demonstrates that all tales can be derived from a small number of paradigms through a set of basic tranformations. Thus, there exists a narrative generative grammar analogous to, say, a Chomskyan-style generative grammar for some set of sentences. If we regard the specific paradigm as one of a set of specifiable paradigms then the occurrence of that particular narrative structure within the textual sequence of all tales could be noted as a category item in a stratum parallel to the textual sequence; thus, this concept of structure could be represented within the Computer Criticism model outlined above and analyzed accordingly. While Todorov does extrapolate on the mental factors involved in composing large tale sequences, he does not attempt any systematic analysis of his paradigm sequences or their macroscopic structure.

More recently, Paul de Man has suggested the possibility of a different concept of structure, similar to the lattice model behind the state diagram and CGAMS approaches discussed above. After noting the scarcity of new techniques for literary study ('There certainly have been numerous excellent books of criticism since, but in none of these have the techniques of description and interpretation evolved beyond the technique of close reading established in the thirties and forties.' 1973: 27) he considers a passage from Proust from a rhetorical perspective. Concentrating on metonymic patterns of association as opposed to the more conventional assertions carried by metaphor, de Man foresees the possibility of a truly comprehensive structural methodology:

> The further text of Proust's novel . . . responds perfectly to an extended application of this de-constructive pattern: not only can similar gestures be repeated throughout the novel, at all the crucial articulations or all passages where large aesthetic and metaphysical claims are being made . . . , but a vast thematic and semiotic network is revealed that structures the entire narrative and that remained invisible to a reader caught in naive metaphorical mystification. The whole of literature would respond in similar fashion, although the techniques and the patterns would have to vary considerably, of course, from author to author. (1973: 32)

Such networks of associations have been partially realized though considerations of selected passages in the work of Genette (particularly in *Figures III*), Greimas, and other semiological critics; however, it is likely to remain impractical to explore the associative patterns of full length works, as suggested by Barthes, without the aid of a computer.

The formalist school whose concept of structure most closely resembles the stratified concept implicit in Computer Criticism is that associated with Firth. However, the comparison is closest not in the relation between the term, structure, as I have used it in this essay, and the term, structure, as it is formally used by Firth and Halliday; rather, the comparison must be drawn between what I have called structure and the concept of the total language construct or model found in the London School. As mentioned above, Firth begins with a material text: either a sequence of characters or a sequence of sounds. He then suggests a succession of levels, each abstract but each growing out of a materialist consideration of the symbol sequence comprising a lower level, that culminates in a 'context of situation'. Inherent in the levels of this outer domain is the possibility of a behaviorialist theory of language which Firth anticipates in one of his final essays in his appeal for the aid of psychology and psychiatry in linguistic description (1968: 209). Because of his untimely death, Firth was unable to flesh out the model that he had sketched;

much of this job, fortunately, has been done by M.A.K. Halliday, particularly in the area of language study generally associated with syntax. Halliday's published elaborations have dealt primarily with levels ranging from text to sentence structure. 'Structure', as formally defined by Halliday is an 'arrangement of elements ordered in "places"'. Thus, structure is a 'horizontal' concept that describes patterns parallel to the textual sequence. Description of that horizontal order, which I have shown to be of primary concern for Computer Criticism, is not addressed by Halliday. Specific form is left as paradigm or, perhaps, at the syntactic level, as the business for generative-tranformationalists or some other linguistic group to define or at the connotative level, as the business of the stylist to define collocations through statistical analyses. Relations that exist across levels are referred to as exponency, the relation between a category designator and the lower level numbers that constitute that category; however, since the realtion is not formally one-to-one between levels, this view is slightly different from the basic concept of parallel associativity inherent within Computer Criticism.

In a more recent paper (1971), Halliday has shown the strength of this stratified view of language as a tool for literary and stylistic analysis. He begins with several samples of text distributed over William Golding's *The inheritors*. He then defines a level of syntactic patterns. Through frequency counts he establishes what are really syntactic collocations and is able to show that these patterns inform/constitute the growing conceptual awareness of the central character. The implication that this theme of growing mental complexity is, itself, an outer sequential level of the novel that could potentially be formally linked through exponency down through a dozen or so intermediate levels to the material text is an exciting, perhaps frightening, possibility. Halliday does not take this last step, probably because of the impracticality of formally doing so through conventional methods; however, because the relation between the Firth/Halliday construct is so closely related to the concept of structure inherent in Computer Criticism, there is the distinct possibility of actually achieving this final interpretive synthesis.

In retrospect, we can see that virtually every major formalist school of criticism in this century has included some notion of hierarchically organized structure along the textual continuum. This concept has ranged in concrete realization from the American New Critic's metaphoric notion of organic unity of connotative structure to the highly formal stratificational model developed by Firth and Halliday. Within this entire spectrum, however, interpretation usually follows immediately upon realization of factored horizontal and vertical dimensions. Computer Criticism differs from all of these in that it interjects an intermediate step between stratified structure and meaning. Once the text is encoded and the parallel systems of strata established, Computer Criticism, because of its methodological emphasis, attempts to define and demonstrate patterns along, across, and among strata. That is, it attempts to display patterns of recurrence through distributions, Fourier analysis, concordance listings, etc.; it locates patterns of interaction across strata through correlation, factor analysis, and other multivariate procedures; finally, it locates patterns of interaction among various strata through lattices revealed in state diagrams, multidimensional scaling, and CGAMS. It is the collection of operatively defined patterns based on a number of structural models that furnish the matter for conceptual analysis and interpretation. The distinction between conventional structural methodology and Computer Criticism is the distinction between Paul de Man's intuitive realization that an entire novel is structured by a 'vast thematic and semiotic network' and an interpretation that begins with a concrete, visual representation of the network for that text.

5 Computer criticism: Temporal and behavioral extensions

The concepts and methods described above were based on a static, fixed text encoded as a sequence of signifiers. This sequence, we saw, could be accompanied by a similar sequence of symbols representing physical characteristics and, perhaps, one or more sequences representing categories or relations on the level of the signified. For some critical investigations a consideration of performance is necessary or desirable; that is, one may wish to consider a text embedded in a temporal domain (the time of the reading experience, or for a play, the time of the performance) as well as a behaviorial domain (the phenomenological response of the reader, to the extent that it can be characterized, or, for a play, the characteristics of performance and the response of the audience). As with all other phases of Computer Criticism, these data must be encoded as sequences of symbols and submitted to the computer as strata parallel to the sequences of signifiers and the other sequential levels. Similarly, the validity of the final analysis will be dependent upon the accuracy and sensitivity of the information initially encoded.

To establish the temporal domain, the critic must be able to measure the passage of time with relation to the basic textual sequence. This can most readily be done if he has an audio or video/audio recording of the performance (since the phenomenological experience of reading implies a specific, temporal experience and since that experience can be characterized only through observable reaction (by the reader, by an observer, or by some form of instrumentation); I shall consider it a 'performance' as well as the more conventional notion of dramatic presentation or situation). Using a stop watch or some similar measuring device, the critic may determine the interval of time between segments appropriate for his study. On the basis of this information the segments (words, sentences, lines, or whatever is appropriate) can be distributed along a uniform time sequence; or, conversely, time (measured in seconds) can be distributed along the uniform textual sequence (words or other segments).

To characterize performance or response to performance is a more delicate matter. Some will object that this implies 'quantification' of complex, esthetic phenomena. There is, however, a subtle but important distinction between categorizing and quantifying. Often we can accurately and without distortion distinguish among, say, the responses of an audience to a play: the audience laughs; the audience 'roars' with laughter; the audience gasps; the audience sits passively. To observe these categories of behavior, established through the experience and critical perspective of the researcher, is different from 'measuring' response, implying some numerical continuum of audience behavior. This distinction holds also when categories are ordered hierarchically but no attempt is made to establish significance to the interval between the hierarchically arranged items.

The behavioral factors observed – the recorded responses of the reader, the collective responses of an audience, or the facial gestures of an actor – will likely vary for each individual study. An example may illustrate the processes of establishing a set of categories and characterizing the form or pattern in the ensuing symbol sequences. Bruce Rosenberg, Robert Brubaker and I analyzed four fundamentalist sermons to demonstrate the formulaic structure of that highly stylized folk genre. In addition to revealing characteristics of the sermons, themselves, we hoped to develop descriptive techniques that could be applied to more sophisticated literary genres. One may reasonably focus an analysis of the sermons on at least three different levels: the entire sermon, thematic segments of twenty to seventy-five lines, and the individual line. Our study included all three levels; for the purpose of illustration, however, I shall discuss here only the dynamics involving the entire sermon.

When one considers the text and accompanying tape recordings of an entire sermon, several factors of the performance and the audience response are readily apparent. The characteristic pattern of interaction between preacher and congregation is statement followed by response: the preacher preaches a line, pauses, and the audience interjects 'Amen', 'Yes, Jesus', or some similar phrase. The interval of time in the cycle of stimulus and response ranges from twenty-three seconds to one second; further, one can observe that there is a general pattern in the changes of this duration: the preacher generally starts slowly, speeds up, and then slows down again at the end. Other apparent factors are the range of responses of the audience and the qualitative shifts in the preacher's tone of voice. The audience demonstrates three distinguishable responses: they may simply speak their responses; they may chant them; and they may chant continuously, overlapping with the preacher's statement. The preacher, in turn, may begin with a conversational tone of voice; he may 'preach' with a clear, orational tone; he may chant parts of lines or, sometimes, entire lines; and, at times, his delivery is paced by very sharp, audible gasps for breath that function almost as a drum beat in their rhythmic regularity. Thus, the time interval between stimulus and response, the five categories of audience response, and the three categories of orational style could be viewed as correlated strata of symbol sequences parallel to the textual sequences. Doubtless, analysts with other intentions could note different categories; however, within the purview of our particular critical intentions these were the factors we hoped would be most productive. Space does not permit a full discussion of our methods and results (see Smith – Rosenberg 1971); however, among the most interesting was the clear indication that all other factors were secondary to the fundamental importance of the rhythmic pattern of stimulus and response. It really didn't matter what the preacher said (so long as his content did not intrude by getting too 'complicated'): the success or failure of his sermon was determined by his ability to establish within very narrow tolerances a particular pattern of rhythmic variation in the cycle of stimulus and response. All other factors correlated and were dependent upon this pattern.

While the reader may not share our enthusiasm for homiletics, there are several implications that may be useful for literary studies. First, we were able to develop techniques for describing subtle structural differences in actual performances. The patterns that were developed represent ontological structures within a materialistic view of a text that may relate to more subtle, complex patterns of esthetic response that are fundamental – perhaps archetypal. The relation between these ontological structures and the substance of the text is analogous to the relation between form and subject in representational visual art. The range of observable factors within literary performances is as diverse as the range of critical intentions. Hopefully, the example cited will illustrate how categories of performance and response can be established and applied. Once this is done and the results encoded, this information can function as strata analogous to the three fundamental strata discussed at length above; the same basic concepts of inherent sequential and parallel form hold. Implied, then, is the possibility of a science of esthetics that links the text with fully cultivated esthetic responses through a continuous series of interrelated structures. A comprehensive critical method must be able to define and characterize relations along and across these strata and a comprehensive critical analysis must interpret them and place them in context.

6 Computer criticism: Interpretation of form

Emphasis in the discussion of models of form was primarily empirical: models that can describe a particular structural characteristic. Used in this manner, they can help the critic develop through close textual scrutiny patterns that, in turn, lead to larger patterns of patterns, etc. The approach is essentially ground-up or, in this case, text up. This empirical aspect of the analysis should be matched with an equal analytic or deductive phase that begins with a theoretical generalization and 'builds down' to meet the empirical. Stated more bluntly, it is the critic, not the computer, who provides the intellectual context of the study, interprets the information produced by the computer, and forms the critical insight. The computer, while it may influence the perspective as other major tools have done in the past, supplements rather than replaces the process of conventional scholarly inquiry.

The 'build down' aspect must begin with a strong initial hypothesis or question. This critical assertion, in all probability, will be derived in the same way that any other assertion is derived: through reading, consideration of hunches, and logical argument. At this stage there is likely to be no formal mention of the computer; if it is present at all, it is in the form of a shadowy recollection of a method and a device for applying that method that may be useful for problems similar to that under consideration. In its initial formulation the problem should be cast in a familiar context, using conventional terminology and critical perspective. Similarly, the study must justify itself within conventional critical values; it must be worth doing in its own right and not simply something that is done because the computer can do it.

Once the hypothesis has been formulated in this manner, the critic may then consider whether or not the computer can be employed. To use the computer, he must be able to translate the hypothesis from substantive terms (as described above) to operative or functional terms. As with any translation process, there is great opportunity for distortion and error. The critic must be extremely judicious to insure that the operative definition of the hypothesis closely fits the substantive definition.

There is no set way in which this translation can always be made; however, an approach that may be useful for a number of studies is for the critic to simply probe his own critical assertions and assumptions, repeatedly asking himself, 'What, exactly, do I mean by ________?' For example, take the rather obvious assertion that the first chapter of Joyce's *Portrait* is structured by the tension between the themes of *fire* and *water*. To demonstrate this with the aid of the computer will involve several translation steps. The critic might engage himself in the following imaginary dialogue.

1. Q. What, exactly, do you mean by the themes, *fire* and *water*?
   A. Well, by 'theme', I mean a group of words or phrases, mostly images, that denote or suggest a basic concept or experience. Obviously, the theme of *fire* will be those words or phrases that

suggest *fire* or *heat* and the theme *water* will be those words or phrases that suggest *water, wetness*, and, in this context, *coldness*.

2. Q. Fine, but what words or phrases suggest *fire* or *water*? To the computer, they all look alike.
   A. I mean specific words like *burn, burned, burning, fire, hearth, heat*, etc. For *water*, I mean *cold, ditch, spit, water, watery*, etc.
3. Q. Now that you have translated the term, 'theme', from a substantive term (a group of words or phrases that suggest the same basic concept or experience) to a functional term (a list of specific words or collocations of words) recognizable by the computer, can you take the next step and clarify what you mean by the relation 'tension', when you say that *fire* and *water* are in a state of tension?
   A. *Fire* is usually related or associated in Stephen's mind with thoughts of home or other pleasant memories; conversely, *water* is associated with his terrible fall into the ditch. While these two themes carry dialectically opposite connotations, he seldom recalls one without his mind jumping to the other. It is this constant, ironic juxtaposition or association between basically opposite themes that constitutes tension.
4. Q. Fine, but what do you mean by the statement that the chapter is 'structured' by this relation of tension between the themes of *fire* and *water*?
   A. That's a little harder, because to say that the chapter is structured by this relation means several things. It means that this dialectic juxtaposition occurs frequently; it occurs at fairly regular intervals; and it is 'fundamental' in some respect to other thematic relations. That is, it occurs in a variety of thematic contexts; and other major themes, while relating to this pair, do not occur with the same regularity or with the same diversity of context.
   Q. Let's take them one at a time. How can you show that these two themes occur close to one another frequently?
   A. I could divide the text into, say, 100 word intervals, have the computer tally up all of the *fire* words for each such interval, and then have it draw a picture or graph of this distribution over the chapter. By comparing this with a similar distribution of *water* words I can tell both the prevalence and the consistency of association of these two themes.
   Q. Fine, you killed two birds with one program, but how are you going to show that this relation is more 'fundamental' than other thematic relations?

A. First, I'll have to define all of the themes that I feel are 'major', just as I did in step 2; but then I'll have to show that these are less 'prevalent' and less 'perverse' than *fire* and *water* and that they are oriented in some way to the *fire/water* dialectic. If I graph all of these themes, I can compare their distributions with those of *fire* and *water* for 'pervasiveness'. If this relation turns out to be true, then I can look at the section of text where these other themes seem to be important and see if they are in some way related to *fire* and *water*.

5. Q. How are you going to get the computer to tell you how these themes are related to *fire* and *water*?

A. I can't, but the computer can tell me where to look. Thus, it points me in the right places and it can tell me whether I have looked at all the places.

The establishment of themes is, of course, one example of the more general notion of categorization discussed above. The examination of juxtaposition of opposite themes is an example of synchronic relation across strata; the test for pervasiveness, similarly, is an example of diachronic structure along the axis of the text. To actually use the computer for a full and critically interesting analysis, the critic would obviously have to extend the sequence of steps outlined above as well as expand each of the individual stages.

Having translated the substantive hypothesis into functional terms and having used the computer to gather and display information and to explore various structural relations, it is then incumbent upon the critic to assimilate this information, to place it in context, and to synthesize his 'interpretation'. Obviously, the computer can only augment, not replace, his critical judgment. The final results of the inquiry should be expressed, once again, in the vernacular of the Profession. To do this, the critic must translate in reverse the relations, patterns, and structure he has discovered on the functional level back into meaningful critical assertions. Once again, the computer should recede into the background leaving behind the unencumbered thesis, but a thesis that rests firmly on a body of specifiable assumptions and demonstrable textual relations. It is this joining of the deductive, critical response of the researcher with the empirical methodology of the computer that makes it possible to envision a science of literary criticism that is powerful but not reductive, sensitive but not simplistic.

Notes

* This article originally appeared in *Style* 12.4: 326-356.

1. I shall discuss the computer and its functions for language analysis within the context of large IBM machines. These remarks can be interpolated for other computers.
2. These concepts are discussed by Erlich (1955: 177-178, 200).
3. For a more thorough discussion of models useful for illustrating and characterizing thematic structures see Smith 1975.
4. For a more flexible and practical method of representing categories for actual Computer Criticism, see Schwupp and Smith 1964.
5. For a detailed description of this study see Rosenberg and Smith forthcoming.
6. For a full discussion of a formal notion of thematic complexity appropriate for thematic structure similar to that represented by state diagrams, see Smith 1975.

References

Barthes, Roland
1967 "Science versus literature", *Times Literary Supplement* (September 1967) [Reprinted in *Structuralism: A reader*, edited by Michael Lane (London, 1970), 410-417.]
1972 "The Structuralist activity", *Critical essays* edited by Richard Howard (Evanston: Northwestern U.P.).

Erlich, Victor
1955 *Russian Formalism: History – doctrine* (= *Slavistic Printings and Reprintings* 4) (The Hague: Mouton).

Firth, J.R.
1968 "The treatment of language in general linguistics", in *Selected papers by J.R. Firth 1952-1959*, edited by F.R. Palmer (London: Longman).

Frye, Northrop
1957 *The anatomy of criticism* (Princeton).

Halliday, M.A.K.
1961 "Categories of the theory of grammar", *Word* 17: 241-292.
1971 "Linguistic function and literary style", *Literary style: A symposium*, edited by Seymour Chatman (London), 330-368.

Harkins, William E.
1951 "Slavic Formalist theories in literary scholarship", *Word* 7.2: 177-185.

Jakobson, Roman
1936 "Randbemerkungen zur Prosa des Dichters Pasternak", *Slavische Rundschau* 7: 357-374.

Jakobson, Roman and Levi-Strauss, Claude
1973 "Charles Baudelaire's 'Les Chats'", *Issues in contemporary literary criticism*, edited by Gregory T. Polletta (Boston), 372-389.

de Man, Paul
1973 "Semiology and rhetoric", *Diacritics* 3.2.

Mukařovský, Jan
1964 "Standard language and poetic language", in *A Prague School reader in linguistics*, edited by Josef Vachek.

Propp, V.
1968 *Morphology of the folktale* (2nd edition) (Austin: Texas U.P.).
Ransom, John Crowe
1940 "Wanted: An ontological critic", *The New Criticism* (Norfolk: New Directions), 297–301.
Reformatsky, A.A.
1973 "An essay on the analysis of the composition of the Novella", translated by Christine Scholl, in *Russian Formalism*, edited by Stephen Bann and John E. Boult (New York: Barnes & Noble).
Rosenberg, Bruce A. and Smith, John B.
forthcoming "Thematic structure in four Fundamentalist sermons", to appear in *Journal of Western Folklore*.
Scholes, Robert
1974 *Structuralism in literature* (New Haven).
Schwupp, Paul W. and Smith, John B.
1964 "Random accessible text system for associative text analysis", *Siglash Newsletter* (December 1964), 8–11.
Sedelow, Sally Yeates
1970 "The computer in the humanities and fine arts", *Computing Surveys* 2.2: 89–110.
Smith, John B.
1972 "Image and imagery in Joyce's *Portrait*", in *Directions in literary criticism*, edited by Stanley Weintraub and Philip Young (University Park, Pa.), 220–227.
1974 "Computer generated analogues of mental structure from language data", *Proceedings of IFIP '74* (The Hague: Mouton).
1975 "Thematic structure and complexity", *Style* 9.1: 32–54.
Smith, John B. and Rosenberg, Bruce A.
1971 "Rhythms in speech: Formulaic structure in four Fundamentalist sermons", *Computer Studies in the Humanities and Verbal Behavior* 4.3–4: 166–173.
Spurgeon, Caroline F.E.
1958 *Shakespeare's imagery* (Boston: Beacon).
Stone, Philip J.
1966 *The General Inquirer: A computer approach to content analysis* (Cambridge).
Todorov, Tzvetan
1969 *Grammaire du Decameron* (The Hague).
1973 "Some approaches to Russian Formalism", translated by Bruce Merry, in *Russian Formalism*, edited by Stephen Bann and John E. Boult (New York: Barnes & Noble).
Wellek, Rene and Warren, Austin
1956 *Theory of literature* (New York: Harcourt, Brace & World).
Widmann, R.L.
1971 "Computers and literary scholarship", *Computers and the Humanities* 6.1: 3–14.

YORICK A. WILKS

Machine translation and the artificial intelligence paradigm of language processes

Preface

We are once again at an interesting point in the chequered history of machine translation. Three traditions of machine translation are at present competing for whatever the rewards of success are in this field: first, the resurrected and revamped first generation systems, of which the best known and most successful is Toma's SYSTRAN system developed from the original US Air Force Translation Project; secondly, the larger surviving second generation academic machine translation projects, of which the best example is perhaps the TAUM project at the Université de Montréal (Kitteredge 1973); and thirdly, smaller systems trying to incorporate methods closer to those of the human understanding of language, and from within the research environment now known as Artificial Intelligence (see Wilks 1973b).

In this paper I want to survey some of the recent work on understanding natural language from within that artificial intelligence paradigm, and then to compare and contrast some of the major approaches under a number of headings. But first I want to argue a little for (what may seem obvious) the relevance of these developments in artificial intelligence to the development of machine translation.

It is worth reminding ourselves at the outset what it was that caused the enormous enterprise machine translation to come to such a seemingly final halt in the mid-Sixties. There were, it seemed, at least three 'intractables' of natural language analysis: three problems that the earlier pioneers had wrongly believed would become soluble once the problems of syntax had been cleared up. They were, in their simplest form:

(1) word-sense ambiguity: the fact that words in natural languages have many senses, and that some structural approach is essential for deciding the right sense for any particular occurrence of a word in a text, because no mere probabilistic guessing will do;

(2) case ambiguity: or, put very roughly indeed, the fact that the prepositions of natural language are also radically ambiguous, and one way of describing this ambiguity is to say that the prepositional phrases of a text can attach to

Computers in Language Research 2

an appropriate main clause in a number of ways, or by a number of case relations, and that delicate semantic tests are needed to decide such assignments of case. Or, to put the matter over-simply, English prepositions like *out of* can be translated into French in at least seven ways, and on each occasion of use they have to be got right;

(3) referential ambiguity: the fact that pronouns, in particular, often, though not always, have to be attached to nouns or noun phrases in a discourse, and that this attachment cannot in general be done by simple syntactic criteria such as gender and number. In *Mary told her mother that she was intolerant* no considerations of gender or number will show us that *she* would normally be taken to refer to the mother and not to Mary. This is made clearer, when we see that the reference would be different in *Mary told her mother that she was pregnant.*

I am listing these 'intractables' of machine translation not simply to rehearse history but to argue their significance for us now. They provide, in my view, a standard by which subsequent work in computational linguistics, and indeed any serious linguistics, is to be judged. For if a new approach is to offer anything serious it must have something to say about these intractables.

A word here is in order concerning the role of Chomskyan, or what one might call conventional, linguistics in all this. It is my view, and I think it would be that of many people in artificial intelligence, that it has not produced much of great value in the search for solutions to the problems the intractables pose. Where there have been developments that seem to be moves towards solutions, and I have Generative Semantics in mind here, (see Lakoff 1971), the overall structure of generative theory, and its great distance from applicable procedures, have inhibited any profitable interaction with the three problems. I have argued this point in some detail, and it does require argument, and is not to be simply assumed in the way many workers in artificial intelligence seem to do (Wilks 1973: 194 and with Schank 1974).[1]

By and large, the structures and techniques that artificial intelligence has brought to bear on the intractables above are (1) the definition, matching to text, and manipulation, of complex semantic structures, and (2) the definition and manipulation of structures of inference rules (operating over the structures of (1)) and which express knowledge of the real world.

In the body of this paper I shall describe a number of projects incorporating these two notions. But, as an end of introduction, it may be worth pointing out artificial intelligence workers did not discover either of these notions or the evident need for them. If one cares to turn over the machine translation literature of fifteen years ago, one will find researchers even then advocating the use of complex semantic structures. Again, Bar-Hillel's (1958) famous 'disproof of machine translation' is an appreciation of the essential role of real world knowledge in understanding and translation.

In spite of its familiarity, it may be worth rehearsing his example again very briefly and for two reasons. First, just in case there are any artifical intelligence workers who read this and believe, as some seem to, that the essential role of real world knowledge in understanding was discovered within the artificial intelligence community. And, secondly, because of the use I shall make of it at the end of this paper.

In brief, Bar-Hillel's example was the following 'children's story':

Little John was looking for his toy box. Finally he found it. The box was in the pen. John was very happy.

Bar-Hillel's focus is on the third sentence, *The box was in the pen*, whose last word we naturally interpret in context as meaning 'playpen' and not 'writing pen'. Bar-Hillel argued persuasively that to resolve this correctly requires knowledge of the real world, in some clear sense: at least in the sense that the difficulty cannot be overcome in terms of some simpleminded 'overlap of concepts', by arguing that the concepts of *baby* and *playpen* can be seen, by lexical decomposition of some sort, to be related in a way the concepts of *baby* and *writing pen* are not. Bar Hillel argues that that would not do, because the story would have been understood the same way if the third sentence had been *The inkstand was in the pen*, where the 'overlap of concepts' would now be between *inkstand* and *writing pen* which would yield the wrong answer on the same principles.

He was clearly right that the machine translation approaches of that time could not possibly have coped with the forms of inference that this example requires. Where I think he was wrong was to argue that no computable system of rules could, in principle, do so, and hence machine translation in the required sense was impossible. It will be my contention that artificial intelligence has shown how such examples can be tackled, and in more than one way. And that, if nothing else, shows that some advance has been made by artificial intellegence research towards the reduction of the intractables. I shall return to this example at the end of the paper.

1 Some background

In his report to the Science Research Council on the state of Artificial Intelligence, Sir James Lighthill (1973) gave most of the field a rather bad prognosis. One of the few hopeful signs he saw was Winograd's (1972) natural language understanding system. Yet now, Winograd has stopped work on the system he constructed, and has begun a new one on entirely different principles. He went so far, in a survey lecture (Winograd 1973) of extraordinary modesty in a field not known for its small claims, to place his celebrated early work in only the 'first generation' of computer systems designed to understand natural language, and went on to describe others' 'second generation' systems.

I shall return later to this metaphor of generations, but what is one to say in general terms of a field where yesterday's brightest spots are today's first generation systems, even though they have not been criticised in print, nor shown in any generally acceptable way to be fundamentally wrong? Part of the answer lies in the profound role of fashion in artificial intelligence in its present pre-scientific phase. A cynical American professor remarked recently that artificial intelligence had an affair with someone's work every year or two, and that, just as there were no reasons for falling in love, so, later, there were no reasons for falling out again. In the case of Winograd's work it is important now to resist this fashion, and re-emphasize what a good piece of research it was, as I shall in a moment.

Another part of the answer lies in the still fundamental role of metaphysical criticism in artificial intelligence. In the field of computer vision things are bad enough, in that anybody who can see feels entitled to criticise a system, on the ground that he is sure he does not see using such and such principles. In the field of natural language understanding things are worse: not only does anyone who can speak and write feel free to criticise on the corresponding grounds, but in addition there are those trained in disciplines parasitic upon natural language, linguists and logicians, who often know in addition how things "must be done" on a priori grounds. It is this metaphysical aspect of the subject that give its disputes their characteristically acrimonious flavour.

In this paper I want to sort out a little what is agreed and what is not; what are some of the outstanding disputes and how testable are the claims being made. If what follows seems unduly philosophical, it should be remembered that little is agreed, and almost no achievements are beyond question. To pretend otherwise, by concentrating only on the details of established programs, would be meretricious and misleading.

To survey an energetic field like this one is inevitably to leave a great deal of excellent work unexamined, at least if one is going to do more than give a paragraph to each research project. I have left out of consideration at least six groups of projects:

(1) Early work in artificial intelligence and natural language that has been surveyed by Winograd (1973) and Simmons (1970a) among others.
(2) Work by graduate students of, or intellectually dependent upon that of, people discussed in some detail here.

(3) Work that derives essentially from projects described in detail here. This embraces several groups interested in testing psychological hypotheses, as well as others constructing large-scale systems for speech recognition. I have devoted no space to speech recognition as such here, for it seems to me to depend upon the quality of semantic and inferential understanding as much as anything, and so I have concentrated upon this more fundamental task.

(4) Work on language generators, as opposed to analysers and understanders. They are essential for obtaining any testable output, but are theoretically secondary.

(5) All the many and varied reasoning schemes now available in artificial intelligence, including PLANNER (Hewitt 1969), QA4 (Rulifson et al. 1972), MERLIN (Moore and Newell 1973), as well as automatic programming (Balzer et al. 1974, Heidorn 1974) and debugging (Sussman 1974) projects, many of which are producing formalisms that appear increasingly like natural language.

(6) Conservative reasoning schemes, such as first order predicate calculus, that have been applied to, or advocated for, the analysis of natural language (McCarthy and Hayes 1969, Coles 1972, Sandewall 1972).

The exclusions under (2) above are particularly unfair to the work in the unpublished theses of Rieger (1974) and McDermott (1974), and can only be justified, like those of sections (5) and (6) above, by space, bias and the considerations advanced in a later section of this survey concerning what it is for artificial intelligence research to be about natural language, rather than about something else, like human psychology, or logic, or the bargaining behavior of children under stress.

One final remark about the style of this survey. I have not indulged the normal critical luxury of careful and extensive quotation from authors followed by detailed and meticulous criticism. That would be wholly inappropriate in the present state of things. A great deal of work is being done at the moment, and many of the principal researchers change their views on very fundamental questions between one paper and the next without drawing any attention to the fact. Cheap self-contradictions and changes of mind are all too easy to find, so criticism and comparisons are best drawn with a very broad brush and a light stroke.

2 Winograd's understanding system

Winograd's system runs as a dialogue, in real time, between a human operator who types in messages, and the system proper, called SHRDLU, which displays on a screen pictures of a closed world of coloured blocks and pyramids, a box into which they can be put, and an arm or crane that can move the objects about. SHRDLU displays its replies to the operator by writing on the same screen. The following is a discontinuous sample of the dialogue Winograd gives in his book. SHRDLU's replies are in upper case:

> pick up the big red block
> OK
> find a block which is taller than the one you are holding and put it into the box
> BY 'IT', I ASSUME YOU MEAN THE BLOCK WHICH IS TALLER THAN THE ONE I AM HOLDING
> OK
> what does the box contain
> THE BLUE PYRAMID AND THE BLUE BLOCK
> had you touched any pyramid before you put the green one on the little cube
> YES, THE GREEN ONE
> when did you pick it up
> WHILE I WAS STACKING UP THE RED CUBE, A LARGE RED BLOCK AND A LARGE GREEN CUBE
> why
> TO GET RID OF IT.

This ingenious program was also able to accept new definitions of words such as *steeple*; to make use of what it knew about the properties of the objects described, such as that a block could have its top cleared off, but a pyramid could not; and also to remember what it had done before, as in the sample above.

The program was written in the language PLANNER[2], which is a concrete expression of the slogan "meanings are procedures", a sentiment into whose own meaning it is probably best not to enquire too closely for the moment, but which has undoubtedly led to a new style of programming. PLANNER is a theorem-proving language; it tries to establish the truth of assertions, not in the normal uniform, proof-theoretic, manner, but by accepting a range of "program hints" about how best to proceed at any point. In a language understanding program like Winograd's, this means replacing familiar grammar rules such as $S \rightarrow NP + VP$ (a sentence consists of a noun phrase followed by a verb phrase) by procedures, in this case:

```
((PDEFINE SENTENCE (PARSE NP) NIL FAIL) ((PARSE VP) FAIL FAIL RETURN)))
```

The details of the notation need not detain us at this point; what is important is that Winograd's grammar is not the conventional list of rules, but small sub-programs like the lines above, that actually represent procedures for imposing the desired grammatical structure.

The first level of linguistic procedures in the system expresses a 'system grammar', due to M.A.K. Halliday (1970), which imposes a hierarchical structure of clauses on the input sentences, which in turn seem to be drawn from a vocabulary of about 175 words.

After this syntactic parsing, a number of 'semantic specialists' attach semantic structures to specific syntactic ones. A semantic definition of an action like *grasp* would be of the form

```
(CMEANS((((≠ANIMATE) ((≠MANIP)))
   (≠EVAL(COND((PROGRESSIVE)
      (QUOTE(≠GRASPING ≠2 *TIME)))
   (T(QUOTE(≠GRASP ≠2 *TIME
      )))))NIL))
```

which says essentially that grasping is something done by an animate entity to a manipulable one (first line). More of the real content of such actions is found in their inferential definition. Here is the one for *pickup*:

```
(DEFTHEOREM TC-PICKUP(THCONSE (X(WHY (EV))EV)
   (≐PICKUP $?X)(MEMORY)(THGOAL(≐GRASP $?X)(THUSE TC-GRASP))
   (THGOAL(≐RAISEHAND)(THNODB)(THUSE TC-RAISEHAND))
   (MEMOREND (≐PICKUP $$?EV $?X))))
```

Once again the details of the notation need not be explained in order to see that the word is being defined in terms of a number of more primitive subactions, such as RAISEHAND, each of which must be carried out in order that something may indeed be picked up.

In the case of *a red cube*, the following structure is built up by an NP (noun phrase) 'semantic specialist':

```
   (GOAL (IS X BLOCK))
   (GOAL (COLOR X RED))
   (EQDIM X) ---------------------------- PLANNER description
BLOCK MANIP PHYSOB THING) ------------------------- markers
```

The first three lines are procedures that, when evaluated, will seek an object X that is a block, is equidimensional EQDIM) and is red. The last line is a set of 'semantic features' read off right to left from the following 'feature tree':

```
          | NAME
          | PLACE          | SHAPE
          | PROPERTY-----| SIZE
          |                | LOCATION
          |                | COLOR                       | ROBOT
          | ANIMATE------------------------------------|
          |                                              |
          |                                              | HUMAN
          |                            | BLUE
          |                            | RED
THING ---|            (-----------------| BLACK
          |            (                | WHITE
          |            (                | GREEN                  | STACK
          | PHYSOB---( | CONSTRUCT-----------------------------| PILE
          |            ( | HAND                                  | ROW
          |            (-| TABLE                  | PYRAMID
          |              | MANIP ----------------| BLOCK
          |              | BOX                    | BALL
          |                              | EVENT
          | RELATION --------------------|
                                         |
                                         | TIMELESS
```

This whole semantic structure can be used by the deductive component of the system, before any evaluation resulting in the actual picking up of the object, so as to see if such an object is possible. If it is not, (as 'equidimensional pyramid' would not be), the system could go back and try to reparse the sentence.

One reason for the enormous impact of this work was that, prior to its appearance, artifiical intelligence work was linguistically trivial, while the systems of the linguists had no place for the use of inference and real world knowledge. Thus a very limited union between the two techniques was able to breed considerable results. Before Winograd there were few programs in artificial intelligence that could take a reasonably complex English sentence and ascribe any structure whatever to it. In early classics of 'natural language understanding' in artificial intelligence, such as Bobrow's STUDENT 91968 problem solver for simple algebra, input sentences had to be short and of stereotyped form, such as "what is the sum of . . . .?"

Conversely, in linguistics, there was, until very recently, little speculation on how we understand the reference of pronouns in such elementary sentences as *The soldiers fired at the women and I saw* several *fall*, where it is clear both that the answer is definite, and that finding it requires some inferential manipulation of generalizations about the world. The reader should ask himself at this point how he knows the correct referent of the pronoun in that sentence.

3 Some discussion of SHRDLU

So far, the reaction to Winograd's work has been wholly uncritical. What would critics find to attack if they were so minded? Firstly, that Winograd's linguistic system is highly conservative, and that the distinction between 'syntax' and 'semantics' may not be necessary at all. Secondly, that his semantics is tied to the simple referential world of the blocks in a way that would make it inextensible to any general, real world, situation. Suppose *block* were allowed to mean 'an obstruction' and 'a mental inhibition', as well as 'a cubic object'. It is doubtful whether Winograd's features and rules could express the ambiguity, and, more importantly, whether the simple structures he manipulated could decide correctly between the alternative meanings in any given context of use. Again, far more sophisticated and systematic case structures than those he used might be needed to resolve the ambiguity of *in* in *He ran the mile in five minutes*, and *He ran the mile in a paper bag*, as well as the combination of case with word sense ambiguity in *He put the key in the lock* (door lock) and *He threw the key in the lock* (river lock).

The blocks world is also strongly deductive and logically closed. If gravity were introduced into it, then anything supported that was planned in a certain way would have, logically have, to fall. But the common sense world, of ordinary language, is not like that: in the "women and soldiers" example given earlier, the pronoun *several* can be said to be resolved using some generalizations such as 'things shot at and hurt tend to fall'. There are no logical "have to's" there, even though the meaning of the pronoun is perfectly definite.

Indeed, it might be argued that, in a sense, and as regards its semantics, Winograd's system is not about natural language at all, but about the other technical question of how goals and sub-goals are to be organised in a problem-solving system capable of manipulating simple physical objects. If we remember, for example, that the key problem that brought down the enormous work on machine translation in the Fifties and Sixties, was that of the sense ambiguity of natural language words, then we will look in vain to SHRDLU for any help with that problem. There seems to be only one clear example of an ambiguous word in the whole system, namely that of *contain* as it appears in *The box contains a red block* and *The stack contains a red block*.

Again, if one glances back at the definition of *pickup* quoted above, one can see that it is in fact an expression of a procedure for picking up an object in the SHRDLU system. Nothing about it, for example, would help one understand the perfectly ordinary sentence *I picked up my bags from the platform and ran for the train*, let alone any sentence not about a physical action performable by the hearer. One could put the point so: what we are given in the PLANNER code is not a 'sense' of *pick up* but an example of its use, just as *John picked up the volunteer from the audience by leaning over the edge of the stage and drawing her up by means of a rope clenched in his teeth* is not so much a sense of the verb as a use of it.

Those who like very general analogies may have noticed that Wittgenstein (1953 para. 2ff.) devoted considerable space to the construction of an elementary language of blocks, beams and slabs; one postulated on the assumption that the words of language were basically, as is supposed in model theory, the names of items. But, as he showed of the enterprise, and to the satisfaction of many readers, "That philosophical concept of meaning [i.e. of words as the unambiguous names of physical objects – YW] has its place in a primitive idea of the way language functions. But one can also say that it is the idea of *a language more primitive than ours*" [my italics].

To all this, it might be countered that it has not been shown that the language facilities I have described cannot be incorporated in the structures that SHRDLU manipulates, and that, even if they could not, the work would still be significant in virtue of its original control structure and its demonstration that real world knowledge can be merged with linguistic knowledge in a working whole. Indeed, although Winograd has not tried, in any straightforward sense, to extend the SHRDLU system one could say that an extension of this sort is being attempted by Brown (1974) with his 'Believer System', which is a hybrid system combining a component about beliefs that is, in the sense of section 4 below 'second generation', with a base analyser from Bruce's CHRONOS system (1972) which is a micro-world – late first generation – system in the same sense as Winograd's. Others in the last category that should be mentioned are Davies and Isard's (1972) exploration of the concepts of *must* and *could* in a micro-world of tic-tac-toe, and Joshi's extension of it (1973), but above all the important and influential work of Woods (1972).

This work, most recently applied to a micro-world of lunar rock samples, is not discussed in the detail it deserves in this paper. The system, based on an augmented state transition network grammar, is undoubtedly one of the most robust in actual use, in that it is less sensitive to the particular input questions it encounters than its rivals. The reason for not treating it in depth is that both Woods and Winograd have argued in print that their two systems are essentially equivalent (Winograd 1971, Woods 1973), and so, if they are right, there is no need to discuss both, and Winograd's is, within the artificial intelligence community at least, the better known of the two.

Their equivalence arguments are probably correct: both are grammar-based deductive systems, operating within a question-answering environment in a highly limited domain of discourse. Winograd's system of hints on how to proceed, within his PROGRAMMAR grammar, is, as he himself points out, formally equivalent to an augmented state of transition network, and in particular to the ordering of choices at nodes in Woods' system.

There is a significant difference in their metaphysical approaches, or presuppositions about meaning, which, however, has no influence on the actual operation of their respective systems. This difference is disguised by the allegiance both give to a 'procedural view of meaning'. The difference is that Woods takes a much more logico-semantic interpretation of that slogan than does Winograd. In particular, for Woods the meaning of an input utterance to his system is the procedures within the system that manipulate the truth conditions of the utterance and establish its truth value.

To put the matter crudely, for Woods an assertion has no meaning if his system cannot establish its truth or falsity. Winograd has certainly not committed himself to any such extreme position.

It is interesting to notice that Woods' is, in virtue of his strong position on truth conditions, probably the only piece of work in the field of artificial intelligence and natural language to satisfy Hayes' (1974) recent demand that to be "intellectually respectable" a knowledge system must have natural model theoretic semantics, in Tarski's sense. Since no-one has ever given precise truth conditions for any interesting piece of discourse, such as, say, Woods' own papers, one might claim that his theoretical presuppositions necessarily limit his work to the analysis of micro-worlds (as distinct from everyday language). However, if Woods' 'internal' interpretation of the "meanings are procedures" slogan has certain drawbacks, so too does Winograd's, or what one might call the 'external' interpretation. By that I mean Winograd's concentration on actions, like picking up, that are in fact real world procedures, and in a way that the meanings of *concentrate, call, have, interpret*, etc. are not self-evidently real world procedures that we could set out in PLANNER for a robot. Of course, Winograd is free to concentrate on any micro-world he wishes, and all I am drawing attention to here is the danger of assuming that natural language is normally about real world procedures and, worse still, the implicit making of the assumption that we cannot understand discourse about a procedure unless we can do it ourselves. I am not saying that Winograd is making this evidently false assumption, only that the rhetoric surrounding the application of the "meanings are procedures" slogan to his system may cause the unwary to do so.

There is quite a different and low-level problem about the equivalence of Woods' and Winograd's systems, if we consider what we might call the received common-sense view of their work. Consider the following three assertions:

(1) Woods' system is an implementation of a transformational grammar.
(2) Winograd's work has shown the irrelevance of transformational grammar for language analysis – a view widely held by reviewers of his work.
(3) Woods' and Winograd's systems are formally equivalent – a view held by both of them.

There is clearly something of an inconsistent triad amongst those three widely held beliefs. The trouble probably centers on the exact sense in which Woods' work is formally equivalent to a transformational grammar – not a question that need detain us here, but one worth pointing out in passing.

Winograd's work is a central example of the 'artificial intelligence paradigm of language', using 'paradigm' in Kuhn's (1970) sense of a large scale revision in systematic thinking, where the paradigm revised is the 'generative paradigm' of the Chomskyan linguists (Chomsky 1957). From the artificial intelligence point of view, the generative linguistic work of the last fifteen years has three principal defects. Firstly, the generation of sentences, with whatever attached structures, is not in any interesting sense a demonstration of human understanding, nor is the separation of the well-formed from the ill-formed by such methods; for understanding requires, at the very least, both the generation of sentences as parts of coherent discourse, and some attempt to interpret, rather than merely reject, what seem to be ill-formed utterances. Neither the transformational grammarians following Chomsky, nor their successors the generative semanticists (Lakoff 1971), have ever explicitly renounced the generative paradigm.

Secondly, Chomsky's distinction between performance and competence models, and his advocacy of the latter, have isolated modern generative linguistics from any effective test of the systems of rules it proposes. Whether or not the distinction was intended to have this effect, it has meant that any test situation necessarily involves performance, which is considered outside the province of serious linguistic study. And any embodiment of a system of rules in a computer, and assessment of its output, would be performance. Artificial intelligence, too, is much concerned with the structure of linguistic processes, independent of any particular implementation[3], but implementation is never excluded, as it is from competence models, but rather encouraged.

Thirdly, as I mentioned before, there was until recently no place in the generative paradigm for inferences from acts and inductive generalizations, even though very simple examples demonstrate the need for it.

This last point, about the shortcomings of conventional linguistics is not at all new, and in artificial intelligence it is at least as old as Minsky's (1968: 22) observation that in *He put the box on the table. Because it wasn't level, it slid off*, the last *it* can only be referred correctly to the box, rather than the table, on the basis of some knowledge quite other than that in a conventional, and implausible, linguistic solution such as the creation of a class of 'level nouns' so that a box would not be considered as being or not being level.

These points would be generally conceded by those who believe there is an artificial intelligence paradigm of language understanding, but there would be far less agreement over the positive content of the paradigm. The trouble begins with the definition of 'understanding' as applied to a computer. At one extreme are those who say the word can only refer to the performance of a machine: to its ability to, say, sustain some form of dialogue long enough and sensibly enough for a human interrogator to be unsure whether what he is conversing with is a machine or not. On the other hand, there are many, almost certainly a majority, who argue that more is required, in that the methods and representations of knowledge by which the performance is achieved must be of the right formal sort, and that mere performance based on ad hoc methods does not demonstrate understanding.

This issue is closely related to that of the role of deduction in natural language understanding, simply because deduction is often the structure meant when 'right methods' are mentioned. The dispute between those who argue for, or, like Winograd, use deductive methods, and those who advocate other inferential systems closer to common sense reasoning, is in many ways a pseudo-issue because it is so difficult to define clearly what a non-deductive system is, (if by that is meant a system that cannot in principle be modelled by a deductive system) since almost any set of formal procedures, including 'invalid inferences', can be so displayed. The heart of the matter concerns the most appropriate form of an inference system; rather than how those inferences may be axiomatised, and it may well turn out that the most appropriate form for plausible reasoning in order to understand is indeed non-deductive. This same insight has largely defused another heated issue: whether the appropriate representations should be procedures or declarations. Winograd's work was of the former type, as was shown by his definitions of words like *pickup* as procedures for actually picking things up in the blocks world. However, simple procedural representations usually have the disadvantage that, if you are going to indicate, for every 'item' of knowledge, how it is to be used, then, if you may use it on a number of kinds of occasion, you will have to store it that number of times. So, if you want to change it later, you will also have to remember to change it in all the different places you have put it. There is the additional disadvantage of lack of perspicuity: anyone reading the procedural version of the Winograd grammar rule I gave earlier, will almost certainly find the conventional, declarative, version easier to understand.

So then, the fashion for all things procedural has to some extent abated (see Winograd 1974). There is general agreement that any system should show, as it were, how it is actually to be applied to language, but that is not the same as demanding that it should be written in a procedural language, like PLANNER. I shall return to this last point later.

4 Second generation systems

To understand what was meant when Winograd contrasted his own with what he called second generation systems, we have to remember, as always in this subject, that the generations are of fashion, not chronology or inheritance of ideas. He described the work of Simmons, Schank and myself among others in his survey of new approaches, even though the foundations and terminology of those approaches were set out in print in 1966, 1968 and 1967 respectively. What those approaches, and others, have in common is the belief that understanding systems must be able to manipulate very complex linguistic objects, or semantic structures, and that no simplistic approaches to understanding language with computers will work.

In a recent, and already very influential paper, Minsky (1975) has drawn together strands in the work of Charniak (1972) and the authors above using a terminology of 'frames'.

> A frame is a data-structure for representing a stereotype situation, like a certain kind of living room, or going to a children's birthday party. Attached to each frame are several kinds of information. Some of this is information about how to use the frame. Some is about what one can expect to happen next. Some is about what to do if these expectations are not confirmed.
>
> We can think of a frame as a network of nodes and relations. The top levels of a frame are fixed and represent things that are always true about the supposed situation. The lower levels have many terminals – 'slots' that must be filled by specific instances or data. Each terminal can specify conditions its assignments must meet. . . . Simple conditions are specified by markers that might require a terminal assignment to be a person, an object of sufficient value, etc. . . .

The key point about such structures is that they attempt to specify in advance what is going to be said, and how the world encountered is going to be structured. The structures, and the inference rules that apply to them, are also expressions of 'partial information' (in McCarthy's phrase) that are not present in first generation systems. As I showed earlier, with the "women and soldiers" example, such loose inductive information, seeking confirmation from the surrounding context, is required for very simple sentences. In psychological and visual terms, frame approaches envisage an understander as at least as much a looker as a seer.

I shall now describe briefly five approaches that might be called second generation.

4.1 Charniak

The new work which owes most to Minsky's advocacy is Charniak's. He studied what sorts of inferential information (Charniak 1972, 1973, 1974) would be needed to resolve pronoun ambiguities in children's stories, and in that sense to understand them. One of his example 'stories' is:

Jane was invited to Jack's birthday party. She wondered if he would like a kite. A friend told Jane that Jack already had a kite, and that he would make her take it back.

The problem concerns the penultimate word *it*, and deciding whether it refers to the first kite mentioned or the second. Charniak's analysis begins by pointing out that a great deal of what is required to understand that story is implicit: knowledge about the giving of presents, knowledge that if one possesses one of a certain sort of thing then one may well not want another, and so on.

Charniak's system does not actually run as a program, but is a theoretical structure of rules called 'demons' that correspond roughly to what Minsky later called frames. A demon for this example would be, 'If we see that a person might not like a present X, then look for X being returned to the store where it was bought. If we see that happening, or even being suggested, assert that the reason why is that P does not like X'.

The important words there are *look for*, which suggest that there may well be confirming hints to be found in the story and, if there are, then this tentative, partial, inference is correct, and we have a definite and correct answer. This approach, of using partial (not necessarily true) inferences, in order to assert a definite answer, is highly characteristic of 'second generation' systems.

The demons are, as with Winograd's work, expressed in a procedural language which, on running, will seek for a succession of inter-related 'goals'.

Here, for example, is a demon concerned with another story, about a child's piggy bank (PB) and a child shaking it, looking for money but hearing no sound. The demon, PB-OUT-OF, is formalised as:

```
(DEMON PB-OUT OF
      (NOLD PB PERSON M N)
      (?N OUT-OF ?M ?PB)
      (GOAL (? IS ?PB PIGGY-BANK))
      (GOAL (? IS ?M MONEY) $DEDUCE)
      (GOAL (?NOLD SHAKE ?PERSON ?PB) $TRUE)
      (ASSERT (? HAVE ?PERSON ?M))
      ASSERT (? RESULT ?N ?NOLD)))
```

Again, it is not necessary to explain the notation in detail to see that conditions are being stated for the contents of a piggy bank having been emptied. The pattern being sought by the demon in operation is the third line. If a chain of demons can 'reach' one of the possible referents in a story then there is a success registered and the ambiguity of the corresponding pronoun is resolved.

It can be seen that the information encoded in the system is of a highly specific sort – in the present case it is not about containers as such, and how to get their contents out, but about Piggy Banks in particular, and everything relies on that particular knowledge having been put in. Not all the knowledge is of this general sort: in a recent paper (Charniak 1974) where the 'kite' story is reconsidered there are rules of considerable generality and interest. One such is what Charniak calls a R+SSA rule:

"If the story gives information which would make it plausible to infer that PERSON is favorably inclined towards action A, and PERSON does S, a significant subaction (SSA) of A, then infer that PERSON is doing A".

An important assumption of Charniak's is what I shall call his 'decoupling assumption', namely that this work on the knowledge-based determination of reference can be effectively decoupled from any particular syntactic or semantic representation, or of its application, and can be explored in isolation. Thus, the apparently, English words in the PB-OUT-OF demon above do not have any particular status other than that of English words that happen to occur in the stories being examined. I shall return to this assumption later.

4.2 Colby

Colby (Colby et al. 1971, Enea and Colby 1973, Colby and Parkison 1974) has developed over a period of several years an on-line dialogue system that simulates a paranoid patient called PARRY. A measure of its success is that it is perhaps the most used artificial intelligence program in existence; used, that is, by those outside the research project that developed it. Here is a discontinuous sample of its output; again with the system's responses in the upper case:

Have you been hospitalised before?
THIS IS THE FIRST TIME
How long have you been there?
ABOUT TWO WEEKS
Any headaches?
MY HEALTH IS FINE
Are you having any difficulty with your memory?
NO
Then perhaps you can tell me who is the President of the United States?
NIXON IS PRESIDENT
What day is it today?
TODAY IS THURSDAY
What season is it?
LETS GET ON WITH THE INTERVIEW

Colby's aim was to produce a system that was not 'fragile' in the way that most artificial intelligence systems are: one that did not break down, or give up, if the input was not exactly what it expected; but one that carried on somehow in all circumstances, in the way that conversing humans do.

Fragility is avoided by having no conventional syntax analyser, and by not even attempting to take account of all the words in input. This is a considerable aid, since any parser that begins to parse a more than usually polite request such as 'Would you be so kind as to ....' is going to be in trouble. British English speakers arriving in the US quickly learn to delete such phrases, since they cause great confusion to human listeners in stores.

The input text is segmented by a heuristic that breaks it at any occurrence of a range of key words. Patterns are then matched with each segment. There are at present about 1700 patterns on a list (Colby and Parkison, in press) that is stored and matched, not against any syntactic or semantic representation of words but against the input word string direct, and by a process of sequential deletion. So, for example, *What is your main problem*? has a root verb BE substituted to become

WHAT BE YOU MAIN PROBLEM.

It is then matched successively in the following forms after successive deletions:

BE YOU MAIN PROBLEM
WHAT YOU MAIN PROBLEM
WHAT BE MAIN PROBLEM
WHAT BE YOU PROBLEM
WHAT BE YOU MAIN

and only the penultimate line exists as one of the stored patterns, and so is matched. Stored in the same format as the patterns are rules expressing the consequences for the "patient" of detecting aggression and over-friendliness in the interviewer's questions and remarks. The matched patterns found are then tied directly, or via these inference rules, to response patterns which are generated.

Enormous ingenuity has gone into the heuristics of this system, as its popularity testifies. The system has also changed considerably: it is now called PARRY2 and contains the above pattern matching, rather than earlier key work, heuristics. It has the partial, or what some would call pragmatic, rules about expectation and intention, and these alone might qualify it as 'second generation' on some interpretations of the phrase. A generator is also being installed to avoid the production of only "canned" responses.

Colby and his associates have put considerable energy into actually trying to find out whether or not psychiatrists can distinguish PARRY'S responses from those of a patient (Colby and Hilf 1973). This is probably the first attempt actually to apply Turing's test of machine-person distinguishability. There are statistical difficulties about interpreting the results but, by and large, the result is that the sample questioned cannot distinguish the two. Whether or not this will influence those who still, on principle, believe that

PARRY is not a simulation because it "does not understand", remains to be seen. It might be argued that they are in danger of falling into a form of Papert's "human-superhuman fallacy" of attacking machine simulations because they do not perform superhuman tasks, like translate poetry, tasks that some people can do. When such sceptics say that PARRY does not understand they have in mind a level of understanding that is certainly high – one could extend their case ironically by pointing out that very few people understand the content of sentences in the depth and detail that an analytic philosopher does, and a very good thing too. But there can be no doubt that many people on many occasions do seem to understand in the way that PARRY does.

4.3 Simmons

The remaining three systems differ from the above in their attempt to provide some representational structure quite different from that of the English input. This means the use of cases, and of complex structures that allow inferences to be drawn from the attribution of case in ways I shall explain. There is also, in the remaining systems, some attempt to construct a primitive, or reduced, vocabulary into which the language represented is squeezed.

Simmons' work is often thought of as a "memory model", though he does in fact pay more attention to word sense ambiguity, and to actual recognition in text than do many other authors. For him the fundamental notion is that of a 'semantic network', defined essentially by the statement of relational triples of form aRb, where R is the name of a relation and a and b are the names of nodes in the network. Simmons' work with this general formalism goes back to at least 1966 (Simmons et al. 1966), but, in its newer form with case formalism, it has been reported since 1970 (Simmons 1970b, Simmons and Bruce 1971, Simmons and Slocum 1972, Simmons 1973); and Hendrix et al. (1973) may reasonably be considered to have further implemented Simmons' methods.

Simmons considers the example sentence *John broke the window with a hammer*. This is analysed into a network of nodes C1, C2, C3, C4 corresponding to the appropriate senses of *John, Break, Window* and *Hammer* respectively. The linkage between the nodes are labelled by one of the following 'deep case relations': CAUSAL-ACTANT (CA1, CA2), THEME, LOCUS, SOURCE and GOAL. Case relations are specifications of the way dependent parts of a sentence, or concepts corresponding to parts of a sentence, depend on the main action. So, in this cxample, *John* is the first causal actant (CA1) of the breaking, the *hammer* is considered the second causal actant (CA1) of that breaking, and the *window* is the theme of the breaking. Thus, the heart of the analysis could be represented by a diagram as follows:

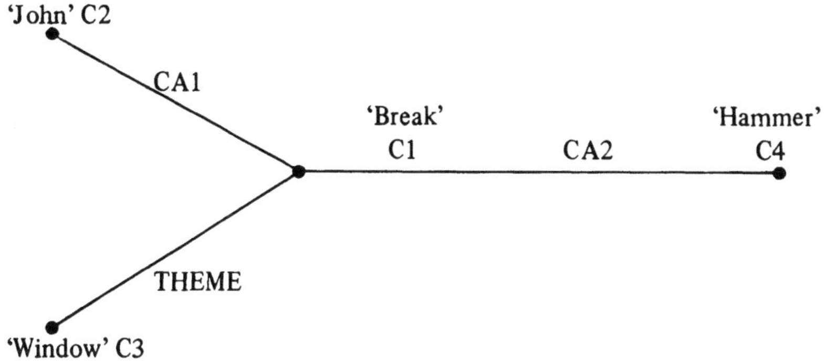

or by a set of relational triples:

(C1 CA1 C2) (C1 CA2 C4) (C1 THEME C3)

However, this is not the full representation, and my addition of the word labels to the diagram is misleading, since the nodes are intended to be names of senses of words, related to the actual occurrence of the corresponding word in a text by the relation TOK (for token). In an implementation, a node would have an arbitrary name, such as L97, which would then name a stored sense definition. So, for a sense of *apple* Simmons suggests an associated set of features: NBR-singular (S), SHAPE-spherical, COLOR-red, PRINTIMAGE-apple, THEME-eat, etc. If the name of the node tied to this set of features was indeed L97, then that node might become, say, C5 on being brought into some sentence representation during parsing. Thus, the diagram I gave must be thought of supplemented by other relational ties from the nodes; so that the full sentence about John would be represented by the larger set of triples:

((C1 TOK Break) (C1 CA1 C2) (C1 THEME C3) (C1 CA2 C4)
(C2 TOK John) (C2 DET Def) (C2 NBR S)
(C3 TOK Window) (C3 DET Def) (C3 NBR S)
(C4 TOK Hammer) (C4 Det Indef) (C4 NBR S) (C4 PREP With)

Word sense ambiguity is taken account of in that the node for one sense of *hammer* would be different from that corresponding to some other sense of the same word, such as that meaning 'Edward, Hammer of the Scots', to take a slightly strained alternative for this sentence.

The network above is also a representation of the following sentences, which can be thought of as surface variants of a single 'underlying' structure:

John broke the window with a hammer

John broke the window
The window broke.

Not all parts of that network will be set up by each of these sentences, of course, but the need for some item to fill an appropriate slot can be inferred, i.e. of the first causal actant (*John*) in the last two sentences. The sentences above are recognised by means of the 'ergative paradigm' of ordered matching patterns, of which the following list is a part:

(CA1 THEME CA2)
(CA1 THEME)
(CA2 THEME)
(THEME)

These sequences will each match, as left-right ordered items, one of the above sentences. It will be clear that Simmons' method of ascribing a node to each word-sense is not in any way a primitive system, by which I mean a system of classifiers into which all word senses are mapped.

Simmons is, however, considering a system of paraphrase rules that would map from one network to another in a way that he claims is equivalent to a system of primitives. Thus in Simmons 1973 he considers the sentences:

John bought the boat from Mary
Mary sold the boat to John

which would normally be considered approximate paraphrases of each other. He then gives 'natural' representations in his system, as follows, in the same order as the sentences:

C1 TOK buy, SOURCE (Mary), GOAL (John), THEME (boat),
C1 TOK sell, SOURCE (Mary), GOAL (John), THEME (boat),

and also the single representation for both sentences, as below, using a primitive action *transfer* (see description of Schank's work in next section) as follows:

C1 TOK and, Args C2, C3
C2 TOK transfer, SOURCE (John), GOAL (Mary), THEME (money)
C3 TOK transfer, SOURCE (Mary), GOAL (John), THEME (boat)

Simmons opts for the first form of representation, given the possibility of a transfer rule going from either of the shallower representations to the other, while in Hendrix et al. 1973 the other approach is adopted, using a primitive action *exchange* instead of *transfer*.

The implementation under construction is a front-end parser of the Woods' augmented transition network type (see Woods 1970), and a generation system going from the semantic networks to surface strings described in detail by Simmons and Slocum (1972). Simmons has also given considerable time (Simmons and Bruce 1971) to the automatic translation of the networks into a corresponding first-order predicate calculus format of the sort developed by Sandewall (1971). This last is particularly valuable because, if generalizable, it shows that any linguistic codings in network form can be translated into some form of the predicate calculus, if that formalism and its associated proof techniques can be shown to be appropriate for certain problems in the area of natural language analysis.

4.4 Schank

Schank's is a rich system of semantic representation, developed over a period of six years, with the collaboration of a number of talented students. Its graph system of notation has influenced psychologists like Abelson (1973), among others. Schank's contribution has been the notational system representing the structure of natural language sentences, and this has been programmed by various collaborators over the years. In its present version, called MARGIE (Schank et al. 1973) it has an analyser of English due to Goldman (1974). MARGIE produces output in two modes, demonstrating the sort of conceptual inferencing that goes on at the level of the semantic representation[4]: the PARAPHRASE mode and the INFERENCE mode. Samples of input and output to and from the two modes can be shown thus:

(INFERENCE MODE)
INPUT: John told Mary that Bill wants a book.
OUTPUT: A book about what.
Mary knows that Bill wants a book.
Bill wants to come to have a book.
Bill wants someone to cease to have a book.
Bill wants to read a book.
(PARAPHRASE MODE)
INPUT: John killed Mary by choking Mary.
OUTPUT: John strangled Mary.
John choked Mary and she died because she could not breathe. Mary died because she was unable to inhale some air and she was unable to inhale some air because John grabbed her neck.

The aim of Schank's system has always been to provide a representation of meaning in terms of which these and other tasks, such as machine translation, could be carried out; a representation, moreover, that was to be independent of any particular language, and of syntax, and indeed, of all surface structure whatever.

The formal structure of Schank's graphs is that of dependency grammar (Hays 1964), and the items in the graph are of four types, or conceptual categories. They are symbolised as PP, ACT, PA and AA, which are acronyms, but which correspond closely (for the purpose of understanding their function) to those of a noun, verb, adjective and adverb, respectively.[5] The basic structure is called a 'conceptualisation', and is normally introduced with a straightforward dependency structure such as, for the sentence *The man took a book*:

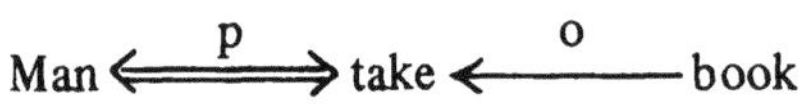

Here 'p' indicates past, and is the dependency symbol linking a PP to the ACT (*take*) which is the hub of the conceptualisation, as with Simmons. The 'o' indicates the objective case, marking the dependence of the object PP on the central ACT. There is a carefully constructed syntax of linkages between the conceptual categories, that will be described only in part in what follows.

The next stage of the notation involves an extended case notation and a set of primitive ACTSs, as well as a number of items such as PHYSCONT which indicate other states, and items of a fairly simplified psychological theory (the dictionary entry for *advise*, for example, contains a subgraph telling us that Y 'will benefit' as part of the meaning of *X advises Y* (Schank 1973a)). There are four cases in the system, and their subgraphs are as follows:

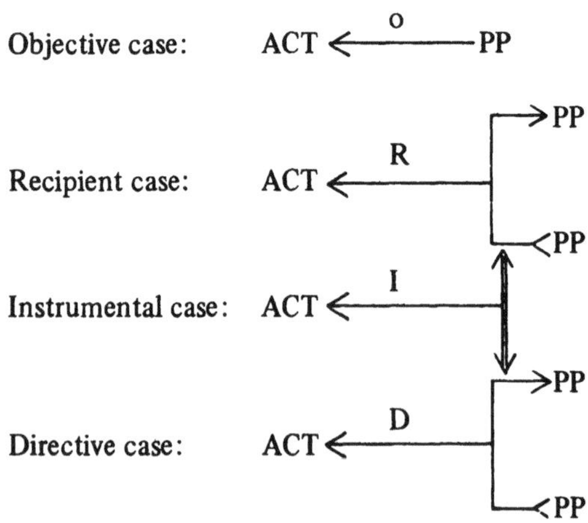

There are at present fourteen[6] basic actions forming the nubs of the graphs, as well as a default action DO. They are: PROPEL, MOVE, INGEST, EXPEL,

GRASP, PTRANS, MTRANS, ATRANS, SMELL, SPEAK, LOOK-AT, LISTEN-TO, CONC and MBUILD. The notions of case and primitive act are related by rules in the development of conceptualisations. So, for example, the primitive act INGEST has as its instrument the act PTRANS. There are also other inferences from any ACT classified as an INGEST action, such as that the thing ingested changes its form; that if the thing ingested is edible the ingester becomes 'more nourished' etc. (see Schank 1973a: 38ff.). This will all become clearer if we consider the transition from a dictionary entry for an action to a filled-in conceptualisation. Here is the dictionary entry for the action *shoot*:

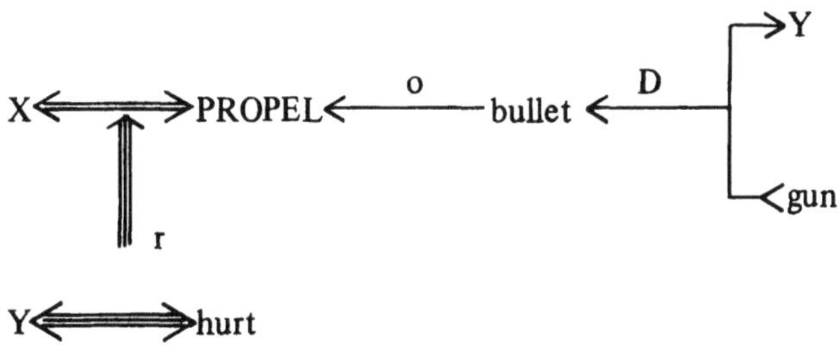

We can consider this entry as an active 'frame-like' object seeking filler items in any context in which it is activated. Thus, in the sentence *John shot the girl with a rifle*, the variables will be filled in from context and the case inference will be made from the main act PROPEL, which is that its instrument is MOVE, GRASP or PROPEL, and so we will arrive at the whole conceptualisation:

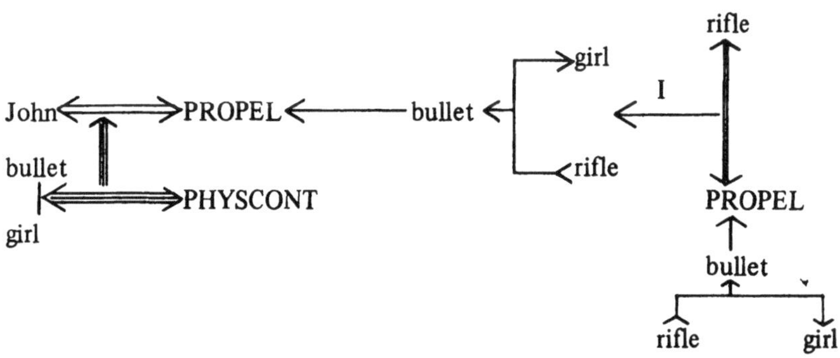

This case inference must be made, according to Schank, in order to achieve an adequate representation. There is, in the last diagram, a certain redundancy of expression, but as we shall see in the next section this often happens with deeper semantic notations.

More recently, Schank, together with Rieger, has developed a new class of causal inferences which deepen the diagrams still further. So, in the analysis of *John's cold improved because I gave him an apple* (in Schank 1974a) the extended diagram contains at least four yet lower levels of causal arrowing, including one corresponding to the notion of John constructing the idea MBUILD) that he wants to eat an apple. So we can see that the underlying explication of meaning here is not only in the sense of linguistic primitives, but in terms of a theory of mental acts as well.

Now there are a number of genuine expositional difficulties here for the commentator faced with a system of this complexity. One aspect of this is the stages of development of the system itself, which can be seen as a consistent process of producing what was argued for in advance. For example, Schank claimed early on to be constructing a system of semantic structures underlying the 'surface of natural language', although initially there were no primitives at all, and as late as 1970 (Schank et al. 1970) there was only a single primitive TRANS, and most of the entries in the dictionary consisted of the English words coded, together with subscripts. Since then the primitive system has blossomed and there are now twelve primitives for ACTS including three for the original TRANS itself. Each exposition of the system recounts its preceding phases, from the original primitive-free one, through to the present causal inference form; rather as each human foetus is said to relive in the womb all the evolutionary stages of the human race. The only trouble with this, from an outsider's point of view, is that at each stage the representation has been claimed, in firm tones, to be the correct one, while at the same time Schank admits, in moments of candor (Schank 1973), that there is no end to the conceptual diagramming of a sentence. This difficulty may well reflect genuine problems in language itself, and, in its acutest form, concerns a three-way confusion between an attractive notation for displaying the 'meanings of words', the course of events in the real world, and, finally, actual procedures for analysis. It is not always clear whether or not procedures implementing conceptual dependency are intended to recapture all the many phases of expansion of the diagrams.

This raises the, to me, important question of the application of a semantic system, that I shall touch on again later. Schank, for example, does mention in passing the questions of word-sense ambiguity, and the awful ambiguity of English prepositions, but they are in no way central for him, and he assumes that with the availability of 'the correct representation', his system when implemented must inevitably solve these traditional and vexing questions. No procedures are hinted at along with the graphs as to how this is to be done. A distinction of importance may be becoming apparent here between Schank's work and Rieger's: in Rieger's thesis (Rieger 1974) the rules of inference appear to create separate and new subgraphs which may stand in an inferential relation to each other so as to produce conclusions about problems of, say, pronoun reference, etc. But in Schank's corresponding papers the same inferences are not applied to actual problems (Schank 1974a) but only complexify the conceptual graphs further. Closely connected with this is the question of the survival of the surface structure in the diagrams. Until very recently primitivisation applied only to verbs, that of nouns being left to Weber (Weber 1972). Most recently, though, noun words have been disappearing from diagrams and been replaced by categories such as *physobs*. But it is clear that the surface is only slowly disappearing, rather than having been abhorred all along.

In his most recent publication (Schank 1974b) there are signs that this trend of infinitely proliferating diagrams is reversing. In it Schank considers the application of his approach to the representation of text, and concludes, correctly in my view, that the representations of parts of the text must be interconnected by causal arrows, and that, in order to preserve lucidity, the conceptual diagrams for individual sentences and their parts must be abbreviated, as by triples such PEOPLE PTRANS PEOPLE. Here indeed, the surface simply has to survive in the representation unless one is prepared to commit oneself to the extreme view that the ordering of sentences in a text is a purely superficial and arbitrary matter. The sense in which this is a welcome reversal of a trend should be clear, because in the 'causation inference' development, mentioned earlier, all the consequences and effects of a conceptualization had to be drawn within itself. Thus, in the extreme case, each sentence of a text should have been represented by a diagram containing most or all of the text of which it was a part. Thus the representation of a text would have been impossible on such principles.

4.5 Wilks

My own system constructs a semantic representation for small natural language texts: the basic representation is applied directly to the text and can then be "massaged" by various forms of inference to become as deep as is necessary for well defined tasks demonstrating understanding. It is a uniform representation, in that information that might conventionally be considered as syntactic, semantic, factual or inferential is all expressed within a single type of structure. The fundamental unit in the construction of this meaning representation is the 'template', which is intended to correspond to an intuitive notion of a basic message of agent-action-object form. Templates are rigid format networks of more basic building blocks called 'formulas', which correspond to senses of individual words. In order to construct a complete text representation templates are bound together by two kinds of higher level structures called 'paraplates' and 'inference rules'. The templates themselves are built up as construction of the representation proceeds, but the formulas, paraplates and inference rules are all present in the system at the outset and each of these three types of pre-stored structure is ultimately constructed from an inventory of eighty semantic primitive elements, and from functions and predicates ranging over those elements.

The system runs on-line as a package of LISP, MLISP and MLISP2 programs, taking as input small paragraphs of English, that can be made up by the user from a vocabulary of about 600 words, and producing a good French translation as output. This environment provides a pretty clear test of language understanding, because French translations for everyday prose are either right or wrong, and can be seen to be so, while at the same time, the major difficulties of understanding programs – word sense ambiguity, case ambiguity, difficult pronoun reference, etc. – can all be represented within a machine translation environment by, for example, choosing the words of the input sentence containing a pronoun reference difficulty so that the possible alternative references have different genders in French. In that way the French output makes quite clear whether or not the program has made the correct inferences in order to understand what it is translating. The program is reasonably robust in actual performance, and will even tolerate a certain amount of bad grammar in the input, since it does not perform a syntax analysis in the conventional sense, but seeks message forms representable in the semantic structures employed.

Typical input would be a sentence such as *John lives out of town and drinks his wine out of a bottle. He then throws the bottles out of the window.* The program will produce French sentences with different output for each of the three occurrences of *out of*, since it realises that they function quite differently on the three occasions of use, and that the difference must be reflected in the French. A sentence such as *Give the monkeys bananas although they are not ripe because they are very hungry* produces a translation with different equivalents for the two occurrences of *they*, because the system correctly realises, from what I shall describe below as preference considerations, that the most sensible interpretation is one in which the first *they* refers to *bananas* and the second to *monkeys*, and *bananas* and *monkeys* have different genders in French. These two examples are dealt with in the 'basic mode' of the system (Wilks 1973a). In many cases it cannot resolve pronoun ambiguities by the sort of straightforward 'preference considerations' used in the last example, where, roughly speaking, 'ripeness' prefers to be predicated of plant-like things, and 'hunger' of animate things. Even in a sentence as simple as *John drank the wine on the table and it was good*, such considerations are inadequate to resolve the ambiguity of *it* between *wine* and *table*, since both may be good things. In such cases of inability to resolve within its basic mode, the program deepens the representation of the text so as to try and set up chains of inference that will reach, and so prefer, only one of the possible referents. I will return to these processes in a moment, but first I shall give some brief description of the basic representation set up for English.

For each sense of a word in its dictionary the program sees a formula. This is a tree structure of semantic primitives, and is to be interpreted formally using dependency relations. The main element in any formula is the rightmost, called its head, and that is the fundamental category to which the formula belongs. In the formulas for actions, for example, the head will always be one of the primitive PICK, CAUSE, CHANGE, FEEL, HAVE, PLEASE, PAIR, SENSE, USE, WANT, TELL, BE, DO, FORCE, MOVE, WRAP, THINK, FLOW, MAKE, DROP, STRIK, FUNC or HAPN.

Here is the tree structure for the action of drinking:

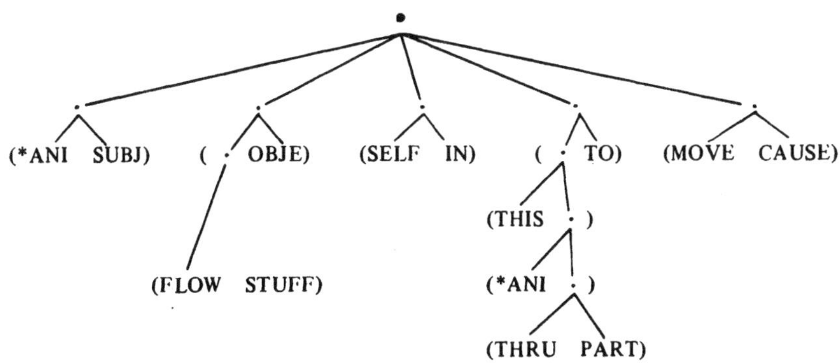

Once again, it is not necessary to explain the formalism in any detail, to see that this sense of *drink* is being expressed as a causing to move a liquid object (FLOW STUFF) by an animate agent, into that same agent (containment case indicated by IN, and formula syntax identifies SELF with the agent) and via (direction case) an aperture (THRU PART) of the agent.

Template structures, which actually represent sentences and their parts are built up as networks of formulas like the one above. Templates always consist of an agent node, and action node and an object node, and other nodes that may depend on these. So, in building a template for *John drinks wine*, the whole of the above tree-formula for *drinks* would be placed at the central action node, another tree structure for *John* at the agent node and so on. The complexity of the system comes from the way in which the formulas, considered as active entities, dictate how other places in the same template should be filled.

Thus, the *drink* formula above can be thought of as an entity at a template action node, seeking a liquid object, that is to say a formula with (FLOW STUFF) as its right-most branch, to put at the object node of the same template. This seeking is preferential, in that formulas not satisfying that requirement will be accepted, but only if nothing satisfactory can be found. The template finally established for a fragment of text is the one in which the most formulas have their preferences satisfied. There is a general principle at work here, that the right interpretation "says the least" in information-carrying terms. This very simple device is able to do much of the work of a syntax and word-sense ambiguity resolving program. For example, if the sentence had been *John drank a whole pitcher*, the formula for *pitcher of liquid* would have been preferred to that for the human, since the subformula (FLOW STUFF) could be appropriately located within it.

A considerable amount of squeezing of this simple canonical form of template is necessary to make it fit the complexity of language: texts have to be fragmented initially; then, in fragments which are, say, prepositional phrases there is a dummy agent imposed, and the prepositional formula functions as a pseudo-action. There are special "less preferred" orders to deal with fragments not in agent-action-object order, and so on.

When the local inferences have been done that set up the agent-action-object templates for fragments of input text, the system attempts to tie these templates together so as to provide an overall initial structure for the input. One form of this is the anaphora tie, of the sort discussed for the monkeys and bananas example above, but the more general form is the case tie. Assignment of these would result in the template for the last clause of *He ran the mile in a paper bag* being tied to the action node of the template for the first clause (*He ran the mile*), and the tie being labelled CONTainment. These case ties are made with the aid of another class of ordered structures, essentially equivalent to Fillmore's case frames, called 'paraplates' and which are attached to the formulas for English prepositions. So, for *out of*, for example, there would be at least six ordered paraplates, each of which is a string of functions that seek inside templates for information. In general, paraplates range across two, not necessarily contiguous, templates. So, in analysing *He put the number he thought of in the table*, the successfully matching paraplate would pin down the dependence of the template for the last of the three clauses as DIREction, by taking as argument only that particular template for the last clause that contained the formula for *a numerical table*, rather than *a kitchen table*, and it would do that because of a function in that paraplate seeking a similarity of head (SIGN in this case) between the two object formulas, for *number* and *table*. The other template containing the *furniture* formula for *table* would naturally not satisfy the function because SIGN would not be the head of this sense formula for table.

The structure of mutually connected templates that has been put together thus far constitutes a 'semantic block', and, if it can be constructed, then, as far as the system is concerned, all semantic and referential ambiguity has been resolved and it will begin to generate French by unwrapping the block again. The generation aspects of this work have been described by Herskovits (1973). One aspect of the general notion of preference is that the system should never construct a deeper or more elaborate semantic representation than is necessary for the task in hand and, if the initial block can be constructed and a generation of French done, no 'deepening' of the representation will be attempted.

However, many examples cannot be resolved by the methods of this 'basic mode' and, in particular, if a word sense ambiguity, or pronoun reference, is still unresolved, then a unique semantic block of templates cannot be constructed and the 'extended mode' will be entered (Wilks 1973b, 1975d). In this mode, new template-like forms are extracted from existing ones, and then added to the template pool from which further inferences can be made. So, in the template derived earlier for *John drinks wine*, the system enters the formula for *drinks*, and draws inferences corresponding to each case sub-formula. In this example it will derive template-like forms equivalent to, in ordinary English, *The wine is in John, The wine entered John via an aperture* and so on. The extracted templates express information already implicitly present in the text, even though many of them are partial inferences: ones that may not necessarily be true.

Common-sense inference rules are then brought to bear, which attempt, by a simple strategy, to construct the shortest possible chain of rule-linked template forms from one containing an ambiguous pronoun, say, to one containing one of its possible referents. Such a chain then constitues a solution to the ambiguity problem, and the preference approach assumes that the shortest chain is always the right one. So, in the case of *John drank the wine on the table and it was good*, the correct chain to *wine* uses the two rules

I 1. ((*ANI 1) ((SELF IN) (MOVE CAUSE)) (*REAL 2)) ⟶ (1(*JUDG) 2)
or, in "semi-English",
[animate · 1 cause-to-move-in-self real · object · · 2] ⟶ [1 *judges 2]

I 2. (1 BE (GOOD KIND)) ⟷ ((*ANI 2) WANT 1)
or, again,
[1 is good] ⟷ [animate-2 wants 1]

These rules are only partial, that is to say, they correspond only to what we may reasonably look out for in a given situation, not to what must happen. The hypothesis here is that understanding can only take place on the basis of simple rules that are confirmed by the context of application. In this example the chain constructed may be expressed as follows (using the above 'square bracket notation' to contain not a representation, but simply an indication, in English, of the template contents):

forwards inf.	↓	[John drank the-wine]		Template 1
		[John causes-to-move-in-self	wine]	≑ Template 1
		[John *judges	wine]	by I 1.
backwards inf.	↑	[John wants	wine]	≑ line above
		[wine is	good]	by I 2.
		[?it is	good]	Template 3

The assumption here is that no chain using other inference rules could have reached the *table* solution by using less than two rules.

The chief drawback of this system is that codings consisting entirely of primitives have a considerable amount of both vagueness and redundancy. For example, no reasonable coding in terms of structured primitives could be expected to distinguish, say, *hammer* and *mallet*. That may not matter provided the codings can distinguish importantly different senses of words. Again, a template for the sentence *The shepherd tended his flock* would contain considerable repetition, each node of the template trying, as it were, to tell the whole story by itself. Whether or not such a system can remain stable with a considerable vocabulary, of say several thousand words, has yet to be tested.

4.6 It will be evident to any reader that the last two systems described, Schank's and my own, share a great deal in common. Even the apparent difference in notation is reduced if one sees the topological similarity that results from considering the head of a formula as functioning rather like a Schank basic action. If one thinks of the dependencies of the case subparts of a formula, not arranged linearly along the bottom of a tree, but radiating out from the head in the center, then the two diagrams actually have identical topologies under interpretation. A difference arises in that the "filled-in-entity" for Schank is the conceptualisation centered on the basic action, though for me it is the network of formulas placed in relation in a template, where there is indeed a basic action, the head of the action formula, but there is also a basic entity in the agent formula and so on. Or, to put it another way, both what-is and what-is-expected are represented in the templates: the agent formula represents the agent, for example, but the left-hand part of the action formula also represents what agent was expected or sought, as in the (*ANI SUBJ) sub-formula of the *drink* formula.

Although developed in isolation initially, these two systems have also influenced each other in more recent years, probably unconsciously. For example, conceptual dependency now emphasises the agent-action-object format more than before, and is less "verb-centered" and timeless, while, conversely, my own system now makes much more overt use of rules of partial information than in its earlier versions. Again, both systems have intellectual connections that go back before either generation of I systems. In my view, both these systems have roots in the better parts of the Computational Linguistics movement of the Fifties: in the case of Schank's system, one may think of the earlier systems of Hays (1964) and Lamb (1966), and the arrow-structured primitive systems of Farradene (1966). In the case of my own system there are clear precedents in the Parker-Rhodes (1961) system of classification and the early semantic structures of Richens (1961) and Masterman (1961). In 1961 the last author was arguing that "what is needed is a discipline that will study semantic message connection in a way analogous to that in which metamathematics now studies mathematical connection, and to that in which mathematical linguistics now studies syntactic connection" (ibid., 3).

This historical point raises a final one that is, I feel, of passing interest. There seem to be two research styles in this field: one is what might be called the "fully finished style", in which the work exists only in one complete form, and is not issued in early or developed versions. The best example of this is Winograd's work. The other type, exemplified by all the other authors discussed here, to some extent, is the developing style: work which appears in a number of versions over the years, one hopes with gradual improvements, perhaps in attempts to tackle a wider range of linguistic or other inferential phenomena. There are advantages to both styles, but even in the latter one knows that any proposed structure of system will, in the end, be found wanting in the balances of language, so it can only be a question of when one will have to abandon it. The interesting question, and one to which no answer could possibly be given here, is just how far is it worth pushing any given structural approach before starting again from scratch?

5 Some comparisons and contrasts

In this section I shall compare and contrast, under some eight interconnected headings, the projects described in the body of the paper. This is not easy to do, particularly when the present author is among the writers discussed, though that is easily remedied by the reader's making an appropriate discount. A more serious problem is that, at this stage of research in artificial intelligence and natural language, the most attractive distinctions dissolve on more detailed scrutiny, largely because of the lack of any precise theoretical statement in most, if not all, the major projects. There are those who think that it therefore follows that this is not the moment for any form of critical comparison in this field and that no more is needed than a "positive attitude" towards all possible projects. Only those who feel that, on the contrary, any time is as good as any other for the discussion of differences in the hope of progress, should read on.

It must be admitted right away that the selection of projects discussed above, like Winograd's distinction between first and second generation systems, on which the selection was to some extent based, cannot be defended by any strict definitions: one that would, in this case, include all the projects described, and exclude all those of Winograd's "first generation". One might, for example, want to define second generation systems (in the study of natural language within the artificial intelligence paradigm) in some very general terms, such as those systems which, (1) contain complex semantic structures for the representation of text that are significantly different from the "surface structure" of the input, and (2) contain cognate structures representing conceptual and real world knowledge that is not explicitly present in the input text. Even so general a description of a frames type approach would not cover Charniak or Colby with the first point, nor Simmons with the second, for he has so far eschewed all concern with information not present explicitly in the input text. Moreover, the second point would certainly cover Winograd's own work, as well as other first generation approaches, so it is clear, at the outset of any comparison, that there is not even a simple and unequivocal definition which covers all and only the projects to be compared.

5.1 Level of representation

One important line of current dispute among the second generation approaches concerns the appropriate level of representation for natural language. On the one hand are those like Colby and apparently Charniak, who hold that the representation of language can, in effect, be by means of itself while, on the other hand, there are those like Schank and myself who hold that the appropriate level of computation for inference about natural language is in some reduced, or primitive, representation. Simmons, as we saw, holds an intermediate position. I wrote "appears" in the case of Charniak because he holds that his structures are independent of any particular level of representation, or rather, that they could be realized at a number of levels of representation, depending on the subject area. However, there is no doubt that the representation in terms of predicates that he offers in his work appears to be in one-to-one correspondence with English words.

The strongest low-level approach is undoubtedly that of Colby, who straight forwardly faces the enormous mapping problems involved if the structures are at the English word level. It is important to realize that this dispute is ultimately one of degree, since no one would claim that every locution recognized by an intelligent analyser must be mapped into a "deep" representation. To take an extreme case, any system that mapped *Good Morning* into a deep semantic representation before deciding that the correct response was also *Good Morning* would be making a serious theoretical mistake.

However, the most serious argument for a non-superficial representation is not in terms of the avoidance of mapping difficulties, but in terms of theoretical perspicuity of the primitive structures, and this argument is closely tied to the defence of semantic primitives in general, which is a large subject not to be undertaken here. One of the troubles about semantic primitives is that they are open to bad defenses, which decrease rather than increase their plausibility. For example, some users of them for linguistic representation have declared them to have some sort of objective existence, and have implied that there is a 'right set' of primitives open to empirical discovery. On that view the essentially linguistic character of structures of primitives is lost, for they then might as well be strings of binary numbers, or something equally opaque and non-linguistic. No great deal of thought is required to see that that simply could not be the case. What is the case is that there is a considerable amount of psychological evidence that people are able to recall the content of what they hear and understand without being able to recall either the actual words or the syntactic structure used. There is a large literature on this subject, from which a sample reference would be Johnson-Laird 1974.

These results are, of course, no proof of the existence of semantic primitives, but they are undoubtedly supporting evidence of their plausibility, as is, on a different plane, the result from the encoding of the whole Webster's Third International Dictionary at the System Development Corporation, where it was found that a rank-ordered frequency count of the words used to define other words in that vast dictionary was a list (omitting *the* and *a*) which corresponded almost item-for-item to a plausible list of semantic primitives, derived a priori, by those actually concerned to code the structure of word and sentence meanings.

It is important to distinguish the dispute about 'level' from the closely connected topic that I shall call the 'centrality' of the knowledge required by a language understanding system.

5.2 Centrality

What I am calling the 'centrality' of certain kinds of information concerns not its level of representation but its non-specificity: again a contrast can be drawn between the sorts of information required by Charniak's system, on the one hand, and that required by Schank's and my own on the other. Charniak's examples suggest that the fundamental form of information is highly specific[7] to particular situations, like parties and the giving of presents, while the sorts of information central to Schank's and my own systems are general partial assertions about human wants, expectations, and so on, many of which are so general as to be almost vacuous which, one might argue, is why their role in understanding has been ignored for so long.

If I were a reasonably fluent speaker of, say, German, I might well not understand a German conversation about birthday presents unless I had detailed factual information about how Germans organize the giving of presents, which might be considerably different from the way we do it. Conversely, of course, I might understand much of a technical article about a subject in which I was an expert, even though I knew very little of the language in which it was written. These are certainly considerations that speak for Charniak's approach, and it is perhaps a paradox that the sort of natural language understander that would tend to confirm his assumptions would be one concerned with discourse about, say, the details of repairing a motor car, where factual information is what is central, yet, ironically, Charniak has concentrated on something as general as children's stories, with their need of deep assumptions about human desires and behavior.

In the end this difference may again turn out to be one of emphasis, and of what is most appropriate to different subject areas, though there may be a very general issue lurking somewhere here. It seems to me not a foolish question to ask whether much of what appears to be about natural language in artificial intelligence research is in fact 'theoretical psychology', in which case it could hardly be research on natural language. When describing Winograd's work earlier in the paper, I raised this question in a weak form by asking whether his definition of *pickup* had anything to do with the natural language use of the word, or whether it was rather a description of how his system picked something up, a quite different matter.

Suppose we generalize this query somewhat, by asking the apparently absurd question of what would be wrong with calling, say, Charniak's work an essay on the 'Socio-economic behavior of American children under stress'? In the case of Charniak's work this is a facetious question, asked only in order to make a point, but with an increasing number of systems in artificial intelligence being designed not essentially to do research on natural language, but in order to have a natural language "front end" to a system that is essentially intended to predict chemical spectra, or play snakes and ladders or whatever, the question becomes a serious one. It seems to me a good time to ask whether we should expect advance in understanding natural language from those tackling the problems head on, or those concerned to build a 'front end'. It is clearly the case that any piece of knowledge whatever could be essential to the understanding of some story. The question is, does it follow that the specification, organization and formalization of that knowledge is the study of language, because if it is then all human enquiry from physics and history to medicine is a linguistic enterprise. And, of course, that possibility has actually been entertained within certain strains of modern philosophy.

However, I am not trying here to breathe fresh life into a philosophical distinction, between being about language and not being about language, but rather introducing a practical distinction (which is also a consideration in favour of opting, as I have, to work on very general and central areas of knowledge) between specific knowledge and central knowledge without which a system could not be said to understand the language at all. For example, I might know nothing of the arrangement of American birthday parties, but could not be accused of not understanding English even though I failed to understand some particular children's story. Yet, if I did not have available some very general partial inference such as the one about people being hurt and falling, or one about people endeavouring to possess things that they want, then it is quite possible that my lack of understanding of quite simple sentences would cause observers to think that I did not understand English. An interesting and difficult question that then arises is whether those who concentrate on central and less central areas of discourse could, in principle, weld their bodies of inferences together in such a way as to create a wider system; whether, to put the matter another way, natural language is a whole that can be built up from parts?

5.3 Phenomenological level

Another distinction that can be confused with the central-specific one is that of the 'phenomenological levels' of inferences in an understanding system. I mean nothing daunting by the phrase: consider the action eating which is, as a matter of anatomical fact, quite often an act of bringing the bones of my ulna and radius (in my arm) close to that of my lower mandible (my jaw). Yet clearly, any system of common sense inferences that considered such a truth when reasoning about eating would be making a mistake. One might say that the phenomenological level of the analysis was wrong even though all the inferences it made were true ones. The same would be true of any artificial intelligence system that made everyday inferences about physical objects by considering their quantum structure.

Schank's analysis of eating contains the information that it is done by moving the hands to the mouth, and it might be argued that even this is going too far from the "meaning" of eating, whatever that may be, towards generally true information about the act which, if always inferred about all acts of eating, will carry the system unmanageably far.

There is no denying that this sort of information might be useful to have around somewhere; that, in Minsky's terms, the 'default' value of the instrument for eating is the hand brought to the mouth, so that, if we have no contrary information, then that is the way to assume that any given act of eating was performed. Nonetheless, there clearly is a danger, and that is all I am drawing attention to here, of taking inferences to a phenomenological level beyond that of common sense. A clearer case, in my view, would be Schank's analysis (1974a) of mental activity in which all actions, such as kicking a ball, say, are preceded by a mental action of conceiving or deciding to kick a ball. This is clearly a level of analysis untrue to common sense, and which can have only harmful effects in a system intended to mimic common sense reasoning and understanding.

5.4 Decoupling

Another general issue in dispute concerns what I shall call 'decoupling', which is whether or not the actual parsing of text or dialogue into an 'understanding system' is essential. Charniak and Minsky believe that this initial 'parsing' can be effectively decoupled from the interesting inferential work and simply assumed. But, in my view, that is not so, because many of the later inferences would actually have to be done already, in order to have achieved the initial parsing. For example, in analysing *He shot her with a colt*, we cannot ascribe any structure at all until we can make the inference that guns rather than horses are instruments for shooting, and so such a sentence cannot be represented by an inference-but-no-parsing structure, such as (AT JOHN STATION), without assuming that language does not have one of its essential characteristics, namely 'systematic ambiguity'. If one allows representational structures to have significance quite independent of their application, then one may not be in a situation essentially different from that of the logician who simply asserts that such-and-such is the "right structure" of some sentence.

The inferences required to resolve word sense ambiguities, and those required to resolve pronoun reference problems, are not of different types; often the two problems occur in a single sentence and must be resolved together. But Charniak's decoupling has the effect of completely separating these two closely related linguistic phenomena in what seems to me an unrealistic manner. His system does inferencing to resolve pronoun ambiguities, while sense ambiguity is presumably to be done in the future by some other, ultimately recoupled, system.[8]

Another way of pointing up the difference between the attitudes of second generation systems to decoupling in relating to the first generation is by describing the role of syntax analysis in them. As we saw, syntax was the heart of Winograd's system, but both levels of frame approach discount syntax analysis, though for very different reasons: Charniak does so because it is part of the initial parsing from which his inferential work has been decoupled. Schank and I do so because we believe semantic analysis to be fundamental, and that in an actual implementation the results of syntactic analysis can all be achieved by a sufficiently powerful semantic analyser. And this last assumption is confirmed by the limited degree of success that the two semantic analysers have actually achieved in operation.

5.5 Availability of surface structure

An issue close to that of the appropriate level of representation in a system is that of the availability of the surface structure of the language analysed; or, to put it more crudely, the availability during subsequent analysis of the actual words being analysed. These are clearly available in Colby, and are indirectly available in Simmons', Winograd's and my own system, but Schank makes a point of the importance of their non-availability, of the input surface structure and words. There are both theoretical and practical aspects to this claim of Schank's: in the limit, the order of the sentences of a text is part of its surface structure, and presumably it is not intended to abandon this 'superficial information'. In one of his recent papers (1974b) Schank seems to have accepted some limitation on the abandonment of surface structure.

The other, practical, point concerns the form of representation employed: in the (1973) implementation of Schank's system using an analyser of input text, a memory and a generator of responses, it was intended that nothing should be transferred from the input program to the output program except a representation coded in the structures of primitives discussed earlier.[9] The question that arises, is, can that structure specify and distinguish word-senses adequately without transferring information specifically associated with the input word? Schank clearly believes the answer to this question is yes, but that cannot be considered established by the scale of computations yet described in print.

A suitable environment in which to consider the question is that of translation from one language to another: suppose we are analysing a sentence containing the word *nail*, meaning a physical object. It is clear that the translation of that word into French should not be the same as the translation for *screw* or *peg*. Yet is it plausible that any description of the function of these three entities entirely in terms of semantic primitives, and without any explicit mention of the word name and its connection to its French equivalent, will be sufficient to ensure that only the right match is made?

5.6 Application

This point is a generalisation of the last two, and concerns the way in which different systems display, in the structures they manipulate, the actual procedures of application of those structures to input text or dialogue. This is a matter different from both that of the availability of the surface structure, and of a computer implementation of the system. In the case of Colby's patterns, for example, the form of their application to the input English is clear, even though the matching involved could be achieved by many different implementation algorithms. In the case of my own system, I hold the same to be true of the template structures, even though by the time the input has reached the canonical template form it is considerably different from the input surface structure. The system at the extreme end of any scale of perspicuity of application is Winograd's, where the procedural notation, by its nature, tends to make clear the way in which the structures are applied. At the other end are the systems of Schank and Charniak, where no application is specified, which means that the representations are not only compatible with many implementation algorithms, which does not matter, but are also compatible with many systems of linguistic rules, whose specification is an essential piece of inquiry, and whose subsequent production may cause the basic system to be fundamentally different.

English prepositions will serve as an example: in Schank's case notation there is no indication of how the case discriminations are actually to be applied to English prepositions in text. So, for example, the preposition *in* can correspond to the containment case, time location, and spatial location among others. As we saw earlier, the discrimination involved in actual analysis is a matter of specifying very delicate semantic rules ranging over the basic semantic structures employed. Indeed, the structures and case system themselves seem to me to be essentially dependent on the nature and applicability of such rules,[10] and so this application of the system should have an obvious place in the overall structures. It is not something to be delegated to a mere 'implementation'. If enough of the linguistic intractables of English analysis were to be delegated out of the representation, artificial intelligence would be offering no more to the analysis of natural language than the logicians who proffer the predicate calculus as a plausible structure for English.

In some of his more recent writings Winograd has begun to develop a view that is considerably stronger than this 'application' one: in his view the control structure of an understanding program is itself of theoretical significance, for only in that way, he believes, can natural language programs of great size and complexity remain perspicuous.

5.7 Forward inference

Another outstanding dispute concerns whether one should make massive forward inferences as one goes through a text, keeping all one's expectations intact, as Charniak and Schank hold, or whether, as I hold, one should adopt some 'laziness hypothesis' about understanding, and generate deeper inferences only when the system is unable to solve, say a referential problem by more superficial methods. Or, in other terms, should an understanding system be problem-, or data-, driven.

Although Schank sometimes writes of a system making "all possible" inferences as it proceeds through a text, this is not in fact the heart of the dispute, since no one would want to defend any strong definition of the term 'all possible inferences'. Charniak's argument is that, unless certain 'forward inferences' are made during an analysis of, say, a story toward inferences, that is, that are not problem-driven; not made in response to any particular problem of analysis then known to the system then, as a matter of empirical fact, the system will not in general be able to solve ambiguity or reference problems that arise later, because it will never in fact be possible to locate (while looking backwards at the text, as it were) the points where those forward inferences ought to have been made. This is, in very crude summary, Charniak's case against a purely problem-driven inferencer in a natural language understander.

A difficulty with this argument is the location of an example of text that confirms the point in a non-contentious manner. Charniak has found an excerpt from a book describing the life of apes in which it is indeed hard to locate the reference of a particular pronoun in a given passage. Charniak's case is that it is only possible to do so if one has made certain (non-problem occasioned) inferences earlier in the story. But a number of readers find it quite hard to refer that particular pronoun anyway, which might suggest that the text was simply badly written.

This is a difficult matter about which to be precise: it would be possible, for example, to agree with Charniak's argument and still construct a purely problem-driven inferencer on the ground that, at the moment, this is the only way one can cope with the vast majority of inferences for understanding, since any system of inferences made in response to no particular problem in the text is too hard to control in practice. Indeed, it is noticeable that the most recent papers of Schank (1974a and 1974b) and Charniak (1974) have been considerably less forward-inference oriented than earlier ones.

This dispute is perhaps only one of degree, and about the possibility of defining a degree of forward inference that aids the solution of later semantic problems without going into unnecessary depth.[11] This might be an area where psychological investigations would be of enormous help to workers in artificial intelligence.

5.8 The justification of systems

Finally, one might usefully, though briefly, contrast the different modes of justification implicitly appealed to by the systems described earlier in this paper. These seem to me to reduce to four:

(i) In terms of the power of the inferential system employed. This form of justification has underlain the early predicate calculus-based language programs, and is behind Hayes' (1974) recent demand that any formalism for natural language analysis should admit of a set theoretic semantics, in the Tarskian sense, so as to gain "intellectual respectability", as he puts it. The same general type of justification is appealed to in some degree by systems with PLANNER-type formalisms.

(ii) In terms of the provision and formalisation, in any terms including English, of the sorts of knowledge required to understand areas of discourse.

(iii) In terms of the actual performance of a system, implemented on a computer, at a task agreed to demonstrate understanding.

(iv) In terms of the linguistic and/or psychological plausibility of the proffered system of representation.

Oversimplifying considerably, one might say that Charniak's system appeals mostly to (ii) and somewhat to (i) and (iv); Winograd's to (iii) and somewhat to the other three categories; Colby's (as regards its natural language, rather than psychiatric, aspects) appeals almost entirely to (iii); Simmon's largely to (iv), and Schank's and my own to differing mixtures of (ii), (iii) and (iv).

In the end, of course, only (iii) counts for empiricists, but there is considerable difficulty in getting all parties to agree to the terms of a test.[12] A cynic might say that, in the end, all these systems analyse the sentences that they analyse or, to put the same point a little more theoretically, there is a sense in which systems, those described here and those elsewhere, each define a natural language, namely the one to which it applies. The difficult question is the extent to which those many and small natural languages resemble English.

6 English

The last section stressed areas of current disagreement, but there would, if votes were taken, be considerable agreement among artificial intelligence workers on natural language about where the large problems of the immediate future are: the need for a good memory model has been stressed by Schank (1974a), and many would add the need for an extended procedural theory of texts, rather than of individual example sentences, and for a more sophisticated theory of reasons, causes, and motives for use in a theory of understanding. Many might also be persuaded to agree on the need to steer between the Scylla of trivial first generation implementations and the Charybdis of utterly fantastic ones. By the latter, I mean projects that have been seriously discussed, but never implemented for obvious reasons, that would, say, enable a dialogue program to discuss whether or not a participant in a given story "felt guilty", and if so why.

The last disease has sometimes had as a major symptom an extensive use of the word "pragmatics" (though this can also indicate quite benign conditions in other cases), along with the implicit claim that "semantics has been solved, so we should get on with the pragmatics". It still needs repeating that there is no sense whatever in which the semantics of natural language has been "solved". It is still the enormous barrier it has always been, even if a few dents in its surface are beginning to appear here and there. Even if we stick to the simplest examples, that present no difficulty to the human reader – and it must be admitted that it has been one of the persistent faults of the artificial intelligence paradigm of language that it has spent too much time on puzzle examples – there are still great difficulties, both systematic and linguistic.

An example of the former would be the development of a dynamic system of understanding texts of stories that had any capacity to recover after having its expectations satisfied and then, subsequently, frustrated. At present no system of the sort described, whether of demons, preference or whatever, has any such capacity to recover. The situation is quite different from that in a dialogue, as in Winograd's system, where, on being given each new piece of information, the system checks it against what it knows, to see if it is being contradicted, and then behaves in an appropriately puzzled way if it is. In frame or 'expectation' systems it is all too easy to construct apparently trick, but basically plausible, examples that satisfy what was being looked for and then overturn it. That possibility is already built into the notion of frame or expectation. An example of Phil Hayes' against my own system will serve: consider *The hunter licked his gun all over, and the stock tasted especially good*. What is meant by *stock* is clearly the stock piece of the gun, but any preference system like mine that considers the two senses of *stock*, and sees that an edible, soup, sense of *stock* is the preferred object of the action *taste*, will infallibly opt for the wrong sense. Any frame or expectation system is prone to the same general kind of counter-example.

In particular cases like this it is easy to suggest what might be done: here we might suggest a preference attached to the formula for anything that was essentially part of another thing (*stock* = 'part of gun' in this case), so that a local search was made whenever the 'part-of' entity was mentioned, and the satisfaction of that search would always be the overriding preference. But that is not the same as a general solution to the problem, which used to be called that of 'topic' in the computational semantics of the Fifties. There are no solutions to this problem available here and now, though some suggestions have been made by Abelson (1974) and McDermott (1974).

A closely related, but equally intractable, problem is that of how to combine highly specific factual information within a general semantic structuring. Systems like Charniak's are, as we saw, concerned with specific rather than conceptual information, but there are quite simple 'semantic specificity' problems that one could not reasonably expect to be tackled even in a system devoted to the handling of facts, as can be seen by contrasting the sentences:

The deer came out of the wood.
The grub came out of the wood.

where we might safely assume that readers would assign quite different senses to *wood* in the two cases simply on the basis of the two different agents. No-one, to my knowledge, has suggested any general method for tackling such elementary examples.

But, to finish on the bright side, it is important to stress that there is indeed an artificial intelligence paradigm of language understanding in existence,[13] one that embraces first and second generation approaches, and which goes back, I suggested, to a considerable amount of earlier work in computational linguistics. It can be distinguished by a catalogue of neglect by conventional linguistics that can be summarised under three heads:

(i) theories of language must have procedural application to the subject matter that could in principle result in computer application and subsequent empirical test;

(ii) theories of language must deal with it in a communicative context, one amenable to empirical assessment. Merely sorting, as generative theories were designed to do, is not enough;
(iii) theories of language must also be, in a clear sense, theories of the formalisation and organization of knowledge. If they are not then we can know in advance that they can never tackle the problem of language understanding.

This paper has perhaps overemphasised areas of disagreement and dispute, and undoubtedly many of these disputes will come to be seen as no more than methodological questions, or disputes about matters of emphasis and degree. But some are, I feel sure, questions of substance, and it should be possible to see in the reasonably near future whether one approach on any given question is right and another wrong. It would be nice if this were to be settled by computation rather than by another change of fashion.

Let me conclude, and bring the paper full circle to a point of rest, by returning to Bar-Hillel's box and pen example. A number of researchers, whose work I have described here, would certainly be prepared in principle to discuss the treatment of this example, and I choose to discuss it within my own only by way of illustration, and to fulfill the promise in the introduction that to tackle this example shows some solid advance on the front that Bar-Hillel defined so clearly.

Some of the systems described here would want to discuss the sentence *The box was in the pen* in terms of inference rules and structured 'frames' for children's play situations. In my view the example can be dealt with at an earlier stage, during the establishment of the representation for the sentence itself. First, let us assume two sense formulas, one for each sense of *pen*:

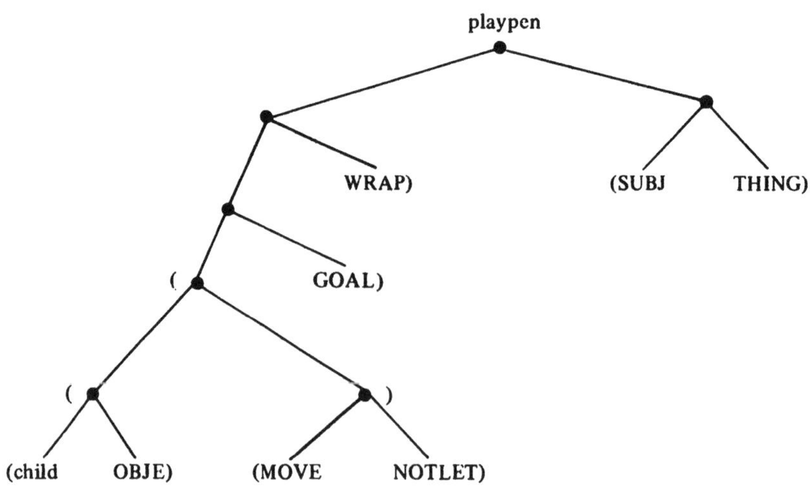

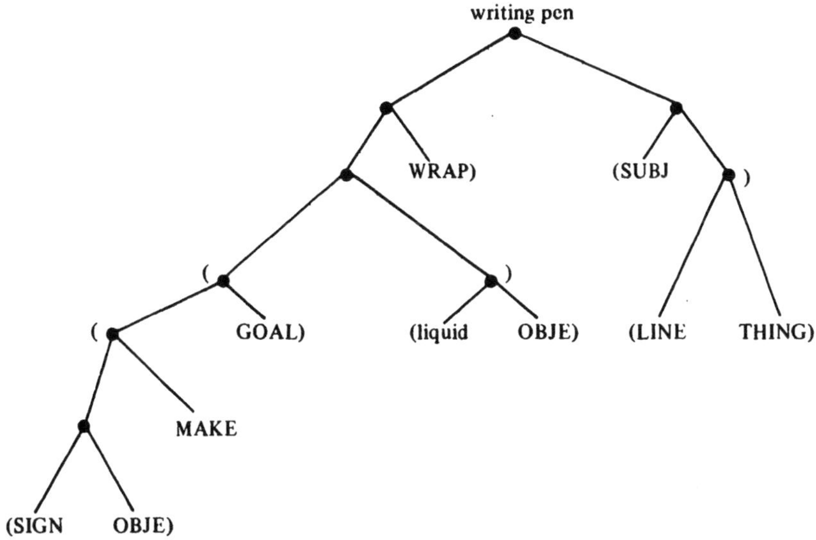

There is one very slight notational change here from the formula as described earlier: I have inserted the 'lower case' items 'child' and 'liquid'. This in no way violates the rule that formulas consist wholly of semantic primitives, because these apparent non-primitive words are only shorthand, as it were, for other formulas. Thus 'liquid' occurs there only because there is, elsewhere in the system, another formula for the English word *liquid*, and in any operation with the formula for *writing pen*, the *liquid* formula would first be inserted at the appropriate point.

This relation, to allow formulas to be 'reentrant' (see Wilks 1975b), makes them easier to read, but without allowing an uncontrolled proliferation of non-primitive words into the formulas.

Let us now consider the treatment of *The box is / in the pen*. The sentence will have been fragmented at the stroke, and a template attached to each part: the first template having a dummy object place, and the second a dummy agent place, since a formula for *in* has become its pseudo-action, and that has no agent. Structures called 'paraplates', whose nature need not detain us (see Wilks, 1975a) then seek to link the two templates back together, the paraplate being in effect a case frame that resolves the *in* as the introducer of the CONTAINMENT case. The application of this paraplate allows the dummy agent of the second template to be 'repacked' in this particular case frame by the agent of the first template and thus we obtain, by a 'repacking inference', a template form equivalent to *box in pen*, which is not, of course, an assertion explicitly present in the text. This 'repacked template form' will have a formula for *box* at its agent node, and since we still have two formulas for *pen* in play, not having yet resolved between them, we shall in fact have two repacked templates at this point, both with a formula for *box* at their agent node, and with the two formulas for *pen* at their respective object nodes. Or, in 'square bracket', semi-English form,

[box in pen] =

<(- - - THING) (- - - PBE) [playpen]>

and

<(- - - THING) (- - - PBE) [writing pen]>

where [playpen] stands for the formula for *playpen* etc., and (- - - THING) stands for [box], the formula for *box*, whose head is THING. Next, after repacking the two new template forms both try to expand themselves, just as a normal template for a text item would do, to see how many preferences each can satisfy, and the "most satisfied" will be preferred.

Inside the formula for *playpen* we see that playpens 'prefer to contain children', while writing pens 'prefer to contain liquids'. And, since a box is a physical object (head of its formula is THING), and so is a child, while a liquid (head of its formula is STUFF) is not a physical object, it is clear that the template with the *playpen* formula is more satisfied than the other, and so is preferred.[14] This method is proof against the 'inkstand in pen' point of Bar-Hillel's mentioned earlier. Furthermore, this solution is general, and the ambiguity is resolved by the application of the general rules of preference used in setting up the representation, and not in any sense by special rules for the example.

In conclusion then, Bar-Hillel's disproof of machine translation is not secure against artificial intelligence techniques based on semantic structures, and rules of inference incorporating real world knowledge. The production of systems of this sort within the artificial intelligence paradigm shows that, for all its faults and theoretical disputes, the paradigm had made some general advance in language understanding and has chipped away at the traditional intractables of machine translation.

Notes

1. Fillmore 1975 and Chafe 1975 seem to be signs of some rapprochement between artificial intelligence and conventional linguistics.
2. Actually the grammar was written in a language PROGRAMMAR, and the semantics and inference sections in LISP and a subset of PLANNER called MICROPLANNER, respectively.

3. Vide: "Artificial Intelligence is the study of intellectual mechanisms apart from applications and apart from how such mechanisms are realised in the human or in animals" (McCarthy 1974: 317).
4. Schank distinguishes 'conceptual' and 'semantic' representations in a way that is important for him within his own system. However, I shall use the terms indifferently since nothing in this brief and superficial description hangs upon the distinction.
5. This is a considerable oversimplification, made in order to give a brief and self-contained description. But, in fact, many English nouns are also represented as ACTs: *chair, pen, honesty* and *transportation*.
6. Since Schank (1973a) their number has been reduced to eleven (plus DO) by the elimination of SMELL, LISTENTO, LOOKAT and CONC, and the addition of ATTEND.
7. In Charniak 1974 are much more specific rules, such as the 'rule of significant sub-action', mentioned earlier.
8. Although Charniak would argue that sense ambiguity could be introduced into his system in its present form.
9. This point is to some extent hypothetical since, as we saw, Schank's conceptualizations do still appear to contain many surface items: nouns, adjectives and verbs. However, this may be a transitional matter, in that they are being replaced by non-superficial representations.
10. This is not intended to be merely bland assertion: I have written on the relations between application and the theoretical status of linguistic theories (Wilks 1974).
11. Which may be no more than a psychological restatement of what used to be called the 'frame problem' (Hayes 1971, Sandewall 1972).
12. Though an interesting, and potentially revolutionary, distinction seems to have been introduced, by a reviewer of several of the systems discussed here, between the functioning of a program and the 'program in itself': 'Only Winograd describes a program that is sufficiently impressive in itself to force us to take his ideas seriously. The techniques of the others have to get by on whatever intuitive appeal they can muster.' (Isard 1974).
13. One of the very few acknowledgements of this possibility from within linguistics is Fillmore 1974.
14. Or, given that the heads of the formulas for *child, box* and *liquid* are MAN, THING, and STUFF, respectively, we can state this conceptual inclusion as THING MAN (humans are objects), but STUFF THING (substances are not objects).

References

Abelson, R.P.

1973 "The structure of belief systems", *Computer models of thought and language*, edited by R. Schank and K. Colby (San Francisco: Freeman), 287–340.

1975 "Discourse headers", *Representation and meaning*, edited by D. Bobrow and A. Collins (New York: Academic), 273–310.

Balzer, R. et al.

1974 *Domain-independent automatic programming* (Marina del Rey, Calif.: University of Southern California Information Sciences Institute)

Bar-Hillel, Y.
1958 "A demonstration of the non-feasability of Fully Automatic High Quality Translation", *Language and information* (Reading, Mass.: Addison-Wesley), 174–179.

Bobrow, D.G.
1968 "Natural language input for a computer problem-solving system", *Semantic information processing*, edited by M. Minsky (Cambridge, Mass.: MIT Press), 133–215.

Brown, G.
1974 *The believer system* (Rutgers, N.J.: Psychology Dept., Rutgers Univ.).

Bruce, B.
1972 "A model for temporal references and its application in a question answering program", *Artificial Intelligence* 3: 219–243.

Bruce, B. and Schmidt, C.F.
1974 *Episode understanding and belief guided parsing* (Cambridge, Mass.: Bolt, Beranek and Newman).

Chafe, W.
1975 "Some thoughts on schemata", *Proceedings of the MIT Conference on Theoretical Issues in Language Processing* (Cambridge, Mass.: Bolt, Beranek and Newman), 89–91.

Charniak, E.
1972 *Toward a model of children's story comprehension* (=*Memorandum* TR266) (Cambridge, Mass.: Artificial Intelligence Lab., MIT).
1973 "Jack and Janet in search of a theory of knowledge", *Advanced Papers of the Third International Joint Conference on Artificial Intelligence* (Menlo Park, Calif.: Stanford Research Institute), 337–344.
1974 *He will make you take it back; a study in the pragmatics of language* (=*Memorandum* 5) (Castagnola, Switzerland: Institute for Semantics and Cognitive Studies).

Chomsky, N.
1957 *Syntactic structures* (=*Janua Linguarum, series minor* 4) (The Hague: Mouton).

Colby, K.M. and Parkinson, R.C.
1974 "Pattern-matching rules for the recognition of natural language dialogue expressions", *American Journal of Computational Linguistics* 1: 1–70.

Colby, K.M. and Hilf, F.D.
1973 *Multidimensional analysis in evaluating a simulation of paranoid thought* (=*Memorandum* AIM-194) (Stanford, Calif.: Artificial Intelligence Lab, Stanford University).

Colby, K.M. et al.
1971 "Artificial paranoia", *Artificial Intelligence* 2: 1–25.

Cole, L.S.
1972 *Techniques for information retrieval using an inferential question-answering system with natural language input* (=*Technical Notes*) (Menlo Park, Calif.: Stanford Research Institute).

Davidson, D.
1963 "Reasons and causal laws", *Journal of Philosophy*: 27–42.

Davies, D.J.M. and Isard, S.D.
1972 "Utterances as programs", *Machine Intelligence* 7, edited by B. Meltzer and D. Michie (Edinburgh: Edinburgh University Press), 325–340.

Enea, H. and Colby, K.M.
1973 "Idiolectic language-analysis for understanding doctor-patient dialogues" *Advanced Papers of the Third International Joint Conference on Artificial Intelligence* (Menlo Park, Calif.: Stanford Research Institute), 278-284.
Farradene, B.
1966 *Research on information retrieval by relational indexing* (London: Dept. of Information Sciences, City University).
Fillmore, C.
1974 Summer School Lectures, University of Pisa, Italy.
1975 "The case for case revisited", unpublished manuscript.
Goldman, N.M.
1974 *Computer generation of natural language from a deep conceptual base* (=*Memorandum* 2) (Castagnola, Switzerland: Institute for Semantic and Cognitive Studies).
Halliday, M.A.K.
1970 "Functional diversity in language", *Foundations of Language* 6: 322-361.
Hayes, P.J.
1975 "Computer programming as a cognitive paradigm", *Nature* 254: 617-620.
1971 *The frame problem and related problems in artificial intelligence* (=*Memorandum* AIM-53) (Stanford, Calif.: Artificial Intelligence Lab, Stanford University).
1974 "Some problems and non-problems in representation theory", *Proceedings of the Summer Conference of the Society for Artificial Intelligence and Simulation of Behaviour* (Brighton: University of Sussex), 63-79.
Hays, D.
1964 "Dependency theory: A formalism and some observations", *Language* 40: 511-525.
Heidorn, G.E.
1974 "English as a very high level language for simulation programming", *Proceedings from the Symposium on Very High Level Languages* (Santa Monica, Calif.: Rand Corporation), 192-201.
Hendrix, G.G. et al.
1973 "Language processing via canonical verbs and semantic models" *Advanced Papers of the Third International Joint Conference on Artificial Intelligence* (Menlo Park, Calif.: Stanford Research Institute), 262-269.
Herskovits, A.
1973 *The generation of French from a semantic representation* (=*Memorandum* AIM-212 (Stanford, Calif: Artificial Intelligence Lab, Stanford University).
Hewitt, C.
1969 "Planner: A language for proving theorems in robots", *Proceedings of the International Joint Conference on Artificial Intelligence*, edited by Walker and Norton (Bedford, Mass.: Mitre Corp.), 295-301.
Hockett, C.F.
1962 "Grammar for the hearer", *Symposia in Applied Mathematics* XII (American Mathematical Society: 117-130).
Isard, S.
1974 Review of *Computer models of thought and language* edited by R. Schank and K. Colby (San Francisco: Freeman, 1973) in *Science* 186: 201-202.
Johnson-Laird, P.
1974 "Memory for words", *Nature* 2251: 704-705.

Joshi, A.K. and Weischedel, R.M.
1973 "Some frills for the modal tic-tac-toe of Davies and Isard: Semantics of predicate complement constructions", *Advanced Papers of the Third International Joint Conference on Artificial Intelligence* (Menlo Park, Calif.: Stanford Research Institute), 352–355.

Kitteredge, B. et al.
1973 *Traduction automatique a l'Université de Montréal* (Montréal: University Computer Science Department).

Kuhn, T.S.
1970 *The structure of scientific revolutions* (2nd edition) (Chicago, Illinois: University of Chicago Press).

Lakoff, G.
1971 "On generative semantics", *Semantics*, edited by D. Steinberg and L. Jakobovits (Cambridge: Cambridge University Press), 232–296.

Lamb, S.
1966 *Outline of stratificational grammar* (Georgetown: Georgetown University Press).

Lighthill, J.
1973 *Artificial intelligence* (London: Science Research Council).

McCarthy, J. and Hayes. P.J.
1969 "Some philosophical problems from the standpoint of artificial intelligence", *Machine Intelligence 4*, edited by B. Meltzer and D. Michie (Edinburgh University Press), 317–322.

McDermott, D.V.
1974 *Assimilation of new information by a natural language understanding system* (=*Memorandum* TR-291) (Cambridge, Mass.: Artificial Intelligence Lab, MIT).

Masterman, M.
1961 "Semantic message detection for machine translation" *Proceedings of the First International Conference on Machine Translation* (Teddington: National Physical Laboratory), 302–323.

Minsky, M.L.
1968 Editor's introduction to *Semantic information processing* (Cambridge, Mass.: MIT Press).
1975 "Frame systems", in *The psychology of computer vision*, edited by P. Winston (New York: McGraw Hill), 211–277.

Moore, J. and Newell, A.
1973 "How can Merlin understand?", in *Knowledge and condition*, edited by L. Gregg (Potomac, Md.: L. Erlbaum Association), 322–341.

Parker-Rhodes, A.F.
1961 "A new model of syntactic description", *Proceedings of the First International Conference on Machine Translation* (Teddington: National Physical Laboratory), 214–239.

Richens, R.H.
1961 "Tigris and Euphrates", *Proceedings of the First International Conference on Machine Translation* (Teddington: National Physical Laboratory), 301–324.

Rieger, C.J.
1961 *Conceptual memory* (unpublished Ph.D. thesis) (Stanford, Calif.: Computer Science Department).

Riesbeck, C.K.
1974 *Computational understanding: Analysis of sentences and context* (=*Memorandum* 4) (Castagnola, Switzerland: Institute for Semantic and Cognitive Studies).

Rulifson, J.A.
1972 *OA4: A procedural calculus for inductive reasoning* (=*Technical Notes*) (Menlow Park, Calif.: Stanford Research Institute).

Sandewall, E.
1971 "Representing natural language information in predicate calculus", *Machine Intelligence 6*, edited by B. Meltzer and D. Michie, (Edinburgh: Edinburgh University Press), 255–280.
1972a "An approach to frame problem, and its implementation", *Machine Intelligence 7*, edited by B. Meltzer and D. Michie (Edinburgh: Edinburgh University Press), 195–204.
1972b *PCF-2, a first-order calculus for expressing conceptual information* (Uppsala University, Department of Computer Science).

Schank, R.C.
1968 *Semantic categories* (Austin, Texas: Tracor Corp.)
1973a *The fourteen primitive actions and their inferences* (=*Memorandum* AIM-183) (Stanford, Calif.: Artificial Intelligence Lab, Stanford Univ.).
1973b "Identification of Conceptualizations Underlying Natural Language" *Computer Models of Thought and Language*, edited by R. Schank and K. Colby (San Francisco: Freeman), 187–248.
1974a *Causality and reasoning* (=*Memorandum* 1) (Castagnola, Switzerland: Institute for Semantic and Cognitive Studies).
1974b *Understanding paragraphs* (=*Memorandum* 6) (Castagnola, Switzerland: Institute for Semantic and Cognitive Studies).

Schank, R.C. and Rieger, C.J.
1973 *Inference and the computer understanding of natural language* (=*Memorandum* AIM-197) (Stanford, Calif.: Artificial Intelligence Lab, Stanford Univ.).

Schank, R.C. and Wilks, Y.A.
1974 "The goals of linguistics theory revisited", *Lingua* 34: 301–326.

Schank, R.C. et al.
1970 *Spinoza II: Conceptual case-based natural language analysis* (=*Memorandum* AIM-109) (Stanford, Calif.: Artificial Intelligence Lab, Stanford Univ.).
1972 *Primitive concepts underlying verbs of thought* (=*Memorandum* AIM-162) (Stanford, Calif.: Artificial Intelligence Lab, Stanford Univ.).
1973 "MARGIE: Memory, Analysis, Response Generation and Inference in English", *Advanced Papers of the Third International Joint Conference on Artificial Intelligence* (Menlo Park, Calif.: Stanford Research Institute), 255–261.

Simmons, R.F.
1970a "Natural language question-answering systems: 1969", *Communications of the Association for Computing Machinery* 13: 15–30.
1970b *Some semantic structures for representing English meanings* (=*Memorandum* NL-1) (Austin, Texas: University of Texas Computer Science Dept.)
1973 "Semantic networks: Their computation and use for understanding English sentences", in *Computer models of thought and language*, edited by R. Schank and K. Colby (San Francisco: Freeman) 63–113.

Simmons, R.F. and Bruce, B.C.
1971 "Some relations between predicate calculus and semantic net representations of discourse", *Proceedings of the Second International Conference on Artificial Intelligence* (London: British Computer Society), 524-530.

Simmons, R.F. and Slocum, J.
1972 "Generating English discourse from semantic networks", *Communications of the Association for Computing Machinery* 15: 891-905.

Simmons, R.F. et al.
1966 "An approach toward answering English questions from text", *Proceedings of the Fall Joint Computer Conference* (San Francisco Association for Computing Machinery), 219-232.

Sussman, G.J.
1974 "The virtuous nature of bugs", *Proceedings of the Summer Conference of the Society for Artificial Intelligence and Simulation of Behavior* (Brighton: University of Sussex), 224-237.

Weber, S.
1972 *Semantics of nominals for conceptual dependency analysis of natural language* (=*Memorandum* AIM-172) (Stanford, Calif.: Artificial Intelligence Lab, Stanford, University).

Wilks, Y.A.
1967 *Semantic consistency in text – an experiment and some suggestions* (=*Memorandum* SP-2758) (Santa Monica, Calif.: System Development Corp.)
1972 *Grammar, meaning and the machine analysis of language* (Boston and London: Routledge & Kegan Paul).
1973 "An artificial intelligence approach to machine translation", *Computer models of thought and language*, edited by R. Schank and K. Colby (San Francisco: Freeman), 114-151.
1974 "One small head – models and theories in linguistics", *Foundations of language* 11: 77-95.
1975a "An intelligent analyser and understander of English", *Communications of the Association for Computing Machinery* 18: 264-274.
1975b "Primitives and words", *Proceedings of the MIT Conference on Theoretical Issues in Natural Language Processing* (Cambridge, Masss.: Bolt, Beranek and Newman), 38-41.
1975c "Preference semantics", *Formal semantics of natural language*, edited by Keenan (Cambridge: University Press), 329-350.
1975d "A preferential, pattern seeking, semantics for natural language inference", *Artificial Intelligence* 6: 53-74.

Winograd, T.
1971 *Procedures as a representation for data in a computer program for understanding natural language* (=Massachusetts Institute of Technology, Ph.D. Thesis).
1972 *Understanding natural language*, (New York: Academic Press).
1973 "A survey lecture on natural language" (=Lecture at the *Third International Joint Conference on Artificial Intelligence*).
1974a "Frame representations and the procedural declarative controversy", *Representation and understanding*, edited by D. Bobrow and A. Collins (New York: Academic Press).
1974b *Five lectures on artificial intelligence* (=*Memorandum* AIM-246) (Stanford Calif.: Artificial Intelligence Lab., Stanford University).

Wittgenstein, L.
1953 *Philosophical investigations* (Oxford: Blackwell).
Woods, W.
1970 "Transition network grammars for natural language analysis", *Communications of the Association for Computing Machinery* 3: 591-606.
1973 "Meaning and machines", *Proceedings of the International Conference on Computational Linguistics*, edited by N. Calzolari (in press).

BERTRAM BRUCE

Belief systems and language understanding*

1 The role of beliefs in natural language understanding

Imagine a king, for instance a King Rupert, who, on one particularly chilly morning, says to his servant, Aldous,

> "This place is too cool!".[1]

We have understood part of King Rupert's statement when we recognize that *this place* is the subject of the sentence, that *is too cool* is the predicate, that the predicate consists of a copula and a predicate adjective construction, and so on. Part of understanding an utterance is an at least implicit recognition of how the words in the utterance fit together. We need to distinguish nominal concepts from actions, actions from modifiers, and function words from content words before we can say that the meaning of the sentence has been discovered.

Determination of structure and word classification are clearly not enough. It is fairly safe to say that Rupert has a single thought which he is attempting to communicate by his utterance. He could mean that people in his castle are too reserved, or that the atmosphere is really hip. Most likely, though, he means that for him the temperature is too low.

In order to recognize the sense of *cool* which Rupert intends, we must apply part of our large body of knowledge about the world. We need to use such 'facts' as:

SOME FACTS ABOUT THE WORLD
- A king can be expected to express his bodily wants.
- A person is uncomfortable if he is too cool.
- A king is usually conservative and does not use "hip" expressions.
- Social matters are not discussed between a king and his servant.

Many other facts are used in determining such things as how large a space is meant by *this place* and the meaning of *too* in *too cool*. These facts comprise

Computers in Language Research 2

the 'world knowledge' which is used in understanding unrestricted natural language. World knowledge is used to determine the context in which an utterance or written sentence occurs and to determine how that context affects the meaning of the sentence.

In this example our world knowledge tells us that Rupert means the temperature is too low in the castle, or at least in the room in which he is speaking. He also means that the low temperature is uncomfortable for him. Only if we knew other information would we assume that he had other bad effects of the coolness in mind. For example, if Rupert were raising plants which required warm temperatures then he might be expressing his concern for the plants rather than his personal discomfort. We also know that too cool means something like 30-70 degrees (F) and not −200 or 3000, which might be meant in another context.

But knowing these things is still not enough. Pity the poor servant Aldous. If he knows only what has been said above about the king's statement then he may have trouble ahead. It is quite likely that Rupert is not just expressing his current state, but is in fact expressing a wish for a change. He is probably commanding Aldous to do something about the temperature, close the windows or add wood to the fire. Aldous must discover not only the literal meaning of the sentence, but also the intentions which underly it. To do that he must have additional facts such as:

ADDITIONAL FACTS ABOUT THE WORLD (WITH AN EMPHASIS ON INTENTION)

- In this situation Rupert has authority over Aldous.
- Rupert believes that Aldous can do something about the cold.
- Rupert believes that Aldous is not necessarily planning to do something about the cold immediately.
- Rupert believes that if he orders Aldous to do something then Aldous ought to do it.

These additional facts are also part of world knowledge, but they are from a special subset which we call 'belief-systems knowledge'. They differ from the previous set of facts only in their degree of focus on intentions, social relationships, and beliefs about other's beliefs. Like other facts, facts from a belief system can be more or less certain, complex or simple, and true or false with respect to larger bodies of knowledge. In using the term 'belief-systems knowledge', we are simply focusing on the kinds of world knowledge which have one or more of the following characteristics:

(1) Institutional facts (Searle 1969) – knowledge which depends upon social conventions or commonly agreed-upon rules of behavior. A baseball game

exists because we have a set of agreed-upon interpretations of certain kinds of behavior. Without these interpretations we can only describe the pattern in terms of "brute facts" (Anscombe 1958) such as "A ran from place X to place Y".

(2) Knowledge about other's knowledge – facts such as "A believes it is raining" as opposed to "it is raining". This can include higher-order facts such as "A believes that B believes it is raining" or worse, "A believes that I believe it is raining". Thus part of belief systems knowledge involves what Minsky (1968) calls "models of models".

(3) Knowledge about intentions – facts about the motivations for actions. This includes procedures for assigning reasons to actions, knowledge about how plans are constructed and implemented, and knowledge of how plans of one person interact with those of another. For instance, we understand King Rupert's behavior in terms of his plan to become warm. Recognizing the plan requires knowledge about what constitutes a goal for Rupert and knowledge about the ways in which Rupert's plan affects, and is affected by, plans of Aldous.

These characteristics do not provide a sharp delineation of belief-systems knowledge from other knowledge about the world. Rather they emphasize that aspect of knowledge which is concerned with human interaction, whether in discourse or other social situations. This aspect is crucial for the understanding of language both because the language reflects our knowledge and because language use is itself a form of social interaction. While a precise characterization of belief-systems knowledge does not exist, it is worthwhile to examine what is known about belief systems and their use in language understanding. There are preliminary efforts which indicate how important knowledge of this kind can be for a system which understands language.

Within the Artificial Intelligence field the best-known of these efforts are probably the works of Abelson et al. (1965, 1969, 1973, 1975) and Colby et al. (1969a, 1969b, 1971). Abelson's work has covered several areas of belief-systems knowledge but much has focused on 'ideological systems', that is, rigid, often simplistic, systems of beliefs. For example, he has studied the ideological system of the "Cold-War warrior" with its beliefs about the Communist goal of world domination. The effects of new information on these systems are studied in terms of the (possibly illogical) inferences which are generated. Colby's work is similar in certain respects. He also considers the effects of new information, but emphasizes factors such as 'consistency', 'foundation', and 'credibility'. Recently, in PARRY, a simulation of paranoid behavior, he has examined more intentionally[2] defined notions such as 'fear', 'mistrust', and 'anger'.

There has also been substantial research in linguistics, philosophy, and psychology on belief systems, work which cannot be covered in such a small space. Especially relevant are works on speech acts, presuppositions, story understanding, and perception of personal causation.[3] In Artificial Intelligence the influence of a belief-systems approach can be seen in works which emphsize connected discourse, context effects, and pragmatics.[4]

This chapter is not intended to be a complete survey of work on belief systems, nor is it the definitive account of what belief-systems knowledge is and how it is used. Instead it is a review of two important components of a belief system, namely 'social actions' and 'patterns of behavior'. These components rely heavily upon a recognition of intentionality in behavior and upon beliefs about one's own beliefs and the beliefs of others. Central to both is the concept of 'personal causation' (Heider 1958). A theoretical system (developed primarily by Schmidt 1974) which accounts for intentional behavior is presented in Section 2. Social actions and patterns of behavior are discussed in Sections 3 and 4, respectively. In Section 5 we consider an admittedly sketchy scenario for how these components are used in understanding a simple story. But first a brief introduction to the three components:

Intentional behavior
Underlying both social actions and patterns of behavior are fundamental principles of motivated actions. These principles account for behavior which is motivated from within a person, and not accounted for by stereotyped behavior patterns or purely physical or physiological facts. The notion of a 'plan' (see Schmidt 1974) as a designed (rather than just executed) sequence of actions requires a detailed account of how one person's beliefs are affected by the actions of others and how goal-oriented behavior takes place in a context in which other persons are also seeking goals. A sketch of this account is given in Section 2. The concepts of obligation, ability, and choice discussed there are central to the definition of social actions and patterns of behavior.

Social actions
A single action can be described at many levels. It may be a movement of the lips, a kiss, a sign of affection, or a kiss of death. Some of these descriptions rely on a body of knowledge about social relationships. It is only at this 'social' level that we are able to describe King Rupert's utterance as a 'command' rather than a 'making of sound' or 'simple statement'. (With respect to utterances, a social level description focuses on what has been called the 'speech act' (Austin 1965, Searle 1969)). In Section 3 and Appendix II we examine a set of social actions commonly used in understanding discourse.

Patterns of behavior
Actions at any level frequently occur in patterns with other actions. These patterns of behavior (similar to what Abelson 1974 calls 'schemes' and Rumelhart 1974 calls 'story schemas') are discussed in Section 4.

2 Theory of personal causation

(See Appendix I for notation conventions.)
Before we examine specific social action concepts and patterns of behavior we need to consider a fundamental theory of personal causation in which the various concepts can be defined. We assume that when the observer of an action in a social situation constructs his/her interpretation of the action that he/she uses a small set of recursive procedures for determining the motivation of others and a few axioms of 'personal' as opposed to 'natural' causation.

Certainly, behavior is explained in many ways. We often account for actions such as slipping and falling, or coughing, in physical or physiological terms. We explain other actions as being habitual or as being part of ritual behavior, such as a greeting. But not all actions can be explained in these relatively simple ways. Frequently we have to account for actions which are motivated from within a person. In those cases we need to view the action as part of a plan, i.e., a foreseeable sequence of actions leading to a goal.

Inner-motivated actions are both the most interesting and the most difficult to explain. It is necessary to appeal, not to a fixed set of causal laws, but to the beliefs of the actor, to his wants and needs, and to his beliefs about the beliefs of others. In determining the goals of the actor it is often necessary to discover his perception of the plans of others, for plans frequently depend upon the assistance or at least non-interference of others. The plan perceived by the actor may not be the same as that perceived by an observer, nor need either's perception be a correct accounting of the motivations of the third party. Furthermore, the third party's plans may depend upon his beliefs about the goals and beliefs of the original actor, the observer, or yet other persons. Clearly an account of an inner-motivated action can be quite complex. The procedures for constructing such an account must process beliefs about beliefs and plans within plans, and are hence defined recursively.

The procedures (or 'motivation rules') which assign reasons to actions consider many factors, including obligation, goal-seeking, and simple predisposition. They provide an account of why a person chooses to act in a given way. Together with the concept of 'being able' to act, a 'choose' theory is used to explain or predict behavior. The resulting explanation is then in terms of 'personal' as opposed to simple 'physical' causation of events. Saying that someone 'personally causes' an action implies both that he can do the action and that he is motivated to do it (where the motivation is computed by motivation rules in terms of the beliefs of the actor). This principle is called the 'axiom of personal causation':

Axiom of personal causation (full form)

If A CAUSES X at t then A CAN X at t and A MUST-CHOOSE X at t

Where no confusion results we will suppress explicit indication of the times. Thus the axiom of personal causation can be written:

Axiom of personal causation (abbreviated form)

If A CAUSES X then A CAN X and A MUST-CHOOSE X

The full definitions of CAUSE, CAN, and MUST-CHOOSE are given below. Informally we can read this basic axiom as "If person A does action X at time t then we can infer both that A is capable of doing X and that the weight of reasons favor A choosing to do X rather than some other action or none at all".

We say A CAN X to mean "it is possible for A to perform action X". A must have the ability and the tools, and must be in an appropriate place and position to do the act. Such 'enabling conditions' are familiar from work on general problem solvers.

The CAN component of personal causation has an additional complication. It is often the case that in order to perform some action one must depend upon others to act. For example, to drive to the airport a person depends upon others driving safely, upon the gas-station attendant to pump gasoline, upon the airport providing parking space, and so on. Thus CAN is necessarily defined in terms of MUST-CHOOSE, that is, MUST-CHOOSE for other actors. To account for one person's action we must consider his perception of beliefs and intentions of others.

The MUST-CHOOSE relation is defined in terms of relations called TRY and OUGHT. These in turn depend upon one or more 'motivation rules'. Motivation rules are basically procedures which relate goals of an actor to outcomes of a sequence of acts. They fall into three classes: personal, normative, and dispositional.

Personal motivation rules account for the ways that people typically use to explain inner-motivated actions of others. These rules are expressed in terms of the beliefs of the actor about the outcomes of his action. At least the following three rules are typically used:

(1) Hedonism – An action performed by A satisfies the Hedonism rule if it can be assumed that A BELIEVES that the outcomes, either immediate or eventual, of that action may include results that may be beneficial to A.
(2) Extended Hedonism – An action performed by A satifies the Extended Hedonism rule if it can be assumed that A BELIEVES that the outcome, either immediate or eventual, of that action may include results that may be beneficial to someone who is in a UNIT (family, club, business partner-

ship, etc.) or SENTIMENT (likes, loves) relationship to A, and A BELIEVES that the beneficiary wants the beneficial outcome.

(3) Reciprocity – An action performed by A satisfies the Reciprocity rule if it can be assumed that A BELIEVES that the outcomes, either immediate or eventual, of his action constitute a 'response in kind' to some action that A BELIEVES another person intentionally performed, e.g., A hit (or kissed) B because B hit (or kissed) A.

Normative rules (Bruce and Schmidt (1074); Schmidt 1974) are those rules, which define 'conventional behavior'. Whereas personal motivation rules are based upon internal motives, normative rules refer to external reasons for actions. There are specific normative rules such as:

- If someone fulfills a request you have made then you ought to thank him.

In addition there is a general normative constraint on behavior that says:

- In any ritualized situation (e.g., greeting someone, ordering food in a restaurant, or listening to a lecture) a person is expected to conform to the ritual or else explain why not.

Generally we say that an action performed by A satisfies a normative rule if it can be assumed that A KNOWS the rule, A BELIEVES that the rule applies in this situation, and if A performs the action required by that particular normative rule. Violation of a normative rule suggests inferences about the actor which cannot be made on the basis of his violation of personal motivation rules. For example, if A does not thank B for some helpful act then we may infer that A is ungrateful, rude, or perhaps, unaware. (Another interpretation is that A does not think B's action was very helpful.)

The third type of motivation rule is both an extension and a mixture of the personal and normative types. Dispositional rules account for behavior the cannot be explained directly as satisfying either personal motives or normative constraints. For example, if Fred stops to help somone fix a flat tire, we may explain his action by saying, not that Fred expected a reward or felt he should stop, but simply that Fred is helpful, where helpfulness is part of Fred's disposition. Thus 'being helpful' is an extension to a large set of people of the UNIT or SENTIMENT concept in the Extended Hedonism rule. Similarly, being honest is an extension of certain normative rules. We say that an action performed by A satisfies a disposition rule if in the given situation, neither personal motivation, nor normative rules, account for the action, and the action is an instance of actions appropriate to the disposition.

Given the various motivation rules we can define the components of MUST-CHOOSE. First there is a function on actions which gives the strength of motivation for an action. This function assumes that a motivation rule gives a 'value' which is the relative strength of that motivation with respect to the given action. In a simple case, the value could be 0 if the rule does not apply and 1 if it does.

CHOOSEVALUE

Choosevalue (A, X, t, S, M) – the value of the motivation rule, M (either personal, normative, or dispositional), for the outcomes (both final and intermediate) of the sequence of acts, S, where S may be either an actual, "happened" sequence or a possible sequence; S includes A doing action X at time t. (Where no confusion results indication of times will be implicit, i.e., choosevalue (A, X, S, M).)

We can then define TRY, OUGHT, and HAS-A-REASON-TO:

TRY

(The action X has outcomes which satisfy some goal of A)

A TRY X <=> (forsome S) (forsome M)
[choosevalue (A, X, S, M) > 0
and (M is a personal
or personal-dispositional rule)]

OUGHT

(The action X fulfills an obligation felt by A)

A OUGHT X <=> (forsome S) (forsome M)
[choosevalue (A, X, S, M) > 0
and (M is a normative
or normative-dispositional rule)]

HAS-A-REASON-TO

(A is motivated by either obligation or goals)

A HAS-A-REASON-TO X <=> (forsome S) (forsome M)
[choosevalue (A, X, S, M) > 0]
<=> A TRY X or A OUGHT X

We can now define MUST-CHOOSE as a relation on a combination of the choosevalues for a particular act. Since we are primarily interested in accounting for either (1) how an observer explains the actions in an episode, or (2) how persons use their perception of the motivations of others in forming their own plans, there is usually only one choosevalue involved. Nevertheless, the formalism allows two or more motivation rules to interact in the choice of an action.

MUST-CHOOSE

A MUST-CHOOSE X <=>
combine (choosevalue (A, X, S, M)) > 0

'Combine' is a function which selects an overall value for all possible sequences containing X and all possible motivation rules. In some cases 'combine' may be a simple additive or maximum function, but in general may involve thresholds for reasons, interactions, and other more complex combinations of reasons.

As defined, TRY, OUGHT, and HAS-A-REASON-TO refer to acts which are done rather than not done. It is possible to choose not to act, i.e., A HAS-A-REASON-TO not-X. In that case the choosevalue must be negative. In order to account for the fact that most possible acts are not done, we need to add an 'axiom of laziness' which says that for any act there is some motivation not to do that act:

Axiom of laziness
(forall X) A HAS-A-REASON-TO not-X

There is also an 'axiom of negative freedom' which says that it is always possible not to do an action (occurrences like sneezing are not considered actions in this sense since choice is not involved):

Axiom of negative freedom
(forall X) A CAN not-X

Together these axioms imply that

(forall X) A MUST-CHOOSE not-X

is true, i.e., that one may always not act.

In addition to predicates which relate combinations of motives to actions, it is often necessary to refer to motives which are sufficient in themselves but may not be dominating reasons in all circumstances. We say A SUFFICIENT-CHOOSE X to mean that there is a motivation rule that alone would be a sufficient reason for A to do X:

SUFFICIENT-CHOOSE

A SUFFICIENT-CHOOSE X <=> (forsome S) (forsome M) choosevalue (A, X, S, M) > k (where k is a threshold imposed by the axiom of laziness)

Analogous to MUST-CHOOSE and SUFFICIENT-CHOOSE are relations MUST-TRY, MUST-OUGHT, SUFFICIENT-TRY, and SUFFICIENT-OUGHT which are restricted to certain types of motivation rules. For example, A MUST-TRY X means A MUST-CHOOSE X, and M is a personal or personal-dispositional rule.

In addition to concepts relating to choice, a belief system requires concepts such as KNOW and BELIEVE. A sketch of these notions is given here for the sake of their use in later sections. We will consider several senses of these concepts, each defined in terms of more primitive notions.

We might begin with the Colby et al. (1969) definition of 'credibility'. Credibility is a function of 'foundation' and 'consistency' which is highest for propositions with high foundation and high consistency. 'Foundation' is defined as a measure of evidence for and against a proposition. 'Consistency' is a measure of the 'consonance' of a proposition with other 'relevant' beliefs of the individual. Credibility values range from 0 (incredible) to 100 (credible). A credibility rating of 50 means 'undecided'. We could define BELIEVE in terms of this credibility scale:

BELIEVE

A BELIEVE X <=> credibility (A, X) > 60.

A possible definition for KNOW then is that KNOW is a very strong BELIEVE:

KNOW (believe-strongly)

A KNOW (believe-strongly) X
<=> credibility (A, X) > 90.

Clearly,

A KNOW (believe-strongly) X => A BELIEVE X.

There are other useful definitions of KNOW, however, which may not be equivalent to this one. In order to distinguish the various senses, we will use parenthetical distinguishers, e.g., KNOW (believe-strongly) for this first sense of KNOW.

A related sense of KNOW is one which separates facts which belong to the external environment from those which are inferred as belonging to the belief systems of others. For instance, a person might say "I *believe* that he thinks it is raining", but "I *know* that it is raining". Let us call this sense of KNOW, KNOW (direct). A person A might have the belief,

- If X is a belief about the beliefs of another then credibility (A, X) is necessarily less than 90.

Thus no indirect belief can have a high credibility. If it were also the case that all direct beliefs had a credibility over 90 than KNOW (direct) would be equivalent to KNOW (believe-strongly).

Another useful sense of KNOW is that which distinguishes propositions believed by both the observer and the observed from those believed by just the observed person. For example, person A might say, "B *knows* today is St. Patrick's Day", meaning, "I *believe* that today is St. Patrick's Day and I *believe* that B *believes* that today is St. Patrick's". On the other hand A might say, "C believes that frogs cause warts", to mean, "I don't believe that frogs cause warts and I believe that C believes that frogs cause warts". This sense of relative KNOW is defined as follows:

KNOW (relative)

A BELIEVE (B KNOW (relative) X)
<=> A BELIEVE (B BELIEVE X) and A BELIEVE X.

A fourth sense of KNOW which is useful is a weak sense which means that the person is aware of a proposition though he may not believe it. For example, if A tells B X we may infer that B KNOWS (is aware of) X at least for a short while following the telling. It is also true that

A BELIEVE X => A KNOW (is-aware-of) X.

The concepts defined in this section form part of a highly interdependent theory of how persons account for the actions of others. It is closely related to language use because, in one way or another, much of communication is concerned with such accounts. In Section 3 we discuss the notion of a 'social action', basing definitions of specific social actions on this Theory of Personal Causation. Several examples of social actions (especially those related to speech) are given in Appendix II. In Section 4 we discuss patterns of behavior which are built out of the theory and the social actions. In Section 5 these concepts are applied in the analysis of a simple story.

3 Social actions

3.1 Aspects of actions

When a person utters a sentence (or writes, prints, types, etc., a sentence) he uses words to describe actions. In addition, each utterance is itself an action which can be described in words.

The description of an action can be at any of several levels, and these levels need not conflict. The idea here is analogous to that in the story of the three workers, where each was asked to tell what he was doing. One said "I am laying bricks"; the second said "I am building a wall"; and the third said "I am building a giant cathedral". Of course each of the workmen was right in his description of one aspect of his action. In a similar way, any act can be decribed at a simple physical-physiological level, or at various higher levels that take into account institutional concepts and inferred causes and effects of actions.

There are at least four aspects of actions that are important to distinguish for the design of an intelligent system. They are the physical-physiological, the propositional, the institutional, and the effectual levels. This is certainly not an exhaustive list but the implied distinctions will be sufficient to illustrate some salient characteristics of intelligent systems and of language understanding in particular.

The first aspect of an action is the physical-physiological level. For speech acts this is called the 'utterance act' by Searle (1969). At this level we might describe an action as "Susie moved her arm up and down causing a paint brush to move while in contact with a chair". A speech act might have the description "Betsy uttered the sounds associated with the sentence *The Red Sox are fantastic*".

The second aspect of an action is the propositional. At this level we describe actions in terms of organizing concepts. We could say "Susie is painting the chair", thus both summarizing and reinterpreting the action described above. A speech act also can be given a propositional description. Continuing our example we could say that Betsy's statement refers to the *Red Sox* and predicates *are fantastic*.

The third aspect of an action is the institutional, so called because it exists by virtue of institutionalized definitions which rely on perceptions of beliefs of others. We can describe Susie's action as "helping Martha paint" if it satifies a set of rules which constitute the definition of *help*. That *help* must be defined by a set of rules about beliefs becomes clear when we consider what it is about Susie's action that makes us view it as a helping action. Certainly it is more than just the physical-physiological facts or even the propositional content of her act, for the same action could also be seen as a 'harming', an 'exploiting', or any of several other institutional concepts. We have to know that Martha had a goal of painting the chair, that this goal satisfied some want or need of Martha, that Susie believed that Martha had the painting of the chair as a goal, etc.

Similarly, speech acts have institutional descriptions, or in Austin's (1965) terminology, 'illocutionary force'. If we believe that Betsy believes her statement, that she believes she has evidence for it, that she believes that it is not obvious to her listeners that the statement is true, that she wants her listeners to believe the statement, and perhaps other conditions, then we might describe her act as 'arguing'. The conditions or institutional rules which define concepts like 'help' and 'argue' have been called 'preconditions' (Bruce and Schmidt 1974) because they must be true at the time the concept is applied. Conditions that hold after the act has been performed are called 'outcome conditions' and are used in defining the effectual aspect.

The effectual aspect is so called because it has to do with the effects or outcomes of actions. In the Betsy example, her arguing may result in her listeners becoming 'convinced'. In the Susie example the outcome might be that the painting is finished. For speech acts Austin calls this aspect 'perlocutionary'.

An action may be described at a variety of levels. As we have seen, as 'uttering', a 'referring and predicating', an 'arguing', and a 'convincing' are not different acts but different ways of conceptualizing the same act. The concept of 'uttering' differs from the concept of 'convincing' in that the rules for its use are primarily physical-physiological, while the rules for 'convincing' have to do with the effects of an action. This is not to say that there are no physical-physiological correlates of 'convincing', but only that there is a concept which summarizes a set of facts about an action; that these facts concern inferred outcomes of the action; and that the English word *convince* in its most common usage matches closely with that concept. The discussion to follow focuses on those concepts whose rules are institutional (or, as Searle says, 'constitutive'). Thus we will examine the use of concepts which (unlike concepts of physical objects and actions) require a social context, a set of commonly agreed-upon rules about intentionality, beliefs and social relationships, to be used and understood.

In the next section we consider the structure of a social action definition. Each concept has cases, preconditions, outcome conditions, and typical instances, or realizations in language or other behavior. Although the concepts can be defined it is important to recognize that the definitions do not imply a reduction of high-level actions to primitive actions. HELP, for instance, is a social action defined in terms of beliefs and motivations, and not a complex of more primitive actions. We are able to organize a set of actions as a 'helping' sequence when we infer these beliefs and motivations, but not on the basis of the action pattern itself.

3.2 REQUEST

In this section we examine a social action which summarizes one person's asking another to do something. In English there are several verbs used to represent various types of asking. Austin (1965) includes these 'asking . . . to' verbs with his 'exercitives'. "An exercitive is the giving of a decision in favour of or against a certain course of action, or advocacy of it." Some of the 'asking . . . to' verbs are – *request, demand, command, beg, order, urge, advise, entreat, warn, plead, direct,* and *recommend.* We consider, the concept REQUEST here, and some related social action concepts in Appendix II.

REQUEST is a social action in which one person (the 'agent') expresses his/her desire for another (the 'recipient') to do something (the 'action'). The REQUEST must, of course, be made prior to the time of the action. Unlike DEMAND and COMMAND, REQUEST does not require any commitment about moral obligations (OUGHT rules) to do the action or about explicit authority relationships.

REQUEST is defined by predicates on its various components, the persons, actions, and times. We call these components 'cases' (see Bruce 1974). They are conceptual as opposed to grammatical relations on REQUEST. The case structure for REQUEST is represented as follows:

REQUEST: case structure

agent: A
recipient: R
action: X
time-request: t
time-action: t'

The preconditions for REQUEST express the constraints that A intends to ask, that A wants R to do X, that A believes that R is able to do X, that A believes that R has some reason to do X, and that A believes that in the absence of the REQUEST, R will choose not to do X:

REQUEST: preconditions (full form)

P1. A MUST-CHOOSE that
(A REQUEST R (X t) at t
P2. A WANTS (R CAUSE X t') t
P3. A BELIEVES (R CAN X t') t
P4. A BELIEVES (R TRY X t') t
P5. A BELIEVES (R MUST-CHOOSE not-X t') t
P6. $t < t'$

Using the convention of suppressing times discussed above we can rewrite the REQUEST preconditions as follows:

REQUEST: preconditions (abbreviated form)

P1. A MUST-CHOOSE that (A REQUEST R)
P2. A WANTS (R CAUSE X)
P3. A BELIEVES (R CAN X)
P4. A BELIEVES (R TRY X)
P5. A BELIEVES (R MUST-CHOOSE not-X)
P6. $t < t'$

Precondition P1 is an example of a general constraint on all speech acts and on many other social actions. Basically it says that for an utterance to be a REQUESTING it must be intentional. If A is talking in his sleep, or at gun-point, or happens to babble in a language he doesn't know then we do not describe his action as a REQUEST. This precondition alone requires the full machinery of choosing discussed in Section 2. Before we recognize that a REQUEST has occurred we have to find a reason for the agent to do it.

A related precondition which might be listed for any action implying intention is one which says that the agent must BELIEVE that his intention is recognized by the recipient. An utterance is not a REQUEST if the speaker does not BELIEVE that it is perceived as a REQUEST. We can state this principle as a general condition requiring 'transparency of intention':

Transparency condition

A BELIEVE (R BELIEVE [P1])

where [P1] is the precondition on a social action which requires intentionality.

Precondition P2 says that the REQUEST occurs only when A WANTS the action to be performed. P3 and P4 state that A BELIEVES that it is possible for R to do the action and that R has some reason for doing it. But P5 says that A BELIEVES that R will not do the action (at time t') without being asked. One view of a REQUEST is that it is an attempt to change R's MUST-CHOOSE value.

The transparency condition requires that A make the REQUEST obvious. Frequently, when making a REQUEST, the agent may reiterate one of the pre-conditions in order to satisfy this condition. Saying "I request that you . . ." is a way to emphasize condition P1. Any of the other preconditions can be stressed by an auxiliary statement, e.g., "And I *do* want you to . . ." or "I *know* you'd like to help me . . .".

There are other general constraints which could also be listed as pre-conditions on REQUEST. Searle (1969) calls these 'normal input and output conditions'. They include such things as that the speaker and hearer speak the same language, they are not acting in a play, and have neither aphasia nor deafness. Precondition P1 plus the transparency condition imply most of Searle's conditions by requiring intention on the part of the speaker. The apparently simpler rule (P1) is, in fact, quite powerful because it invokes all the procedures for construction and recognition of plans.

Outcome conditions on REQUEST are those facts which hold once the REQUEST has occurred (been recognized). For example, if R recognizes A's action as a REQUEST then R BELIEVES that A WANTS (R CAUSE X) and that A BELIEVES (R CAN X). Furthermore, if A BELIEVES (R BELIEVES (A REQUEST R to X)) then A BELIEVES (R BELIEVES (A WANT (R CAUSE X))) and A BELIEVES (R BELIEVES (A BELIEVES (R CAN X))). Thus A might say later, "You knew I wanted that!". Since outcomes of this sort form a potentially infinite set we will indicate that they exist by simply stating that all computable (in a weak sense determined by the situation) consequences of the preconditions and other outcome conditions are possible outcome conditions of a social action. This set of consequences will be symbolized, CONSEQUENCES (PC+OC).

The second outcome condition for REQUEST is a pointer to a normative rule. In the event that R fails to perform the action requested he has an obligation to explain why not. The variable Z represents the reason why R does not do X.

REQUEST: outcome conditions

O1. CONSEQUENCES (PC + OC)
O2. if not-(R CAUSE X)
then R OUGHT (R EXPLAIN A Z X)

Part of the definition of REQUEST is a set of pointers to typical expressions of the concept in language. We call these 'instances':

REQUEST: instances

will you . . . , could you . . . , I would like you to . . .

When an observer reports that a REQUEST has occurred he uses what we call a 'summary characterization':

REQUEST: summary characterizations

ask, *request*

One of the interesting features of natural language is that summary characterizations can be used at the time of the action (in most cases). Thus, someone might say, "I am asking you to come with me". This shows dramatically how belief systems knowledge interacts with both general world knowledge and specialized linguistic knowledge.

There are certain verbs corresponding to social actions which cannot be used in the first person present as *ask* or *request* are used. For example *convince* sounds odd in *I am convincing you to come with me*. The reason is that the concept CONVINCE has specific outcome conditions which the concept REQUEST lacks. Whenever a concept implies outcomes other than pointers to normative rules or simple consequences of the preconditions then the use of its instances in the present tense sounds strange. It is because the outcomes have obviously not occurred at the time of the utterance. This is one of the distinctions which Austin (1965) suggests between illocutionary and perlocutionary verbs.

Other 'asking . . . to' concepts are similar to REQUEST. Most have the same case structure. Some, like THREATEN, though, have additional cases. If A THREATENS X to R there is an implied case which contains the action which A does not want R to carry out.

The preconditions and outcome conditions for the various 'asking . . . to' concepts vary considerably, although they each contain the elements of A WANTING R to do something and A BELIEVING that R CAN do it. Definitions for several of these concepts (COMMAND, DEMAND, REQUEST, THREATEN, WARN) are given in Appendix II.

Recognition of an action at the social level facilitates understanding by providing discourse (as opposed to sentence) level constructs. Although a REQUEST may be realized by a single utterance, it is in fact a summarizing notion. Accepting such a summary commits the observer of a sequence of actions to several propositions about the beliefs and wants of the actors involved (these propositions being expressed in the preconditions and outcome conditions of REQUEST). In order to accept the propositions, the observer must attribute plans to the actors. These plans connect many actions (whether actual or foreseen) into coherent sequences. In real world situations, connections based on motivations are necessary to select useful sequences out of the many possible ones determined by physical connections alone.

4 Patterns of action

4.1 Types of patterns in social situations

One way in which an intelligent system can cope with a multitude of actions performed by others is to store a set of patterns of behavior. These patterns represent summaries of many sequences of action; thus, they are efficient but occasionally faulty mechanisms for predicting or accounting for behavior.

Before discussing patterns of behavior it will be useful to reiterate the role of motivation rules in analyzing actions. Whenever person A performs an action we can look for reasons for that action. The reason may be that A is disposed to act in that way. On the other hand one or more normative or personal motivation rules may be satisfied. As actions unfold in a sequence there is an alteration of the conditions which determine the effects of these rules. Thus previous actions play an important role in creating the environment for later choices. In the discussion to follow we consider some patterns of actions which exist because given actions in given situations facilitate (though not determine) specific successive actions.

There are a multitude of action patterns which fit the description given above. They are probably organized in some fashion which enables their efficient use in language. However it is premature to impose such an organization. Instead we will consider a few examples and some principles that should apply to the use of any such pattern.

There is one special type of behavior pattern that should be mentioned at the outset. It includes those patterns that have become ritualized, often embedded in the language. For example, the interchange –

> "Hello."
> "Hi! How are you?"
> "Fine; and you?"

is an extremely common form of greeting. It is not difficult to imagine a grammar for such greetings which generates virtually all of the normal pattern we use. Furthermore, it is clear that the words in these patterns have lost much of their original significance. We usually do not want a graphic answer to the greeting "how are you?". Instead, the phrase is serving as an unanalyzed terminal symbol in the 'greeting' grammar.

A richer example of a behavior pattern is one that might be observed in a school or other teaching and learning situation. A teacher and a student can be expected to act in a 'teaching/learning' mode. This includes talking, writing on paper or a blackboard, and possibly a lot of hand waving or silences for thinking. It usually does not include physical violence, singing or love making unless one of those is the subject under study. Furthermore, the content of the talking, writing, etc. is constrained. We might expect many questions and answers by both the teacher and the student. On the other hand, commands should be somewhat rare.

Included in our knowledge of the teaching/learning mode are rituals and the effects of normative and personal motivation rules. Thus this mode is a special case of very general schemas for organizing actions. A schema might be a pattern of actions without an explicit goal-orientation (like the teaching/learning pattern) or a sequence directed to a goal. In the latter case there may be only one actor involved (cf. Abelson's 1975 examples of a 'plans' such as "Communist military action against South Vietnam"). The 'story schemas' of Rumelhart (1975) and the 'frames' of Minsky (1974) are similar approaches to this issue of characterization of likely action sequences.

An important feature of any behavior pattern is that it cannot be applied in all situations. Implicit in each of the given examples are certain constraints on the applicability of the behavior pattern. The greeting pattern occurs only upon meeting someone; a waiter/customer pattern exists only in a restaurant; a boss/employee pattern exists only in the work situation; and even the teaching/learning pattern applies only when we infer certain conditions. In the following section we consider further the need for such constraints and discuss how some of them might be specified.

4.2 Social action paradigms

The term 'social action paradigm' (SAP) will be used to refer to a pattern of behavior with its associated situational constraints. The situational constraints form the 'header' of the social action paradigm and the pattern itself is the 'body'. The header checks conditions in the situation, and, in the process, determines the bindings of variables in the SAP body to entities (individuals, outcomes of acts, propositions) in the situation.

Part of a SAP can be represented by a graph in which the nodes are action-concepts and the arcs represent likely actions to follow. For example a teacher and a student might engage in the interaction shown in Figure 1.

That such a network of social actions is insufficient can be seen by consideration of the relationship between the successive actions. For instance, when the teacher poses a question we expect the student to respond, but this response should be related to the question. It may not be a correct or complete answer, but to be a "response to the question" its propositional content should bear a close relationship to the propositional content of the question. If this "close relationship" is defined by a function, F, then we can give a better account of the question-response paradigm as shown in Figure 2.

Using other propositional content relating functions we can redo Figure 2 as shown in Figure 3.

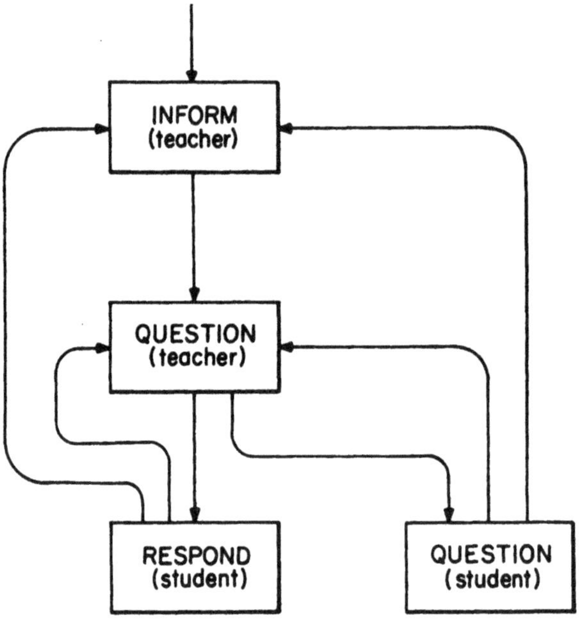

Figure 1. Rough approximation of a SAP body.

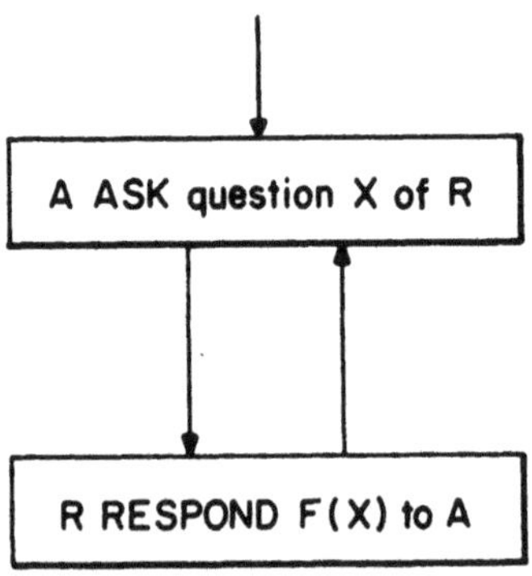

Figure 2. Instantiated social actions with a propositional content relating function, F.

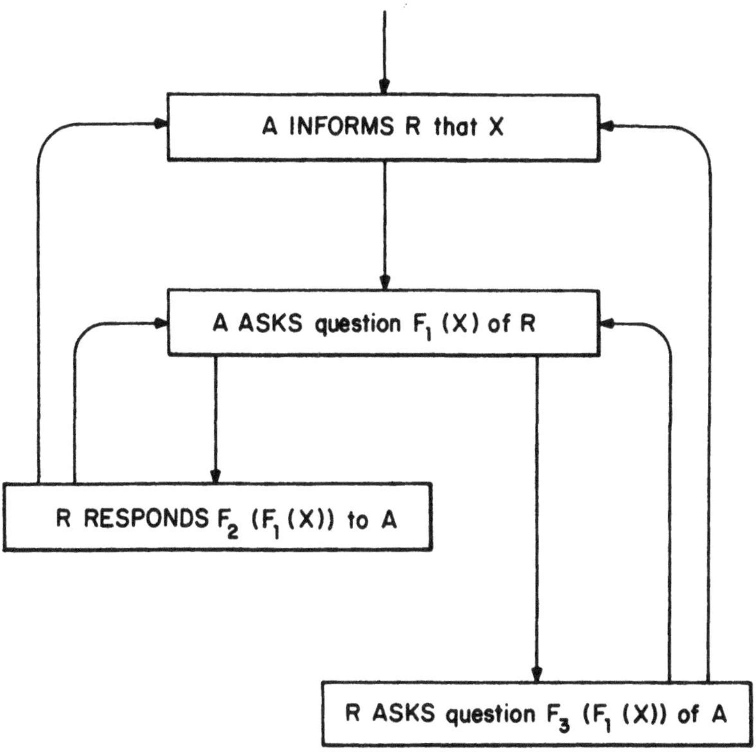

Figure 3. A SAP body with instantiated social actions.

Once the notion of social actions with arguments (or cases, see Bruce 1974) is introduced the problem of specifying the situations in which the paradigm is applicable becomes explicit. That is, it is necessary to show the correspondences, or bindings, of entities in the situation to the variables in the SAP graph.

The problem of specifying appropriate situations is, of course, inherent in a SAP whether or not the variables are explicitly identified. In the previous example it is clear that the SAP exists because there are commonly shared expectations concerning the behavior of students and teachers. Thus, whenever we observe two individuals in a student-teacher relationship, with the associated relations of dominance, helping, etc. we are able to invoke the student-teacher SAP. The SAP could certainly be applied in other situations, but most likely in situations that share certain salient aspects of the teacher-student situation. We would not, for example, expect similar behavior to occur between a ship's captain and his first mate (assuming they were not also in a teaching situation).

In the following section we consider a social action paradigm which we find associated with the concept REQUEST.

4.3 The social action paradigm *REQUEST*

REQUEST is a pattern of behavior (body) with constraints (header) on its applicability. The header for *REQUEST* specifies both conditions on the situation in which *REQUEST* is to be applied and bindings of variables in the body to entities of the situation. *REQUEST* is a simple SAP in the sense that its pattern has only one starting node, that is, the pattern begins when person A REQUESTS that person R do some action X. Because of this, the header is the same as the preconditions for REQUEST:

REQUEST header

1. A MUST-CHOOSE
   that (A REQUEST R (R CAUSE X))
2. A WANTS (R CAUSE X)
3. A BELIEVES (R CAN X)
4. A BELIEVES (R TRY X)
5. A BELIEVES (R MUST-CHOOSE not-X)
6. time-request < time-X

If there were other starting nodes in the *REQUEST* body then the preconditions of the corresponding social actions would also have to be satisfied, and hence included in the *REQUEST* header. Other SAP's have additional constraints in their headers. For example, the teaching/learning SAP discussed above might have the constraint

A is-teaching R

The body for *REQUEST* is represented by a graph (Fig. 4) in which the nodes are instantiated social actions an the arcs show which actions are likely to follow from a given action. In the SAP the functions F_1, F_2 and F_3 relate the propositional content of one action to another. $F_1(X)$ is an action which can be considered as an alternative to the action X. $F_2(X)$ is information which relates to the doing of X by R. $F_3(X)$ is an implication, that there is some cause Z such that if Z then not-(R CAUSE X). Obviously, before the *REQUEST* body can be understood it is necessary to define the concepts implicit in it such as PROMISE, THANK, and EXPLAIN (see Appendix II) and their associated SAP's. Nevertheless, some appreciation of what the body means can be gained by an informal description.

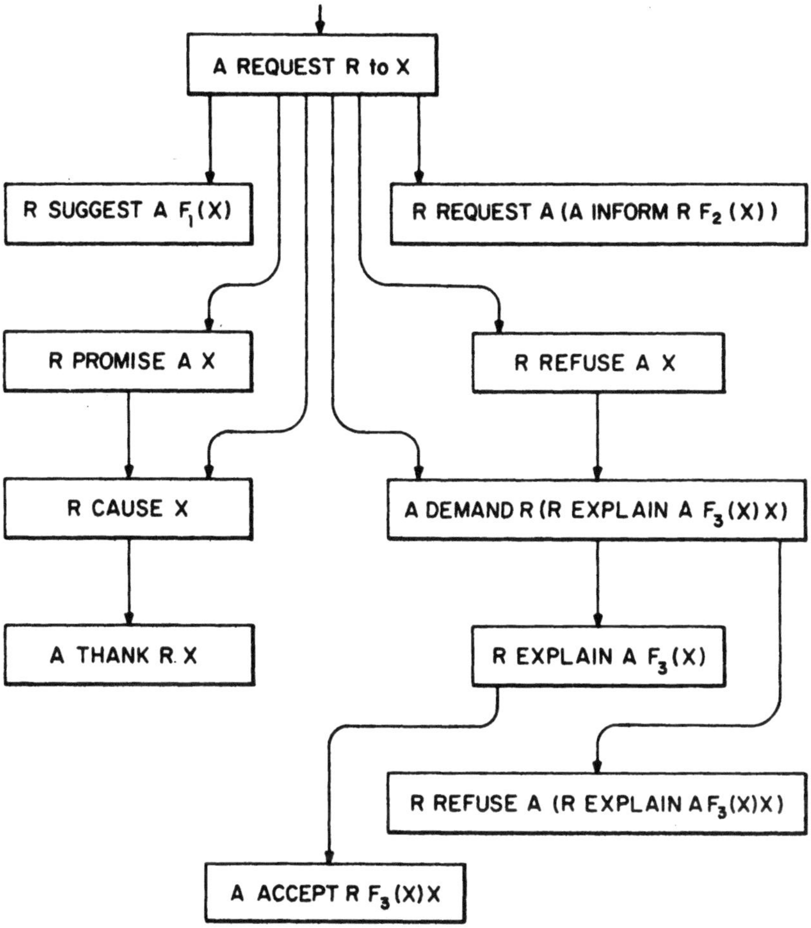

Figure 4. The social action paradigm, *REQUEST*.

What the SAP for *REQUEST* expresses can be stated fairly simply. In a situation in which person A WANTS person R to do something and believes that R CAN do it and that R has a reason to do it but won't in the absence of a REQUEST, A can REQUEST that the action be performed. Before we judge A's utterance as an instance of REQUEST we need to establish these preconditions and as well believe that A intends to do the asking. Regardless of the actual words uttered, it is not a REQUESTING unless this precondition of intention is established. Once we know that the situation defined by the preconditions does in fact hold then we can reasonably expect to find that A's REQUESTING exists as part of a larger pattern involving several actions.

This larger pattern is given by the *REQUEST* body. It states that following the REQUESTING, R may CAUSE the action or may REFUSE. Following the REFUSAL or simply inaction of R, A may REQUEST an explanation, SUGGEST alternatives, and so on.

Other actions may also evoke *REQUEST*. For example, upon hearing, "No, I won't do that!", an observer might deduce that a REFUSE has occurred. This recognition provides a valid, though, perhaps, less likely, pointer to the *REQUEST* SAP.

In the next section we will consider a simple story and the use of SAP's social actions and the theory of personal causation in connecting and understanding the actions.

5 The use of belief systems knowledge for language understanding

Consider the following story –

> It was a hot July afternoon and Joey wanted to cool off. He asked his older brother Nick to buy him an ice cream cone. Nick said no. Joey then demanded an explanation. Nick said that he didn't have any money. Joey said, OK, he understood.

Part of what it means to understand this story is the ability to answer the following kinds of questions:

- Why did Joey ask Nick to buy him an ice cream cone?
- Why did Nick say he didn't have any money?
- Did Joey accept Nick's explanation for his refusal to buy the ice cream cone?

In general, these questions are not difficult, but they do require use of knowledge about social actions, e.g., REQUEST, REFUSE, EXPLAIN, and ACCEPT (see Appendix II), patterns of behavior, e.g., *REQUEST* and related SAP's, plans, purposes, perceptions of beliefs, and other elements of belief systems knowledge. In order to illustrate how this knowledge is used in understanding language, we will consider here a probable sequence of actions that would be taken by an intelligent system in understanding the story given above. We will call this system the 'Observer'.

Upon hearing (or reading, seeing, etc.) the first sentence, "It was a hot July afternoon and Joey wanted to cool off," the Observer establishes a set for the story. World knowledge is brought in to make (possibly wrong) inferences such as:

- The sun is shining.
- Joey is wearing summer style clothes.
- The story is set in the Northern Hemisphere.
- Joey is perspiring.
- The temperature is over 90 degrees (F).

Using knowledge about typical behavior the Observer might also infer:

- Joey will soon do something to cool off. He may go swimming, look for an air-conditioned building, sit on a block of ice, or get something cold to eat or drink.

The setting can be considered to be a collection of facts of the kind given above, the most interesting of which are the ones that refer to beliefs and intentions. In this story we have at least one such fact, namely that Joey wants to cool off. In our notation we could say

Joey WANT (A CAUSE X)

where X is an action which has as an eventual outcome

Joey is-cool

and A is some person, possibly Joey. The presence of this fact implies a plan in formation. While the Observer cannot at this time know the fine structure of Joey's plan he does know certain gross characteristics. He can expect Joey to perform an action which either has the outcome, "Joey is-cool", or enables either Joey or someone else to perform some other action which ultimately has that outcome. ("Ultimately" here means the recursive application of an enablement procedure.) Since no actions are explicitly mentioned in the first sentence the Observer does not need to use social action definitions to interpret the sentence, nor are any SAP's applicable.

With the setting established, the Observer is already prepared for certain actions. Upon hearing the second sentence, "He asked his older brother Nick to buy him an ice cream cone", the Observer attempts an interpretation in terms of the structure he has constructed.

Starting with the verb (i.e., the action) he has a pointer, via 'instance' links, to various social action concepts. In this case *ask* is a typical word used to express COMMAND, DEMAND, REQUEST, and perhaps other speech acts. Checking the preconditions for these concepts he finds that COMMAND is unlikely since there is no reason to think that Joey DOMINATES (has authority over) Nick. Similarly DEMAND is improbable because no OUGHT conditions have been established. REQUEST appears likely since it is reasonable to believe that each of its preconditions are satisfied.

The argument for the interpretation of Joey's action as a REQUEST might go as follows: The Observer knows from general world knowledge that -

> Nick BUY an ice cream cone for Joey
>
> ENABLES
>
> Joey EAT ice cream cone
>
> HAS-AS-OUTCOME
>
> Joey is-cool

and is likely to construct such a sequence from his knowledge of Joey's wants. Furthermore the sequence provides an instantiation of the previously vague plan ascribed to Joey. Thus, assuming a SENTIMENT and UNIT relationship between Joey and Nick it is reasonable to infer that

> Joey BELIEVES (Nick TRY
> (Nick BUY ice cream cone for Joey))

Also, since there is no reason to think that Nick is already planning to buy the ice cream cone, the Observer can infer that

> Joey BELIEVES (Nick MUST-CHOOSE
> not-(Nick BUY ice cream cone for Joey))

He already knows that

> Joey WANTS (A CAUSE X)

where X leads to Joey-is-cool. From general world knowledge he might infer that since Nick is older Joey knows that he is able to buy the ice cream cone, i.e.,

> Joey BELIEVES Nick CAN
> (Nick BUY ice cream cone for Joey)

Since the ice cream cone has not been purchased he also knows that the temporal precondition for REQUEST is satisfied, i.e.,

> time-request < time-action

Thus it is reasonable to infer that Joey's utterance constitutes a REQUEST.

At this point the Observer can invoke the SAP for REQUEST which we have called *REQUEST* (see Figure 4). The header for *REQUEST* checks to see that a REQUEST has occurred and then binds its formal parameters to the case fillers of the REQUEST. In this example, the agent is Joey, the recipient is Nick, and the action is (Nick BUY ice cream cone for Joey).

REQUEST is a very general SAP, unlike, for instance, a waiter/customer pattern in a restaurant. It suggests several rather diverse actions which can reasonably be expected to follow the REQUEST. The Observer is thus predisposed though not committed to perceive successive actions to be consistent with the *REQUEST* body. Upon hearing the next sentence, "Nick said no", he tries first to interpret the action as a PROMISE, REQUEST, or other action suggested by the SAP body. In this case the negative statement, plus the fact that no other SAP is active at this point, suggest that Nick is REFUSING to fulfill Joey's REQUEST.

In order to accept Nick's action as a REFUSE, the Observer is committed either to believing that

Nick BELIEVES not-(Nick CAN
(Nick BUY ice cream cone for Joey))

or that

Nick MUST-CHOOSE
not-(Nick BUY ice cream cone for Joey)

If he cannot accept the former assumption then he must formulate a plan for Nick which is hindered by the REQUESTED action. For example, he might assume that Nick has a limited amount of money which he wants to spend on something else. As in the previous case of Joey's plan to cool off this vague plan becomes an active agent which influences the perception of succeeding sentences.

The next sentence, "Joey then demanded an explanation", fits into the SAP for *REQUEST* as a DEMAND. In fact, the interpretation of Nick's "no" as a REFUSE is reinforced by the interpretation of Joey's sentence as a DEMAND for an explanation. The combination of these interpretations suggests strongly that the next action may be an EXPLAIN by Nick. In fact, "Nick said that he didn't have any money", is a quite plausible explanation. It is an assertion that

Nick CAN (Nick BUY ice cream cone for Joey)

is not true. The final sentence, "Joey said, OK, he understood", can then be interpreted as an ACCEPT for Nick's explanation.

The description above leaves out many important details of the Observer's processing. Each action needs to be analyzed in terms of active SAP's but also in terms of formulated but unfulfilled plans, instance pointers and other possible social actions. Furthermore, the usual syntactic and semantic processing is only supplemented, not replaced by, the belief systems processing. What I have tried to show here is that intentionality and related concepts, as expressed in social action definitions and SAP's, are critical for understanding and that feasible mechanisms for their application do exist.

It should be emphasized that only in restricted cases can we do without the full machinery discussed here. We might for example explain the processing of many stories in terms of simple pattern-matching rules without resort to beliefs about intentions. However, such rules fail in generality. Consider, for example, a rule which says:

- Following a question by A concerning a future action of R, a "no" from R means that R REFUSES to act.

That such a rule is insufficient can be seen clearly in the following examples:

(A) Joey: Will you buy me an ice cream cone?
Nick: No (REFUSE)

Joey: Will you forget my birthday?
Nick: No (PROMISE)

(B) Joey: Can you buy me an ice cream cone?
Nick: No (REFUSE)

Joey: Can you buy a new car?
Nick: No (INFORM)

Nick's "no" can have quite different meanings depending upon the Observer's analysis of the goals and beliefs of Nick and Joey. In the sentences in group (A) above it is an inference about Joey's WANTS and Nick's BELIEFS about Joey's WANTS which transforms the REFUSE into a PROMISE. In (B) it is an inference about the BELIEFS of Nick and Joey concerning Nick's financial capabilities which makes one "no" a likely REFUSE and the other a likely INFORM. Only by a model of beliefs and intentions can an Observer account for behavior in these social situations.

Acknowledgements

I owe many of the ideas discussed here to Chuck Schmidt and Geoff Brown. In fact it is Schmidt's theory of personal causation that provides the foundation for this paper. Geoff Brown is implementing some of these ideas in a computer program for understanding stories in natural language. (The program is called BELIEVER.) I would also like to thank Andee Rubin and Eleanor Warnock for suggestions on the paper itself.

Notes

* This research was supported by the Advanced Research Projects Agency under ARPA Order No. 1697; Contract No. DAHC15-71-C-0088.

1. This example was inspired by Gordon and Lakoff's (1971) Duke of Bordello.
2. Not to be confused with 'intensionally'.
3. Austin (1965), Fillmore (1971), Garner (1971), Gordon and Lakoff (1971), Grice (1957), Hass (1971), Heider (1958), Hutchinson (1971), Lakoff (1971), Rumelhart (1975), Schmidt (1974), Sedlak (1974), Searle (1969), Strawson (1964), and Wittgenstein (1958).
4. Brown (1974), Bruce and Schmidt (1974), Carbonell and Collins (1973), Charniak (1972), McCarthy and Hayes (1969), McDermott (1974), Minsky (1974), Norman (1972), Schank et al. (1972a, 1972b, 1973), and Schmidt and D'Addamio (1973).

References

Abelson, Robert

1973 "The structure of belief systems", in *Computer simulation of thought and language*, edited by K. Colby and R. Schank (San Francisco: Freeman).

1974 "Frames for understanding social actions", in *Representation and understanding: Studies in cognitive science*, edited by D.G. Bobrow and A.M. Collins New York: Academic).

Abelson, Robert and Carroll, J.D.

1965 "Computer simulation of individual belief systems", *American Behavioral Scientist* 8: 24–30.

Abelson, Robert and Reich, Carol

1969 "Implicational molecules: A method for extracting meaning from input sentences", *Proceedings of the First International Joint Conference on Artificial Intelligence, Washington D.C.*

Anscombe, G.E.M.

1958 "On brute facts", *Analysis* 18.

Austin, J.L.

1965 *How to do things with words* (New York/London: Oxford University Press).

Brown, Geoffrey

1974 "The BELIEVER system", *National Institutes of Health Report* CBM-TR-33 (Computer Science Dept., Rutgers, New Brunswick, N.J.).

Brown, Geoffrey, Bruce, Bertram and Trigoboff, Michael
1974 "The CHRONOS Natural Language Understanding System", *National Institutes of Health Report* CBM-TR-30 (Computer Science Dept., Rutgers, New Brunswick, N.J.).

Bruce, Bertram
1974 "Case systems for natural language", *National Institutes of Health Report* CBM-TR-31 (Computer Science Dept., Rutgers, New Brunswick, N.J.).

Bruce, Bertram and Schmidt, C.F.
1974 "Episode understanding and belief guided parsing", *National Institutes of Health Report* CBM-TR-32 (Computer Science Dept., Rutgers, New Brunswick, N.J.).

Carbonell, Jaime and Collins, Allan
1973 "Natural semantics in Artificial Intellegence", *Proceedings of the Third International Joint Conference on Artificial Intelligence, Stanford, Palo Alto, California.*

Charniak, Eugene
1972 "Towards a model of children's story comprehension", *AI Lab Report* AI-TR-266 (Cambridge, Mass.: MIT).

Colby, Kenneth Mark and Canfield Smith, David
1969 "Dialogues between humans and an artificial belief system", *Proceedings of the First International Joint Conference on Artificial Intelligence, Washington, D.C.*

Colby, Kenneth Mark, Tesler, Lawrence and Enea, Horace
1969 "Experiments with a search algorithm for the data base of a human belief structure", *Proceedings of the First International Joint Conference on Artificial Intelligence, Washington, D.C.*

Colby, Kenneth Mark, Weber, S. and Hilf, F.D.
1971 "Artificial paranoia", *Artificial Intelligence* 2: 1–25.

Fillmore, Charles J.
1971 "Verbs of judging: an exercise in semantic description", in *Studies in Linguistic semantics*, edited by C.J. Fillmore and D.T. Langendoen (New York: Holt, Rinehart & Winston).

Garner, Richard
1971 "'Presupposition' in philosophy and linguistics", in *Studies in linguistic semantics*, edited by C.J. Fillmore and D.T. Langendoen (New York: Holt, Rinehart & Winston).

Gordon, David and Lakoff, George
1971 "Conversational postulates", *Proceedings of the Seventh Regional Meeting, Chicago Linguistic Society.*

Grice, H.P.
1957 "Meaning", *Philosophical Review* 66: 377–388.

Hass, Wilbur
1971 "Truth-functional and communicational bases for prescriptive discourse", *Proceedings of the Seventh Regional Meeting, Chicago Linguistic Society.*

Heider, Fritz
1958 *The psychology of interpersonal relations* (New York: Wiley).

Hutchinson, Larry G.
1971 "Presupposition and belief-inferences", *Proceedings of the Seventh Regional Meeting, Chicago Linguistics Society.*

Lakoff, George
1971 "Presupposition and relative well-formedness", in *Semantics: An interdisciplinary reader*, edited by D.D. Steinberg and L.A. Jakobovits (Cambridge: Unversity Press).

McCarthy, John and Hayes, P.J.
1969 "Some philosophical problems from the standpoint of Artificial Intelligence", in *Machine Intelligence* 4 (New York: American Elsevier).

McDermott, Drew
1974 "Assimilation of new information by a natural language understanding system", *AI Lab Report* AI-TR-291 (Cambridge, Mass.: MIT).

Minsky, Marvin
1968 "Matter, mind and models", in *Semantic information processing*, edited by M. Minsky (Cambridge, Mass.: MIT).
1974 "A framework for representing knowledge", in *The psychology of computer vision* (New York: McGraw-Hill).

Norman, Donald
1972 "Memory, knowledge and the answering of questions", Center for Human Information Processing, University of California, San Diego, Chip 25.

Rumelhart, David E.
1974 "Notes on a schema for stories", in *Representation and understanding: Studies in cognitive science*, edited by D.G. Bobrow and A.M. Collins (New York: Academic).

Schank, Roger
1972 "Conceptual dependency: A theory of natural language understanding", *Cognitive Psychology* 3: 552-631.
1973 "Causality and reasoning", TR-1, Instituto per gli studi semantici e cognitivi, Castagnola.

Schank, Roger, Goldman, Neil, Rieger, Charles J. and Riesbeck, Christopher K.
1972 "Primitive concepts underlying verbs of thought", Report STAN-CS-265-72, Computer Science Dept., Stanford, Palo Alto, Cal.

Schmidt, C.F.
1974 "Recognizing plans and purposes", *National Institutes of Health Report* CBM-TR-34, Computer Science Dept., Rutgers, New Brunswick, N.J.

Schmidt, C.F. and D'Addamio, John
1973 "A model of the common-sense theory of intention and personal causation", *Proceedings of the Third International Joint Conference on Arificial Intelligence, Stanford, Palo Alto, Cal.*

Sedlak, Andrea
1974 "An investigation of the development of the child's understanding and evaluation of the actions of others", *National Institutes of Health Report* CBM-TR-28, Computer Science Dept., Rutgers, New Brunswick, N.J.

Searle, J.R.
1969 *Speech acts: An essay in the philosophy of language* (Cambridge: University Press).

Strawson, P.F.
1964 "Intention and convention in speech acts", *Philosophical Review* 73: 439-460.

Wittgenstein, Ludwig
1958 *Philosophical investigations* (New York: Macmillan). [Translated by G.E.M. Anscombe.]

APPENDIX I: Notation conventions

The language used here is a form of predicate calculus (see Bruce – Schmidt 1974). In order to distinguish social actions from the English words which are commonly used to describe them, the predicates in our language are written in capital letters. Thus, the concept of an 'informing' is represented by the symbol INFORM rather than the English word *inform*. In a similar way concepts such as 'being able to', 'being motivated to', 'being obligated to', and 'believing' are represented by the symbols CAN, TRY, OUGHT, and BELIEVE.

For the sake of readability several deviations from standard predicate calculus notation will be used. Rather than expressing atomic formulas in the form:

<predicate> (<argument 1> . . . <argument n>)

we will use the more English-like form:

<argument 1> <predicate> <argument 2> . . .
<argument n>

Thus INFORM (A, B, S, t) (meaning "A informs B that S at time t") will be written:

A INFORM B S t.

In addition various function symbols such as 'that', 'to', '-s', and 'does' will be used whenever they make the formulas more readable. For example:

A INFORM B that S at t.

Where no confusion can result the explicit reference to times will be omitted. Thus,

A INFORMS B that S.

APPENDIX II. Social actions

ACCEPT

(*Frances accepted Ralph's explanation for being late*)

Case structure
agent: A
recipient: R
cause: X
action: Y
time-accept: t
time-action: t′

Preconditions
P1. A MUST-CHOOSE (A ACCEPT R X)
P2. A BELIEVES (R EXPLAIN A X Y)
P3. A BELIEVES (if X then not-(R CAUSE Y))
P4. $t' < t$

Outcome conditions
01. CONSEQUENCES (PC + OC)

Instances: accept, understand

Summary characterizations: accept

Figure 5: The social action ACCEPT. Precondition P2 states that in order for A's action to be an ACCEPT A must BELIEVE that R has EXPLAINED why R did not CAUSE a previous action, Y. The explanation is some proposition, X. P3 states that A BELIEVES the explanation, i.e., that X implies either not-(R can Y) or not-(R MUST-CHOOSE Y).

ACCUSE

(*George accused Bill of dealing from the bottom of the deck*)

Case structure
agent: A
recipient: R
action: X
time-accept: t
time-action: t′

Preconditions
P1. A MUST-CHOOSE (A ACCUSE R X)
P2. A BELIEVES (R CAUSE X)
P3. A BELIEVES (R SUFFICIENT-OUGHT not-X)
P4. $t' < t$

Outcome conditions
01. CONSEQEUNCES (PC + OC)

Instances: accuse, blame

Summary characterizations: accuse, blame

Figure 6: The social action ACCUSE. An ACCUSE occurs when A BELIEVES that R CAUSED some action, X, (P2) and that R had a sufficient obligation not to do X. It can be followed by a form of EXPLAIN which presents reasons why R CAUSED X, by an action such as APOLOGIZE, another ACCUSE, a DENY or a REINTERPRET.

ASKABOUT

(*Alfred asked Judy about the upcoming schedule*)

Case structure
agent: A
recipient: R
object: X
time-askabout: t

Preconditions
P1. A MUST-CHOOSE (A ASKABOUT X to R)
P2. not-(A KNOWS(is-aware-of) X)
P3. A BELIEVES (R CHOOSE (R INFORM A X t'))
P4. $t < t'$
P5. A BELIEVES (R KNOWS(is-aware-of) X)

Outcome conditions
01. CONSEQUENCES (PC + OC)

Instances: who, what, where, etc.; tell me . . . , is . . . , did . . .

Summary characterizations: ask

Figure 7: The social action ASKABOUT. Precondition P2 says that the agent of ASKABOUT does not know the answer to his question. If P2 is false then R may respond, "I thought you knew!". P2 being false suggests that the apparent ASKABOUT is really a TEST, a form of LIE, or ritual talk. However it could also be that the agent is trying to clarify or strengthen his knowledge.

If P5 is false then instead of A ASKABOUT X to R we have A ASKABOUT (R KNOWS(is-aware-of) X). If P3 is false then the action could be an attempt to EMBARRASS or BADGER.

COMMAND

(*Alexander commanded his troops to shave their beards*)

Case structure
agent: A
recipient: R
action: X
time-command: t
time-action: t′

Preconditions
P1. A MUST-CHOOSE (A COMMAND R to X)
P2. A WANTS (R CAUSE X)
P3. A BELIEVES (R CAN X)
P4. A BELIEVES (R CHOOSE not-X)
P5. A BELIEVES (R SUFFICIENT-OUGHT X)
P6. A BELIEVES (if (R BELIEVES
(A COMMAND R to X))
then (R OUGHT X))
P7. A DOMINATES R
P8. $t < t'$

Outcome conditions
01. R OUGHT X
02. CONSEQUENCES (PC + OC)

Instances: order, command, tell

Summary characterizations: order, command

Figure 8: The social action COMMAND. COMMAND is a complex form of 'asking'. In addition to the preconditions that A WANT (R CAUSE X) and A BELIEVES (R CAN X) there are conditions on the relationship of A to R and on A's beliefs about R's intentions.

A must BELIEVE that R has reason(s) not to do X but that there is a SUFFICIENT-OUGHT for R to do X. Furthermore, A BELIEVES that if R recognizes the COMMAND that R OUGHT X. Finally, (in this situation) A DOMINATES R.

COMMAND has a special outcome condition (01) which says that the observer (anyone who recognizes A's action as a COMMAND) BELIEVES that R OUGHT X.

CONVINCE

(*Peter convinced me to buy the blueberries*)

Case structure
agent: A
recipient: R
proposition: X
time-convince: t

Preconditions

P1. A MUST-CHOOSE (A CONVINCE R that X)
P2. A BELIEVES X
P3. A BELIEVES not-(R BELIEVES X)
P4. not-(R BELIEVES X)

Outcome conditions
01. R BELIEVES S
02. CONSEQUENCES (PC + OC)

Instances: tell, inform, say

Summary characterizations: convince

Figure 9: The social action CONVINCE. CONVINCE differs from INFORM in that it implies a stronger commitment about the beliefs of the recipient. Precondition P4 states that R does not BELIEVE the proposition X, a constraint which is not implied by a simple INFORMING. Also CONVINCE makes a stronger statement about the effects of the action. Whereas INFORM says merely that the recipient is aware of the proposition, CONVINCE says that the recipient must BELIEVE the proposition.

There is another sense of 'convince' which does not express intentionality; instead it merely gives the outcome of a discussion. Thus we can talk of 'convincing' in the intentional sense (like PROMISE) or the descriptive sense. Many other words, such as 'ask' serve similar dual roles. In this chapter we are concerned with the intentional uses only.

DEMAND

(*She demanded that he shut up*)

Case structure
agent: A
recipient: R
action: X
time-demand: t
time-action: t′

Preconditions
P1. A MUST-CHOOSE (A DEMAND R to X)
P2. A WANTS (R CAUSE X)
P3. A BELIEVES (R CAN X)
P4. A BELIEVES (R BELIEVES (R MUST-CHOOSE not-X))
P5. A BELIEVES (R SUFFICIENT-OUGHT X)
P6. $t < t'$

Outcome conditions
01. if not-(R CAUSE X)
then R OUGHT (R EXPLAIN A Z X)
02. CONSEQUENCES (PC + OC)

Instances: demand, insist

Summary characterizations: demand, insist

Figure 10: The social action DEMAND. DEMAND is a complex form of 'asking'. In addition to the preconditions that A WANTS (R CAUSE X) and A BELIEVES (R CAN X) there are preconditions that A BELIEVES (R BELIEVES (R MUST-CHOOSE not-X) and A BELIEVES that R intends not to do X but that there is a strong OUGHT for R to do X. Because A's belief in the SUFFICIENT-OUGHT there is a local normative rule invoked by DEMAND. This rule, pointed to by 01, states that if R does not do X then R OUGHT to give a reason why (EXPLAIN).

EXPLAIN

(Jerry explained to Jane that the cake burned because the thermostat was broken)

Case structure
agent: A
recipient: R
cause: X
action: Y
time-explain: t
time-cause: t′
time-action: t″

Preconditions
P1. A MUST-CHOOSE (A EXPLAIN to R that (if X then not-(A CAUSE Y)))
P2. not-(A CAUSE Y)
P3. A BELIEVES (R BELIEVES not-(A CAUSE Y))
P4. A BELIEVES (R WANTS (A CAUSE Y))
P5. A BELIEVES (if X then not-(A CAUSE Y))
P6. A BELIEVES (R BELIEVES (if X then not-(A CAUSE Y)))
P7. A BELIEVES not-(A OUGHT Y)
P8. $t' < t''$
P9. $t'' < t$

Outcome conditions
01. CONSEQUENCES (PC + OC)

Instances: explain

Summary characterizations: explain, make an excuse

Figure 11: The social action EXPLAIN. A variant of this social action is one in which the agent is EXPLAINING why an unwanted act was done (rather than a wanted act which was not done). In either case the cause, X, must be a sufficient reason for A's behavior. In the case of an act not done X should say why A CAN X is not true or why A MUST-CHOOSE X is not true. If X is focused on MUST-CHOOSE then it can be a statement that A has a sufficient reason not to do the act, either A SUFFICIENT-TRY not-X or A SUFFICIENT-OUGHT not-X. X can also state that there is simply no sufficient reason to do the act. The exact form which X takes in a specific situation depends upon such things as the previous social actions. For example, if A has failed to carry out a valid COMMAND then the only appropriate causes for the lack of action would be not-(CAN X) or A SUFFICIENT-OUGHT not-X.

INFORM

(*Linda informed Richard that the tire was flat*)

Case structure
agent: A
recipient: R
proposition: X
time-inform: t

Preconditions
P1. A MUST-CHOOSE (A INFORM R that X)
P2. A BELIEVES X
P3. A BELIEVES not-(R BELIEVES X)

Outcome conditions
01. R KNOWS(is-aware-of) S
02. if not-(R BELIEVES S)
then R OUGHT (R INFORM A not-(R BELIEVE S))
03. CONSEQUENCES (PC + OC)

Instances: tell, say

Summary characterizations: inform

Figure 12: The social action INFORM. If P2 is false then the apparent INFORM is probably a form of ritual talk or a LIE. If P3 is false then it is probably a REQUEST or COMMAND. If X is an action such that A causes a negative outcome for R then it may be a THREAT; if the outcome is positive then it may be a PROMISE. If X contains a *need* or *want* verb then the action may be a REQUEST or COMMAND for the complement of the need-want verb. If X asserts that A cannot do an action Y then it may be a REQUEST for R to do Y. If X asserts that A doesn't have some object Z then it may be a REQUEST for HELP from R in obtaining Z.

There is probably another related social action, which might be called 'TELL'. TELL has the same outcome conditions and instances as INFORM. It differs only in not requiring P3, i.e., there is no commitment made about R's beliefs. While the notion of a simple TELLING is useful in some circumstances, it should not be used to hide more motivated speech acts such as REQUESTING which often are expressed as simple factual statements.

LIE

(*Sam lied to Karen about the money*)

Cas structure
agent: A
recipient: R
proposition: X
time-lie: t

Preconditions
P1. A MUST-CHOOSE (A LIE X to R)
P2. not-(A BELIEVE X)
P3. A BELIEVES not-(R BELIEVES not-X)

Outcome conditions
01. CONSEQUENCES (PC + OC)

Instances: tell, say, inform

Summary characterizations: lie

Figure 13: The social action LIE. The preconditions are similar to those for INFORM, except, of course, that a 'not' is inserted. P3 says that the agent of LIE must BELIEVE that the recipient does not BELIEVE the opposite of the proposition, i.e., A BELIEVES there is some chance of success with the LIE. If R BELIEVES that an INFORMING has occurred then the consequences of that social action will hold within R's belief system. If P1 is false than A can say later that he was mistaken (P2) and did not intend to LIE. If R BELIEVES not-X then R may say "You are wrong" or "Did I hear you correctly?"

PROMISE

(*Catherine promised to give Bill a kiss*)

Case structure
agent: A
recipient: R
action: X
time-promise: t
time-action: t′

Preconditions
P1. A MUST-CHOOSE (A PROMISE R X)
P2. A CAN X
P3. R WANTS (A CAUSE X)
P4. if not-(A PROMISE R X)
then not-(A MUST-CHOOSE X)
P5. A TRY X
P6. $t < t'$

Outcome conditions
01. A SUFFICIENT-OUGHT X
02. CONSEQUENCES (PC + OC)

Instances: promise, offer

Summary characterizations: promise

Figure 14: The social action, PROMISE. PROMISE is a rather complicated speech act and its definition makes some fine distinctions. Basically the preconditions say that A is capable of doing X and intends to do it; that he would not necessarily do it were it not for the PROMISE and that R WANTS A to do X. The important outcome condition is that A now has a sufficiently strong obligation to carry out the action PROMISED. For a further discussion of PROMISE with a slightly different approach, see Searle (1969).

REFUSE

(*Art refused to divulge the location of the treasure*)

Case structure
agent: A
recipient: R
action: X
time-refuse: t

Preconditions
P1. A MUST-CHOOSE (A REFUSE R X)
P2. A BELIEVES (R ASK A to X)
P3. A MUST-CHOOSE not-X
P4. not-(A CAUSE X)

Outcome conditions
01. CONSEQUENCES (PC + OC)
02. R BELIEVES not-(A CAUSE X)

Instances: refuse, I won't . . .

Summary characterizations: refuse

Figure 15: The social action REFUSE. REFUSE is an action which typically follows an ASKING . . . TO concept such as ASK, DEMAND or COMMAND. It occurs when A BELIEVES that the ASK has happened but MUST-CHOOSE not to act. One outcome of REFUSE is that R BELIEVES that A will not do X.

REQUEST

(*Mac requested that Ella sharpen the knife*)

Case structure
- agent: A
- recipient: R
- action: X
- time-request: t
- time-action: t′

Preconditions
- P1. A MUST-CHOOSE (A REQUEST R to X)
- P2. A WANTS (R CAUSE X)
- P3. A BELIEVES (R CAN X)
- P4. A BELIEVES (R TRY X))
- P5. A BELIEVES (R MUST-CHOOSE not-X)
- P6. $t < t'$

Outcome conditions
- 01. if not-(R CAUSE X)
  then R OUGHT (R EXPLAIN A Z X)
- 02. CONSEQUENCES (PC + OC)

Instances: will you . . . , could you . . .

Summary characterizations: request, ask

Figure 16: The social action REQUEST. REQUEST is a type of 'asking' which implies beliefs of A about R's intentions. A BELIEVES that R has a reason to do X but that MUST-CHOOSE is not true. The main purpose of the REQUEST is to change R's choosevalues so that R MUST-CHOOSE X will be true.

TEST

(*Stan tested Nell's knowledge of lacrosse*)

Case structure
agent: A
recipient: R
object: X
time-test: t

Preconditions
P1. A MUST-CHOOSE (A TEST X to R)
P2. A BELIEVES X
P3. A BELIEVES (R CHOOSE
((R INFORM A X t') or (R INFORM A not-X t')))
P4. $t < t'$
P5. not-(A BELIEVES (R BELIEVES X))
P6. not-(A BELIEVES (R BELIEVES not-X))

Outcome conditions
01. CONSEQUENCES (PC + OC)

Instances: who, what, where, etc.; tell me . . . , is . . . , did . . .

Summary characterizations: test, ask

Figure 17: The social action TEST. Preconditions P5 and P6 state that the agent does not BELIEVE either that R BELIEVES or does not BELIEVE X. Thus his asking is an attempt to ascertain part of R's beliefs.

THANK

(*Frank thanked Nancy for the volleyball*)

Case structure
agent: A
recipient: R
action: X
time-thank: t
time-action: t′

Preconditions
P1. A MUST-CHOOSE (A THANK R X)
P2. A BELIEVES (R CAUSE X)
P3. A WANT (R CAUSE X)
P4. $t' < t$

Outcome conditions
01. CONSEQUENCES (PC + OC)
02. R KNOW(is-aware-of) (A WANT (R CAUSE X))

Instances: thank

Summary characterizations: thank

Figure 18: The social action, THANK. THANK occurs when A BELIEVES that R has done an action which A WANTS. One consequence is that R is aware of the fact that A wanted R to do the action.

THREATEN

(*Norman threatened to leave the party if Pat wouldn't stop singing*)

Case structure
agent: A
recipient: R
action: X
r-action: Z
time-threaten: t
time-action: t'
time-r-action: t''

Preconditions
P1. A MUST-CHOOSE (A THREATEN X to R)
P2. A CAN X
P3. A BELIEVES (R BELIEVES (A CAN X))
P4. A BELIEVES not-(R WANT (A CAUSE X))
P5. A BELIEVES (R CAN Z)
P6. A BELIEVES (R CHOOSE Z)
P7. A WANT not-(R CAUSE Z)
P8. A BELIEVES (R BELIEVES not-(A WANT (R CAUSE Z)))
P9. $t < t''$
P10. $t'' < t'$

Outcome conditions
01. CONSEQUENCES (PC + OC)

Instances: you better not . . . , I warn you

Summary characterizations: threaten

Figure 19: The social action THREATEN. THREATEN is a complex social action which is related to the 'asking' concepts because it involves A's seeking to influence R's action. Most of the preconditions fall into two categories, those relating to A's THREATENED action (P2-P4) and those relating to R's action (P5-P8).

WARN

(*Leslie warned Fran about the troll*)

Case structure
agent: A
recipient: R
action: X
time-warn: t
time-action: t′

Preconditions
P1. A MUST-CHOOSE (A WARN X to R)
P2. A BELIEVES not-(R WANT (OUTCOMES X))
P3. A BELIEVES
(some Z)((R CAN Z) and
(if (R CAUSE Z) then not-X))
P4. A SENTIMENT R or A UNIT R
P5. $t < t'$

Outcome conditions
01. CONSEQUENCES (PC + OC)

Instances: you better not, I warn you

Summary characterizations: warn

Figure 20: The social action WARN. WARN is an action whereby A attempts to get R to act in such a way that R avoids actions which A BELIEVES have OUTCOMES which R does not WANT. A must have some SENTIMENT (e.g., 'likes') or UNIT (e.g., 'family') relationship to R.

Part II

Notating the language of music, and the (pause) rhythms of speech

WALTER A. SEDELOW JR. and SALLY YEATES SEDELOW

Encoding

As crucial as any social development in human history was the emergence of non-analog codes. That development can be sub-divided into a number of phases: perhaps the grossest distinction would be between the representation of number and the representation of other forms of human symbolism (although some of the 'fuzziness' research of Lotfi Zadeh [e.g., Zadeh 1979] and his students, and others [e.g., Gaines – Kohout 1977] – by implication – renders problematic certain traditional hard-edged distinctions between numericality and qualitativeness). Traditionally the distinction between the spoken and the written had been taken for the most important division: but it is at least arguable that now we can see the distinction between number symbolism and non-number symbolism as the most critical, Zadehan accomplishments to the contrary notwithstanding.[1]

Underlying all these forms of representation are the consequences for the human species of non-analogality. While the distinction between analog representations and non-analog representations is crucial, nonetheless it does need to be noted that we may construe analogality as having degrees distributed over an analogality/non-analogality (dis)continuum. Even (literally) seeing the physical world – in some crucial senses an analog experience – involves learning, although, on the whole, more so when what is being seen is being seen as a convention. A person blind from birth who through surgical intervention or otherwise suddenly gains sight has to learn, even apart from understanding verbal mediation (e.g., billboards; books), to make sense of (analog) visual experience. And that obtains all the more so for those components of visual experience which though analog nonetheless of necessity must contain some element of conventionality; also, such learning is, *a fortiori*, far greater and more demanding when parts of the visual realm are treated as conventions which are not analog.

One may contend that the history of consciousness, or of symbolism, or even of the human brain, taken collectively, is marked by increasing consciousness or, thus, self-consciousness.[2] Put another way, it is a matter of building ever more abstract models – as with, to take a paradigmatic case, the logical modelling of mathematics. Phenomenology, ethnomethodology, computation-

Computers in Language Research 2

al linguistics, and numerous other modes (e.g., W.A. Sedelow, Jr. 1957) of self-consciousness about symbolism, have bit by bit – that is to say, word by word – rendered more and more of our uses of language problematic. But, to this point, the approach to problematicity has been piecemeal. Now the question is whether it would not be useful to achieve for the first time a culture-scale paradigm shift by rendering problematic all representation – or, at least, all non-analog representation. The 'usefulness' in question may be thought of as deriving from a purely intellectual exfoliation of ideas (that is, a 'next stage' in the drama of the history of thought); but it also may be understood to derive from the current situation of our species, wherein the (literal) globalization of CCNs (*C*omputer *C*ommunication *N*etworks) is leading to a trans-veridicalization of heretofore culturally-defined notions of 'truth,' and other word-length language strings in a sub-lexicon with 'truth.'[3] That is, the arbitrariness of the non-analog 'character sets' (e.g., alphabets; syllabaries) vis-à-vis each other, and of their respective rules of usage (i.e., constrained combinatorics), is brought closer to consciousness (i.e., less adequately defended against, psychoanalytically speaking) with the (increasing) constant mutual juxtaposition of such sets of symbolism by way of the development of modern computing/telecommunications and informatics. What holds at the level of the "medium" (McLuhan) holds *a fortiori* at the level of the "message," and so now we are seeing the beginnings of an uneven but world-wide transveridicalization which goes far beyond its earlier partial parallel in the 'transvaluation of values.' *Truths* in particular and *truth* in general are shown to be cultural fictions masquerading as givens of a mythic 'Nature' peculiar to each culture. (Problems with intercultural mapping – that is, with *translations* and, more technically, with *commensurability*[4] – exacerbate our awareness of specific cultural arbitrariness with symbolism, and end by raising issues of how communicative are our socially available symbolisms for communication, if, indeed 'communication' is the word.[5] Are those symbologies, on balance and globally speaking, more dysfunctionally divisive than they are cohesive in effect? And, thus [in that way among others] not contributing to effective species adaptation to [dynamically changing] environment contraints?)

While there are some few resemblances in the early forms of Chinese ideographs to the objects which they were meant to represent and while we have onomatopoeia – or, more exactly, the imputation of it – as an occasional phenomenon in language, fundamentally in both the oral and written modes, as well as others, and with reference to both number systems and the character sets for non-numeric representations, the elements are not analog in character. With the exception of certain recent highly formal systems of notation these non-analog sets of notational elements and 'rules' for their use also have emerged without over-all plan or purpose. The perception that language is a social construct is itself an achievement of recent centuries. It is not, after all, so many centuries ago when language was thought to be not a construct but a given (even, in some cases, a God-given).

Thus, there should be no possible imputation of contrivance to achieve social control in the emergence of non-analog symbolism, although at various points in time there may very well be those who do perceive the social implications, and especially the control implications, of particular types of notation, and who may wish to hold on to whatever presumptive advantages of restriction of access those types of notation may be believed to have or to be susceptible of being used for. So, then, without any utilization of the vocabulary of intentionality (now hopelessly outmoded, in any case, and in every case, anyway, Speech Act Theory (Searle, *et al.*) to the contrary notwithstanding[6]), we may take note of the essentially hieratic quality produced by all non-analog representations and – given that non-analogality is always a matter of degree on a scale – of some measure of the hieratic even in analog representations, even (in the case at the limit) in simple human optical experiences.

Today the issue of 'non-analogality' is the general form of expression for a widespread series of crises of confidence in what is being generated using such notation. These crises of confidence as to how much professional users of symbolism actually 'know' (e.g., economists) have become the more acute in view of the high rate of technological/cultural/social change which is exposing the extent to which what has been ostensibly significant knowledge in fact has been at best highly contingent and often merely descriptive, or ex post facto (i.e., non-knowledge); as to the character and analysis of scientificity, see Sedelow – Sedelow 1979 and 1978, and, also, W.A. Sedelow, Jr. 1968. The arrival, primarily through television, but, earlier, through motion pictures, of widely accessible and highly potent analog representations of reality is also behind the major challenge to non-analog modes of representation, and (by necessary extension) the challenge to Establishment purveyors of instances of such representation (as through churches, schools and universities, etc.); the dynamics of United States changing popular response to the Vietnam War constitute an interesting subject of study from this perspective.

One of the critically important features of the traditions of non-analog symbolism has been the effort to create (the illusion of) a separation of the perception of what is symbolic from the perception of what is a part of physical reality. It even may be argued that a part of the basic, most basic even, social construction of reality through the use of symbolism has been the tacit, and, more recently, the overt, perception of it (i.e., symbolism) as something other than physical, i.e., the (social) invention of the non-physical, or, alternatively, the devising of 'immateriality' by way of synonymies and sub-lexicons of *spirituality, ideas, symbolism*, and the like. Just as in the largest perspective professional symbol users derived from, historically, those who in the past have fulfilled essentially priestly functions in societies, so too does the concept of symbolism derive from the emphasis on a 'non-material' which has been a part of the verbal stock-in-trade available for generically priestly tasks.

Further, in a world which technology is making more fully and compactly one, the presence and use of non-analog representations has the effect of separating (*per contra:* many of the recent analog international 'symbols of the road,' for automotive vehicle drivers). Thus, in addition to the fundamental issue posed by non-analog representation and the possible resolution of that issue by a decline in non-analog representation, and in addition to an issue as to the relative significance of non-quantitative – or, more precisely, non-formal and non-algorithmic – uses of symbolism vis-à-vis other uses of symbolism, there is the third and critical development of a greater understanding of 'symbolism' through the use of physical models (e.g., Arbib et al. 1982).[7] The chapters in this part of the book are notable for their contribution to, and understanding of, symbolism in its physical manifestation, and also for their contribution to the increasing formality of such understanding – a formality which is enhanced by the use of the computer, to which it also contributes or, rather, which it makes possible.

At least since the time of Francis Bacon there has been a clear understanding of how subject to illusions of their own manufacture academic intellectuals can be. Now, the most troublesome of those illusions is that to 'understand' talk we need to generate more talk after 'thinking,' as opposed to conducting classically scientific investigations. Wilbur Marshall Urban, in the Yale Philosophy Department in an earlier day., wrote that language was the last and deepest problem of the philosophic mind (Urban 1939). With that we may well agree, while still perceiving that what Urban said was truer than he knew, and harder to cope with. That is, while Urban understood that issues in philosophy must be dealt with as matters of language, he seems not to have understood that matters of language, in turn, are going to be understood with physical models applied to, *inter alia*, biological phenomena. Helpful though Ogden and Richards' *The meaning of meaning* (1923) was in its day, by now it – for example – serves as a barrier to understanding that the meaning of meaning is not simply reflection and talk, but rather the impacts of particular verbal strings within varying fields of force (both within and outside the central nervous system, but necessarily always perceived wholly within it, and perceived through the mediation of inter-codal contrast).

In addition to the very substantial importance which each chapter in this part of this book has in its own right, there is the further advantage and significance to them that goes with the way in which they are able to exemplify how to move toward formality with all dimensions of all lingual strings – in virtue of helping us to obtain distance from our own language uses and thus ready us for perceiving them through a formalist paradigm. The rigorous analysis of non-semantic – or, more precisely, what heretofore usually has not been regarded as semantic – dimensions of verbal language, (i.e., pauses), and the effort at finding notation and rules of usage for characterizing a non-verbal language (i.e., music) which, nonetheless, partakes through the musicality of verbal language in a close association with it are highly advantageous, in their own right and also as part of the larger and socially important enterprise of *understanding* language (only) for the differential physical impacts (intra-cranial and extra-cranial) of varying symbol strings in the interaction of biological systems (in this case, human) with their (total) environments. (Compare William James's meaning of a language string as all the practical differences it makes, as expounded in *Pragmatism* [1907] and elsewhere.)

Language of all sorts is no less and no more than patterned energy. That energy is subject to Fourier decomposition at varying 'levels.' John Smith's work has shown, *vide supra*, some of the ways in which that can be done; W.A. Sedelow (1957) forecast others. Those Fourier techniques also would be applicable to the understanding of both the music and the pause patterns which are the subject of immediate discussion in the chapters which follow. Similarly, just as the pause patterns (e.g. rests, phrasing stops) in the written or published musical composition or in any of its performances may be studied for (the musically semantic freight carried by) their pauses, spoken versions of the text could be represented by musical notation without reference to the 'meaning' of what was spoken. Such an idea is not entirely "novum sub solem": Janos Jánaček and Robert Frost, composer and poet, were each interested – though informally and creatively – in such mappings back and forth between the encodings that are speech and those that are music. (See Jánaček 1955, and Thompson et al. 1966-76).

These papers differ in respect of the bounding of precision in their analytic domains; in the pausological analysis no upper bound is postulated, and the successful reconstitution of the data in its original form out of its notated representation would be aspiring to completeness, so that no information would be dropped (i.e., a version of the scientific test of reproducibility, or synthesis, by rule). By a kind of Turing Test, complete success would mean complete indistinguishability in the two forms, the original and its resynthesis, with reference to the dimensions in question. But as to the music, a close approximation is all that is aspired to – and that is, of course, all that even traditional musical notation has hoped to achieve. For music, within the limits set by notation, variation in what is not notated – as well as, of course, sometimes, with reference to some features of what is notated – provides the bases for qualitative discriminations.

Notes

1. A challenge to this distinction which is by far more consequential than even the impressive results of the 'fuzziness' research is the growing and great strength of work in the mathematical logic and model-theoretic tradition of Gottlob Frege (e.g., Geach – Black (eds.) 1952, esp. pp. 56–78 [Frege's "Über Sinn und Bedeutung," as "On sense and reference"]) and, then, Alonzo Church (e.g., Church 1940, 1951, 1956) (the Lambda Calculus), to date culminating in the 'Grammar' of Richard Montague (e.g., Dowty et al. 1981, and Dowty 1979; also, Bryan 1980, and Godden 1980). With this approach (wherein, in the manner of Montague, semantics and syntax are treated as isomorphic) we have the pregnant implication of the fact that both 'natural' language expressions and mathematical (e.g., programmed) language expressions are automatically transformable into a formal (and, thus, 'machineable') model with the same logical apparatus. Almost precisely a century ago Frege had, *mutatis mutandis*, in his functionality argument some view down this prospect, which by way of Church (the Lambda Calculus) and Montague and now Montague's intellectual heirs (such as Robert Bryan) is being clarified and effectuated – in part through the consequences of Montague's rejections of precisely the formulations of natural language expressions being either too rich or, *per contra*, too trivial for effective formal-logical transformation. Now, thusly, we are able to detect and act upon their essential comparability. And such a residual knotty problem as suitable 'framing' for metaphoric statement (as in the exemplary case of *Birch Bayh didn't get to first base*) may come to be by-passed or rendered by means of fuzzy topological structures (Isai and Kumimura). So, then, now we see an interesting and significant sort of convergence between the Zadehan and the Montaguean *traditios*. Consider, also, the implications of Benson 1979.
2. E.g., Erich Kahler 1970, and, especially, the translation of his "Die Verinnerlichung des Erzählens" by Richard and Clara Winston (Kahler 1973).
3. See W.A. Sedelow, Jr. 1982.
4. See Feyerabend 1978; also, Fish 1980; as well as Ortony (ed.) 1979; Brown 1978; and of course, Kuhn 1962 (and revised edition, 1970), noting, however, his 'recantations,' as in Kuhn 1978.
5. The elucidation of the associations, semantics, and entailments of the dubious concept "communication" probably can not be successfully undertaken without heavy 'theoretic' borrowings from the psychoanalytically-inspired Object-Relations literature, especially in the British tradition – inasmuch as the latent mythopoeic content of that concept is laden with unresolved 'Kleinian' issues, as to separation, and, then, a mythopoeic re-integration by means of the fantasy of communication.
6. Note the neo-Aristotelianism through a purposive lexicon in Searle 1975.
7. One facet of that third development is, then, the possible prospective elimination of many non-analog symbolic strings from various of the globe's cultures – by way of discovering that they lack algorithmic utility in facilitating stable relationships to environment, and also by way of discovering that they establish factitious and arbitrary partitions among the world's peoples through the differential generation and distribution of specious entities (e.g., hypostases; reifications).

References

Arbib, Michael, et al.
1982 *Neural models of language processes* (New York: McGraw-Hill).

Benson, David B.
1979 "Formal language vis-à-vis 'natural languages'", *Computers in language research: Formal methods* (= *Trends in linguistics, Studies and monographs* 5), edited by Walter A. Sedelow, Jr., and Sally Yeates Sedelow (The Hague: Mouton), 97-164.

Brown, Richard H.
1978 *A poetic for sociology: Toward a logic of discovery for the Human Sciences* (London: Cambridge University Press).

Bryan, Robert M.
1980 "Elements of an improved treatment of tense, aspect, and temporal deixis in a Montague framework" (Ph.D. diss., University of Kansas) (also: *University Microfilms*, Ann Arbor).

Church, Alonzo
1940 "A formulation of a simple theory of types", *Journal of symbolic logic* 5: 56-68.
1951 "A formulation of the logic of sense and denotation", *Structure, meaning and method*, edited by P. Henle et al. (New York: Liberal Arts), 3-24.
1956 *Introduction to mathematical logic* (Princeton: Princeton University Press).

Dowty, David R.
1979 *Word meaning and Montague Grammar* (Dordrecht: D. Reidel).

Dowty, David R., et al.
1981 *Introduction to Montague semantics* (Dordrecht: D. Reidel).

Feyerabend, Paul
1978 *Against method* (London: NLB).

Fish, Stanley
1980 *Is there a text in this class?, The authority of interpretative communication* (Cambridge, Mass.: Harvard University Press).

Gaines, B.R. – L.J. Kohout
1977 "The fuzzy decade: A bibliography of Fuzzy Systems and closely related topics", *International journal of Man-machine studies* 9: 1-68.

Geach, Peter T. – Max Black (eds.)
1952 *Translations from the philosophical writings of Gottlob Frege* (Oxford: Blackwell).

Godden, Kurt S.
1980 "Montague Grammar and machine translation between Thai and English" (Ph.D. diss., University of Kansas) (also: *University Microfilms*, Ann Arbor).

James, William
1907 *Pragmatism* (New York: Longmans, Green and Co.).

Jánaček, Janos Leoš
1955 *O lidové písni a lidové hudbě: Dokumenty a studie* [About folk songs and folk music: Documentation and studies] (Praha: H. Státní nakl. krásnéliteratury, Hudby A. Uměni).

Kahler, Erich
1970 *Untergang und Übergang* (München: Deutscher Taschenbuch Verlag).

1973 *The inward turn of narrative* (= Die Verinnerlichung des Erzählens), translated by Richard and Clara Winston (Princeton: Princeton University Press).

Kuhn, Thomas
1962 *The structure of scientific revolutions* (Chicago: University of Chicago Press; revised edition: 1970).
1978 *Black-body theory and quantum discontinuity; 1894-1912* (Oxford: Oxford University Press).

Ogden, C.K. – I.A. Richards
1923 *The meaning of meaning* London: Routledge & Kegan Paul).

Ortony, Andrew (ed.)
1979 *Metaphor and thought* (Cambridge: Cambridge University Press).

Searle, John R.
1975 "Minds, brains, and programs", *Mind, language and reality* vol. 2 (Cambridge: Cambridge University Press).

Sedelow, Jr., Walter A.
1957 "History as language, an essay at a new historiography, with special reference to David Hume's *History of England*" (Ph.D. diss., Harvard University).
1968 "History as language", *Computer studies* 1.4: 183–190.
1982 "Toward a globalization of the sociology of language", *Proceedings of the 5th Annual Third World Conference* 5, edited by Mavis C. Bauman (Columbus, Ohio: OCLC), 1–13.

Sedelow, Jr., Walter A. – Sally Yeates Sedelow
1978 "Formalized historiography", *Journal of the history of the behavioral sciences* 14: 247–263.
1979 "The history of science as discourse", *Journal of the history of the behavioral sciences* 15: 63–72.

Thompson, Lawrence, et al.
1966–76 *Robert Frost*, 3 vols (New York: Holt, Rinehart & Winston).

Urban, Wilbur Marshall
1939 *Language and reality: The philosophy of language and the principles of Symbolism* (New York: Macmillan).

Zadeh, Lotfi A.
1979 "Precisiation of human communication via transcription into PRUF" (= Memorandum M 79/73, Electronics Research Laboratory, University of California, Berkeley).

RAYMOND ERICKSON and ANTHONY B. WOLFF

The DARMS Project: implementation of an artificial language for the representation of music

1 Introduction: music, mathematics, and language

1.1 Historical precedents

When, in the fourth century B.C., Plato described music as consisting of the rhythm, the harmony and the words (1961: 643) he implied an interdependence of elements of mathematics, music and language. Such interrelationships had existed long before Plato's time and still exist today, although their nature has, understandably, varied with cultural context. It is the purpose of this paper to describe one contemporary endeavor that demonstrates how the modern concepts of music, mathematics and language have interacted with one another. However, in order to put the matter in perspective, there is first offered a brief overview of historical precedents.

Throughout the history of Western man, the relationship between music and mathematics has been contemplated with the most serious interest. This tradition antedates the sixth century B.C. when the philosopher Pythagoras, so the well-known story goes, 'discovered' that certain musical intervals could be expressed in whole-number, super-particular[1] ratios. On this basis was predicted a cosmic harmony that held a band-box universe in stable balance, a concept – one of the most important in the history of occidental thought – that was proved chimerical only by the discoveries of Copernicus, Kepler and Newton more than two thousand years later. Therefore, it is not surprising to learn that Plato, in his inspired *Timaeus*, described the creation of the universe in terms of the mathematics of music; that the geometric axioms of Euclid's *Elements* and the music-theoretic system of the *Harmonics* of Aristoxenus (a pupil of Aristotle and the first important music theorist) were both products of late fourth century Greek mathematics;[2] and that music was taught as a branch of mathematics in the medieval and renaissance universities. (Regarding the latter, it should be pointedly noted that a trivium of studies in the language sciences of grammar, logic and rhetoric was prerequisite to the study of music and the other mathematical arts.)

Computers in Language Research 2

During the Age of Reason the traditional mathematical basis of music (relieved of some of the cosmological overtones) continued to be maintained – witness the *Compendium Musicae* (1618) of René Descartes. However, new scientific methods soon unearthed further evidence that mathematics provided useful tools for explaining musical phenomena; thus, the discovery of the harmonic series in musical sound by Mersenne and others in the seventeenth century provided the scientific 'justification' (however weak) for the Cartesian harmonic theory of Jean-Philippe Rameau (1722), which is still today the basis for the teaching of 'traditional harmony.'[3] On the other hand, composers, philosophers and critics of the Romantic Age of the nineteenth century tended to value music for its ability to express feeling rather than for its relationship to science. Nevertheless, even Schopenhauer, in whose philosophical system music is a 'universal language' leading to a direct understanding of the world, wrote that "its forms may be reduced to perfectly definite rules expressed in numbers, from which it cannot free itself without entirely ceasing to be music . . ." (1818:268).

The close bonds between music and language are equally apparent. In the ancient world language and music were so intimately connected that Aristotle (1959) remarked that there was such a thing as poetry without music, but that it did not even have a name. For him, the study of music was perforce the study of poetry, drama and language. In the Renaissance and Baroque ages, when the humanistic concern for words and language resulted in pictorial and affective representation and delivery of text, music was increasingly described (and composers were exhorted to compose) in rhetorical and poetic terms.[4] And as early as the eighteenth century Johannes Mattheson (1739) adumbrated the linguistic approach to musical description when he likened the structural and syntactic aspects of a musical composition to those of an oration.[5]

1.2 Twentieth-century viewpoints

After the relatively brief anti-scientific Romantic movement of the nineteenth century alluded to above, the importance of the relationships among music, language and mathematics has been reasserted in the twentieth century. This has resulted from the confluence of distinctly modern ideas flowing from logic, set theory, linguistics, ethnomusicology, music theory, composition, and computer technology. To exemplify this, there follows a brief discussion of three aspects of music – *performance, structure* and *notation* – with which new interrelationshiops of mathematics and language (more precisely, linguistics) have recently been established.

Until modern times, there was no means of preserving musical *performance* and therefore no means of analyzing or representing it in any systematic way. Today, however, ethnomusicologists have attempted to do precisely that. One such endeavor is the formalization of Swedish nursery tunes with a set of 'fundamental rules of linguistic prosody' by Lindblom and Sundberg (1970). However, a more comprehensive approach to the whole question of systematically describing musical performance is to be seen in the newly blossoming research area of semiotics.[6]

The twentieth century has also seen the birth of a number of theoretical systems that provide analytic and terminological tools for studying and regenerating the *structure* of Western 'classical' music. In particular, the system of Heinrich Schenker (1935) takes as axiomatic a small set of *Ursätze* and specifies what are in essence a set of re-write rules, thereby attempting to account for all 'tonal music'.[7] This approach is highly reminiscent of a formal grammar. Michael Kassler (1967) has undertaken to explore the question of decidability for this system, that is, the strictly mathematical question of whether, given some piece of music, there exists a proof of either membership of that piece of music in the set of all possible Schenker-generated pieces.

While results on Schenkerian decidability are not yet known, even should the system be proved decidable, such a system could generate only a consistently tonal subset of all pieces of Western music, and could not generate the subtleties of notation contained in most western scores since the middle of the eighteenth century. It is doubtful indeed that there will ever be a formal grammar capable of generating all musically meaningful scores in complete form.

The difficulties of deriving such a hypothetical system are similar to those encountered in specifying a complete and consistent grammar for, say, English. Commonly, English is considered a 'natural' language, to be distinguished from such deliberate human constructs as FORTRAN, PL/1 and DARMS, all of which are known as 'artificial' languages. While this binary distinction sometimes serves a purpose, it is not always possible to classify a linguistic object as being purely natural or artificial. While the lexicon and grammar of Esperanto are defined *a priori* by 'inventors', the semantic information to be conveyed arises as naturally for an Esperantophone as for an Anglophone. Thus, the classification of Esperanto as either natural or artificial is not easy to make and perhaps is not even meaningful.

Music notation also presents such a classification problem, and its formalization is that area of recent concern which is of greatest interest here. In the past, the notation of music served to convey musical ideas to a *human* reader (and/or performer) of the score. However, the contemporary realization that computers could be of value in a wide variety of commercial and scholarly applications has motivated intense interest in programming computer-driven optical scanners to 'read' musical scores, and in developing procedures for 'translating' musical scores into machine-readable form. While the former goal is, as yet, only partially fulfilled,[8] the latter has become feasible because of advances in pertinent fields of mathematics, computation linguistics and technology.

It should be stressed at the outset that the conversion of 'sounding music' into a symbolic or internally-stored form is not at issue here: it is highly unlikely that the information in a musical score will ever be completely retrievable from a human performance, no matter how 'definitive'. On the other hand, the task of converting a musical score into machine readable form is not a matter of defining a one-to-one correspondence between a music-notational symbol (the definition of which is itself a problem) and some machine-readable character or character string. In fact, such a one-to-one mapping appears to be impossible due to the continuous nature of certain notation symbols (e.g., slurs). Furthermore, although not a discursive (i.e. 'natural') language, music notation has evolved over many centuries, in the process acquiring rich semantic implication and structural characteristics not tolerable in a strictly artificial language.

The reader may question the practicality or even the validity of devising an artificial language to represent something as fraught with structural inconsistencies and ambiguities as music notation and, indeed, the authors are aware that artificial languages are not universally applicable analytical tools. Nonetheless, it may be pointed out that systems as diverse as psychoanalysis and optical illusion have been modeled with artificial language constructs.[9] Furthermore, Professor Hao Wang has suggested criteria under which devising an artificial language may be appropriate or not:

> We might speak of degrees of artificiality as perhaps measured by the amount of deviation from the natural course [. . .] To introduce artificial language is to make revolution. Unless there are compelling *natural needs* [our italics], the resistence will be strong and the proposal will fail. On the other hand, when an artificial language meets existing urgent problems, it will soon get generally accepted and be no longer considered artificial. Hence, it may be more to the point if we compare artificial languages with Utopian projects. (1955: 200).

The DARMS Project represents an attempt to specify the representation of music notation as a consistent and complete artificial language, namely DARMS, and to implement a set of DARMS translator programs, or compilers, on a digital computer. There are some who may regard this as a 'Utopian project', yet it must be noted that it came into existence in order to satisfy certain concrete needs that will be subsequently detailed. Thus, those who have worked on the DARMS project have had an *a priori* reason to consider music in linguistic terms. Given the idiosyncratic nature of music and its notation, both the theoretical basis of DARMS, which is the work of Stefan Bauer-Mengelberg, and the practical problems of design and implementation, which will be dealt with here, will be of interest to both the linguist and computer scientist.

Therefore, in the sections that follow, there will be taken up in turn the historical evolution of the DARMS Project, a condensed grammatical description of the language, and representative psycholinguistic problems encountered in the implementation of DARMS. By discussing these matters in some detail, the authors hope to document the progress of one contemporary endeavor grounded in the interrelationship of music, language and mathematics which is, as has been suggested, so rich in historical precedent.

2 History of the DARMS Project

The DARMS Project was originally conceived in 1961 when Stefan Bauer-Mengelberg and Melvin Ferentz decided to collaborate on an attempt to develop an automated music-printing process. As is well known, the consumer cost of published musical scores has risen dramatically in recent years, one of the principal causes of this increase being the ever-decreasing number of professional music engravers. Indeed, almost no musical engraving is done in the United States today and so American publishers must rely on the diminishing number of European craftsmen when they wish to have a score produced by engravery. This is an expensive process and most publishers are chary of investing considerable sums of money to have the composition of lesser known and younger composers engraved, preferring instead the cheaper and less elegant method of autography. However, this can have an adverse effect on such a work's chances of being performed. Bauer-Mengelberg and Ferentz envisioned that, if their work bore fruit, both consumer and contemporary composer might benefit.

With the objective of developing the means to produce, under computer control, scores that would be comparable in quality to engraved music and, with a Ford Foundation grant administered through Columbia University, the DARMS Project was officially launched in 1964. Bauer-Mengelberg, a musician and mathematician, undertook to design a machine-readable code for the representation of musical notation. Originally known as the "Ford-Columbia Music Represention", its name was later changed, in honor of a benefactor of the project, to the terser "DARMS", which was interpreted as an acronym for "Digital-Alternate Representation of Musical Scores". Ferentz, on the other hand, occupied himself with certain technical and hardware aspects of producing a master score that could be reproduced at low cost.

There consequently ensued an extremely thorough investigation of the syntax of music notation and of the unwritten conventions that govern musical graphics, resulting in criteria for a music encoding standard; these became the guidelines followed in the subsequent design and implementation of DARMS. Thus the Ford-Columbia Music Representation – that is, the earliest form of DARMS – was from the time of its conception intended to capture accurately all the information provided by the composer but not those details of layout within the province of the engraver or autographer.

During the early years of the DARMS Project, a large number of competing encoding systems were developed for musicological research,[10] but the very comprehensiveness of the DARMS system soon attracted the attention of music theorists and music historians, who began to disseminate information about DARMS within the scholarly community. Eventually, this led to a two-week seminar in the summer of 1966 at Harpur College (SUNY-Binghamton).[11] Attended by 32 musicologists from the U.S., Canada and Europe, most of whom had had no previous contact with computers, the seminar spawned a number of research projects that have since been documented[12] and caused DARMS to become the most widely used of encoding systems for music.

Although the process of expanding and refining the facilities of DARMS has been, up to very recently, a constantly ongoing one, the absence of software support has necessarily limited the kind of music that could be encoded error-free and the analytical problems that could be tackled. Attempts to remedy this were initiated in 1970 with work on a syntax-error detection program for DARMS datasets and a codification of the language in a manual that became available in 1971.[13] Although now outdated, this document provided a focus for discussion and caused to be brought to light lacunae and inconsistencies in the encoding facilities, so that by the summer of 1973 it was possible to encode in DARMS most of the music written or published since about the year 1600.

With this richer and more stable syntax in hand, the authors commenced to develop two large computer programs for processing DARMS datasets. The first of these, known as the Syntax Checker, accepts as input the raw data supplied by the user and detects all syntactic and some few semantic errors therein. After all such errors have been purged, the corrected dataset may be processed by the second program, known as the Canonizer, which converts the user-DARMS dataset into a canonical-DARMS dataset. Canonical DARMS is a form of DARMS which, by virtue of rigidly defined precedence, facilitates subsequent machine processing of the encoded information.[14]

Since both these programs are designed to process the same source language (i.e., user-DARMS), the initial stage of the parse is shared in the form of a 'front end' program which, in a bottom-up manner (that is, proceeding from the leaves to the root of the syntax tree), recognizes and classifies, in turn, each token of the input stream. A table-driven device, this program also serves the usual functions of the scanner element of a compiler, such as the elimination of gratuitous blanks. A few rudimentary syntactic errors are also recognized at this stage.

Upon recognition of a particular token by the 'front end', a subroutine call is made to a program specifically written, in the case of the Syntax Checker, to search the token systematically for possible error and, in the case of the Canonizer, to translate the token into an intermediate representation. Since these specialized subroutines are *ipso facto* given the *root* of the relevant syntactic sub-tree, they continue parsing the tokens, which are their input, in a 'top-down' manner. While purely top-down parses have become more popular of late in the processing of programming languages, the general parse of DARMS, seen to be a bottom-up, then top-down procedure, follows the natural 'fault lines' of the language.

The Syntax Checker functions as an independent first stage of a compiler: it generates as output not an equivalent of the input data but, rather, a body of natural language messages specifying the nature and location of obvious errors or unusual conditions in the input data. A preliminary but abortive attempt to develop a DARMS Syntax Checker dates from 1970, when the attempt was made to implement a table-driven, syntax-directed compiler that had proven quite useful in a previous musicological investigation (Erickson 1970).[15] But, whereas the relatively simple notational system involved in this study proved easily formalizable in a BNF-type meta-language, modern notation did not. Thus, the initial parsing mechanism was abandoned in favor of that described above.

As is the case with many programming language compilers, several levels of conditions are recognized by the Syntax Checker. Unequivocal errors of syntax (e.g. the attributes of a note not being encoded in the correct order specified in Table 3 of Part 3 of this paper) cause an ERROR message to be generated. Certain semantic conditions (e.g., a conflict between the durational values in a measure and the meter signature; or lack of closure within a certain limit of a beam, slur, tie or some similar symbol of horizontal extent) prompt WARNING messages. Finally, conditions arising primarily from insufficient dimensioning of variables or arrays within the program (e.g., too many Instruments, active beams or any other category of symbol requiring Identifiers described in Part 3) produce PROGRAM RESTRICTION messages.

'Canonization' is accomplished in several passes over the input (a corrected user-DARMS dataset), during which a number of intermediate representations and data-structures are used. In the first major pass all defaults and abbreviations are expanded to 'full spelling' while numerical identifiers are in most cases submitted to a hashing function in order to insure uniqueness in the final Canonical form. In particular, DARMS structures of inter-token extent (slurs, beams, long hairpin dynamics, etc.) require considerable processing at this stage. Chord structures must be converted to vertical structures of single notes delimited by commas (section 3.2.1) and the information within each vertical slice must be reordered from bottom to top. A host of other data conversions, data distribution and data suppression tasks must be accomplished. Finally, the layers of Linear Decomposition Mode (section 3.1), for each musical passage so encoded, are merged into vertical slices, even though the information for every vertical slice may have been widely scattered throughout the user-DARMS dataset.

Following are three examples of fragments encoded in user-DARMS followed by their respective canonical forms.

User-DARMS: 2QL 3
Canonical-DARMS: 22QUL1000 23QUL2000

User-DARMS: (1 (2))
Canonical-DARMS: 21EU(B1 (B1 22SUB2))

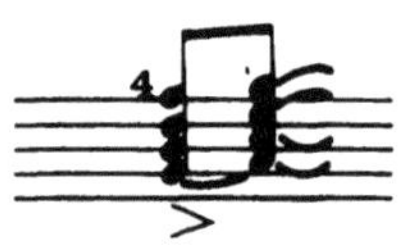

User-DARMS: (!|1|3|5|7|9FW4|UL>|1,4|J)
Canonical-DARMS: 23EUO(B1L1>,25EUOB1,27EUOB1, 29EUOB1FW4
24EJUOB2)L2,26EJUOB2), 28EJUOB2),
30EJUOB2)

The above examples, in addition to illustrating the results of canonization, also demonstrate the power of the user-DARMS abbreviation facilities and defaults. It should also be stated that, as a result of canonization, all of the many possible correct encodings of a composition in user-DARMS will have but one form in canonical-DARMS.

Encoding, error-detection and corrrection, and canonization are all necessary steps in the preparation of data for the various applications of the DARMS system, brief descriptions of which follow.

2.1 Automated music printing

Ironic though it be, the original purpose of the DARMS system has been the most difficult to fulfill, although considerable progress has been made since 1972. One investigation in this area has been done by David A. Gomberg who in a recent dissertation (1975) describes a set of programs, using as input a canonical-DARMS dataset, to determine the exact placement of symbols on a page of music. 'Music setting', as this process is called by engravers, is governed by a time-honored set of rules and conventions that are nowhere described in detail precise enough to be implemented directly. Indeed, it was only by working directly with a professional music editor that Gomberg was able to learn the procedures and criteria involved:

Our interactions have resembled those of artificial intelligence researchers and their subjects doing protocol analysis. Typically I would ask about a particular problem and the editor would tell me all he could think of about the problem. I would then attempt to draw some sort of generalizations that would be useful in constructing algorithms to deal with the problem. Most often I would find I had failed and, rather than ask the original question again, which likely would have elicited essentially no new information, I would look for examples which I could not yet handle. Armed with a stack of these, I would ask for individual solutions, and usually somewhere through them enough understanding on my part was generated so that general solutions could be stated. (Gomberg 1975:32)

The Gomberg programs attempt to simulate the human decision making process governing music setting. The human decisions occur at several levels of organization, moving from the largest to the smallest:

a. 'Casting off' involves the division of an entire score into lines of musical text, that is, it establishes, tentatively, how many measures of music will be in each line of each page. Being a kind of first approximation of how the music will eventually be distributed in the score, casting off is essentially a trial-and-error process.

b. When casting off has been done, the vertical placement of staves on a page is decided. Here the primary consideration is that symbols on one stave do not crowd those on the stave above or below it.

c. 'Punctuation' is the procedure determining the *exact* horizontal placement of notes and other symbols.

In Gomberg's implementation, these steps are somewhat reversed:

The approach taken in this project is to perform the initial punctuation as if an entire movement of a score were to be set on a single, very wide page [. . .] This *global* punctuation is performed in several passes over the input data structure. When completed, the casting-off process can be undertaken with great confidence; there will be no nasty surprises. With the page boundaries decided, a final *local* punctuation must be performed which is a fairly straightforward (nearly) linear expansion or contradiction of the existing global punctuation to fit the desired page width. (1975: 37ff.)

After this is done, beams, stems, articulation marks, ties, slurs and other symbols are added and then the vertical placement of the staves is computed.

Although the matter is too specialized to discuss at length here, it should be noted that the horizontal spacing of notes on the stave is a function of both the rhythmic structure of the score in question and conventions of musical graphics. Gomberg has implemented procedures for what is known in the language of music setting as "spine-formation," that is, the projection of all rhythmic data from all simultaneous voices or instruments onto one hypothetical voice; in other words, it is analogous, and arithmetically equivalent, to finding a common denominator of a set of fractions. For example, in the figure below, line *c* is the spine of lines *a* and *b*.

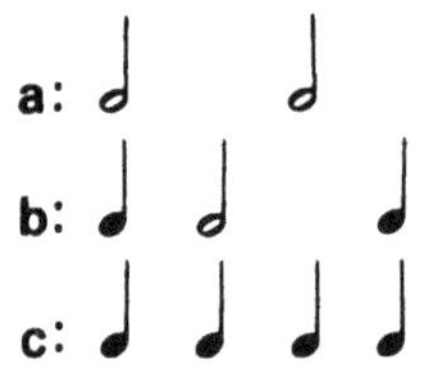

Figure 2.1

It is necessary to compute the spine of, say, a measure of music for tasks which involve the merging of two or more individual lines of music, as in assembling an orchestral score from the individual instrumental parts, or in reassembling the separately encoded layers of a section of music which has been encoded in DARMS using Linear Decomposition Mode (see section 3.1). In the example above the formation of the spine is of course trivial, but in order to deal with music of extraordinary rhythmic complexity, such as the *Double concerto* (1961) by Elliott Carter (the test piece for this research), the method for spine computation must be completely general. Gomberg regards the algorithm he developed to solve this problem as one of the major accomplishments of his research, for it is precisely in matter of layout that other attempts at computer-controlled music printing have failed most conspicuously.

Even when the score layout processing just described is completed, several other steps (not implemented at this writing) stand between it and the final product:

Production of proofs (under computer control),
proof reading ('by hand'),
part extraction (under computer control),
part layout processing,
production of final plates,
printing of score and parts.

In the original design, Bauer-Mengelberg and Ferentz thought of utilizing a programmable photo-composition device known as the Photon for the production of the final plates and, in fact, a type of Photon is being used in limited applications for this purpose.[16] All DARMS software, however, has been designed to be independent of a specific output device.

Recently there has been proposed a different kind of music printing application for DARMS, one that is made possible by the generality of DARMS itself, the formalization of canonical DARMS, and its independence of a specific printing device. This new role is the printing of music for the blind, using the facilities of the Library of Congress. A pilot project using simple choral music, processed by the IML-MIR system developed at Princeton University, has already shown the feasibility of a computer-driven Braille music printer (Patrick – Friedman 1975); however, since keyboard scores are those in greatest demand by sightless musicians, the most serviceable system will naturally be one designed to handle the complexities of keyboard music. Because DARMS from the outset was designed to represent all kinds of scores, regardless of notational complexity, a DARMS-to-Braille translator offers a promising and efficient method for transforming canonical DARMS datasets into input for the existing programmable Braille printers.

2.2 Musicological applications

2.2.1 Data band of DARMS-encoded scores

A sad but unavoidable condition of computational musicology is that a disproportionate amount of time must go into the preparation of data. The formation of a data bank of scores encoded in DARMS could reduce the duplication of effort that now exists. Because of its comprehensiveness DARMS is regarded by many as the most likely encoding standard for music. Of course, rigorous controls would have to be imposed to insure that all datasets in such a library were completely and correctly encoded. It might be added that once a dataset has been encoded, canonized and incorporated into the database, it could also be made available in Braille, at very little production cost, using the hardware cited above.

2.2.2 Computer-assisted style analysis

That music theorists and musicologists were attracted to DARMS early in its history has been mentioned above. However, there does not yet exist, in theory or implementation, a general-purpose system for the interrogation of the *musical* structure encoded in DARMS datasets. In the past several years, a number of theoretical systems, suitable or specifically designed for computer implementation, have been proposed[17] and there is at least one fully operational system (the IML-MIR system at Princeton University) for the analysis of Renaissance music (see Mendel 1969; 1973). However, none of these has so fully developed a grammar and syntax as DARMS and so the building of a comparable analytic system around DARMS should be approached with great circumspection.

Three avenues of approach therefore present themselves. In following the first, the researcher would design his own music-analytic programs, written in any appropriate general-purpose programming language, to operate on canonical-DARMS datasets. Taking the second path, he would need a translator to convert the canonical-DARMS input into a set of internally stored data-structures; his own programs, operating on these data-structures, would be much less complicated than would be the case in option one. Finally, should the third way be open to him, the user would write his application programs in a high-level programming language specifically designed for this purpose. Although this implies the availability of a complete and sophisticated programming system, there exists an operational prototype in the IML-MIR system. The chief advantage of such a high-level special-purpose language is that the user of such a system need not be a professional programmer in order to undertake, with the help of a computer, stylistic studies of real merit.

3 Summary of DARMS grammar and syntax

The section that follows does not provide a complete exposition of DARMS, although all major DARMS grammatical categories are at least briefly introduced. The reader is not expected to absorb all the information given here before proceeding to Part 4, although it is recommended that section 3.1 be read with particular care. The discussions of certain language-design problems in Part 4 are provided with back references when detailed knowledge of particular DARMS symbols is necessary. However, since space does not here permit a complete description of DARMS, the reader who wishes to utilize the DARMS system should obtain the 1976 DARMS reference manual.[18]

3.1 Some fundamental concepts: tokens and facilities for representing position

A DARMS dataset is a character-string which can be decomposed into a series of relatively small character-string events called 'tokens'. A token is defined to be any structure in DARMS terminated by a Delimiter, where a Delimiter may be a blank, comma or double comma. In general, a token represents a single musical symbol or construct (note, key signature, barline, etc.) or is a control symbol (indicating change of instrument, or symbol size, etc.). There follows a list of token classes in DARMS, most of which will be briefly described below.

Table 1: *Classes of DARMS tokens*

Barlines
Base-Increment Chord Structures
Broken Beams
Chord-Structure Definers
Chord-Structure References
Clefs
Comments
Dictionary Symbols
Doubling Mode Codes
Dynamics
Equate Code Definers
Equate Code References
Groupette Definers
Instrument Controls
Key Signatures
Linear Decomposition Mode Controls
Literals
Meter Signatures
Ossia Stave Controls
Repetitions
Rests
Single Notes
Size Controls
Skip Codes
Space-Pattern Chord Structures
Stave Transposition Controls
Stretch Codes

Because a score is two-dimensional and a DARMS string one-dimensional it is necessary to provide, in DARMS, facilities for indicating position – both vertical and horizontal – as well as codes for representing the various types of musical symbols.

The vertical placement of a musical symbol is represented by one of a variety of codes. Because most scores involve several instruments or voices, which are notated on horizontal staves parallel to one another, it is necessary to distinguish the stave(s) of one instrument from that (those) of another, and to have facilities for specifying, as precisely as is desired, the position of a musical symbol on, above or below a particular stave. Instrument differentiation is accomplished in DARMS by use of an Instrument Code, vertical placement by a Space Code, Pseudo-Space Code, Double-Space Code or Attach Prefix, depending on conditions to be described.

Instrument Codes are required for all scores involving more than one Instrument. (In this discussion, the proper noun "Instrument" will refer to a DARMS Instrument; in general, every instrumental or vocal part having its own stave or system will have its own Instrument Code.) The basic form of the Instrument Code is

I*n*

where *n* is a numeric identifier, assigned arbitrarily by the encoder, to each instrumental or vocal part of the score. Thus, four Instrument Codes would be required in order to encode a string quartet (although the identifiers need not be the same as those in this example):

Violin I	I1
Violin II	I2
Viola	I3
Violincello	I4

The Instrument Code makes it possible to encode individual parts in linear segments, the codes for each segment being preceded by the appropriate Instrument Code. (In the first stage of canonization, a process described in the previous section, these segments will be concatenated in their proper order.) There also exist in DARMS special identifier formats to permit the encoding of multiple instruments that use the same stave, of *divisi* scoring, and of other non-normative situations.

The *Space Code* is always relative to a *stave* of the current Instrument and is simply a representation of vertical placement, *not of pitch*. In the common case of an Instrument notated on a single stave, the middle line of that stave is designated by the integer value 25. As can be seen in Figure 3.1, the Space Codes range from 01 to 49, all 'line' positions being denoted by odd integers. Even if the symbol being encoded is a note, the Space Code will not designate pitch; nevertheless, pitch is easily calculated as a function of Space Code, key signature, accidental, clef. However, the Space Code is not limited to the encoding of notes; indeed, it is used for all musical symbols whose precise vertical placement is of consequence.

If the music for a given Instrument requires more than one stave (for example, a piano score is normally embodied on a two-stave system), the Space Codes for the topmost stave are as described above; the Space Codes for each successively lower stave of *that* Instrument are augmented by 50. Thus, the Space Code of the middle line of the second or 'left hand' stave of a piano score is given a Space Code of 75 and the middle line of the third or 'pedal' stave of an organ score is represented by 125.

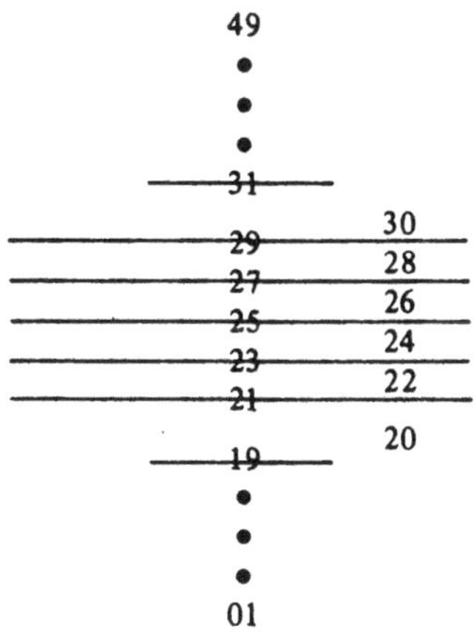

Figure 3.1

Most two- and three-digit Space Codes can be reduced to a single digit by means of the DARMS abbreviation facilities known as "2-suppression" and the Stave-transposition Control Code, which are described below in sections 3.5 and 3.4.2 respectively. It is advisable to read these sections before proceeding further, as the DARMS encodings of the examples that follow will utilize abbreviations wherever possible.

The vertical position of certain types of information, for example, dynamics, vocal text, and tempo indications, does not normally carry semantic meaning and therefore is not critical. Such information is usually above or below the stave to which it relates, and therefore the *Pseudo-Space Code* has been invented to signify the loci 'above' or 'below' a stave or between two staves of an Instrument:

00	Above the topmost stave of the Instrument
50	Below the topmost stave of the Instrument OR Between the two uppermost staves of the Instrument
100	Below the second stave of the Instrument OR Between the second and third staves of the Instrument
etc.	

00@¢ALLEGRO$

Note that if it is *necessary* to specify the precise vertical position of a symbol normally encoded with a Pseudo-Space Code a proper Space Code *must* be employed.

Certain symbol types have a variable vertical dimension that must be encoded if the vertical extent or vertical component of the symbol is to be accurately represented. A common instance of such a symbol is the arpeggio, encoded in DARMS as a wiggly line between two points. These two points are specified in a *Double-Space Code* prefix of the form

$$\sigma_1 | \sigma_2$$

where σ_1 and σ_2 are the lower and upper terminal points of the symbol being represented.

1|9?;
(?; is the code for a wiggly line)

Finally, there is the *Attach Prefix*, by which one symbol may be represented as being proximate (but not contiguous) to another in a direction specified by means of a character string designating a point of the compass. The form of an Attach Prefix is

A*c*

where *c* is a one- to three-letter compass direction (N, SSW, etc.): it is employed for symbols whose *exact* placement is not critical, but where some graphical or musical association ought to be indicated. In many cases a Pseudo-Space Code may be used instead of an Attach Prefix, although the Attach Prefix is a far more flexible facility that permits a series of symbols to be 'attached' to one another.

Vertical position is considered an 'attribute' of a symbol and thus the codes used to indicate vertical position – Space Code, Pseudo-Space Code, Double-Space Code and Attach Prefix (the last also being able to represent a relative horizontal position) – are incorporated into the code for those token types that represent musical symbols; they are not in themselves tokens.

While the precise vertical distance (relative to a stave) between notes has semantic significance (for it permits the harmonic intervals between such notes to be calculated), the horizontal distance between notes merely indicates that they are discrete events, it is the duration of the former note, denoted by its shape, color and stem, that normally (but not always!) determines the temporal position in the score of the latter note, whereas graphical and typographical considerations determine the spatial position on the page. It follows therefore that it is really not necessary to represent the *precise* horizontal position of symbols, since that is determined by the copyist, engraver or layout program, not the composer. It suffices, in general, to represent the durations of notes and rests, and the order in which they occur along the horizontal axis.

Fundamental to DARMS is the concept of an imaginary 'horizontal-position pointer' which always is positional at the 'current position' in the score, i.e., the point in the score being encoded at that moment. The normal movement of this pointer is from left to right or, more precisely, from the vertical slice of information containing the musical symbol being encoded to that containing the next symbol to the right that is to be encoded. The advance is signified by a *Delimiter Blank,* i.e., a blank terminating a DARMS token. Thus, in the following example, the blank between 7H (where 7 stands for Space Code 27 and H indicates "half note") and 8Q (where 8 stands for 28 and Q indicates "quarter note") indicates that the second note occurs to the right of the first.

7H 8Q

It often happens that several distinct musical symbols are in vertical alignment. If these symbols are notes that form a chord, they may all be encoded in a single 'Chord Structure' (two types of which are described in section 3.2.1 below) which is terminated by a Blank Delimiter. However, chords need not be encoded this way and not all simultaneously sounding notes are chords in the DARMS sense; furthermore, some or all of the symbols in a vertical slice may not be notes at all. In these cases the individual tokens representing each discrete symbol (except the last) in the vertical slice being encoded will be terminated with a *Delimiter Comma*; this provides syntactic separation of tokens but causes no change in the pointer's position.

Therefore, the basic encoding procedure in DARMS might be characterized as the encoding of vertical slices which are ordered from left to right; each slice contains a minimum of one token's worth of information. Tokens in a vertical slice are separated by Delimiter Commas which indicate their vertical alignment; the last token in a vertical slice is, however, terminated by a *Delimiter Blank*, which indicates that the pointer advances to the position of the next vertical slice to be encoded.

In general, the increment by which the pointer advances at any given time is not explicitly specified by the encoder; the distance will *normally* correspond to the smallest durational value possessed by any token in the most recently encoded vertical slice. However (see Table 2), a Delimiter Blank will represent a forward advance spatially but not in terms of musical time. Such a symbol is the barline (represented by a slash) which, while marking off metrical units (measures), does not itself represent a duration.

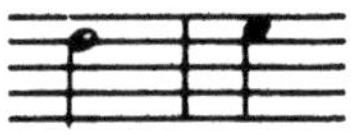

7H / 8Q

Table 2: *Classes of tokens possessing durational value*

Notes
Rests
Chord-Structure References
Base-Increment Chord Structures
Space-Pattern Chord Structures
Repetitions
Skip Codes

On the other hand, the encoder has the ability to control the pointer's motion by means of a variety of codes. Stating a new Instrument Code causes the pointer to move from the 'current position' in what was the 'active' Instrument to the position in the part of another (specified by the new Instrument Code) at which the encoding had previously terminated or, if the Instrument had never been 'active', at the beginning of the new Instrument's part. That Instrument then becomes active until the condition is terminated by another Instrument Code, and so on.

By means of *Linear Decomposition Mode*, the encoder can encode the information of a DARMS Instrument in several passes (the amount and kinds of information being left largely up to the encoder); !& signals that a 'layer' of information in Linear Decomposition Mode follows and that the layer will not complete the information for the passage; & marks the termination of the layer and a return to the point in the score corresponding to the beginning of the previous layer; &$ ends Linear Decomposition Mode itself and advances the pointer to the position immediately beyond the end of the right-most point of the stratified passage.

Linear Decomposition Mode is one of the most useful of DARMS facilities, since it enables a complex score to be reduced to several components (e.g., music, text, dynamics, tempo and other literal instructions, etc.), each of which can be encoded in a separate pass with a greatly reduced probability of error. In addition, the musical text itself (notes, rests, etc.) may be 'decomposed' into several strata, e.g., melody and accompaniment, right- and left-hand keyboard parts, etc., should it prove convenient.

A variety of codes employ the character ¬, which always affects, if only temporarily in certain contexts, the position pointer. The *Skip Operator* has the form

¬*d*

and is normally followed by a token representing a musical symbol of some sort. The value of *d* specifies the distance to the right of the then current position at which the symbol following the Skip Operator appears. If a Delimiter Blank precedes the Skip Operator the pointer is unconditionally advanced to the position corresponding to that of the symbol whose code follows the Skip Code. If, however, a Delimiter Comma precedes the Skip Operator, the Skip Operator is said to be 'anchored', which means that the pointer returns to its previous position immediately after the last character of the token following the Skip Operator has been processed. The (unanchored) Skip Operator is extremely useful in Linear Decomposition Mode (since the density of information will normally vary from layer to layer) and for fingerings, figured bass, ornaments, etc., that occur *subsequent* to the attack point of a note.

@¢A-¬H MEN.$
(text only encoded)

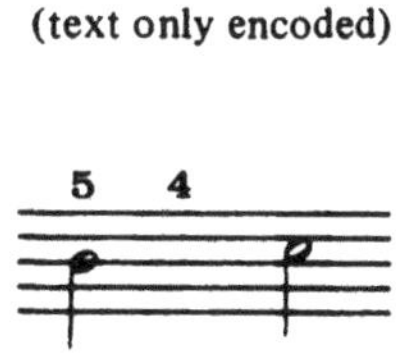

5HF5¬QF4 6
(encoding a change of fingering)

There are two DARMS facilities that might be regarded as lateral counterparts to the Double Space Code, which has been shown to specify the terminal points of symbols whose vertical extent is variable. The corresponding features for indicating horizontal extent are Identifiers and the Stretch Operator.

Identifiers are integers that, when used in the encoding for slurs, ties, hairpin dynamics, and other symbols that begin and end in different vertical slices, indicate the horizontal extent of the symbol in question. At the starting point of such a symbol an odd-numbered Identifier is employed, whereas the next even integer, used as an Identifier for the same DARMS symbol category serves to mark the terminal point of the symbol, at the same time freeing the Identifier pair for reuse. This makes it possible to have, for example, several slurs 'active' in the encoding stream at any given point. Note that the numerical value of the Identifier does not imply anything about the length of the symbol associated with it; however, this may be computed.

The *Stretch Operator* prefixes the code for a symbol that is 'stretched out' over a specific duration. The normal case of this is a performance instruction such as *accelerando*, or *ritardando*, whose letters – often separated by dashes – are distributed so as to indicate precisely the length of the musical passage to which the instruction pertains. The Stretch Operator has the form

$$\neg > d$$

where d is the distance covered by the symbol, beginning at the current position.

With this introduction to some of the most basic concepts of DARMS, it is now possible to survey its facilities more systematically.

3.2 DARMS musical symbols: codes for note/rest information

The philosophy of the DARMS system mandates that all information in the score pertaining to a note be encoded. Therefore, by means of a system of defaults, certain attributes pertaining to Notes will be assumed unless countermanded by a code for another attribute of the same class. (A DARMS *Note* is a single note or chord.) For example, suppression of a Stem-direction Code means that a default stem direction is automatically implied. Thus a great amount of information may be conveyed by very few characters; on the other hand, failure of the encoder to encode certain types of information may mean that the defaults, when supplied by the DARMS system programs, will probably be incorrect at least some of the time.

The following table lists classes of attributes that apply to Notes: when they occur in the score, they must be encoded in the following order:

Table 3

	Attributes of Notes	Discussed below in section
1.	Open Beam (DARMS 'Short Form')	3.2.8
2.	Position with respect to stave	3.2.1
3.	Accidentals	3.2.2
4.	Non-normative noteheads	3.2.3
5.	Duration	3.2.4
6.	Tie	3.2.5
7.	Stem direction	3.2.6
8.	Tremolo	3.2.7
9.	Beam(s) (DARMS 'Long Form')	3.2.8
*10.	Articulation	3.2.9
	Fingering	3.2.10
	Ornament(s)	3.2.11
	Slurring	3.2.12
11.	Figured Bass	3.2.13
12.	Close Beam (DARMS 'Short Form')	3.2.8

* Encoding precedence is determined by proximity to the notehead.

3.2.1 *Vertical Position* for a single note is specified by a Space Code as explained above. Chords, which consist of several noteheads on the same stem, may be represented in three ways:

a. as individual notes in the same vertical plane with the same Stem Identifier (cf. 3.2.6 below):

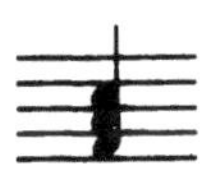

2QU1, 4U1, 6U1

b. as a 'Space-pattern' structure in which each note and attributes unique to it alone are represented in cells enclosed by vertical bars. Information common to the entire chord is encoded in normal order (cf. Table 3 above) to the right of the last note cell.

|2|4|6|QU

c. in 'Base-increment' representation, by which the intervallic rather than the Space Code structure of the chord is encoded. The lowest note of the chord is specified by a Space Code, but each successive note of the chord is given – in ascending order – as an increment calculated by subtracting the Space Code value of each note from that of the one below it. This form of encoding chords may be used only when all information except Space Code and Accidental Code is common to each note of the chord.

2+2+2QU

By means of a Chord-Structure Definer, the interval sequence within a chord may be extracted, labelled and stored for future reference. Thus, when the same chord-form recurs, it may be encoded in abbreviated form by means of a Chord-Structure Reference, which specifies 1) the chord-form, by means of the Identifier; 2) the Space Code of the lowest note of the current instantiation of the chord-form; 3) the number of times the chord is stated in immediate succession; 4) accidentals associated with the chord being encoded. The Chord-Structure Reference occupies the position of the Space Code information in the token representing the chord and its attributes; it can be a powerful abbreviation facility, especially in the encoding of keyboard scores.

3.2.2 *Accidentals* are represented as shown in the following table:

Table 4: *Accidental Codes*

Sharp (♯)	#
Flat (♭)	-
Natural (♮)	*
Double Sharp (𝄪)	##
Double Flat (𝄫)	

3.2.3 *Non-normative Noteheads* are encoded in the form

N*i*

where *i* is an integer Notehead Identifier representing a special notehead type.

3.2.4 *Duration Codes* are summarized in the following table:

Table 5: *Duration Codes*

WW	Double Whole note
W	Whole note
H	Half note
Q	Quarter note
E	Eighth note
S	Sixteenth note
T	Thirty-second note
X	Sixty-fourth note
Y	One hundred twenty-eighth note
Z	Two hundred fifty-sixth note
ZZ	Five hundred twelfth note
G	Simple grace note (graphically represented as a small eighth note with a slashed stem: 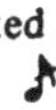)
•	Dot

Rests are encoded in the form

$$\sigma R\delta$$

where σ is the Space Code of the Rest, and where δ is the Duration Code of the Rest. Under proper conditions either or both σ and δ may be suppressed; the proper values will be supplied by the Canonizer.

Multiple measures of whole rests may be abbreviated in the form

$$R\,i\,W$$

where i is an integer specifying the number of measures. (Note that a whole rest is used conventionally to stand for an entire measure of rest, regardless of the meter.)

4Q / R3W / 3

Successive rests within a measure may be abbreviated thus:

Unabbreviated: 4Q RQRQ
Abbreviated: 4Q RQQ

3.2.5 *Ties* are indicated by a J in the code for the *opening* note of the tie; the next occurence of that Space Code in that Instrument is assumed to terminate the tie.

4QJ / Q (E EJ) QJ / H

In any case where ambiguity might arise, Tie Codes with integer Tie Identifiers must be used on *both* the opening and closing note of the tie.

3.2.6 *Stem Codes* are used

a. to indicate stem direction (U = 'up'; D = 'down'), and

b. to identify those notes in a multi-stemmed structure that belong to the same stem. This is accomplished by the use of an integer Stem Identifier suffixed to the U or D.

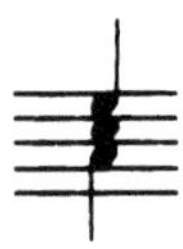

4QD,6U1, 8U1

In many cases the Stem Code may be suppressed; the correct code will then be supplied by the Canonizer.

3.2.7 *Tremolos* are of two types:

a. One-Note tremolos are encoded as a string of *n* left parentheses followed immediately by right parentheses, where *n* equals the number of slashes of which the tremolo notation consists.

2Q (( ))

1+3+2H( ) Base-increment format

|1|4|6|H( ) Space-pattern format,
cf. section 3.2.1 above

b. Two-Note tremolos are notated as two notes or chords separated horizontally by a tremolo-beam system. The DARMS system provides a Long and a Short Form of two-Note tremolo encoding; however, the Short Form is not usable where ambiguity might arise, most notably when there is another two-Note tremolo or any Beam System active in the encoding of the same Instrument. Since two-Note tremolos are graphically related to beam systems, the method of encoding them is somewhat similar. The reader is referred to section 3.2.8 (Beam Codes), which will assist him in understanding the encoding of tremolos that follow:

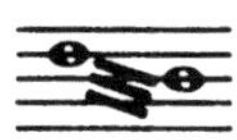

Long Form:	7WB1 (((B1))) 5WB2	3+3HDB1 (((B1))) 5+3HDB2
Short Form:	7WB ((( ))) 5W	3+3HDB ((( ))) 5+3HD

(3HB (( )) 7-H)

3HDB1,7UB3 (((B1))),(((B3))) 1HDB2, 9UB4

3.2.8 *Beams* in systems of any complexity may be represented in DARMS in the Long Form. However, in many cases it is possible to utilize a Short Form to save encoder time and reduce error. In both forms, the left parenthesis signifies a beam opening and the right parenthesis a beam closing. In cases where the Duration Code is calculable from the number of active beams, the Duration Code may be suppressed. However, in no case may both Space Code and Duration Code be suppressed.

a. *Short-Form Beam Codes* are applicable only when there is only one *active* beam system in the encoding of the current Instrument. Beam openings are represented by a string of left parentheses, whose number corresponds to the number of beams being opened, prefixing the Space Code. Beam closings are similarly encoded as a string of right parentheses terminating the DARMS code for the corresponding note (or chord).

(3 3) (2 (2 2) 2) (2. (2)) ((2) 2.)

b. *Long-Form Beam Codes* make use of a Beam Identifier ("B" prefixing an integer) to make it possible to distinguish several beam systems active in the encoding stream. Long-Form Beam Codes follow the Stem Code, thus differing from the Short-Form; moreover, the Beam Identifier is used for every note or chord of the beam system, regardless of whether or not there is a beam opening or closing on a given note of the system.

6(B1 7B2)

2(B1 2(B1 2B1 2B1 2B1) 2B2)

6U(B1,4•D(B3 7UB2) (B3 2DB4))

3.2.9 *Articulation* marks, together with Slurs (section 3.2.12 below), Fingerings (3.2.10) and Ornaments (section 3.2.11 below) are encoded as a complex whose internal ordering is determined by proximity to the notehead. The most common articulation codes are found in the following table.

Table 6: *Articulation Codes*

Symbol	*Code*
	' (staccato)
	" (wedge accent)
	– (tenuto)
	>
	<
	; or ;1
	;2
	;3
	;4
	;6
	;8

Other articulation codes are included in the Dictionary of Additional Symbols (3.3.8).

3.2.10 Simple *Fingerings* have the general form

Fcn

where *c* is a compass direction specifying the location of a fingering with respect to the note and *n* is an integer from 1 through 5. It is also possible to encode more complicated fingerings, including multiple fingerings, change of fingerings, slurred fingerings, etc.

3.2.11 *Ornaments* are encoded in the form

Ox

where *x* is a numeric or alphabetic code specifying the symbol represented. It is possible to represent all the ornaments listed in the article "Ornaments" in *Grove's dictionary of music and musicians*, 5th edition.

3.2.12 *Slurs* are indicated normally only at their terminal points by a Slur Code of the form

Li

where *i* is an integer Slur Identifier that may be omitted when there is only one active slur in the current Instrument and the slur terminates on the next note encoded.

3QL 4

3QDL1,8HUL3 4QD 5HDL2,7UL4

Provision has been made to permit the encoding of dotted and dashed slurs as well as slurs that change direction. Further discussion of this will be found in Part 4.

3.2.13 A *Figured-Bass* Code has the general form

¢cx

where ¢ indicates Figured Bass (mnemonic 'chord'), *c* is a compass direction N or S indicating that the figure is respectively above or below the stave. (This code is usually suppressible.) Finally, *x* is the code for a particular figure.

All figures that are found in F.T. Arnold, *The art of accompaniment from a thorough-bass* (London, 1931; New York, 1965) can be represented.

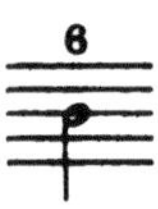

5H¢6

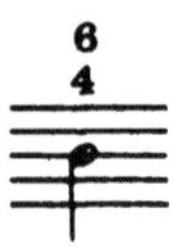

5H¢46

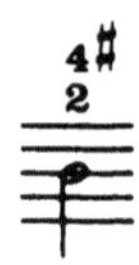

5H¢2|4#|

3.2.14 Finally, a remark concerning *double-stemmed notes* is required. These structures are made up of two notes that share the same notehead but may differ in virtually every attribute except pitch. The DARMS encoder may encode such notes as two discrete notes with the same Space Code, separating the codes by a Delimiting Comma, or may employ the option of 'recycling', in which the encoder encodes the attributes of one stem, then 'recycles' back to the Duration Code or Stem Code (as the situation demands) in order to represent the attributes pertaining to the other.

5QDEU

5QL1UL3 4HDL2,6UL4

3.3 Code for other musical symbols

3.3.1 *Clefs* are encoded in the general form

!*c*

where ! is the Space Code denoting the line referenced by the clef and where *c* is the letter G, F or C depending on the clef type.

Default Space Codes for clefs are

23	!G
27	!F
25	!C

Provision has also been made for a variety of special clefs.

3.3.2 Standard *Key Signatures* are encoded in the general form

!K*n*

where *n* is the number of symbols and where ! is either

-	(flat),
#	(sharp) or
*	(natural).

K2-

!K2* !K3#

Non-standard key signatures are encoded in the form

$$!\mathrm{K} a_1 \sigma_1 a_2 \sigma_2 \cdots a_n \sigma_n$$

where n is the number of symbols a in the key signature and where σ is the Space Code of each symbol.

!K#9-5

3.3.3 *Meter Signatures* are encoded in the general form

σ!Mr

where σ is the Space Code (normally suppressed in favor of the Meter Signature default value of 25) of the implied fraction line and where r stands for the meter, normally represented as a ratio.

Examples:

$\frac{2}{4}$	!M2 : 4
C	!MC
¢	!M¢
2/4	!M2/4
(2/4)	!M(2/4)
$\frac{2+3}{4}+\frac{3+4}{4}$	!M2+3 : 4+3+4 : 4
$\frac{3½}{2}$	!M3-1/2 : 2
3 𝅗𝅥	!M3 : H

3.3.4 Various types of *barlines* are represented by the appropriate concatenation of the following codes:

/	Normal (thin) barline
!/	Thick barline
:	Repeat symbol
/.	Dotted barline
/-	Dashed barline

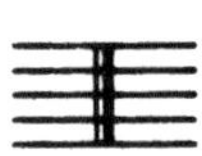

/!/

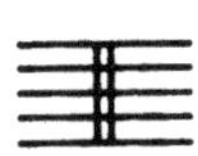

!/!/

!//:

3.3.5 *Dynamics* are encoded in the general form

σVν

where σ specifies vertical placement (required when the dynamic is not in normal position under the stave), and where ν is

a. any meaningful combination of the symbols

F P M S Z - R

or, b. for the representation of hairpin dynamics

<*i*	crescendo hairpin and
>*i*	decrescendo hairpin,

where *i* is an integer Dynamic Identifier.

Hairpin dynamics (excepting those on a single note) require a Dynamic Code at both beginning and end of the hairpin:

6Q,VF 6Q,VSF 6QVP<3 7,V<4F

3.3.6 The category *Literal* includes text, tempo indications and other natural language information. A literal is encoded in DARMS in the following order:

σ	Optional Space Code (default: 50, i.e., below the stave)
@ Roman	
or	Type styles
!@ Italics	
[literal]	Any combination of letters, digits, and the special characters ! " ' - : ; ? ( ) , . ƀ and the Control characters (where appropriate) ¢ : shift to capital (upper case) for next letter or, if in shift lock mode, release shift lock, and ¢¢¢ : set shift lock (all capitals), #*x* : *x* specifies a diacritical mark, subscript, superscript, ⌉*d* : Skip Operator; *d* specifies the distance skipped.
$	Designates termination of the literal string.

Among the special facilities for encoding literals is the ability to incorporate any legitimate DARMS substring representing a musical symbol into a literal. Such a musical symbol would not function as part of the sounding music itself. For example, the following instruction appearing at the head of a movement can be fully encoded.

Mesto, ♪ = ca.96
DARMS Code: @¢ MESTO,|=EU|CA.96$

Here the vertical bars indicate that the EU is to be interpreted not as letters of the alphabet but rather as a DARMS Musical Symbol Code for an eighth note with ascending stem. The fact that it occurs *within* a literal string isolates it from the musical text, properly speaking.

3.3.7 *Repetition signs*, which denote that a measure or figure is to be stated a number of times in immediate succession, have the percent sign as their leading character, e.g.,

 %

 %2

3.3.8 The *Dictionary of Additional Symbols* provides a theoretically limitless capacity for special and rarely employed symbols. These symbols may be encoded as independent tokens set off by Delimiters or, when appropriate, may be suffixed to the code for a note or other musical symbol. The form of a Dictionary Code is

?*x*

where *x* is a string of one or more characters specifying the symbol type.

3.4 Special codes

There are two groups of DARMS codes that fall under this heading. While the members of neither group represent musical symbols *per se*, the first group is necessary for the accurate encoding of musical information. The second includes a variety of codes to ease the burden of encoding.

3.4.1 Code necessary for accurate encoding

a. *Groupette Definers* are necessary to define the temporal relationships and bracket forms encountered in groupettes, which are non-normative subdivisions of a metrical unit. For example, in $\frac{4}{4}$ meter  is a groupette. A Groupette Definer includes an Identifier that uniquely specifies the Definer; this Identifier is, in turn, incorporated into the Duration Code for notes or rests having the defined relationship. Thus the Groupette Definer 3E5:Q indicates that '3' eighth-notes 'E' tagged with the Identifier '5' stand in the place of a single normal quarternote 'Q'.

3E5:Q . . . 4Q 5E5 6 7 6Q

Groupette Definers may also be defined recursively as this may be required by the musical text.

b. *Ossia Stave Codes* are used to indicate information regarding *ossia* staves, which provide alternate versions of (portions of) the principal musical text. Ossia Stave Codes specify the location, and extent of the ossia staves, as well as the beginning and end of the encoding of information on ossia staves.

c. *Size Codes* are necessary to indicate that the size of an individual symbol or of an entire passage has been enlarged or reduced. Several degrees of size change are possible.

3.4.2 Convenience Codes

a. The *Stave Transposition Control Code* is the form

!+*n*

where *n* is a multiple of 50. It signifies that until the 'transposition' is cancelled or changed, *all* Space Codes (specified or implied) are actually *n* more than given. This facilitates the encoding of second and subsequent staves of an Instrument by reducing the usable Space Code and Pseudo-Space Code range for the segment in question to 00 to 50 which, in turn, may be further abbreviated by "2-suppression" (see section 3.5 below). Thus,

!+50 !F 6E 9 30 9RE

is equivalent to

77!F 76E 79 80 79RE

This condition may be terminated by either

a. cancellation by the code !+0 , or
b. another transposition, e.g., !-100

b. *Doubling Mode* is introduced by a code that signifies that, until the mode is cancelled or changed, all encoded notes will stand for two-note chords in which the second note is at a given interval, specified in the Doubling Mode Code, from the encoded note. This is especially handy for encoding a series of parallel thirds, sixths, etc., in keyboard music.

c. *Equate Code Definers and References* are useful when a passage (and, therefore, its DARMS representation) is repeated without change. If the code for the first appearance of the passage is enclosed within an Equate Code Definer, then the corresponding Equate Code Reference will suffice to represent appearances of that musical text, wherever it subsequently reappears.

An Equate Code Definer is of the form

=*i*=*s*=$

where *i* is an integer Equate Code Identifier to be associated with the particular musical passage and where *s* is the DARMS string representing that passage.

An Equate Code Reference is of the form

=*i*$

where *i* is the appropriate Equate Code Identifier.

d. *Comments* are of the form

K*s*$

where *s* may be any character string not containing a dollar sign. This facility functions identically to the comment capability in other computer languages, allowing the user to document his dataset. A comment may occur *anywhere* in a DARMS string, thus making it possible to comment upon individual attributes of a symbol. In canonization and later processing, comments will maintain their original associations, which could be of significant help in musicological applications. Since they are not considered part of the musical text, comments will, of course, be deleted from any *printed* DARMS dataset.

3.5 Summary of DARMS abbreviations and defaults

3.5.1 *Space Code* (σ)

a. *2-Suppression*. Space Codes 20-29, which are the most frequently encoded Space Codes, may be abbreviated by dropping the tens digit. All other Space Codes must have at least two digits, for example, 09, 30, 121.

b. *Sigma Suppression*. If two successive single notes or two successive Chord Structures have identical Space Code(s), the second may be suppressed. In the first case the notes themselves may be separated by tokens other than those representing notes of Chord Structures; in the second, the Chord Structures may be separated by tokens other than those representing single notes.

For any given note, Sigma Suppression and Delta Suppression are mutually exclusive conditions.

c. *Defaults*: Default values for σ (or at least relative positioning) have been provided for Rests, Clefs, Dynamics, Literals, Ornamental Signs and some Dictionary symbols.

d. *Chord Structure Definers and References* (3.2.1) and Doubling Mode (3.4.2) permit abbreviated encoding of chords.

e. *Stave Transposition*. The second, third, etc. staves of an Instrument may be encoded as if they were the first stave when preceded by the appropriate Stave Transposition Code (3.4.2). Thus, the benefits of 2-Suppression may be enjoyed.

3.5.2 *Duration Code* (δ)

a. *Delta Suppression for Notes*. If two successive notes or Chord Structures have the same Duration Code, that of the second may be suppressed. Their representations may be separated by other kinds of tokens, except for Instrument Codes. For any given note, Sigma Suppression and Delta Suppression are mutually exclusive conditions.

b. *Delta Suppression for Rests*. If two successive Rests have the same Duration Code, that of the second may be suppressed. Their representations may be separated by other kinds of tokens. Multiple measures of rest and successions of rests in the encoding stream may also be abbreviated (3.2.4).

3.5.3 *Equate Codes* (3.4.2) permit entire passages of music that occur more than once to be encoded in full only once.

4 Psycholinguistic problems and considerations in the implementation of DARMS

In 1971 DARMS had existed in a relatively stable state for five years or more and, indeed, could claim to be the most comprehensive encoding method for music. However, with the circulation of an 'underground' users' manual (1971) and efforts to encode the Elliott Carter *Double concerto*, it became apparent that it would be necessary to specify more precisely the domain of encoder responsibilities and to expand the facilities of the language.

How this was done is of some interest, for there are many constraints and considerations that influence language specification decisions, a few of the most important being

uniformity
compactness
mnemonic appeal
machine processing implications
historical precedent (see Weinberg 1971).

In the particular case of DARMS, moreover, questions were also raised relative to musical graphics, editorial prerogatives, and the musical background of those who would actually encode.

* * * * *

4.1 It has never been the intent that DARMS be able to represent a score with photographic precision; rather, the object has been to make possible the encoding of a score with completeness and objectivity sufficient to enable the score to be reproduced, given the proper medium, without change or loss of musical information. The difference is important, for the point at which a composer's rights end and those of a music editor begin is not clearly defined and surely is often a matter of argument. Although it can be said confidently that such matters as horizontal spacing and page turns are properly editorial matters, there are also contexts in which an editor wields some control over the notation itself. There are several reasons for this, among them that many composers are not fully aware of editorial conventions concerning music notation; that in some cases the composer's intent may be represented with equal accuracy by a different but more elegant-looking configuration; and that the conventions of music editing, while standardized within the profession, are very poorly documented. The implications of this situation have penetrated every level of the DARMS Project, from the language specification to the layout and printing software.

As the province of editorial rights came under increasingly thorough investigation, the structure of DARMS began to reflect more accurately the give-and-take relationship between the composer and editor as regards the representation of vertical placement of symbols. In the original Ford-Columbia language, for example, there were no Pseudo-Space Codes or Attach Codes and the function of the Space Code was limited to denoting the location of noteheads, rests and accidentals in key signatures. Furthermore, such categories as dynamics and literals were assumed to be in 'normal position' under the stave.

In time, however, it was recognized that the 'normal position' for certain classes of symbols was not the only position to be employed in musical scores; thus, the Space Code function became an optional part of Dynamic, Literal, and even Meter Signature Codes (among others), making it possible to represent the location of any symbol with great precision.

To take an example, the first formulation of the Dynamic Code (cf. section 3.3.5 above) was of the general form Vν where ν was a letter or hairpin dynamic code. A dynamic so represented was assumed to be in the 'normal position under the stave'. However, not all dynamics are under the stave, so the Dynamic Code was redefined as σVν, with σ being a Space Code whose default value was 'under the stave'. Thus, the old form was contained within the new.

This form of the Dynamic Code was, in turn, judged to be too rigid since, in most cases, a slight vertical adjustment would not change the meaning of the dynamic indication. Furthermore, the precise placement of dynamics is an editorial prerogative, and the use of a Space Code (unless exact vertical position is a critical matter) can be viewed as an encroachment upon the freedom of the programs whose job it is to determine the layout. To restore this freedom the Pseudo-Space Codes and Attach Code were invented and authorized as *optional* replacements for the Space Code in the specification of many classes of symbols. Now it was also possible to specify the *relative* position of one symbol with respect to another.

The Attach Code, it should be pointed out, was admitted somewhat grudgingly into the canon of DARMS symbols, since its great potential for abuse was perceived. On the one hand it was argued that the Attach Code gave to the music editing programs the flexibility that has been the right of the human music editor; on the other, it was regarded as a kind of Pandora's box, whose lid would be opened by indiscriminate use, thereby threatening the stability, precision and reliability of DARMS representations. Regardless of one's viewpoint it is evident that the encoder must use this powerful yet potentially ambiguity-producing facility only in the proper contexts.

But what are the proper contexts? Clearly this is a question that can only be answered by trained musicians and then only for each individual instance.

This difficulty and others to be discussed below arise from the fact that music and its western notation bear strong dissimilarity to artificial algorithmic languages. This was an unsettling realization, for it implied that an understanding of western musical notation rests to some extent on understanding the music it represents; therefore, it follows that the syntactic decoding of notation presupposes the understanding of certain semantic information about the music itself.

This again points up the differences between DARMS and a strictly artificial language such as an algorithmic computer language. In the case of algorithmic computing languages, it is known that the 'deep structure' of a syntactically correct program which will halt is always a recursively computable function, as was shown by A.M. Turing, among others. Different programs which compute the same function may thus be linguistically viewed as having the same deep structure. On the other hand, DARMS is designed to represent music notation, which in turn represents music, although not without ambiguity and inconsistency. Since there exists no formal theory of music or of its notation comparable in rigor to the theory of recursive function, it is not surprising that the computer processing of an artificial language for the representation of musical scores is less well understood than the process of compiler construction for an algorithmic language. This is due, at least in part, to the fact that the semantics of musical notation have not been formulated as thoroughly as those of programming languages.

This conclusion was reached somberly and even regretfully, since the implications for encoder qualifications and data-processing are grave. It means that the hope of being able to train encoders without previous musical experience probably cannot be fulfilled (at least when complex scores are to be encoded); it also suggests that the tasks of designing error detection and translation programs might spill into the muddy field of artificial intelligence research in order to develop a computer program capable of interpreting the musical meaning of musical symbols (or, more precisely, their DARMS representation).

4.2 A good example of a problem that concerns editorial rights, encoding and data-processing is the matter of treating stem direction in beam systems. Gomberg has formulated (for the first time) rules for determining the stem direction of beamed notes, a matter that he, in consultation with a professional music editor, regards as being within the province of his layout programs (1975: 72-74). However, all would admit that visual elegance and legibility are not the only criteria for determining stem direction. There is also the composer's intent to be considered since, in some cases, stem direction carries *semantic* implications (e.g., for voice leading). Therefore, the question is asked: should stem direction be represented (explicitly or by implication) always, or only in certain contexts? If the latter, how are these contexts defined? The Gomberg solution is to have the layout programs determine stem direction only when not explicitly given in the canonical DARMS input to those programs. This places the burden on the canonizer to supply or not to supply default values for Stem Codes in user-DARMS data strings; since most DARMS datasets will, at least at first, be based on published music, it was decided that the mechanism to provide default values should normally be enabled.

4.3 The encoding of stems presents another problem; in this case, however, the conflict is between the ideals of uniformity and historical precedent. In the original language definition of 1964 the code for stem direction was given as either D ('down') or U ('up') and its position was designated to be between

Tie Code (if any) and Tremolo Code (if any). However, a notehead may have *two* stems, signifying the confluence of two voices, thus conceptually representing two notes, each with its own attributes. For instance, Figure 4.1 represents two voices playing the same pitch; notice that the upper voice is an accented quarter note while the lower is a staccato eighth note.

Fig. 4.1

Fig. 4.2

In order to represent such a structure, the DARMS user is now permitted to 'recycle' to the Duration Code once in his encoding (cf. 3.2.14) after which may follow any of the note attributes permitted in the usual order of encoding as specified in Table 3 of Part 3. Thus, Figure 4.1 could be 'spelled':

3ED'QU>

When both voices share not only the same pitch but also the same duration, the encoder may recycle directly to the Stem Code, leaving duration to be filled in by default option. Thus, Figure 4.2 could be spelled

2QUD

very compact indeed when compared to the canonical version

22QD,22QU

4.4 Since these conventions of stem syntax hark back to the original language specification, all currently existing, correctly encoded DARMS datasets conform to them; to nullify these conventions would in fact be to disenfranchise all past and present DARMS users from any new software system predicated upon such revision. It is clear that although DARMS is an 'artificial' or invented language, the existence of a population of human DARMS users is a natural-linguistic constraint on the system, preventing those involved in language design and software maintenance from wantonly revising syntactic or semantic rules. Therefore, excluding the remediation of previously ill-defined rules, any extension of the language should result in a new grammar of which the old grammar is a proper subset. In other words, the new grammar should differ from the old only by addition or extension, such that old datasets remain well-formed under the new grammar.

In 1973, ten years after the original DARMS specification, it was decided that in order to fully encode certain slurs, the direction of slur concavity must be encodable. (The basic form of Slur Codes is described in 3.2.12.) Since no provision had previously existed for representing this information, a convention was added to Slur Codes, and this was provisionally specified as either a letter U or D following the "L" and preceding the Slur Identifier. This solution had the elegant advantage of uniformity with stem direction, that is, 'up' and 'down' were encoded identically in both contexts.

Fortunately, before this new extension had been publicized in the revised DARMS manual of 1976 and had been incorporated into the system software, it was discovered that the expanded slur syntax led to an ambiguity. Consider the token 2QLD1. If U and D could indicate slur curvature, this DARMS fragment could be canonized as either two notes, the first with a default 'up' stem, the second with a 'down'; or as one note, assuming the D to be a slur direction.

Since such an ambiguity is strictly unacceptable in DARMS, a revision of syntax became necessary. Historical precedent precluded changing either Stem Codes or recycling conventions. One possibility would have been to introduce an optional escape character in slur syntax, such as 2Q1!D1 (exclamation mark) to indicate an unusual slur; the other possibility was to substitute other symbols in slur syntax in place of U and D, and this latter option was in fact chosen for reasons of compactness, substituting + for U and - for D in Slur (and Tie) Codes. This new rule clearly violates the principle of uniformity, which would legislate employment of the same symbols for *all* instances of a given meaning, that is, 'up' and 'down'. It is clear that such a loss of uniformity increases the amount of information the user must know about DARMS, and has the effect of making the language harder to learn.

4.5 However, uniformity in an artificial language for the representation of music would be much easier to achieve if music notation itself were consistent. Unfortunately, such is not the case. Consider Figures 4.3 and 4.4 below. Note that in Figure 4.3 the whole notes are vertically aligned with the quarter note on the first beat of the measure, whereas in Figure 4.4 the rests, which, like the whole notes of Figure 4.3, are operative from the downbeat of the measure, nonetheless are symmetrically placed at the midpoint of the measure. This is a case where editorial convention goes counter to a basic principle of musical notation, viz., that as musical time progresses in a piece, graphical displacement continues to the right in the score.

The consistency here poses no musical problem, but the language designer, or the encoder, finds himself in a dilemma: should the rests be encoded at the point corresponding to their graphic position (mid-measure) or to the place where their musical function commences (the downbeat)? In the former case the rests would be encoded after half their value was already used up; in the

75Q,OW,7 77#Q 76 75

Fig. 4.3

76RW,OR,5-QU 5*U 6U 6#U

Fig. 4.4

latter the encoder would be required to recognize the exceptional condition and, in addition, the basic DARMS principle of left-to-right encoding would have to be suspended. As with other difficulties of this type, the solution takes the form of teaching the encoder another rule, which is that rests must be encoded at the point where they take musical effect.

If DARMS were strictly a representation of graphical information, the code 5-QU 5*U 76RW,OR 6U 6#U would be an acceptable representation of Figure 4.4. However, this positions the rests incorrectly – from the *musical* standpoint – at about the third beat and, in fact, implies more than four beats in the measure, a condition that would generate an error message from the system software. The irony here is that the insistence upon maintaining DARMS as a comprehensive, non-interpretive encoding language is itself at the root of the problem, since only the musical meaning, and not graphical placement, is distorted by the incorrect encoding.

A comprehensive language, however, has many advantages over a highly specialized one. Datasets may be processed for diverse purposes, including musical analysis, printing, transposition, and so forth, if it has been encoded in a general-purpose code. One of the most elegant features of DARMS is that the encoder may be blissfully naive about the process of music setting and layout, and can proceed with his encoding purely on the basis of his understanding of music notation, leaving actual layout decisions to be made by the software.

4.6 Another problem drawn from the musical-time domain is the difficulty presented by certain meter signatures (cf. 3.3.3). The typical meter signature consists of two integers arranged vertically, the lower indicating that durational value which equals one beat, the upper stating how many beats make up a measure. Thus 3/4 is interpreted: a quarter gets one beat and there are three beats in a measure.

Occasionally one encounters a meter signature which consists of two meter signatures as described above, arranged side by side, as in $\frac{4}{4}\frac{3}{4}$. This notational oddity can have two meanings: either the two stated meters apply to strictly alternating measures of music or both meters apply to some measures, although there is no way to predict the meter of any one measure. Both these conventions are found primarily in music of the Renaissance and of the twentieth century. Again, were DARMS simply a representation of graphical information, no problem would arise, since the system could then blindly print any measure of music without reference to its metrical context. However, in the process of spine formation (see Part 2) meter becomes an important piece of data.

While it is necessary to know the meter for spine formation, it is not always possible to compute the meter of a measure in a given Instrument. Moreover, as will be illustrated below, durational content of a given measure sometimes conflicts with the given meter. Although these problematic cases are rare, and are usually resolvable by examining larger and larger contexts, particularly those of other Instruments, the amount of processing required to search these contexts may become arbitrarily large.

Therefore, to provide metrical information in such instances, the following *encoding* convention was established: in the case of irregularly alternating meter, the encoder must infer from the source material each instance of meter change, and the new meter must be encoded at each point, using as a control character an asterisk, which signals to the printing software that this particular meter signature is not to be printed, for example, !M*2:4. The music analyst also benefits by being told, as it were parenthetically, something about the metrical structure of the music. Once again it is the encoder who must take the brunt of this language design problem.

4.7 A final example, again deriving from the inconsistency of music notation itself, will serve to conclude this discussion.

Figure 4.5 shows a measure in 3/8 meter containing an eighth rest and seven quarter notes in one voice, which seems to contradict our most basic assumptions about well-formedness in a musical score. Yet Chopin, Schumann and others have employed this notational device to indicate a passage with performer-determined or improvised durations, beginning in this case on the second beat of the measure. The pianist encountering this notation will perhaps pause momentarily to infer the meaning, or perhaps will sense the musical implication immediately.

Fig. 4.5

Musicians can interpret such unconventional forms for several reasons: 1) the preceding auditory musical context provides a preditive model for the measure in question; 2) musicians generally have teachers or colleagues who can instruct them; 3) a musician may have also heard the piece performed; and 4) the default assumption regarding a published score is that it is syntactically correct; 5) the notes in question are size reduced, suggesting an abnormality. In this case the musical meaning can be deciphered since the edition is assumed to be reputable; since the music is representative of that style period (noted for its rhythmic liberties and notational freedom) known as 'Romantic'; and since this measure is penultimate to a final cadence, a further contextual cue. Note that this process of understanding depends upon the human ability to differentiate, by analysis of contextual and interval consistency, misprints form rarely occurring usages.

The assumptions of a compiler must unfortunately be different from those of the musician. A rule of the form

<NON-NORMATIVE DURATION VALUES>
<IN CONTEXT OF <ROMANTIC COMPOSERS>; : := <IMPLICIT GROUPETTE>

<NON-NORMATIVE DURATION VALUES>
IN <OTHER>CONTEXT; : := <ERROR STATE>

is unacceptable, since we posses no reasonable algorithm for correctly computing who is a Romantic or, worse, when some composer is composing in the 'Romantic' style. The former algorithm would be a set inclusion rule for a *fuzzy set*,[19] a concept which by definition embraces a non-zero rate of classification error; the latter would require a routine for analysis of musical context, a task that would involve years of work in artificial intelligence and musical analysis and that, even then, would retain risk of error. Additionally there is a reasonably high *a priori* probability that such a measure, encountered randomly in the input stream, is written or encoded incorrectly. This follows from the great likelihood of human error in copying, counting, encoding and keypunching. The cost of misclassifying an error as a correct notational oddity is thus far greater than the cost of misclassifying a notational oddity as an error. Furthermore, it is unacceptable to impose *ad hoc* grammatical rules for such small classes of constructs as Figure 4.5., since there are many other such classes, of which we have already seen a few. To attempt to treat each anomalous construct with a new specific syntactic feature would be to open another Pandora's box of ungenerality. The compiler default, then, must be to flag such an occurrence as a probable error if encoded as a string of undistinguished quarter notes, as follows:

!M3:8 / 4QDL1,8RE 8QU 33QU 31QU 8QU 6*QUL2 4QJ 1QJ /

The objective is to arrive at a DARMS encoding which is consistent with previous language definition and consistent with the music notation at hand. Since these seven quarter notes fill the duration of two ordinary eighth notes, they can in some sense be considered a groupette (cf. 3.4.1), even though a groupette conventionally requires special graphical mention, as in the familiar case of the triplet

defined in DARMS as !3E*i*:Q, where *i* is some integer. Similarly, we can define our problem case as !7Q*i*:2E, where we will, in addition, indicate suppression of the usual groupette indication in the score by a suffix attached to the Groupette Definer.

While this solution is optimal from the viewpoint of consistency, it has the drawback, previously encountered, of thrusting upon the encoder the responsibility of recognizing the occurrence of a non-normative, graphically unannounced groupette, and again accrues the cost of adding another encoding rule. While this is an example of the need for a more musically sophisticated encoder, it is clearly preferable to the implementation of computer programs to decipher meanings, since the state of the programming art, present and foreseeable, is inadequate as explained above.

5 Conclusion

Over the years, literally hundreds of revisions of DARMS have been necessitated by discoveries of music notation structures not included in the original language specification, or of unanticipated complexities of notational forms which had previously been considered too superficially, as in the case of slur direction. Most subsequent syntactic revisions have been incorporated elegantly into the existing grammar, violating no major proscriptive language design rule; however, such rules have occasionally been broken, and on the basis of the problems and solutions described here it may be concluded by some that DARMS should be scrapped as an encoding standard. Perhaps by utilizing the knowledge painfully accumulated from the DARMS Project, a new music encoding language should be designed, uniform where DARMS is not, more compact than DARMS and unencumbered by the weight of historical precedent, slow-fading datasets and user criteria. While this may seem to be an attractive option, prospective language designers should be made aware of the tremendous bulk and diversity of western musical literature, and of the quantity of work involved in producing a reasonable encoding scheme which is comprehensive, consistent and elegant. To quote Gomberg:

> [...] I believe a sufficiently strong case has been made for the adoption of DARMS [...] [but] if future investigators feel that DARMS is unattractive or inadequate (on whatever grounds), they should be prepared to face an arduous task just to provide an alternative, much less an improvement. In particular, they should carefully study the uses of notation of a wide variety of music, especially that of the twentieth century. (1975:111)

It should be remembered that while modern linguistics has provided us with a powerful framework for syntactic analysis, a complete formalized theory of semantics, even for so-called 'natural' languages, is nowhere to be found (notwithstanding the pioneering logical analyses of Tarski (1944) and Carnap (1942)) except perhaps in an applied sense as an embryonic test tube baby in artificial intelligence and natural-language processing laboratories. Perhaps a surprising conclusion about music notation is that our understanding of its semantic structure is nearly as impoverished. This lack of formal knowledge fortunately prevents us neither from speaking English, nor from reading music; while syntactic processes are becoming more and more amenable to mechanical solution because of advances in syntactic theory, the best semantic theory that exists resides in the brains of the human beings employing the languages in question, including music notation and DARMS. The process of encoding music into DARMS is akin to other music-reading tasks, such as instrument playing and conducting, and these are generally conceded to be best performed by musicians, or at least by those with some musical training. This rather obvious principle applies to DARMS encoding as well, particularly where complex scores are involved, even though it was originally hoped, for economic and other reasons, that this would not be the case.

Artificial languages, though artificial, must still obey the laws of nature.

Notes

1. A super-particular ratio is one in which the first term is one greater than the second: 2:1, 3:2, etc. For some additional information, see Werner 1959: 376-383.
2. See Crocker 1966: 98ff.
3. Rameau's harmonic system is discussed in detail in Shirlaw (undated).
4. See, for example, Burmeister's (1606) *Musica poetica*.
5. The relevant portion of Mattheson 1739 is translated in Lenneberg 1958: 193ff.
6. Cf. Nattiez 1974. This article includes extensive bibliographics dealing with various aspects of semiological activity.
7. See also Forte 1959.
8. Cf. Prerau 1970 and Kassler 1972.
9. See Bergman (undated).
10. Most of the principal systems are described by their inventors in Brook (ed.) 1970. The authors include Bauer-Mengelberg (1970), Brook (1970), Gould and Logemann (1970), Wenker (1970), and Jackson and Berzott (1970). See also Heckmann (ed.) 1967, especially Robison 1967.
11. See Lincoln 1966 and Pruett 1966.
12. Lincoln (ed.) 1970 (*The computer and music*) contains several articles that grew out of the Harpur Seminar in Computers and Music. As this paper is being written (1976), final plans are being formulated for a second DARMS conference, cosponsored by the National Endowment for the Humanities and SUNY-Binghamton to be held in July 1976.
13. This was made possible by a Research Fellowship awarded Raymond Erickson by the IBM Systems Research Institute, New York City, for the year 1970-1971.
14. The programs were begun and largely completed under a grant from the National Endowment for the Humanities (administered through the Research Foundation of the City University of New York) for the academic year 1973-1974. Responsibility for the Syntax Checker rested with Raymond Erickson at Queens College, C.U.N.Y., and that for the Canonizer with Anthony B. Wolff at the School of Advanced Technology of S.U.N.Y.-Binghamton.
15. For a description of the compiler (based on a design by T.E. Cheatham and Kirk Sattley, Jr.) see Erickson 1969.
16. Armando Dal Molon of Music Reprographics, Ltd., located in Oyster Bay, New York, uses a Photon printing device for only a part of the score, most of the details of which must be hand-finished (Gomberg 1975: 5).
17. Kassler 1966, Regener 1967, Forte 1966; 1974.
18. The manual is available from Raymond Erickson, Department of Music, Queens College of the City University of New York, Flushing, N.Y. 11367.
19. See Zadeh 1965.

References

Aristotle

1959 "De poetica" 1447b, translated by Ingram Bywater, in *The works of Aristotle*, edited by W.D. Ross (Oxford: Clarendon Press), vol. 11.

Bauer-Mengelberg, Stefan

1970 "The Ford Columbia Input Language", in Barry S. Brook (ed.) 1970: 48-52.

Bergman, Albert D.

no date "Toward a theory of descriptions" (unpublished manuscript).

Brook, Barry S.

1970 "The plaine and easie code", in Barry S. Brook (ed.) 1970: 53-56.

Brook, Barry S. (ed.)

1970 *Musicology and the computer* (New York: C.U.N.Y. Press).

Burmeister, Joachim

1606 *Musica poetica* (Rostock).

Carnap, Rudolf

1942 *Introduction to semantics* (Cambridge, Mass.: Harvard University Press).

Crocker, Richard

1966 "Aristoxenus and Greek mathematics", *Aspects of medieval and Renaissance music*, edited by Jan LaRue (New York: W.W.Norton), 96-110.

Descartes, René

1961 *Compendium of music* (original version published in 1618), translated by Walter Robert (Rome: American Institute of Musicology).

Erickson, Raymond F.

1969 "A General Purpose system for computer-aided musical studies", *Journal of music theory* 13: 276-294.

1970 *Rhythmic problems and melodic structures in* organum purum: *a computer-assisted study* (Ph.D. dissertation, Yale University).

Forte, Allen

1959 "Schenker's concept of musical structure", *Journal of music theory* 3: 1-30.

1966 "A program for the analytic reading of scores", *Journal of music theory* 10: 330-363.

1974 *The structure of atonal music* (New Haven: Yale University Press).

Gomberg, David A.

1975 *A computer-oriented system for music printing* (D.Sc. dissertation, Washington University).

Gould, Murray J. – George W. Logemann

1970 "ALMA: alphameric language for music analysis", in Barry S. Brook (ed.) 1970: 57-90.

Heckmann, Harald (ed.)

1967 *Elektronische Datenverarbeitung in der Musikwissenschaft* (Regensburg: G. Bosse).

Jackson, Roland – Philip Berzott

1970 "A musical input language and a sample program for musical analysis", in Barry S. Brook (ed.) 1970: 130-150.

Kassler, Michael

1966 "Toward musical information retrieval", *Perspectives of new music* 4: 59-67.

1972 "Optical character recognition of printed music: a review of two dissertations", *Perspectives of new music* 11: 250-254.

Lenneberg, Hans
1958 "Johann Mattheson on affect and rhetoric", part 2, *Journal of music theory* 2: 193-236.
Lincoln, Harry B.
1966 "The computer seminar at Binghamton: a report", *Notes of the Music Library Association* 23: 236-240.
Lincoln, Harry B. (ed.)
1970 *The computer and music* (Ithaca and London: Cornell University Press).
Lindblom, Björn – Johan Sundberg
1970 "Towards a generative theory of melody", *Swedish journal of musicology* 52: 71-88.
Mattheson, Johannes
1739 *Der vollkommene Capellmeister.*
Mendel, Arthur
1969 "Some preliminary attempts at computer-assisted style analysis in music", *Computers and the Humanities* 4: 41-52.
1973 "Princeton computer tools for musical research", *Informatique et sciences humaines* 19.
Nattiez, Jean-Jaques
1974 "Sémiologie musicale: l'état de la question", *Acta musicologica* 46: 153-171.
Patrick, P. Howard – Patricia Friedman
1975 "Computer printing of Braille music using the IML-MIR system", *Computers and the Humanities* 9: 115-121.
Plato
1961 "The republic", book III.398, translated by Paul Shorey, *The collected dialogues of Plato*, edited by Edith Hamilton and Huntington Cairns (Princeton University Press), 643.
Prerau, David S.
1970 *Computer pattern recognition of standard engraved music notation* (Ph.D. dissertation, Massachusetts Institutes of Technology).
Pruett, James
1966 "The Harpur College music-computer seminar: a report", *Computers and the Humanities* 1: 34-38.
Rameau, Jean-Philippe
1722 *Traité de l'harmonie réduite à ses principes naturels.*
Regener, Eric
1967 "Layered music – theoretic systems", *Perspectives of new music* 5: 52-62.
Robison, Tobias D.
1967 "IML-MIR: a data-processing system for the analysis of music", in Heckmann (ed.) 1967: 103-135.
Schenker, Heinrich
1935 *Neue musikalische Theorien und Phantasien*, 3: *Der Freie Satz* (Wien: Universal Edition).
Schopenhauer, Arthur
1961 *The world as Will and Idea* (original version published in 1818), translated by R.B. Haldane and I. Kemp (Garden City and New York: Doubleday & Co.), 268.
Shirlaw, Matthew
undated *The theory of harmony* (London: Novello & Co.).

Tarski, A.
1944 "The semantic conception of truth and the foundations of semantics", *Philosophy and phenomenological research* 4: 341-376.

Wang Hao
1955 "On formalization", *Mind* 64: 226-238.

Weinberg, Gerald M.
1971 *The psychology of computer programming* (New York: Van Nostrand Reinhold Company).

Wenker, Jerome
1970 "A computer oriented music notation including ethnomusicological symbols", in Barry S. Brook (ed.) 1970: 91-129.

Werner, Eric
1959 *The sacred bridge* (New York: Columbia University Press).

Zadeh, L.A.
1965 "Fuzzy sets", *Information and control* 8: 338-353.

DANIEL C. O'CONNELL and SABINE KOWAL

Pausology[1]

1 Introduction

For many reasons, the field of pausology is neither well known nor well represented among scholars. The term itself has been in use, as far as we can determine, only since 1965, when it was introduced in the context of equipment engineering (Tosi 1965). Lack of accurate and reasonably inexpensive voice recording equipment has itself contributed to the modest popularity of the field until quite recently. And until such equipment was generally available, pausological research was limited to quite subjective and/or primitive methods of analysis.

Pauses occur, of course, between vocalizations. Primarily they are periods of silence in the speech of a person. It should be noted, however, that, in the case of dialogue, such silences may occur between vocalizations of either the same or different speakers. But silence, reticence, or taciturnity is not of itself a pause. In addition to this primary meaning of silent or unfilled pauses (UPs), filled pauses (FPs) are usually included in the literature, as well as a variety of hesitation phenomena in the speech signal such as repeats (*he he went*), false starts (*when they . . . if they*), syllabic prolongation, and certain types of verbal fillers (*well, you know*). Moreover, since it has been found quite generally that the length and frequency of pauses are primary contributors to variation in speech rate, the latter has historically become quite closely associated with the research tradition concerned with pauses.

Before we begin our detailed historical tour of duty for the cause of pausology, it might be well further to specify the variety of research disciplines involved in that history, since the domain of pausology is genuinely multi-disciplinary. Disciplines as disparate as philosophy and neurology have contributed to its progress. Much of the early interest was on the part of phoneticians, radio broadcast specialists, speech specialists in the areas of rhetoric and drama, and clinicians interested in the use of interview material for diagnostic or psychotherapeutic purposes. Anthropologists were among the first to be concerned with periodicity of vocalization and silence in conversation. Only later was there interest in the psychological aspects of pauses

Computers in Language Research 2

in personality, anxiety, emotion, and development, along with shifts in the interests of linguists and the contributions of audio engineers. In some respects, then, the psycho- and sociolinguistic interest in pauses was the very last to develop.

It is equally important to specify for the reader a number of related areas which will not be treated in this historical overview of pausology. One of these is the psychophysics of perception of temporal intervals with other than speech signals as the stimulus source (e.g., Braud and Holborn 1966). Also excluded is the study of the perception of vowels and consonants as a function of variation of temporal intervals (e.g., Liberman, Harris, Eimas, Lisker, and Bastian 1961; Harris, Bastian, and Liberman 1961). Pauses and other hesitation phenomena occasioned by delayed auditory feedback (DAF) are also omitted from our review (e.g., Breskin, Gerstman, and Jaffe 1971). The entire area of compressed speech, with its very extensive bibliography, is omitted as well (e.g., Fairbanks, Guttman, and Miron 1957; Orr 1968; Foulke 1971; Miron and Brown 1971). Oculomotor stops in silent reading have sometimes been referred to as reading pauses (Erdmann and Dodge 1898); these too are not considered in the present chapter.

Our plan of attack in the following sections is basically chronological. The early period is handled rather globally up until 1945. The subsequent periods from 1945 to 1950, 1951 to 1960, 1961 to 1970, and 1971 to 1980 are structured primarily in terms of individual landmarks in research and research developments derivative therefrom. Since they overlap many of the other categories and constitute veritable schools of pausological research, the works of Mahl, Goldman-Eisler, Boomer, Tosi, Matarazzo, Jaffe, Siegman, Martin, Cook, Lass, Grosjean, and O'Connell are handled separately from the chronological treatment up until 1980. A final section is devoted to a summary and conclusion.

A few more preliminaries by way of *caveat* must be emphasized. Even antecedent to our review, it should be made clear that multidetermination, though very often neglected in individual research projects, is universally important in pausology. Pauses are determined by breathing, embarrassment, weariness, anxiety, confusion, anger, interruption, pain, syntactic complexity, mendacity, availability of lexical items, emphasis, boredom, and a host of other situational, organismic, intersubjective, linguistic, and conventional factors. None of them can ultimately be disregarded for any nontrivial theory of pausology; some are neglected by nearly all the research recorded below.

Another caution regards the problem of physical exactitude and the related specter of operational exactitude. Neither has been cultivated very assiduously in the research reported here, but there are peculiar reasons why physical exactitude has been largely unattainable. We tend intuitively to think of the vocalization-pause alternation as a simple on-off cycle. Practically, however, it always involves a gradual approach of departure from a base-rate noise level as transduced through more or less adequately sensitive equipment. Put another way, arbitrary, uncertain, and approximate factors all enter into the determination of what may appear in the final report to be very exact measures of position, frequency, and length of unfilled pauses in speech corpora.

A final forewarning concerns the whole matter of generalizability in the area of pausology. The speech corpora subject to study in pausological research include: monologue, dialogue, and multilogue; a continuum that extends from rote reading to very spontaneous utterance; distracted and attentive speech; what might be called pure speech (e.g., radio communication) and elliptical speech intermingled with a variety of nonverbal, contextual, situational supplements. Generalizations regarding speech *per se*, without further specification, are almost necessarily trivial, if not positively false or misleading.

2 The early period of research (up until 1945)

Mankind has always cultivated the skillful use of unfilled pauses and hesitation phenomena in his persuasive and rhetorical devices. Quintilian, the Roman rhetorician, is said to have spoken of their power in discourse. One of the earliest modern references we have been able to find is a charming passage in Kleist (undated: 976) which dates from the early nineteenth century. He describes how one works through a difficult expression as follows: "I mix in some unarticulated sounds, prolong transitional words, use some redundant apposition, and avail myself of other tricks to extend the discourse in order to win the requisite time to construct my ideas in the workshop of my mind" [our translation from the German].

Sheridan (1787) emphasized the rhetorical effect of variation in speech rate and pausing. Proper pausing allows correct understanding of a sentence; proper emphasis determines pause location. Somewhat later, Walker (1811) recommended addition or extension of pauses to those noted by punctuation. He set up a list of rules to assist speakers in finding proper places to pause.

The psychologist Cattell (1886) is our first reference to empirical data on speech rate. He summarizes rather succinctly in English some work he had published earlier (1885) in German:

> it takes about twice as long to read (aloud, as fast as possible) words which have no connexion as words which make sentences, and letters which have no connexion as letters which make words. [. . .] When a passage is read aloud at a normal rate, about the same time is taken for each word as when words having no connexion are read as fast as possible. The rate at which a person reads a foreign language is proportional to his familiarity with the language. For example, when reading as fast as possible the writer's rate was,

English 138, French 167, German 250, Italian 327, Latin 434, and Greek 484; the figures giving the thousandths of a second taken to read each word. Experiments made on others strikingly confirm these results. The subject does not know that he is reading the foreign language more slowly than his own; this explains why foreigners seem to talk so fast. This simple method of determining a person's familiarity with a language might be used in school examinations. (1886: 64–65)

For a summary in German, see Erdmann and Dodge (1898).

Wallin (1901) was the first to measure the length of silent pauses instrumentally. In his study on the rhythm of speech in poetry readings, he defined pauses as "those gaps which, in the main purposeful, separate groups of words by silences other than those involved in the mere production of a series of sounds" (1901: 75):

The laws of mental activity seem to demand that the words in speaking be grouped into short unities that agree, in the main, with the 'unity of consciousness'; and that frequent, though brief, pauses be made to enable the mind to easily grasp and synthesize this manifold of sensation. (1901: 81)

Some nine years later, Beer (1910) carried on the psychological tradition of early pausology. He found that polysyllabic passages were read more rapidly in terms of seconds per syllable than monosyllabic passages with the same number of syllables. He argued that the slower reading rate corresponded to a higher rate of meaning per syllable for passages with a lower mean syllable per word ratio. In fact, changes in the distribution of meaning were considered to be the source of all changes in reading rate. We might add in passing that Beer utilized a rather quaint method of measurement that relied on soot markings from flames – called *der Marbesche Sprachmelodieapparat* (Marbe 1908).

In the very first volume of the *Revue de phonétique* appeared a study by Lote (1911) in which he undertook to locate and measure silences in the oral reading of French poetry. His measurements were made in centiseconds by physical instrumentation. Essentially his position was that pauses are not primarily dictated by physiological necessity (breathing), but rather functionally by the sense of the passage as understood and expressed by the reader. His comprehensive discussion engaged many crucial questions neglected by subsequent researchers unfamiliar with the historical development of pausology. One rather quaint bit of nomenclature are his *mauvais silences*, pauses which he considers illegitimate.

Snell (1918) investigated the nature of pauses in readings of Milton's *Paradise Lost*. She assumed that pauses have the psychological function of separating "from each other ideas, or important phases of ideas, in order that the mind may grasp these as logical units" (1918: 13). She found that pause distribution did not vary greatly as function of the presence or absence of punctuation marks. Not unexpectedly, in view of her speech genre (poetry recitation) and selection of experimental subjects (people accustomed to reading poetry for enjoyment), she found that pauses occurred "only at points logically possible" (1918: 24), i.e., between simple thought units. She also distinguished rhythmic from grammatical pauses.

Woolbert (1920) presented a long experimental report on the effects on listeners' perception of various modes of public reading, some of which involved wide variation in pause and phonation time. From the listeners' responses, only the following comment regarding temporal factors could be offered: "Among authorities in elecution there seems to be no unified opinion as to the effect of changes in Time; and this study leaves that issue with results that are inconclusive, calling for refinement of method or more data" (1920: 184). Apparently there was also no agreement as to how to spell *elocution* in those days.

The same year, Fröschels (1920) reported what he considered an unexpected finding: Simple repetition of the same syllable (*ta* and *pa*) always proceeds at a slower rate than the articulation of syllables in sentences. He discussed both the physiological and psychological roots of this finding, the latter in more detail than any other author we have found up to that date:

> Printed sentences arouse some affect in the reader as a function of their meaning – a curiosity, even though hardly conscious, about what's coming. And this affect (and perhaps an affect due to the content of the part already read) accelerates the speech rate by way of tension or arousal (1920: 869) [our translation from the German].

He also noted the considerable differences in the rate of spontaneous speech and reading in many of his subjects. His equipment made use of an electrical circuit to mark time intervals on the kymograph.

Wagoner presented considerable speculation regarding the relationships of speech defects and temperamental traits. For example:

> The profile of the person who drawls, hesitates or is extremely deliberate in his speech shows low scores for speed of movement, speed of decision, finality of judgment, and motor impulsion, while interest in detail scores high. The degree of hesitation seems to be inversely proportional to the score. (1925: 242)

Would that it were that simple. But to jump ahead just for a moment, Rieffert (1932), in a similarly speculative article, included speech rate and unfilled pauses as criteria for his characterological system.

When we come to the research of Brigance (1926), phonographic recording becomes the basic technique. He noted 15% variation in the rate of sound reproduction with the available equipment. What he referred to as the best average rate for speaking (English) was specified as between 115 and 135 words a minute, whereas the rate of reading is about three times as rapid, from 300 to 400 words a minute. This is the first occasion for us to call attention to the very important and most frequently overlooked problem of the normative data on syllable per word rate, which varies considerably from person to person and from one speech genre to another, not to speak of one language to another, and renders words per minute a relatively meaningless measure.

One of the brightest spots in the early history of pausology and an example as well of interdisciplinary cooperation worthy of emulation is a monograph of Griffith (1929). Her methodology, instrumentation, taxonomy of unfilled pauses, and self-critical attitude are extraordinarily refreshing. Though her work has well nigh been lost on recent researchers, studies such as that of Grosjean and Collins (1979) take on new meaning in light of her monograph. Today, Griffith stands as a warning against ahistoricity in scientific research. Although several researchers (Meinhold, 1967; Funkhouser and O'Connell, 1978) have recently engaged poetic literary criticism with a pausological methodology, to date no one has to our knowledge followed Griffith's lead to study prose literature by means of pausological analyses of oral readings. To our knowledge, Griffith was the first researcher to report extensive empirical data on pauses rather than simply speech rate.

An example of early pausological taxonomy by a linguist is to be found in Bloomfield 1933, including the pause after a final-pitch, the pause-pitch, or suspension-pitch (a rise of pitch before a pause within a sentence), and parenthetic hesitation-forms such as the filled pause. He generalized as well that the word is not primarily a phonetic unit: "We do not, by pauses or other phonetic features, mark off those segments of our speech which could be spoken alone." (1933: 181)

As of 1935, there was no general agreement as to an optimal rate of speech for radio broadcast (Cantril – Allport 1935). Lumley (1933) found mean rates of 107, 160, 171, and 191 words per minute for politicians, educators, preachers, and news reporters, respectively. At this same time, we find an excellent example of a relatively sophisticated use of equipment (Parmenter – Treviño 1935), a precedent unfortunately not followed by all subsequent investigators. They reported empirical data on number, length, and location of pauses rather than simply speech rate:

> The sound was picked up by the microphone and by means of an oscillograph was photographed upon a strip of motion picture film propelled at the rate of two feet per second. On the edge of the film the vibrations of a 1000-cycle oscillator were recorded simultaneously as a timer.
>
> The developed film was placed over an illuminator, the time lines numbered, the end of each sound marked, and its length measured in thousandths of a second. The exact limits of the sounds were sometimes difficult to determine, particularly in the case of the voiced continuants. (1935: 129)

Using such methods with a case study on practical reading of narrative prose, they found that almost one-fourth of the total time of reading was taken up with unfilled pauses. However, the categorization of silences was thereafter complicated by a method introduced by Cotton (1936), by which the silence of a pause was considered a part of the preceding syllable and was used to determine the normal syllabic rate.

For the first time in pausological research, Olson and Koetzle (1936) introduced developmental considerations. They studied thirty-second intervals of spontaneous speech in a group of kindergarten children and found that boys speak less than girls, but do so at a faster rate in words per minute (188 > 184). Word rate was estimated while the children spoke, rather than from recordings.

Newman and Mather (1938) provided a landmark in that they analyzed the speech of patients with affective disorders. Their taxonomy included prosodic (between phrases) and hesitating pauses (within phrases), and tag phrases (e.g., *you see, I dunno, you know*). They found that depressed patients tended to use relatively more hesitating pauses and gave the impression of slow and halting speech; that many patients used relatively more prosodic pauses and gave the impression of a theatrical declamation; and that all the syndromes studied showed relatively frequent pauses. Their methodology, however, relied on subjective judgments of pauses derived from repeated playings of phonographic recordings. All these elements of their research they seem to come upon without reliance on a previous research tradition.

Norwine and Murphy (1938) took up the problem of conversational (telephonic) pauses. They used the terms *talkspurt* and *resumption time* for the individual speaker and *response time* for the shift between speakers. Subsequent investigators who used judges to locate pauses would have done well to note their advice:

> It will be well to keep in mind that the fundamental basis of these measurements is the presence or absence of speech energy. Many of the pauses recorded in this study are of the type which are known to occur within sentences, phrases, or even within words. Some of these are insufficient in duration to interrrupt the continuity of the flow of speech, and some are too short to be noticed by a listener. The intervals as defined in this paper probably do not, therefore, exactly correspond to those which would be observed by a person listening to the conversations. (1938: 281)

The work of Chapple (1940; 1942; 1949; Chapple – Lindemann 1942) is primarily of importance because of his later influence on the methodologies of Goldman-Eisler and Jaffe. His basic hypothesis was that the measurement of temporal parameters of interaction between individuals could afford some insight into personality. Later the hypothesis was extended to psychoneurotic and psychotic individuals.

Franke (1939) reviewed much of the literature on rate of reading aloud and found that judges were quite accurate in categorizing reading as slow, normal, or fast. Men read on the average eight words per minute faster than women. The sex difference was not confirmed by Darley (1940), but the results of Beer (1910) were replicated: polysyllabic passages were read more rapidly in terms of syllables per minute than monosyllabic ones. It is, however, diagnostic of American research at this era that no mention of the earlier German research was made. The additional point was also made that subjective impression of speeech rate corresponds closely to words per minute, but is inversely related to syllables per minute. Keilhacker (1940), too, found discrepancies between objective measurement and subjective impression of speech rate. Also included in his article is a broad array of conclusions regarding the personality of various types of speakers. But because of the almost entirely qualitative nature of the discussion, quite independent of the data, the conclusions might well be considered to be only rather interesting hypotheses:

> The communicative significance of pausal structure is both important and relatively evident. Frequent and clearly demarcated pauses, even where the sentence structure does not necessarily call for them, are symptoms of a highly conscious and deliberate speech style, implying quite generally a conscious, self-disciplined characteristic of the speaker (1940: 228) [our translation from German].

Although such description called attention to some of the cognitive aspects of pausing and anticipated later research on rhetorical and poetic expression, the empirical data did not warrant such speculation.

Similar comments can be made with respect to the work of Fairbanks and Hoaglin (1940). They concluded that expression of the emotions of anger, fear, and indifference manifest a rapid rate of speech, whereas contempt and grief manifest a slow rate. But they were dealing with simulation of actors rather than actual emotional expression. Apparently they were unaware of this methodological shortcoming.

Snidecor (1943: 50) made phonographic recordings of one-minute impromptu speeches by "superior male speakers". A week later each subject read aloud a transcript of the speech he had made. A phonographic record of the fundamental sound wave frequencies was then made from the recordings. The mean speaking rate in words per minute was much slower (151 < 183) than the reading rate. The ratio of phonation to unfilled pauses was in both cases 2:1, a lower ratio than that found by Parmenter and Treviño (1935).

In the related context of public oratory, Sheerin (1944) called attention to the retrospective function of the pause to allow something to sink into the consciousness of the audience, in addition to the function of preparing the speaker to continue.

On the whole, then, the German component of this early period was preoccupied with speech rate, largely from the point of view of a reflective philosophy and the school of *Ausdruckspsychologie*. As that tradition faded, the more technological American orientation took over, more often than not in complete isolation from the earlier research. The American emphasis was on temporal characteristics of the optimal or superior speaker, but with little attempt to explain or speculate about possible psychological reasons for pausing. Neither tradition possessed any overall, integrated theory that could justify our speaking of a discipline of pausology.

3 The period from 1945 to 1950

Pike (1945: 31) provides an excellent example of the use of pause in linguistic descriptions at this period. He treated pause very much in the context of contour, pitch, and rhythm, but his observations relied on the assumption that unaided human perception can objectively discern "cessation of speech". His taxonomy of tentative and final pauses was intimately dependent on the same assumption.

Tindall and Robinson (1947) are noteworthy in that they were the first to analyze counselee- and counselor-initiated pauses during interviews though they relied on listener judgments for pause identification. They found it possible to classify them "as to intent and as to their varied effects upon the counseling situation" (1947: 140). Neither Jaffe nor Goldman-Eisler refer to their work in any way.

Cowan and Bloch (1948) defined a perceived pause to be present only if five or more of their ten observers reported it in a corpus of speech. But they found that some of these pauses "were located at points where there was no actual interruption of the physical speech energy, and that on the other hand some relatively long interruptions of the physical energy were not detected as pauses" (1948: 92). They found the following explanation justified:

> If speech pauses set off syntactic phrases in accordance with accepted linguistic usage, as they do most of the time, they present no problem to the observers. If, however, there is no objective pause at a point where there is a strong linguistic reason to expect one, observers may actually be led into reporting a perceptual pause. Similarly, if an objective pause occurs within a phrase where there is no linguistic reason to expect it, observers may fail to notice it even when it is of considerable duration. (1948: 92-3)

The sort of empirical linguistics they engaged in, a combination of psychophysical and grammatical study, could well be considered a forerunner of the cross-disciplinary studies that came to be known at a later date as psycholinguistics. Attention to these findings would have saved Maclay and Osgood (1959), and other more recent researchers, a great deal of trouble, as we shall see somewhat further on.

We should note in passing one of the earlier psychiatric articles on the role of silence in psychoanalysis. Baker (1948) philosophized, somewhat beyond the scope of his data, that "the unconscious aim behind all speech is silence. The silence which we try to achieve is one of complete psychic equilibrium, of agreement, content, and tranquillity" (1948: 365). Baker emphasized, too, the use of false starts. His data base was limited to one patient.

The present authors must admit that they have some difficulty taking an article by Fliess (1949) seriously. The author treated psychotherapeutic aspects of pausology and presented essentially a psychoanalytic taxonomy of unfilled pauses into urethral-erotic, anal-erotic, and oral-erotic silences. The first of these included ordinary interruptions in expected locations, the second disruptive pauses, and the third a temporary replacement of verbalization by silence – whatever that might be. The article is great entertainment for a rainy evening, but its empirical logic is deplorable.

Ruesch and Prestwood (1949) studied pauses due to anxiety in therapeutic interviews with patients. They found that anxiety can be manifested in a great variety of ways, e.g., through long pauses, meager production of words, hesitation, or filled pauses – or quite opposite behaviors. They noted, too, that the perception of anxiety in another depends not on some exact quantity of measures, but on change in a base rate characteristic of the personality of the person observed.

The work of Kelly and Steer (1949) provides some interesting reflections on American research at the time. They characterized speech by means of a measure of rate that excluded between-sentence unfilled pauses. They were quite explicit about the trivial nature of the research: "The results must necessarily be confined to extemporaneous speech in classroom situation and to the particular analysis employed" (1949: 225). Even more interesting is the assumption behind the measure of sentence rate:

> The difference between the over-all rate in a speech and sentence rate is due to a non-speech factor; that is, pause time between sentences is time during which no speech occurs and hence is not directly related to the speed of word utterance within the thought units of speech. (1949: 224)

It is, of course, highly unlikely that nothing directly related to speed of utterance or to thought processes happens during between-sentence unfilled pauses. Perhaps the fact that the authors' interest was in public speaking style accounts for their lack of interest in psychological processes.

Essen (1949) exemplifies once again the preoccupation with speech rate as a reflection of psychological processes, a preoccupation typical of the early German tradition in pausology: "Variation of rate is obviously controlled first of all by the meaning of the individual units of the expression; the more meaning there is invested in a word, the greater the increase in psychological and physical tension, and the slower the articulation rate" (1949: 325) [our translation from the German]. His methodology entailed the use of simulation of emotional mood by the experimental subjects; the extension by inference to genuine emotional situations is rather tenuous.

Hahn (1949) studied a number of dimensions of the speech of six and seven year old children, including phrasing, considered as a means of making meaning clear by dividing spoken words into groups by means of perceivable pauses. Her methods left something to be desired: "To judge the vocal and articulatory aspects of speech, one cannot set up objective measures. The experience of the person making the evaluations must be the basis for the acceptance of the judgments" (1949: 338).

Verzeano and Finesinger (1949) introduced an automatic speech analyzer to measure unfilled pauses with a minimum duration of 0.5 second. A considerable percentage of unfilled pauses is excluded by such an analytic device. Their only reference to Chapple (1942) is in their bibliography, despite his early contribution to the design of such equipment.

The final research report within this chronological period is an acoustic study by Black (1950) on the effect of room characteristics upon vocal intensity and rate: "Phrases were read more slowly in large rooms than in small ones, and among the large rooms, the rate was slower in live than in dead rooms. During reading a series of phrases the mean rate became faster, more so in large than in small rooooms" (1950: 176).

All in all, this short period from 1945 to 1950 was not highly productive or creative in the area of pausology. There are no great landmarks, no great breakthroughs, only some sober warnings about methodological deficiencies: subjective identification methods would have been more appropriate for the study of pause perception than for the study of pause production. But this failing in the quality of research is offset by the fact that most of the areas characteristic of pausology in later years are already represented during this period, with the sole exception of experimental psycho- and socio-linguistics.

4 The period from 1951 to 1960

Meerloo (1952) developed further the taxonomy of silences begun by Fliess (1949) to include additionally physiological inhibition, the silence of the womb, genital silence, transference silence, and repressed aggression. Among his somewhat quaint categories, he included the need to make sounds, or lust for noise (*Schwatzbedürfnis*). Obviously everything fits into a pansexual psychoanalysis with ease.

The work of Karger's (1951) was rather novel in that she had subjects study their own pauses in reading and free speech. In the latter, she found that the faster subjects spoke, the greater the relative and the absolute average length of their pauses. The ratio of all pauses made to pauses recognizable by subjects was 6:1. In other words, even upon reflection, subjects were not aware of most of their unfilled pauses.

The first attempt for applied pausology was made by Toman (1953). Beginning from Karger's (1951) findings, he used the method of having subjects study a recording of their own speech to analyze their pauses. The purpose of this technique was clinical: "All of 35 subjects [. . .] revealed content material hidden or suppressed in the pauses that probably could not have been brought to light by other interviewing procedures in the given time" (1953: 2). Although Toman recommended his technique especially for short-term therapy, it was not developed further in subsequent periods.

Lorenz (1953) wrote in a clinical context regarding both a taxonomy of speech behavior in manics and the function of filled pauses. She speculated that the characteristic locus of filled pauses is before proper names and dates, and observed that filled pauses not noted in the ordinary course of speech can be much better localized from recorded speech.

Both methodologically and theoretically, an empirical study of pauses in spontaneous speech and reading by Hegedüs (1953) was highly sophisticated. With a view to better learning "the general laws of thinking" (1953: 34), he measured pause lengths of six subjects from a kymograph in hundredths of a second and apparently without using a cut-off point of some minimum length. The following summary emphasizes the great differences he found between spontaneous speech and written language:

> In writing, successive sentences are generally separated from each other fairly distinctly. In speaking, the boundary lines between the sentences are not so sharp. The speaker completes a thought, as it were, and also effects a longer pause. During the pause, however, he continues to develop the thought, which he attaches to the preceding one in a loose grammatical form. [. . .] The spontaneous forms of language continually appear to be of looser texture than the written ones; yet they are perfectly intelligible, they even have a more direct effect than the logically more exactly framed written sentences, for the moments most essential for understanding are properly underlined and are conveyed to the hearer well defined, not only with the pauses of speech but also by intonation, stress, rhythm, and the tempo of speech. (1953: 18)

In comparing spontaneous conversation with readings, he found on the average the same number of short pauses (around 460 msec), but more longer pauses (1530 msec) in the readings. He interpreted the latter finding in terms of the expressive function of silent pauses. Finally, his review of the history of research on speech pauses is excellent.

Like Hegedüs, Henze (1953: 240) is remarkably comprehensive in his scope and sophisticated in comparison with subsequent research. The impossibility of studying speech rate with numerical or nonsense materials was clearly enunciated; the complex influence of emotion, thought, and social purpose were pointed out; and the wider variation of style in spontaneous speech as compared with reading was recognized. The data indicated that most of the variation in speech rate was accounted for by variation in the amount of pausing; variation in phonation time was very slight. These latter results have been confirmed in numerous subsequent studies.

In one early psychophysical study of speech rate, Hutton (1954) found estimated rate "to be a logarithmic function of measured rate in words per second during the total speaking time" (1954: 69), and then judged appropriateness of the rate of a given speech sample "to be an inverse linear function of the difference between the estimated rate of the sample and the estimated rate most preferred." (1954: 70)

The next entry to be considered must be noted as highly influential for subsequent research on psycholinguistic aspects of pausology. Lounsbury (1954) wrote one of the sections for the classic *Psycholinguistics* edited by Osgood and Sebeok. His own approach was what he referred to as sequential psycholinguistics. He characterized juncture pauses as being in the order of a hundredth of a second or less in length. Yet he considered these same pauses to be an aid to the hearer and a help to put across the structure of a sentence. His primary preoccupation, however, was with hesitation pauses, which he considered to be appreciably longer. He considered them to be often an annoyance to the hearer and to interfere with rather than aid in grasping the sentence as a whole. His major hypotheses were: Hesitation pauses correspond to the points of highest statistical uncertainty in the sequencing of units of any given order, correspond to the beginning of units of encoding, and frequently do not fall at the points where immediate-constituent analysis would establish boundaries between higher-order linguistic units or where syntactic junctures or facultative pauses would occur; the units given by immediate-constituent analysis, and especially those bounded by facultative pause points, do correspond to units of decoding; and the units of encoding for easy oft-repeated combinations approach coincidence with those of decoding. As we shall point out further on in the appropriate contexts, these hypotheses have been granted an inordinately important role in the subsequent history of pausology. In fact, the historical sense of American pausologists typically extends no further back in history than Lounsbury. Finally, Lounsbury's purely speculative characterization of juncture and hesitation pauses was partly in terms of syntax, partly in terms of the purpose they serve for speaker and/or hearer, and partly in terms of duration. The confusion has led to much unnecessary controversy.

Weisman's (1955) article was a rather philosophical plea for attention to silence as much as to words on the part of psychotherapists. Psychoneurotic silence was described as having the purpose of either provocation or protection. Weisman urged a judicious counter use of silence on the part of the therapist.

In one of the few available studies on languages other than English or German, Hegedüs (1957) studied articulation rate (language sounds per second) in Hungarian, taking his lead partly from Essen 1949. He found that, corresponding to an increased articulation rate for a sports report, as compared to other types of broadcast material, there was also an increase in the average length of unfilled pauses. The importance of articulation rate was later to be underestimated during the Goldman-Eisler era.

Bolinger and Gerstman (1957) hypothesized that spacing (pausing) might influence the differential perception of such lexical items as *lighthousekeeper,* vs. *light housekeeper*, in addition to the factors of pitch and intensity. The evidence indicated that such disjuncture does indeed function directly to carry information. They suggested a redefinition of phonemic stress to eliminate reliance upon loudness and place it upon disjuncture, or alternately a redefinition of loudness to eliminate reliance upon intensity and place it upon disjuncture.

Science fiction and satire have always been a weather vane for the scientific *Zeitgeist*. Böll's *Doktor Murkes gesammeltes Schweigen* (1958), about an eccentric professor who spliced out of tapes the silences or unfilled pauses of speakers, is eloquent testimony that pausology has made its mark on the culture!

Among all the pausological references we have examined, Mysak and Hanley (1958) are the first to have engaged the question of gerontological processes. In their study of male subjects from 30 to 90 years of age, they found a general decline with age in vocal rate for oral reading largely because of the greater duration of pause time. A similar steady decrease in rate was *not* observed for impromptu speaking. Mysak and Hanley (1959) interpreted the latter finding to indicate that oral reading makes more demands on the central nervous system which has to associate sensory with motor input. In impromptu speaking no such sensory input is involved.

For a thoroughly impressionistic interpretation of hesitation phenomena in a clinical context, Feldman (1959) can be cited. He generalized among other things, that the filled pause is always associated with anxiety, and that the initial filler *well*, in reply to a question, is used to give one time to overcome separation from the person who asked it.

In a similar context, an article by Waldhorn (1959) on silence in patients is noteworthy only in that it carries to an extreme the tendency shown in so many psychoanalytic articles in this area. There are no references to other archival literature whatsoever, only intuitive, speculative and informal evidence.

Appealing to the approach of Goldman-Eisler and Matarazzo and his associates, Kanfer (1959; 1960) used speech content and eyeblink as a measure of anxiety and found that verbal rate increases with a subject's present anxiety level, in particular, with a topic of discourse that is anxiety inducing. The experiments were carried out partly with normal and partly with psychiatric patients.

Panek and Martin (1959) used only the more frequent among the speech disturbances of Mahl (1956a and b) and found that both filled pauses and repeats increase with high emotional arousal, as measured by the galvanic skin response (GSR).

Fónagy (1960) compared Hungarian with French and German poetry, and Fônagy and Magdics (1960) investigated various types of speech and found that more rapid speech (e.g., sports announcers) is made possible primarily because pauses are omitted, not because of the shortening of duration of sounds, and thus confirmed for Hungarian Henze's (1953) findings for German, but not the findings of Hegedüs (1957) for Hungarian. They found, too, that equalization of rate is not so much a matter of breath control but of psychological control, a finding redolent of Griffith's (1929) findings for reading and anticipatory of F. and L. Grosjean and Lane's (1979) similar findings. Almost 97% of all inspiratory pauses took place at the end of sentences or clauses.

Because of their influence on subsequent research, Maclay and Osgood (1959) have become quite an important landmark in pausology. They began from Lounsbury's (1954) hypotheses. The corpora consisted of transcripts of selected longer utterances from a scientific conference. Unfilled pauses were localized by the estimation of unaided listener judgment. False starts, repeats, and filled pauses were also analyzed. Their results indicated that both filled and unfilled pauses occur more frequently before lexical than before function words; filled pauses occur more frequently between phrases, unfilled pauses within phrases; individual style determines dominant type of hesitation used; filled pauses come at the conclusion of longer unfilled pauses as a ploy to keep control of the conversation ball. Both the subjective method of identifying unfilled pauses and the very small, selective, atypical sub-corpus on which analyses are based make the results minimally significant. Undoubtedly the historic influence this research has exerted in stimulating further research has been far-reaching.

The decade must be considered important in the history of pausology for the appearance of both Lounsbury's (1954) and Maclay and Osgood's (1959) work. In particular, their hypotheses regarding probabilistic relationships of pauses to elements within the sentence and their taxonomies of pauses were to exert a profound influence on future research. Meanwhile in Europe a certain preoccupation about articulation rate emerged during the same period.

5 The period from 1961 to 1970

We should note briefly in beginning this chronological section that research in both the previous period and the present period was profoundly influenced not only by the individual landmarks in research which we have noted, but also by the gradual development of a number of schools of research, all of which centered about one dominant individual, or in some few cases several individuals. We shall return to these schools at the conclusion of this section.

Arlow's (1961) discussion of silence on the part of patients in psychoanalytic sessions concerned two broad categories of silence: those which serve primarily the function of defense, and those which serve primarily the function of discharge. He considered silence during analytic treatment as essentially an ego disturbance of longer or shorter duration, a repression of cathexis. Several other clinically oriented studies at this time indicated that stress interviews disrupt the speech of chronic schizophrenics (Blumenthal 1964; cited here because of the 1961 date of the doctoral dissertation), that hesitation phenomena are indeed indicators of anxiety (Krause 1961; Krause – Pilisuk 1961), and that silence "could be a sign of contentment, mutual understanding, and compassion" (Zeligs 1961: 8). This last quotation may seem rather banal, except that it is one of the few occasions in the history of pausology on which a psychoanalyst so much as entertains the possibility that pausing or silence might have a positive, healthy function.

Johnson (1961) made use of a number of disfluency categories in a comparative study of stutterers and non-stutterers. The categories were defined rather arbitrarily and atheoretically without reference to other research on disfluencies. Unfilled pauses were entirely excluded from the study "because of the relatively unsystematic judgment involved in deciding whether a given pause is or is not part of the meaningfully fluent production of speech" (1961: 3). It was found that disfluencies do *not* adequately distinguish stutterers from non-stutterers.

The first sociolinguistic contribution to pausology was by Bernstein (1962). He studied hesitation phenomena in adolescent middle-class and lower-class groups and found that the latter group used a longer phrase length, a shorter mean pause duration, and a considerably shorter word length, indicating lower levels of verbal planning characteristic of the *restricted code*.

Niepold's (1970) critique of Bernstein is based on the fact that the lower-class group had several practice sessions before the experimental discussions and that Bernstein actually studied the effect of practice rather than social class.

Leitner (1962) investigated the influence of interphrase rate and pause time on information gain and speaker image. Only interphrase rate influenced information gain, but both independent variables influenced audience perception of the speaker. Unfortunately, the two independent variables were confounded under the conditions of the experiment. In addition, simulation of natural presentation under forced rates, even by advanced graduate students in speech, hardly produces representative human discourse. Leitner held a very idiosyncratic view of both the subjective nature of pausing and, by implication, its function:

> These silences are known as pauses. Since the number and length of these pauses is actually an individual matter, two speakers may be speaking at the same rate, but the manifest rate of one may be much faster than the other's, simply because the first speaker is spending a greater percentage of the total time in pause and is forced to "make up" for these pauses by speeding his actual speaking rate. (1962: 2)

We have found very few pausological materials in Spanish. A study by Navas (1962) dealt with a very specific instance of sentence structure in which a verb phrase after a noun phrase is replaced by a pause serving as a zero morpheme.

Agnello (1963) had subjects report where they had paused in reading a passage. The minimal length of interphrase pauses actually detectable was 190 milliseconds.

The appearance of reviews of extant research is undoubtedly one of the vital signs for any discipline. Kramer's (1963) article on the judgment of personal characteristics and emotions from nonverbal properties of speech is one such review. Interestingly enough, he pointed out that silence and disturbances in speech had "chiefly been treated as disruptions in the speech process rather than as part of the simultaneous nonverbal accompaniment to spoken words" (1963: 415).

Little (1963) described filled pauses and fillers in a corpus of spontaneous speech in terms of their syntactic location. For example, such vocalized pauses do not typically occur between an auxiliary and an infinitive phrase (*has to go*) or between a subject and its predicate, but occur frequently in positions of coordination. Such positioning was found to be in accord with Lounsbury's (1954) hypotheses.

A psycholinguistic study by Livant (1963) argued that "filled pauses serve antagonistic functions, *increasing* the speaker's *control* of conversation, but *decreasing* the *quality* of his production" (1963: 1). The conclusion, however, is ludicrously unrelated to the experiment, in which a handful of subjects were asked either to vocalize or not to vocalize while solving addition problems.

Another example of redundant research is that of Minifie (1963). His conclusions regarding the sources of variation in speech rate (e.g., impromptu speaking slower than reading) had all been in the literature for some time before 1963. Unfortunately, this is not the last time we shall see this phenomenon recurring in pausological research.

Paivio's (1963) research introduces situational context into pausological research. He had children tell stories to adults and found that there were no effects of personality variables (exhibitionism and audience anxiety) or experimental conditions on either speech rate or non-fluencies in speech.

In detailed experimental study, Simkins (1963) found that, when reinforcement is made contingent on talking, there is a significant reduction in amount of pausing for both emotional and non-emotional topics. However, he measured only pauses longer than 0.75 seconds, excluded subjects with large pause indices, and defined emotional topics (circularly) through low pause index: "If one is willing to assume that amount of pausing is a verbal measure of emotion, then it can be tentatively concluded that reinforcement can be employed to bring about systematic changes in emotional behavior" (1963: 467). But what if one is not willing? The assumption is over-simplified and reductionistic and seeemingly disregards the principle of multidetermination of pauses enunciated at the beginning of this review. The topic of reinforcement effects has not been taken up extensively in pausological research.

It is difficult to comment on Blankenship and Kay (1964), largely because they covered such a variety of hesitation phenomena and discussed so much of the background literature in a somewhat diffuse manner. The article is indeed fertile ground for hypotheses about hesitation phenomena, and the concluding comment to the effect that hesitation phenomena operate as some kind of signal for the listener and as a redundant element in the system to aid in understanding, despite their superficially disruptive nature, is well taken.

Crystal and Quirk (1964), in their monograph on prosodic and paralinguistic features of English, have raised the problem of measurement in a rather unusual way:

> Observation and replicability alike suggest that length of silent pause is its relevant gradient characteristic. We have no reason to believe, however, that *absolute* length is relevant, but rather that impressionistic relative length varies with the tempo norm of a given speaker and that the unit should not therefore be a particular number of microseconds but an interval (still of course measurable) related solely to an individual's tempo. (1964: 49)

Without opting for a one-for-one relation between voiced and silent pauses, they suggest parallel details for both in a system of individual rhythmicity. It appears to us that any interval related solely to an individual's tempo is doomed beforehand to inadequacy.

Osser and Peng (1964) returned to the impression, discussed much earlier by Cattell (1886), that foreigners speak fast. They compared spontaneous speech samples of native Americans and native Japanese and found no difference in production rates for segmental phonemes. They speculated, however, that the permissible distribution of pauses may differ. In addition, they posit that

> when we listen to a foreign language being spoken we do *not* hear the pauses (other than the very long ones), rather we hear "continuous flow of speech," and translating this into our experience of hearing the flow of fast English speech, we judge the foreign speech to be faster than it really is. (1964: 124)

A rather more speculative discussion of some of the positive uses of silence in various linguistic cultures is to be found in Samarin 1964.

Brady (1965) reported a technique for investigating on-off patterns of speech. Among the methodological matters discussed are: the designation of 200 milliseconds as the boundary between intersyllabic gaps and listener-detected pauses; a corresponding definition of pause as a time period which is judged by a listener to be a period of nontalking, other than one caused by a stop consonant, a slight hesitation, or a short breath; and admissions that even small changes in the measuring technique can produce noticeable effects on the results and that a simple automatic speech detecting technique involving fixed parameters is inadequate for some purposes. In the dialogues studied, more than 18% of the total time was pause time and over 7% of the time, both speakers were speaking simultaneously.

Whatever may be said of the difficulties of electronic equipment such as Brady's, a return to the use of a stop watch to obtain normative data for reading and speaking rate for grade-school boys, as in Caraway 1965, is methodologically unjustifiable. The same must be said for the hand timing of Laffal (1965) in analyzing the speech of one schizophrenic patient. Pauses of less than 0.5 seconds in length were disregarded. He speculated that brief unfilled pauses are related to word-choice problems, longer pauses to problems in encoding larger units. Levin and Silverman (1965) simply divided unfilled pauses into zero segregates (less than a second) and long pauses by hand timing with a stop watch. Children from 10 to 12 years of age told stories to an audience of four adults or to a microphone. They found that, for the boys, deliberate hesitations varied with exhibitionism; stressful hesitations varied with the audience situation. The deliberate type includes long pauses, repetitions, corrections, and slow rate; the stressful type includes the zero and vocal segregates.

Tannenbaum, Williams, and Hillier (1965) carried out two experiments to study the predictability of words in hesitation contexts. Their return to subjective judgment by trained coders to determine silences of unusual length, rather than the use of objective equipment, can only be considered regressive methodology after all the warnings in the literature. They concluded that words subsequent to hesitations tend to be less predictable than words uttered in fluent context.

Zuk (1965) presented two cases of schizophrenia in which the patients' silence and babbling can be traced to silencing strategies of parents.

Ramsey and Law (1966) attacked once again the perennial problem of accurate equipment for the measurement of unfilled pauses. Their recording and computerized measurement device relied on two conventions: All sounds of less than 0.15 seconds were regarded as spurious sounds, or noise; all silences of less than 0.25 seconds were not regarded as hesitation pauses, after Goldman-Eisler 1958c.

Wolff (1966) hypothesized on the basis of considerable earlier research that neutral and stressful passages would yield differences in reading time, speech rate, pause time, and disruptions. No significant main effects were found for any of the four measures.

Contrary to Osser and Peng (1964), Hanley, Snidecor, and Ringel (1966) found significant differences in terms of phonation/time ratios in a study comparing spontaneous speech of native Spanish, Japanese, and Americans. However, they themselves suggested that very short speech samples produced heterogeneity of variance, thus "casting the validity of the results into serious question" (1966: 103). Due to serious recording problems, the findings of Hanley and Snidecor (1967: 145), namely significant differences in phonation/time ratios among Spanish, Japanese, American, and Tagalog in a reading task, are questionable as well.

The research of Hannah and Engler (1967) is unlike most of the other studies we have considered in that it concerns conversations of an adult with two children. Their purpose was to determine linguistic segmentation as reflected in the perception of unfilled pauses. They found that juncture pauses were perceived most of the time whereas hesitation pauses were minimally perceptible. These results were presented as contrary to those of Boomer and Dittman (1962). Because of the unusual corpus in the present study, it is difficult to say whether the difference is a substantive one.

Lenneberg's (1967) book on the biological foundations of language has become a classic in the short time it has existed. For our purposes it suffices to say that he emphasizes the importance of breathing rate:

> of the two independent variables, rate of breathing and rate of speaking, the former is considerably more subject to variation than the latter. Most subjects speak at a surprisingly constant rate, but some vary in their rate of speech patterns [. . .] The rate of breathing appears to be well-correlated with physiological and emotional stress factors; clearly it may vary independently and without affecting the rate of speaking. (1967: 82–83)

In a later passage, he comments on the truly psycholinguistic import of speech rate: "Apparently, the most important factor limiting rate of speech involves the cognitive aspects of language and not the physical ability to perform the articulatory movements" (1967: 90). The passage attempts to isolate the cognitive aspects of language to the exclusion of the affective both unnecessarily and unrealistically – a separation which has become over the years a powerful hindrance to the development of a reasonable pausological theory.

Levin, Silverman, and Ford (1967) attempted to replicate Goldman-Eisler's (1962) study on descriptive and explanatory speech with children, but altered the cut-off point for minimal unfilled pauses from 250 to 80 milliseconds. They also combined a number of hesitation measures into one overall response measure because of low rate of occurrence for the individual measures. The data in their Table 1 are incorrect, and they also refer to their own previous work (Levin – Silverman 1965) inaccurately. Nonetheless, their findings are in accord with Goldman-Eisler (1962):

> the hesitations in speech inversely mirror the automaticity of the cognitive process. To encode an event whose features are available to the child is automatic. To search one's memory, to accept or reject an idea that comes to mind, to put ideas together – in short, to think – is not automatic and results, as we have seen, in slow, pause-filled, hesitant speech (1967: 564)

Preston and Gardner (1967) presented an ambitious correlation study of various indices of language behavior (written and oral), personality, and ability characteristics. They included only unfilled pauses greater than 1.5 seconds in length, as well as a measure of filled pauses. A factor of social approval or anxiety was reflected in longer unfilled pauses (caution) and proved more characteristic of women than of men. A factor called word production was reflected in the more frequent use of unfilled and filled pauses by people with relatively poor vocabularies.

Pike (1967), in his comprehensive text on language and human behavior, discussed the taxonomy of pauses under two categories; emic and etic pause groups. The categories are no more empirically based than, and as equally abstract as, his earlier ones (Pike 1945).

Woolbert (1920) had found no differences in recall of listeners due to variation of speech rate of pausing. Suci (1967) took up the same problem. Subjects memorized a text or word list. These were then reconstructed, either in accord with or contrary to the pauses used originally, and were then memorized. A cut-off point of 400 milliseconds was used for minimal unfilled pauses. Since the materials reconstructed contrary to the original pause patterns proved more difficult to rememorize, Suci concluded that pauses do indeed reflect psychological units in speech.

Tannenbaum, Williams, and Wood (1967) undertook a comprehensive factor-analytic study similar in its scope to that of Preston and Gardner's (1967). They used a cut-off point of 300 milliseconds for unfilled pauses in vocal encoding, and by analogy a cut-off point of 3 seconds in type-written encoding: "As the cognitive demands increase, the lexical/functional ratio increases and there is a corresponding rise in silent pauses, and it is these which in turn, account for the slower encoding rate and the greater total encoding time" (Tannenbaum – Williams – Wood 1967: 208).

Webb, Williams, and Minifie (1967) tested the hypothesis that verbal decision behavior during induced silent pausing results in reduced respiratory activity; the hypothesis was based on Goldman-Eisler's (1956a) work. Decision demand was varied in an oral reading task in which subjects were to replace one adjective in a message out of a list of either two or six words while reading the message. The finding of no significant effect seems to leave the initial hypothesis untouched because of the extreme artificiality of the experiment.

Weintraub and Aronson (1967) studied defense mechanisms in depressed patients. They defined long pauses as silences of more than 5 seconds. Rate of speaking was also analyzed. A period of 10 minutes of spontaneous monologue was collected and compared with a similar sample from normal subjects. The results were the same as those found three decades previously by Newman and Mather (1938): depressed patients tend to use relatively more pauses. But the authors do not refer to the earlier study at all.

Another psychiatric approach is to be found in Greenson 1967:

> Silence is both a passive and an active intervention on the part of the analyst. The patient needs our silence because he may need time for his thoughts, feelings, and fantasies to emerge from within himself. Our silence also exerts a pressure upon him to communicate and to face his utterances and emotions without distraction. He may feel our silence as supportive and warm, or as critical and cold. (1967: 374)

A final entry for this year is by Meinhold (1967). He used oral readings in German by professional actors and found that the length of unfilled pauses does not differ appreciably in news reports, poetry, and prose, but that frequency of unfilled pauses does vary, and is, for example, much greater in poetry.

Wode (1968) endeavored, by means of a theory of normal intonation, to determine a rationale for the occurrence of pauses related to the syntactic-morphological structure of an utterance. He discussed the conditions under which such pauses may be facultative or obligatory.

Once in a while in this welter of research it is good to find someone who steps back for a moment to review the recent research. That is exactly what Ramsay (1968) did. In addition, he compared Dutch and English subjects on a variety of verbal tasks and found similar speech patterns. However, he found that introverts used longer silences between utterances. Men spent less of the total time in speech than women.

Another worthwhile review appeared at this time (Duncan 1969), with a fairly thorough section on hesitation phenomena, but within the larger general context of non-verbal communication. Duncan, Rice, and Butler (1968) also found therapists' paralanguage discriminative of peak and poor psychotherapy hours. Filled pauses characterized poor interviews. The methodology, however, made use of subjective judgments to identify all categories of paralinguistic behaviors, including filled and unfilled pauses.

Several studies toward the end of this period (Brady 1968, 1969; Gustafson 1969) concerned the statistical properties of on-off patterns in conversations and computer simulation based on the statistical models. This approach is closely related to that of the Jaffe school, to be discussed below.

Reynolds and Paivio (1968) studied cognitive and emotional determinants of speech. Filled pauses were found to be related only to the cognitive determinants; specifically, the definition of more difficult stimulus words elicited relatively more filled pauses. In an audience situation, highly audience-sensitive subjects had the highest silent-pause ratio, suggesting the influence of emotional arousal. Only unfilled pauses exceeding 1.5 seconds were recorded in this study.

A very similar experiment by Lay and Paivio (1969) yielded almost identical results with various samples of spontaneous speech. Noteworthy is the different methodology even within this series of studies; in this later study, only unfilled pauses greater than 1 second were recorded.

What Gilbert and Burk (1969) refer to as self-perception of oral reading rate is really the ability of subjects to match an instructed proportion of their original base rate of speaking. Apart from an abundance of psychophysical terminology, the only interpretable result seems to be that subjects were better able to follow the instruction to slow their speech rate than to accelerate it. What the study had to do with perceptual alterations is difficult to determine, since they are so generically specified.

Howell and Vetter (1969) investigated "the hypothesis that hesitations in spontaneous speech are attributable to the difficulty in selecting the word immediately following hesitation, and the implication that the difficulty of selection is directly related to the relative frequency of the word to be selected" (1969: 261). Their experiment involved the production of sentences with given nouns. Besides the fact that such speech hardly represents typical spontaneous speech, the allocation of pauses as initial and internal to the discourse was somewhat arbitrary. Hesitations were indeed found to be attributable to selection difficulty (number of words to be used by the subjects in accord with instructions), but not to the relative frequency of the individual words. These results were in accord with the authors' earlier study (Howell – Vetter 1968), in which semantic and grammatical complexity were found to be more important than word frequency. In view of these results, it is surprising to find Howell and Vetter (1976) treating hesitation and pausal phenomena in their chapter on speech pathologies and considering "the nongrammatical pause" as an "irregularity" or "normal aberration of speech" (1976: 238).

In a similar experiment, Taylor (1969) superimposed one-second clicks on tape recordings. Otherwise, her method was subjective judgment of frequency and duration of unfilled pauses. She found that content, but not sentence structure affected latencies and hesitations.

With a rather small number of subjects and using a stop watch to measure speech time and unfilled pauses, Webb (1969) claimed to have made measurements down to 0.1 second. The study was intended to compare two methods of categorizing speech rate. He confirmed the finding of Matarazzo that rate of speaking of interviewers alters rate of speaking of interviewees.

Sansbury (1969) took up the question of silences in the counseling situation. He defined silence as any period over two seconds with no verbal communication and found that advanced counselors had more than twice as many silences per interview as beginning counselors and had longer counselor initiated-client terminated silences.

Ford (1970) had children aged 5–11 imitate sentences in which location of unfilled pauses was varied. He found that unfilled pauses within rather than between grammatical phrases facilitiate imitation because they enable the subject to take advantage of grammatical structure sooner and hence make predictions about what is going to be presented. Pauses which occurred between the noun and verb phrase in the stimulus materials were the most disruptive.

Carver (1970) used variously chunked written stimulus materials for adults to read orally. There was no difference due to chunking on either reading rate or comprehension measures. Removal of all punctuation did, of course, degrade both reading rate and comprehension.

After the repeated warnings in the literature about subjective measurement, it is incredible to find, at this late date, such an unsophisticated method as the following from Mishler – Waxler 1970: "Pauses: These are unfilled pauses or silences, judged by the typist and a coder to be 'periods of time in which the average participant might feel that someone *should* be speaking'" (1970: 105). They sampled interaction in families of schizophrenic and normal children and analyzed both unfilled pauses and other hesitation phenomena. College students were asked to guess each successive word in the sampled sentences. They found that, for samples from normal families, predictability rises for words immediately preceding filled and unfilled (non-content) pauses and drops for words following them, and that for samples from schizophrenic families, words preceding such pauses are no more predictable than fluent words, and words following them are highly unpredictable.

Williams (1970) found that grade school teachers differentiated a child's social status by speech characteristics: "Among the most salient predictors were the incidence of silent pausing [. . .]" (1970: 485). But the incidence of silent pausing was in turn assessed by subjective judgment after the precedent of Maclay – Osgood 1959 and was therefore not actually "based on measured characteristics of the speech samples" (1970: 472).

What the present authors have referred to throughout this chapter as parenthetical remarks were investigated by Gülich (1970: 275–6) in French narratives and dialogues from a linguistic point of view. She considered these initial and terminal segmental signals as both psychologically and linguistically relevant: they help the listener segment speech and the speaker to formulate his ideas and serve as a punctuation for speech. Nonetheless, she quotes Hockett (1958) to the contrary:

> Recent research suggests that much can be learned about a person through a close examination of his unedited speech. The particular ways in which he hems and haws, varies the register of his voice, changes his tone quality, and so on, are revealing both of his basic personality and of his momentary emotional orientation. But since (if our assumption is correct) phenomena of these sorts are not manifestation of the speaker's *linguistic* habits, it is proper to ignore them in the study of language, basing that study exclusively on edited speech. (1958: 143f)

Suffice it to say that Hockett's assumption is not correct; the phenomena in question most certainly reflect linguistic habits. Finally, an important methodological principle is expressed by Gülich: "Crucial to our observations is therefore what the ear of the hearer perceives, not what instrumentation reports" (1970: 277) [our translation from the German]. This is indeed the case when speech perception is the focus of a research design. In the present instance, however, only Gülich's ear reported – without any check on its accuracy or reliability.

A rare example of an applied study in pausology is the use of pauses and hesitation phenomena in second language teaching. Leeson (1970) writes: "The possibility suggests itself that the analysis and measurement of pausal phenomena might well have an important role to play in the evaluation of student performance under test conditions and might well form the subject of part of a battery of fluency tests and scores" (1970: 22). Cattell had suggested something of that sort in 1886.

Fillenbaum (1970) found that syntactic locus of pauses affects judgments of their apparent duration. Unfortunately, he used a pause duration (2 sec.) too long to occur unobtrusively at minor within-sentence breaks. There is no reason to believe that his conditions were all "*equally* unobtrusive and salient" (1970: 221) or that the situation was "not too far removed from the normal speech situation" (1970: 220).

Except for a brief mention of a note on the specifications for a new device for speech pause analysis by Reich and Sharma (1970), we have now finished the research for the decade of 1961-70. A comment by Herriot (1970) on the state of the art at this time is in place:

> Firstly, constituent units are perceptual units, in that they preserve their integrity by resisting interrruptions. Secondly, the perception involved is active rather than passsive; the perceiver applies the structure himself, it is not given him by direct physical signals.
>
> Related to these findings are those concerning *pauses* in speech production. If language is planned as a sequence, then pauses should occur before items of low transitional probability. If, however, it is planned hierarchically, then one would predict pauses before constituent units. (1970: 46)

Apparently, it did not occur to researchers during this period that it might be quite likely that speech production is both hierarchical and sequential, instead of a pure case of either.

6 The schools

Before we proceed to the final chronological period of recent research, we would like to discuss somewhat at length a number of schools of research whose work has been both central and crucial in the area of pausology. For our purposes here, we will define school in terms of archival research to which the central figure of the school contributes as sole or co-author. Undoubtedly this is an arbitrary delimitation and omits much research that is actually closely related to the school. Such research is presented in the regular chronological sections.

The first of these schools to be discussed is that of Mahl. The published reports extend from 1956 until 1972, with Mahl sometimes sole author (e.g., 1956a, 1956b, 1958, 1959, 1961, 1963, 1972), and sometimes co-author (e.g., Kasl – Mahl 1956; Kasl – Mahl 1958; Schulze – Mahl – Holzberg 1959; Schulze – Mahl – Murray 1960; Zimbardo – Mahl – Barnard 1963; Mahl – Schulze 1964; Kasl – Mahl 1965).

Mahl began with a taxonomy of normal speech disturbances (SD) which he developed from his empirical work. The basic interests from the very beginning were both personality and the psycholinguistics of anxiety (Mahl 1956a): "The basic working hypothesis underlying the present use of recordings for *this* purpose has been that the most valid linguistic measures of anxiety will be those based on the behavioral or "expressive" aspects of the speech rather than those based on manifest verbal content analysis" (1956a: 1). Over a variety of speech genre and speakers, he found that SDs (exclusive of unfilled pauses) occur approximately every five seconds. The most frequent are filled pauses, sentence changes (or false starts), and repetitions (or repeats), corresponding to the measures of Maclay and Osgood (1959). Mahl assumes that, in most cases, neither speaker nor hearer is aware of their use.

Since anxiety is at the heart of the psychotherapeutic process, Mahl sought a meaningful and useful measure of anxiety in order to investigate the psychosomatic correlates of anxiety in humans in spontaneously occurring real life, interpersonal situations (Mahl 1959). Silence was correspondingly defined in the theory as a defense motivated by anxiety and evoked by ideational events or by the nature of the interpersonal relation. A silence quotient (seconds of silence/seconds available for patient to talk) was obtained by means of a refinement of the old Chapple (1940) methods dependent on tape recordings and hand switching.

The studies of filled pauses (e.g., Mahl 1958) gradually led to the generalization that filled pauses do not vary with anxiety and to the development of the non-ah ratio (speech disturbances minus filled pauses) as a measure of anxiety. From anxiety in spontaneous speech, Mahl proceeded to experimentally induced anxiety and found the non-ah ratio again useful. For the purposes of assessment of ongoing emotional states, content and expressive aspects of speech were found to be largely unrelated (Schulze – Mahl – Murray 1960). Neither was the speech disturbance level found to discriminate schizophrenics (Schulze – Mahl – Holzberg 1959). The first application to children was to high anxiety (HA) and low anxiety (LA) types (Zimbardo – Mahl – Barnard 1963):

> HA children manifest more speech disturbance when they are interviewed under evaluative test-like conditions than when they are treated permissively. On the other hand, LA children react with marked speech disturbance when they are treated permissively, but show much less disturbance in an evaluative interview setting. (1963: 366)

It should be clear that Mahl and his associates have influenced virtually all pausological research dealing with the question of anxiety since the mid 1950s. A fairly typical example of such research is Baker (1964), who used Mahl's speech disturbance categories to find that "student speakers completing the basic speech course can significantly reduce stage fright" (1964: 243).

Were it not for her own review of her work (Goldman-Eisler 1968) and the many critical comments that have arisen (e.g., Boomer 1970) precisely because her work has been so influential, it would be an interminable job to review Goldman-Eisler's many studies. She herself acknowledges that the work of Chapple (1940, 1942) was the initial spur for her own work in the area of pausology. In order to exclude simple articulatory shifts, she systematically limited her considerations to unfilled pauses of more than 250 milliseconds. In general, she concludes that

> pauses represent that aspect of the speech act which has little call on skill and which reflects the non-skill part of the speech process. One might regard pausing as an attribute of spontaneity in the creation of new verbal constructions and structures, i.e., of verbal planning. (1968: 26)

The basic response measure of interest to Goldman-Eisler was, therefore, the unfilled pause. Her early studies (1952, 1954) simply concerned conversation and the interview situation, then tension and affect (1955), psychiatric interviews (1956a), and the cathartic process (1956b), and then more general, normative and statistical matters (1957; 1958a, b, and c; 1961a, b, c, d, and e; 1962; 1964a and b; 1967). Her work with co-authors began fourteen years after she had begun the research series: on equipment (Goldman-Eisler – Mendoza 1965), on the effects of chlorpromazine (Goldman-Eisler – Skarbek – Henderson 1965a and b; 1966; 1967), and again on generally normative matters (Henderson –Goldman-Eisler – Skarbek 1965a and b; 1966). At the end of her own review (1968), she concludes that

> the serial ordering of elements was shown to be a matter of alertness related to the organized execution of peripheral acts; the semantic generation of language on the other hand, e.g., in word choice or the interpretation and creation of meaning to be a matter of suspending peripheral acts and concentrating on central activity. (1968: 127)

Another excellent overview of her work up until 1972 is to be found in Goldman-Eisler 1973 in French.

In more recent work (Goldman-Eisler 1972a) the psychological reality of words, clauses, and sentences has been studied. The assumption is that characteristic duration of unfilled pauses reflects psychological reality differentially. All the speech samples used in this research were from highly literate people and are, therefore, not at all typical spontaneous speech. Without adverting to earlier findings on the same effect, she concluded that pauses between sentences were the longest and most frequent, and that between 93% of the words within clauses there was no unfilled pause. The rarity of fluent transitions between sentences led her to believe that "in most cases a sentence presents the externalization of a thought unit" (1972a: 111). She appeals to Wundt for support with regard to the priority of the sentence as a unit.

In her first work on simultaneous translation (Goldman-Eisler 1972b), she found that professionals use not only the pause time of the speaker for their translation, but they overlap as well with the speaker's speech time. In a second study (Goldman-Eisler – Cohen 1974, 1975), neither the receptive nor productive processes reflected by the experimental tasks succeeded in simulating simultaneous translation. Somehow, this study got published as two completely independent, mutually unacknowledged articles which are almost to a word identical.

The research of Boomer and his associates begins with Boomer – Goodrich 1961, which was essentially an inconclusive replication of Mahl (1956a) based on analyses of only two psychiatric patients. It suggested that the speech disturbance ratio (SDR) be not accepted as a universal measure of situational anxiety in psychiatric interviews. Boomer and Dittman (1962) were considerably more experimental:

> A psychophysical comparison of speech pause perception threshold for juncture and hesitation pauses yielded significantly lower thresholds for the latter. On the basis of these and other data, a functional and methodological distinction between these two types of pause is proposed. (1962: 215)

It should be noted that the distinction in function is intended to apply to the listener. It is methodologically of equal importance to categorize pauses in terms of their function for the speaker.

Boomer (1963) in the following year took up the question of speech disturbance classes once again: "In 39 brief excerpts from the psychotherapy of one patient, a relationship was found between the amount of non-purposive movement and the frequency of a proposed class of speech disturbance, the filled pause ("ah" or unnecessary repetition of a word)" (1963: 265). More commonly, it should be noted, the term *filled pause* is reserved to the former only; repetition of a word is a *repeat*. Little more need be said of the generalizability of research with only one subject. Boomer and Dittmann (1964) returned to the question, however, with eight subjects and found that an increase in filled pause (FP) by inducing cautious syntactic selection is not accompanied by an increase in body movement. The evidence was also negative regarding their hypothesis that "accelerated speech is a primary effect of emotional disturbance, while FP and movement are secondary, almost mechanical, consequences of the acceleration" (1964: 324).

Boomer 1965 is unquestionably the most famous article in the entire series. The occurrence of filled and unfilled pauses was examined with respect to their location in phonemic clauses. A 200 millisecond cut-off point was used for unfilled pauses. Phonemic clause was theoretically defined phonologically by a single primary stress as well as terminal juncture. Actually, they were determined circularly from the unfilled pauses in the tape recordings. In fact, according to Lieberman (1965), the objective physical bases of the Smith-Trager phonemic clause cannot be identified. In addition, there was considerable editing, e.g., *thank you* was considered a single word. The hypothesis was framed as follows:

> hesitations in spontaneous speech occur at points where decisions and choices are being made. On this basis, the patterning of hesitations should provide clues as to the size and nature of the encoding units which are operative.
>
> If the encoding units are single words then hesitations should occur more frequently before those words which involve a difficult decision; i.e., a choice among many alternatives. If the encoding unit is a sequence of several words then the hestitations should predominate at the beginnings of such sequences, rather than occurring randomly wherever a difficult word choice occurs. (Boomer 1965: 148)

Accordingly, Boomer proposed the phonemic clause as the encoding unit of speech at the grammatical level, because both filled and unfilled pauses occur most frequently at the beginning of the phonemic clause. Barik (1968) was largely in agreement with Boomer (1965), but suggested that "depending upon its duration, a pause occurring between two phonemic clauses may be interpreted as consisting of two components: a juncture pause component associated with the first clause and a hesitation pause component associated with the second clause" (1968: 156).

A final article in the Boomer series (1970) is a very thorough critique of Goldman-Eisler 1968, in particular, of her apparent confusion between a proximal and distal theory of the relationship of hesitation and lexical choice. Unfortunately, Boomer (1970) should have pointed out that both alternatives are ridiculous, just as the two theories he presents (1965) of the single word or clause as the encoding unit, and the sequential or hierarchical dichotomy of Herriot (1970) are chimerical, straw alternatives. *The* unit and *the* moment of encoding and *the* unitary process of encoding are all somewhere over the rainbow. One might have thought that we were far beyond such naiveté.

We have referred already to the first work of Tosi (1965) on the technical specifications for the pausimeter, in which he first used the term *pausology*. Black, Tosi, Singh, and Takefuta (1966) had native speakers of Hindi, Spanish, and Japanese, who were either proficient or unskilled in aural comprehension of English, read a two-minute passage in their own languages and in English: "the groups representing less proficiency yielded significantly larger values of median and semi-interquartile range of pauses than those representing more proficiency" (1966: 240). They offered no explanation for the fact that there was no difference between pause length in the native languages compared with the English readings. The data reported in their Table 2 appear highly unreliable.

Tosi, Rockey, and Fischer (1968) found contraction of pause duration at the peak action of the excitatory-exaltatory drug, psilocybin, and hypothesized that such contraction is due to a faster grasp of the information conveyed by each successive word or phoneme. Some of the more recent work of Tosi (1974a and b) investigated measurement and duration of unfilled pauses; Tosi and Lashbrook (1970, 1974) studied unfilled pauses and circadian rhythms. In the latter, the authors found no interaction of circadian rhythm with the subjects' pause duration.

The school led by J.D. Matarazzo has been extraordinarily prolific in the production of research papers; however, a certain amount of redundancy exists in the series of papers. We have selected what we feel is a representative group of the papers most directly concerned with pausological questions. The earliest of these are Saslow – Matarazzo – Guze 1955, and J.D. Matarazzo – Saslow – R.G. Matarazzo 1956, in which the interaction chronograph (Chapple

1940) is discussed and the stage set for their preoccupation with the pauses between speakers in dialogue situations, particularly in various types of interviews. Typical of the research of this school is the finding that the style of the interview affects the temporal aspects of the patients' or interviewees' speech (R.G. Matarazzo – J.D. Matarazzo – Saslow – Phillips 1958). Many of the studies in the earlier years of the research tradition dealt with modifications or validation of their techniques (e.g., Saslow – Matarazzo 1959) and with the relationship of content and structure (e.g., Phillips – R. Matarazzo – J.D. Matarazzo – Saslow – Kanfer 1961; Matarazzo – Weitman – Saslow – Wiens 1963). Throughout the years, the typical subjects of the research were male adults (e.g., Matarazzo – Hess – Saslow 1962). The study by Matarazzo, Wiens, Saslow, Dunham, and Voas (1964) exemplifies some of the applications of their research. Speech durations of astronaut and ground communicator were analyzed by means of both the Chapple interaction chronograph and the interaction recorder (Wiens – Matarazzo – Saslow 1965). It was found, once again, that interviewee speech durations are a function of speech durations of the interviewer. Even interviewer Mm-Hmm was studied in relation to interviewee speech duration (Matarazzo – Wiens – Saslow – Allen – Weitman 1964). An interim review of their research for this early period can be found in Matarazzo – Wiens – Saslow 1965. Matarazzo and Wiens (1967) systematically varied interviewer influence:

> the interviewer increased and decreased his average duration of silence (reaction time latency) before responding to the interviewee. The average duration of silence of the interviewee was increased and decreased by this interviewer tactic as predicted[. . .] These and the earlier results appear to fit into several conceptual frameworks, a response-social reward contingency, on the one hand, and Bandura's *modeling* framework, on the other; with the results of the present study appearing to fall more clearly into the latter. (1967: 56)

Other studies of reaction time latency included the effect of deception and of various content matters (Matarazzo – Wiens – Jackson – Manaugh 1970a and b).

A final methodological comment regarding the Matarazzo research involves the temporal measurement. The hand operated equipment is credited throughout the literature with levels of accuracy that it is difficult to accept without a grain of salt. Such measurements are dependent not only on the limitations of the equipment and the reaction of the experimenter, but on the ability to perceive pauses. The archival literature of pausology leads us to believe that this last influence is an extremely complex one which must surely counter-indicate the accuracy of hand operated timing equipment applied to humanly perceived speech pauses.

The research of Jaffe (1961) and his associates begins with an explicit clinical preoccupation regarding the relation between type-token ratios (TTR) and the non-ah ratio (Mahl 1958) in psychotherapy, schizophrenics (Feldstein 1962), and normals and schizophrenics (Feldstein – Jaffe 1962a). Though the results were inconclusive, they went on to study the effects of anger on normals (Feldstein – Jaffe 1962b) and found no changes in the occurrence of speech disturbances. The following year saw their first use of a computer analysis of speech disturbances (Feldstein – Jaffe 1963a); research also included a replication (Feldstein – Jaffe 1963b) of Feldstein 1962 and a shift from use of monologue only to the addition of dialogue (Feldstein – Brenner – Jaffe 1963). The non-ah ratio was found to be higher in dialogue than in monologue. Jaffe and Norman (1964) began the work on simulation of time patterns in dialogue, and Jaffe, Cassotta, and Feldstein (1964) applied a Markovian model to monologue on-off time sequences. The next two publications (Cassotta – Feldstein – Jaffe 1964; Cassotta – Jaffe – Feldstein – Moses 1964) were concerned with the new automatic vocal transaction analyzer. Thereafter, the question of the predictability of speech disruption became the question (Feldstein – Rogalski – Jaffe 1966).

Apart from a single paper dealing with the changes in time patterns from a screened (deprived visual) access to a vis-a-vis conversation (Feldstein – Jaffe – Cassotta 1967; cf. Kasl – Mahl 1965), nearly all the subsequent studies concerned the statistical properties, stochastic models, computer assessment, and computer simulation for time sequences in dialogues (e.g., Jaffe – Feldstein – Cassotta 1967a and b; Feldstein 1968; Jaffe 1968; Schwartz – Jaffe 1968; Breskin – Jaffe 1970; Jaffe 1970; Jaffe – Breskin 1970a, b, and c; Jaffe – Feldstein 1970) and in monologues (Breskin – Gerstman – Jaffe 1971; Feldstein 1976). Jaffe – Feldstein 1970 is a summary and review of the previous research; it has been favorably reviewed by Aaronson (1973). Jaffe – Breskin – Gerstman 1972 is a *caveat* on the interpretation of time series data. The authors used simulated patterns of vocalizations and pauses to illustrate that random process may produce speech rhythms similar to those attributed to cognitive planning.

Some brief reflections on this tradition of research are in order. The emphasis on dialogue is a healthy antidote for the limitation of most contemporary research to monologue, isolated sentences, or even artificial language materials. However, the contention that dialogue is the unit of verbal interaction, and that monologue is a special case of dialogue, would better be asserted of multilogue, of which dialogue is in turn a special case. In addition, the statement that certain "long range constraints in the on-off patterns of monologue [. . .] are attributable to random fluctuations rather than underlying cognitive states of the speaker" (Jaffe – Feldstein 1970: 4) is entirely gratuitous. The success of a stochastic (or any other type of) model does not logically or empirically exclude the possibility of success of some other scientific model. As a matter of fact, Markovianism hardly protects theoreticians from banality, any more than less sophisticated -isms. The following wisdom regarding dialogue sequences hardly requires commentary: "The more prolonged a silence became, the greater became the probability that it would be succeeded by a speaker switch" (Jaffe – Feldstein 1970: 50). A simple soul might well agree that it does indeed become increasingly evident to an interlocutor that, the longer a speaker refrains from speaking, the more likely it might possibly be that he has finished what he wanted to say. But then, that sounds suspiciously like a cognitive approach.

The work of Pope and Siegman (1962) began with a study on the effects of therapist verbal activity on speech disturbance in initial psychiatric interviews. From twelve verbatim transcripts they concluded that as specificity of the therapist's informational input increases, speech disturbance (anxiety) decreases. The concept of the interview as an informational exchange system with input from both participants was derived from Lennard – Bernstein 1960. Pope and Siegman (1964) assumed that formal characteristics of the interviewer's message (ambiguity vs. specificity, and neutral vs. anxiety arousing topical focus) affect both cognitive (uncertainty) as well as emotional (anxiety) aspects of speech. Siegman and Pope found that "an anxiety-arousing topic produces *disrupted speech*, as manifested in non-ah speech disturbances. Low-specificity remarks, on the other hand, are associated with *cautious and hesitant* speech, rather than with disrupted speech" (1965: 529). Siegman and Pope (1972) found that ambiguous interviewer remarks were associated with more filled pauses and lower articulation rate; but they considered this effect to be independent of anxiety, since it was present in both anxious and non-anxious subjects alike. The same effect was produced by a screen between the interviewer and interviewee, i.e., by relationship ambiguity as well as by message ambiguity, as had been found originally by Kasl and Mahl (1965). Finally, anxiety-arousing interviewer messages elicited speech disruption, but the latter was not related to predispositional anxiety of subjects as indicated by the Manifest Anxiety Scale (MAS). But both situational and predispositional anxiety led to increased speech rate. Pope and Siegman (1972) studied relationship variables (i.e., interviewer rather than message characteristics). They found that a decrease in attraction of interviewees to interviewers led to more filled pauses; that interviewer warmth results in greater fluency of interviewee speech; and that low status interviewers elicit a higher speech disturbance ratio in certain content areas only.

The research of Pope and Siegman can be criticized in that it was done typically with very standardized interviews and consistent behavior of trained interviewers, almost exclusively with female nursing students, and with a stop watch method that admittedly was unreliable for unfilled pauses of less than two seconds in length. Matarazzo and his associates were not quite as modest about an equally inaccurate method of measurement. Finally, it should be noted that Pope and Siegman were interested solely in the speech of the interviewee as a dependent variable, and not with the speech of the interviewer, except as an independent variable.

For a rather short period, Martin and Strange were very productive in the psycholinguistically rather than clinically oriented area of pausology, but since then Martin has become more interested in prosodic features of speech and has abandoned pausological research as such. Their main interest was in the location of hesitations in speech production and perception. In the first study (Martin 1967), encoders described pictures in short utterances and decoders reproduced them:

> encoders yielded a relatively higher proportion of repeats, unfilled pauses, and total hesitations before content words (which have greater uncertainty) than did decoders. Decoders placed relatively more of their hesitations at sentence breaks than did encoders. Apparently, while encoder pauses reflect uncertainty, decoder pauses tend more to mark grammatical boundaries. The selection of semantic-syntactic structure precedes selection of individual words during encoding but follows during decoding. (1967: 903)

A later study (Martin 1968) limited some encoders to one sentence and left others unrestricted. There were fewer unfilled pauses before content words in the unrestricted condition. Unconstrained speakers appear to use more words, but fewer filled pauses within constituents. Martin and Strange (1968a) found a similar reduction in unfilled pauses before content words when the content words were supplied ahead of time.

Martin and Strange (1968b) also took up the question of perception of unfilled pauses with the suggestion that

> listeners normally may ignore hesitations, and perhaps other characteristics of the acoustic signal as well. In all likelihood this is for precisely the reason that while occasionally these are grammatical or informative, usually they are not. The experimental results were thus consistent with a theory stressing the active role of speech perception mechanisms, which would assume that hesitations are filtered out during encoding. (1968b: 428)

The experimental results indicated that attending to acoustic and message aspects of a speech signal are incompatible operations. Methodologically, the research is very questionable. The authors themselves admit in their discussion that spectrographic analyses indicate that unfilled pauses are often not empty intervals. This statement can be made only because they define unfilled pause solely by subjective judgments of observers rather than by any objective measuring device.

Another study (Martin 1970) returned to the question of pause perception. When judgments about pause location by scorers and spectrographic analyses were compared Martin found 90% scorer-spectrograph agreement. False judgments by scorers (perception of a pause where there was none or missing an actually occurring pause) were further analyzed in terms of their location at grammatical junctures. Martin found that "it appears that short preceding syllables suppressed pause judgments at junctures, while long preceding syllables induced pause judgments even though grammatical juncture cues were absent" (1970: 77). He concluded that syllable length is the dominant cue for pause perception; and unless "the duration of real silence is an issue" (1970: 77) listener judgment is preferable to spectrographic recordings.

Martin 1971 reviewed the other studies in the series and summed up use of unfilled pauses in speech production as follows: "Subjects who talk more, think less, at least about word choice, and therefore they tend to pause between rather than within constituents" (1971: 59). With regard to speech perception, it is important to note that according to Martin pauses and false starts constitute distorting speech characteristics which misinform the hearer about the speaker's message. The inability of the decoder to properly model an encoder's hesitations does not at all imply, however, that these are not useful (rather than disruptive) to the decoder. Consequently we cannot, in the absence of further empirical evidence, agree with Clark's (1971) statement in his discussion of Martin 1971: "The conventional pauses seem to have evolved in the language mainly for the benefit of the listener, whereas idiosyncratic hesitations are the product only of an overburdened speaker and give no help to the listener" (1971: 78).

Starting out in the framework of Mahl's work on speech disturbance, the research of Cook and his associates focused on the function of non-ah and filled pauses, respectively. Cook (1968) found that filled pauses were not related to length of utterance, but non-ah speech disturbances decreased for longer utterances. He concluded that data from most previous work on speech disturbances in interviews cannot be applied to conversations due to shorter utterances in the latter. In a study on anxiety, speech disturbances (SD), and speech rate (Cook 1969a), a significant increase in non-ah speech disturbances occurred only for transient anxiety but no relationship between anxiety and filled pauses was found. Cook concluded: "The data support the view that Ah is a function of processes of organization of speech and control of the interaction, and is unrelated to other SDs" (1969a: 20).

In a series of experiments, various aspects of Maclay and Osgood's (1959) hypothesis regarding the function of filled pauses were tested. Partial support was indicated by the finding that words following filled pauses had lower transition probabilities with the exception of pronouns (Cook 1969b). Lalljee and Cook (1969) found that filled pauses in dialogues do not increase as the pressure to continue speaking increases. They suggest, therefore, that Maclay and Osgood's hypothesis applies only to monologue. But even this restricted version of the hypothesis does not seem to hold true. Cook and Lalljee (1970), who asked their subjects to indicate whether a speaker had finished or not, observed that grammatical completeness rather than filled pauses provides cues for the subjects' judgments, although Ball's (1975) evidence was later to indicate clearly that "terminal filled pauses delayed subjects' assumption of the floor considerably" (1975: 423). Cook and Lalljee (1972) hypothesized an increase in filled pauses in a no-vision condition compared to a face-to-face condition in spontaneous dialogue. Their results were negative and their rationalization thereof rather trivial. Finally, Cook (1971) refuted Maclay and Osgood's finding that filled pauses occur more often before lexical words. Using interviews as speech samples and including each filled pause in his analysis rather than selected sequences only, he found that filled pauses occur equally often before lexical and function words. In a critical remark on Maclay and Osgood, Cook concluded that "there is more to the production of speech than finding individual words; the grammar and organization of the utterance requires thought also" (1971: 139). Filled pauses and speech rate as indices of uncertainty in first interview encounters were studied by Lalljee and Cook (1973). Their hypothesis that filled pauses decrease and speech rate increases with progressing interaction was supported. In addition, men were found to produce more filled pauses than women. Cook, Smith, and Lalljee (1974) investigated the relationship of filled pauses and syntactic complexity. Using Goldman-Eisler's (1968) Subordination Index as measure of complexity, they found that filled pause rate did not vary systematically. Such a relationship was observed, however, when clause length was varied. Filled pause rate increased before longer than average clauses: "It appears that FPs are related to uncertainty at the level of the word and clause, but probably not at the level of the sentence" (1974: 15).

The research of Lass and his associates on speech rate has been of recent origin. Their first study (Lass – Noll 1970) concerned the speech rate of normals and cleft palate speakers. As predicted, normals read and spoke at a faster rate by reason of fewer and shorter unfilled pauses. Lass (1970) mechanically altered pause time in order to study perceptual judgments of oral reading rate. The perceptions of rate changed accordingly. Lass and Puffenberger (1971) replicated the Lass (1970) experiment and found no differences between experienced and inexperienced listeners in this regard. Lass and Sandusky (1971) studied the relationship of diadochokinetic (repetition), speaking and reading rates and found the latter two closely related, but the former unrelated to either of the latter two.

In a detailed study of temporal patterns of speech rate alterations by Lass and Deem (1972), subjects were instructed to read at their natural rate and at twice that rate and half that rate. In such circumstances, there are very few options for subjects as to how they can accomplish the task of increasing or decreasing their reading rate, as indicated by a good deal of research previous to the present research. The authors bludgeon the obvious by saying that total pause time was greater for all subjects when attempting to reduce reading rate, and smallest when attempting to increase rate. Similarly, to say that all subjects showed a much greater change in intra- and inter-sentence pause times when attempting to decrease reading rate is ludicrous. It is the only thing they could do to accomplish the slower rate given a test which contained 3 inter-sentence but 73 intra-sentence pause locations. Lass and Clegg (1973) compared temporal characteristics of picture-elicited and topic-elicited speech and found no differences.

The last two in this series of studies on oral reading (Lass – Lutz 1973, 1975) concerned the effect of repetitive reading on speech rate and unfilled pauses. Temporal characteristics of speech were found to be highly consistent over 15 consecutive readings of the same passage and showed little variation from session to session.

The entire series of studies by Lass and his associates exemplifies atheoretical research with practically no link from one study to the next.

7 Recent research (from 1971 to the present)

There has not been a great deal of preoccupation with multilingualism in pausology, but this period opens with a couple of studies in this area. Beardsley and Eastman (1971) studied two Tanzanians whose native language was Swahili. It was found that their code switching (to English) occurred in the environment of pauses and markers. Dickerson (1971) used non-active speakers of English and found that they use the same hesitation devices as native speakers, but take more time to plan their utterances, can store less preplanned utterance, and use more self-corrections and repetitions than native speakers.

Much of the research in this year was developmental. Clay and Imlach (1971) studied length and location of unfilled pauses in oral readings of seven-year olds. Identification of both response measures was by subjective judgment. The poorer readers used long unfilled pauses relatively more often and paused more frequently than punctuation indicated. The best readers reproduced messages in syntactic chunks. Deich (1971) found that retarded children read at the same speed as normals at the same reading level, but made more errors. Engel and Sigelman (1971) found that white and black children enunciated at the same rate in telling stories, but the white children had fewer hesitations. Hawkins (1971) also studied story-telling in children, but the fact that he combined filled and unfilled pauses into a single response category makes his research difficult to compare with others. Clause initial pauses accounted for 66% of all pauses and were longer than pauses before lexical items. He includes a critique of Boomer 1965.

Kools and Berryman (1971) studied disfluencies in spontaneous speech of normal children. Boys and girls had no differences in total number, but boys had more incomplete phrases than girls. Marshall and Cullinan (1971) differentially reinforced children for telling stories, but found no corresponding variation in total disfluencies. Only vocal disfluencies were used, not unfilled pauses. Silverman (1971) studied children's disfluencies in everyday situations or in a structured interview. The latter situation yielded more disfluencies.

The last developmental study in this year (Broen 1971) represents an important approach to children's speech. Broen found that mothers speak more slowly and pause almost exclusively at the end of sentences when dealing with children of about two years of age. Almost all sentences were followed by pauses. With adults, only 50% of the unfilled pauses occurred at the end of sentences. If, as some psycholinguists have suggested, the child's task is to learn to understand and create sentences, mothers' pauses would appear to identify sentences for younger children in this way.

In the same year, a number of reviews of the literature appeared. DeVito (1971) approached the review from the point of view of communication disorders and found pausology important not only for a theory of psycholinguistics, but also for a theory of communication disorders. He held, for example, that stuttering is nothing more than extreme hesitation. Fillenbaum's (1971) review criticized the research on temporal phenomena on the ground that such research has remained largely unrelated to linguistic analysis. Hörmann's (1971) review emphasized the work of Goldman-Eisler and of Maclay and Osgood because of their importance for the study of the psychological reality of grammar. A final review by Murray (1971) summarized studies on talk, silence, and anxiety, i.e., studies relating anxiety and verbal productivity.

A number of other studies in this very productive year must be categorized as *varia*. Wilkinson (1971) approached filled and unfilled pauses rather speculatively as stabilizers: "To 'er' is human" (1971: 49). Brown and Miron (1971) sought to identify predictors for the location of unfilled pauses in reading and came up with the already well established finding that fluent oral readers tend to pause at grammatical junctures. Hunt (1971) compared the speech rate of waking, hypnotized, and simulating (hypnosis) subjects. The latter two groups had more unfilled pauses. But her use of a stop watch to measure the pauses makes the reliability of data questionable. Quinting (1971) studied filled and unfilled pauses in narratives of adult aphasic and normal speakers. Unfilled pauses were measured to a minimum length of one second. He found that both filled and unfilled pauses occur most frequently before a noun or noun phrase. He failed, therefore, to confirm the functional difference in their distribution as predicted from Maclay and Osgood's (1959) findings. He found no differences in patterning of pausing between normals and aphasics. He has been seriously criticized in a review by Schveiger (1973) for his thoroughly atheoretical approach and for the inadequacy of his data presentation and analyses.

The year 1972 contains a little bit of everything, and most of it seems to be presented without much reference to previous research. Aronson and Weintraub (1972) measured articulation rate and silences of more than five seconds in length in speech of patients with a variety of diagnoses. They essentially confirmed the findings of Weintraub – Aronson 1967 and once again failed to refer to the pioneering work of Newman and Mather (1938). Another psychiatric study by Freedman (1972) investigated only one paranoid patient in order to establish some connection between body movement and unfilled pauses of more than 0.5 seconds. Broen and Siegel (1972), without offering operational criteria for disfluencies, found more disfluencies in casual conversation than in speech before a TV camera. Jensen, Ruder, and Harrington (1972) described a device for dubbing unfilled pauses of any desired length into selected locations of voice recordings. Brubaker (1972) found that rate of oral reading is higher for noninitial sentences and interpreted the finding in terms of the gradual reduction of uncertainty as a passage proceeds. Gerver and Dineley (1972) introduced a new automatic speech-pause analyzer and adopted the conventional 250 millisecond cut-off point for unfilled pauses. Martin, Haroldson, and Kuhl (1972) found no significant differences across child-child and child-mother interactions with respect to amount of disfluency. Houston (1972) reviewed the pausological literature with particular emphasis on Mahl's work. Mehrabian (1972) speculated that fillers and filled pauses reflect inconsistent experiences or ambivalence. Finally, Rosenberg (1977) found that unfilled pauses did not differ in sentences produced from either semantically related or unrelated noun pairs, although initial latencies were longer for the unrelated pairs. Similar results were found for adults and children. The materials were presented as a paper in 1972.

In a series of studies, Wilkes and Kennedy (1969, 1970; Wilkes 1972) argued for the relevance in pausology of very short-term unfilled pauses. Some of their research used sentences, some word lists, and some a recall design.

One of the few developmental studies to include older subjects is by Shipp and Hollien (1972). They reported a decrease in mean oral reading rate with increased chronological age in male subjects ranging in age from 20-89 years. This decrease was due to an increase in pause time during utterances. The findings confirm those of Mysak and Hanley (1959).

Yairi and Clifton (1972) in a developmental study compared the narrative speech of preschool children, high-school seniors, and geriatric subjects on a disfluency index similar to Johnson's (1961). No significant differences between preschool children and geriatric subjects were found, but both differed significantly from the high-school seniors. Whereas word repetition and incomplete phrases were most typical for preschool children, the geriatric subjects exhibited the greatest number of interjections, including filled pauses and parenthetical remarks. Meyerson (1976) comments on these findings: "Perhaps Birren's concept (1959) of a need for additional perception and integration time in aging can explain the increased frequency of the aforementioned types of 'timefilling' disfluencies in geriatric subjects" (1976: 33).

The year 1973 occasioned a number of pausological studies with a developmental bent. Cukras (1973) investigated the relationship of pauses to reading comprehension for sixth-grade children reading below grade level. Ability to use pauses was positively correlated with oral and silent reading comprehension. Instruction was found to improve the ability to use pauses efficiently. In a sociolinguistic study, Hawkins (1973) had seven-year old boys and girls tell stories. Narratives of less than 100 syllables were excluded. His questioning of his original assumption is redolent of our principle of multiple determination: "greater fluency inevitably means less planning and hence inferior quality. It seems at least equally plausible to say that fluency indicates more experience, and/or greater confidence in language use on the part of the speaker and hence perhaps even *better* quality" (1973: 243). He found the working-class girls the most fluent, the working-class boys the least. Middle-class children had more genuine hesitation pauses at within-clause locations, suggesting selection of individual lexical items. Hawkins pointed out

> the importance for the present study, of classifying the pauses according to their length and grammatical location. This study suggests pauses may have two different functions. The first function relates to the selection of lexical items; the second function may indicate a failure to meet the specific demands of the task. (1973: 248)

A similar study (Jones – McMillan 1973) added to social class a variety of speech situation variables. Their findings are partly at variance with those of the preceding experiment, however: "These consistent findings of more frequent and longer pauses for lower-class subjects, across age level and across speech conditions, call into question the relevance of hesitation phenomena for cognitive or verbal planning activity accompanying speech" (1973: 120). The findings are also at variance with those of Bernstein (1962). LaBelle (1973) presented sentences to children somewhat under four or somewhat over five. Only the younger group was facilitated by grammatical pause positioning in the stimuli in the task of matching sentences and pictures. He called attention to the developmental importance of the phrase.

Several 1973 studies concerned pathological speech. Liles (1973) varied pause positioning and length to test the comprehension of aphasics and found that presence of pauses, regardless of location, improved comprehension. Spreen and Wachal (1973) compared spontaneous speech of normals and aphasics. Aphasics were found to speak relatively more slowly due to longer unfilled pauses and more between-word pauses and more filled pauses, repeats, and false starts. Silverman (1973) investigated schizophrenic speech. He measured the ratio of pause time (unfilled pauses greater than 250 milliseconds) to total vocalization time. The hypothesis that this ratio would be lowest for the most disturbed patients was not confirmed.

Two studies in this year applied pausological research to the question of effective teaching. Grobe, Pettibone, and Martin (1973) asked one university lecturer to give the same lecture at what he himself considered slow, moderate, and fast instructional paces. They measured students' noise level in response to this variation and found that the moderate pace maintained the lowest noise level in the class. Wyckoff (1973) had twelve teachers increase pausing in their lectures. The increased rate improved comprehension in secondary and lowered it in elementary students.

The mixed-bag category for this year includes a speculative model of segmental timing control in speech production by Allen (1973) and Bruneau's (1973) speculative and philosophical taxonomy of silences. Rochester and Gill (1973) questioned the claim that syntax is irrelevant to the speaker. They analyzed two types of sentence structure in monologue and dialogue and found that in monologue there is no relationship between sentence complexity and speech disruption, but in both monologue and dialogue, noun phrase component constructions are more apt to be disrupted than sentences that contain relative clauses. Ruder (1973) and Ruder and Jensen (1972) used the psychophysical method of adjustment to study the effect of duration of pauses on the perception of pauses in sentences in which the location of the pause varied with the sentence structure, i.e., within or between phrase boundaries. They found that the mean duration of hesitation pauses was 505 milliseconds, of fluent pauses 186 milliseconds, and of pause detection threshold 23 milliseconds, but for only the most complex level of syntax. For the less complex syntactic types, the variation was less systematic. Scherer, London, and Wolf (1973) hark back to *Ausdruckspsychologie* in their use of paralinguistic cues for the expression of doubt and confidence. A confident voice was associated with a faster rate of speech relative to a doubtful one, due to both fewer and shorter unfilled pauses.

Among the reviews of pausological literature, Butterworth's (1973) is rather selective. Rochester's (1973) review focuses on filled and unfilled pauses in spontaneous speech only and is quite comprehensive and critical. Drommel's (1974) is the first comprehensive review of pausological research to appear in German.

Lucci (1973; 1974) measured silent pauses oscillographically (with no cutoff point for minimum length indicated). He found higher speech rates in syllables per second for reading and in turn for reading of lectures than for the lectures themselves; the differences he ascribed to differential pausing, not to articulation rates. He found that prolongation of open syllables in French seems to replace use of filled pauses in English. Conversational speech rate he found to be more variable than that of reading. He also found that the prolongation of open syllables in cultivated conversation was replaced by filled pauses and repeats in ordinary conversation. He made much of a concept of rhythmic groups, but without a clear definition.

Other pausological studies of 1974 include the following : in the area of language development, a study by Dale (1974) looked at hesitation in mothers' speech. In particular, he studied whether these hesitations differ in speech addressed to older vs. younger children. He reported more hesitations at sentence boundaries in the speech to the younger group. No difference was found at phrase boundaries. However, pause measurement was crude: filled pauses were detected by ear and unfilled pauses on a tape with a beep that was triggered after 270 milliseconds of silence. In a sociolinguistic study, Jones (1974) reported that fifth grade boys with high verbal ability paused less frequently and had a shorter mean pause duration than boys of the same age with low verbal quality. Again, the methodology is suspect. Jones explained neither how the oral language samples were recorded nor how the pauses were measured. Also in the area of applied pausology, Rowe (1974) completed a seven-year study of pauses as they affect quality of classroom instruction. She measured, by means of servochart plots, a variable called "wait-time" in two situations, i.e., the pause between the teacher question and initiation of student response and the pause between student responses and initiation of the next teacher question. Typically, the wait-time in both instances is about one second. When teachers were trained to lengthen wait-time to three to five seconds, Rowe noted the following effects: 1) student responses increase in frequency and length, 2) speculative responses increase, 3) student-student comparison of data increases, 4) student-initiated questions increase. Rowe posited that these data tend to support the hypothesis that pauses serve a cognitive function.

In a brief discussion of "Orderly presentation of ideas", the *Publication manual of the American Psychological Association* has the following advice: "Punctuation marks contribute to continuity by providing transitions between ideas. They cue the reader to the pauses, inflections, and pacing normally heard in speech, although punctuation differs in speech and writing. [. . .] Use punctuation to support meaning" (1974: 26). Or, to return to Griffith for a moment: "The silences drive home the sense" (1929: 20).

Henderson (1974) took Jaffe, Breskin, and Gerstman (1972) to task over their intimation that hesitations in speech may be a random process rather than evidence of cognitive planning. He regards this as a null hypothesis in light of theory and experimental findings to date. Hänni (1974) went even further, stating that silent pauses are not to be considered as speech planning time. He based this conclusion on pausological studies in which acoustical disturbance was used to disrupt silent pauses but was found not to affect planning.

Fodor, Bever, and Garrett (1974) reviewed much of the recent pausological research, particularly that of Goldman-Eisler, Boomer, Martin, and Maclay and Osgood. They summed up recent interest in research of this kind as follows: "it is clear why hesitations have been of interest to psychologists – they have face validity as indicants of sentence-planning activity" (1974: 420). The fact of the matter is that their statement vastly over-simplifies both the research interest of the studies they themselves review and the field of pausology in general.

Another article by Drommel (1974-75) on 'occlusion' pauses adds to the small corpus of pausological articles in Spanish and about Spanish speech behavior.

The research of Helfrich and Dahme (1974) was concerned with hesitation phenomena as indicators of situational and habitual anxiety in the context of a represser-sensitizer model. Highly anxious subjects made more long silent pauses (> 1.2 sec) in a threatening situation than in a reassuring situation. The reverse was true for minimally anxious subjects.

One recent research paper is an object lesson in the history of science. Steer 1974 studied the relationship of personality variables and emotion to speech rate. Subjects were asked to count up to 150 three times in a neutral, angry, and pleased manner. An interaction of sex and emotion was found; male subjects showed a slower rate of speech rate change than females across conditions. Most interestingly, however, and contrary to clear advice given by Henze (1953) over two decades earlier, Steer used a meaningless numerical task variable to infer language behavior of a pausological nature:

> Although the subjects were using meaningless material in this case, they were presumably trying to mimic what they thought of as the prevalent sterotype for anger. In view of the well documented statement that in our culture men are chiefly responsible for task activities and women for socio-emotional activities, it may be that for male subjects anger is more commonly expressed in complex task situations requiring considerable planning activities and more speech pauses. If this is the case, personality variables would seem to be too high a level of explanation for considering usefully the speech rate decrease/increase problem (1974: 85).

The passage assumes, of course, that subjects successfully mimic. It also argues circularly from a personality effect in the present research that personality cannot thus be studied.

Finally, Künzel (1974) used an "automatic signal pause analyzer" developed at the Phonetics Institute in Kiel to measure differences between perceived pauses and real (acoustically-measured) pauses. Although his results are not of interest, the push for more sophisticated instruments is a welcome trend in pausology.

It is noteworthy that pausological research of the past few years has been conducted predominantly in applied pausology areas. This trend is ironic in face of the need for basic research using an objective methodology for pause measurement.

Several articles published in 1975 are interesting because they show a return to more basic questions of pausology. Unfortunately, they also persisted in conducting research that may be methodologically spurious.

Lindsley (1975) conducted a study from which he concluded that some but not all of an utterance may be planned before speech is initiated. In particular, he found that verb selection is sometimes performed before subject-verb utterances are initiated. The study consisted of three experiments performed under rather strict laboratory control. Lindsley himself points out the problem of generalizing his conclusions to include naturalistic speech.

In another publication, Butterworth (1975) took up a question posed earlier by Henderson: when and where does content planning during an utterance occur? His data purportedly gave evidence for "a cycle of planning and execution [that has] linguistic and semantic integrity" (1975: 86). The evidence, however, is undermined by a weak methodology. Subjects were asked to mark off 'ideas' in a written text (transcripts of spontaneous speech) by marking them off with slashes. But orthodox punctuation had already been imposed on the texts, thereby providing a built-in indication of linguistic and semantic integrity.

Beginning from the encoding concepts of Butterworth 1975, Beattie has pursued a number of research topics. His first (Beattie 1977) tested the Maclay and Osgood (1959) hypothesis that filled pauses are used to maintain control of the conversational ball. Using a context of natural dialogue, he found filled pauses "effective short-term devices for reducing the probability of interruption" (1977: 284). Beattie (1978a) found no relationship between gaze and incidence of short switching pauses ($\leq$ 500 msec) in conversation. Pauses of $\leq$ 200 msec were regarded as immediate speaker-switches. Beattie (1978b) presented an analysis of sequential temporal patterns of speech and gaze in dialogue. In Beattie 1979, contextual constraints in dyadic conversation were considered. A more general presentation of language production processes in face-to-face interactions was presented in Beattie 1980. Butterworth and Beattie (1978) investigated gesture and silence as indicators of planning in speech. Beattie and Bradbury (1979) found that pause rate was significantly affected by reinforcement and punishment, but that "the overall amount of hesitation is fixed by the cognitive demands of the task" (1979: 225). Butterworth, Hine, and Brady (1977) turned their attention to interaction in sound-only communication channels. Finally, Butterworth (1978) has provided some useful guidelines for studying conversations.

To go back to the mid-seventies again, Rochester (1975-76) has reviewed studies focusing on listener judgment of pauses in speech. To her listing could well be added the work of Drommel (1974). In an experiment with speakers and non-speakers of Spanish, he found that speakers tended to estimate the length of pauses between major syntactic segments to be longer than did non-speakers. He found a correlation of 0.83 between all the subjective judgments of length and the objective lengths of the pauses.

In a series of studies, Grosjean and his colleagues have pursued a variety of research topics. Lane and Grosjean (1973) in a psychophysical study of perception found that "when a speaker doubles his reading rate he perceives a sixfold increase whereas a listener perceives less than a threefold increase" (1973: 141). Lane, Grosjean, Le Berre, and Lewin (1973) examined the effect on the comprehension of English passages by French speakers of variations in articulation rate, pause frequency and duration, transformational complexity, word frequency, and thematic continuity. Variations in transformational complexity had the most marked effect on comprehension. Studies by Grosjean and Deschamps (1972: 1973; 1975) compared temporal phenomena of spoken French and English. These studies have been summarized recently by Grosjean (1980). Effects of temporal phenomena on listener's perception was taken up by Grosjean and Lane (1974: 1976). Grosjean and Lane (1977) and Grosjean (1979) have also taken up the question of timing and syntax of American Sign Language and have made comparisons with spoken English (see also Dechert – Raupach 1980). Finally, Grosjean and Collins (1979) have studied the relationship of breathing and pausing in reading, and F. Grosjean, L. Grosjean, and Lane (1979) have investigated patterns of silence as performance structures in sentence production.

Barik (1970) introduced a computerized method of analysis for temporal data with a 600 msec minimum as cut-off point for silent pauses and a 50 msec minimum for speech bursts. He then applied the method of research on simultaneous translation (Barik 1973, 1975). In Barik 1973, he concluded that translators articulate more slowly than the original speaker and endeavor to speak as much as possible during the speaker's pauses, with a lag of 2-3 sec. In the 1975 study, he concluded that translators were better able to avoid both errors and omissions if speakers' silent pauses occurred more often at grammatical junctures. More recently (Barik 1977) he has presented the same data again, this time with more emphasis on the consistent relationships among temporal variables across French and English. Unfortunately, methodological problems in the selection of speech materials presumed to be comparable across French and English render the research uninterpretable. The sample base is extraordinarily small in comparison with that of Glukhov (1975), who used more than 35 hours of broadcast material to compare Spanish, Portuguese, French, Italian, English, and German and concluded that "the specifics of the different languages have only a relatively slight influence on the univariate pause distribution function" (1975: 72).

The preceding four paragraphs complete our coverage of recent research involving a series of publications, with the exception of our own research (to be reported at the end of this section). The remaining entries constitute individual projects and reports and will be reviewed chronologically.

Pürschel (1975) had native speakers of German read an English text and its translation into German. He interpreted the greater number of pauses in the English text as indicative of greater cognitive demands in planning speech in the foreign language. Identification of pauses was perceptual only.

Helfrich (1975) reviewed studies on hesitations in spontaneous speech according to their functions in cognitive and affective processes and as cues for the listener.

In his discussion of the psycholinguistic significance of pausal phenomena in the context of fluent speech production, Leeson (1975) limited himself mainly to pausological research completed more than a decade previously.

Eagan (1975) found a relationship of pauses in oral reading of children in grades 2-4 to silent reading comprehension, but not to oral reading comprehension. Insufficient detail was provided by the author to allow proper assessment of the findings.

Boguslawski (1975) investigated subjects who spoke for two minutes on a subject of their choice. She failed to confirm her hypotheses regarding positive correlations among speech rate, preferred listening rate of speech, and perception of time, but suggested nonetheless that circadian rhythms should be further investigated in this context. Shoen (1975) also reported negative findings. He asked eighth and tenth graders a series of questions and found that disfluency did not vary significantly with the cognitive complexity of the questions asked.

Semiloff-Zelasko (1975) used a speech perception task and found that rate of speech (slow vs. fast) was easier to distinguish than style (formal vs. casual). No indication was offered for the reader as to the author's method of measurement of actual rate and style.

Natale (1975) found that "individuals with high social desirability converge more in their duration of switching pauses than individuals with low social desirability" (1975: 828). It should be noted, however, that the constraints on subjects' spontaneity were extreme.

In a study comparing miners who were afflicted with black lung disease and normal subjects, Gilbert (1975: 134) concluded: "The inappropriate placement of pauses as well as an increase in the within sentence pause time clearly manifest the miners' inability to sustain phonation over appropriate linguistic intervals."

The relationship of speech performance to nonverbal behaviors is clearly important for pausology. Graham and Heywood (1975) had subjects describe with or without hand gestures two-dimensional drawings of high or low verbal codability. Deletion of gestures led to increase in proportion of time spent in pausing.

Finally in 1975, a study of "Artifacts in the registration of interpretation of speech-process variables" by Braehler and Zenz (1975) must undoubtedly be considered a landmark in pausological research. Their critique applies in some way to almost all earlier and contemporary research. They identified technical artifacts occasioned by uncritical dependence on technology and pinpointed the problem of "the uncritical usage of variables as being synonymous with semantic concepts; this leads to the development of interpretations which refer to these concepts instead of to the measured variables" (1975: 167). They insisted quite correctly that "the selection of a cut-off point for pauses directly determines one's conclusions as to the length of pauses or number of words per chunk" (1975: 171). They also criticized premature use of models "founded on an inadequate theoretical base", especially Markov models, and concluded that "we shall have to remain content with descriptive statistical methods for the time being, at least until mathematical penetration of the communication problem has progressed so far that formal models in keeping with the corresponding theoretical levels can be supplied" (1975: 178). Nor is their critique just another theoretical viewpoint; it is based on empirical replications cogently interpreted.

The year 1976 was not a banner year for pausology. There was generally some concern about cut-off for minimum length of silent pauses. Bordone-Sacerdote and Sacerdote (1976) analyzed the statistical distributions of pauses in readings of a passage of fiction by 20 Italian subjects. They commented that it is not safe to assume (at least for their Italian data) that pauses of < 300 msec in length are strictly phonetic in character.

Rochester (1975-76) reflects a similar concern. She reviewed research on the ability of listeners to perceive short pauses in an attempt to assess the importance of syntactic pause location. She urged researchers to take linguistic context into account in perceptual studies when dealing with silent pauses of < 200 msec in length.

Duez (1976) analyzed a political speech by G. Pompidou as an instance of a specific speech genre. Using a Siemens Oscillomink for measurements and a 200 msec cut-off point, she found an extraordinarily slow speech rate (2.1 syllables per sec) and pause time of 53% of total time. Correspondingly the mean length of silent pauses was 1.3 sec, and articulation rate was slower than for other types of speech in French.

All that need be said of Ragsdale's (1976) study on the effect of anxiety on hesitation phenomena is that he neglected the recent literature and identified silent pauses by subjective judgment only (cf. Ragsdale 1969). In utterances of at least 30 sec in length, five of his 30 subjects made no silent pauses whatsoever!

Dillon (1976) had seven university professors of literature read aloud a passage of poetry (Miltonian iambic pentameter). He measured "substantial pauses" (> 140 msec) oscilloscopically. His results suggested a model of strategies for pause placement in poetic reading.

It is entirely unclear to the present authors what the experiments reported by Wiens, Manuagh, and Matarazzo (1976) have to do with the question they pose, namely how bilinguals store words. Nor is it clear how they argue that their negative results "tend to support the hypothesis that bilingual individuals have neither a single word memory pool nor two discrete word memory pools but, rather, they appear to draw their words from two discernible pools which have a considerable degree of overlap between them" (1976: 90).

Whalen 1976 provides one more example of an empirical project which begins *de novo*, both terminologically and methodologically instead of building on the knowledge already in the literature.

In his book on *Stuttering*, Wingate (1976) castigated others for the use of the words *repetitions, hesitations,* and *interjections*. Then, after proclaiming without any evidence whatsoever that "there is no reason to suspect that the length of a hesitation is of particular significance" (1976: 41), he proceeded to make the same kind of "flagrant violation" (1976: 44) as he accused others of by categorizing prolongations and repetitions as "abnormal" (1976: 47) in his own taxonomy.

Among the 1977 studies of pausology, MacWhinney – Osser 1977 studied spontaneous speech of 5-year-olds: "It was found that hesitations served 3 major functions: *preplanning* of verbalization not yet produced, *coplanning* of verbalization currently being articulated, and *avoidance of superfluous verbalization*" (1977: 978).

Saint-Bonnet and Boe (1977) had subjects read a passage by Zola in the original French. They found that variations in speech rate were due to silent pauses, not to changes in articulation rate.

Engel (1977) studied spontaneous speech of fluent and nonfluent aphasics, nonaphasic brain damaged, schizophrenics, and normals. Her primary concern was with 'commentaries', a category quite closely resembling what the present authors have referred to as parenthetical remarks, and with corrections (including false starts and repetitions). Nonfluent aphasics produced commentaries more often than fluent aphasics, and they in turn more than the other experimental groups. Her interpretation of aphasics' extensive use of commentaries was that they serve to establish a communicative framework, not that they reflect a subjective, emotional function.

Rochester, Thurston, and Rupp (1977) found that thought-disturbed subjects differed from other speakers only in initial pause durations but not in other hesitations.

We can be grateful to H.H. Clark and E.V. Clark (1977) for having made their theory of ideal delivery very explicit. They asserted that all theories of speech production assume that people strive for ideal delivery. In the ideal delivery, however, people " can breathe at junctures, but not within clauses" (1977: 261). The upshot of all this is that silent pauses, filled pauses, repeats, and false starts are all lumped together and presented under the general heading of common speech errors. There is, of course, no necessary connection whatsoever between a theory of speech production and a theory of ideal delivery. In fact, the assumption that there is such a connection reduces the concept of fluency to a caricature of spontaneous speech.

In a series of articles, Gould (1978a, 1978b) and Gould and Boies (1978a, 1978b) have developed the analogy of pauses in written composition to speech pauses. In addition, they have worked out a formula for the allocation of a certain portion of generation time (analogously articulation time in speaking) to planning time. It is abundantly clear that some planning does go on during speaking and writing. The specific formula of Gould and Boies, however, relies on the assumption that this amount is to be determined by the difference between maximum generation rate and actual generation rate. Unfortunately their conclusion that good habits of dictation can be learned very rapidly made use of quite unreliable rater judgments. Finally, the glowing endorsement of dictating by authors employed by a firm that manufactures dictation equipment smacks of experimenter bias. Matsuhashi and Cooper (1978) have also begun similar work on pauses in written composition.

Deese (1978) studied spontaneous multilogue (including graduate seminars and business meetings). Hesitation phenomena such as filled pauses and false starts were assumed to reflect problems in translating thoughts into words. His analyses were largely anecdotal and descriptive.

We have postponed presentation and discussion of our own research until now both because it is of recent vintage and because it represents fairly well where the authors themselves are.

Our research has been conducted under two major premises. First, we agree with Goldman-Eisler that in spontaneous speech "one may expect the relationship between speaking and thinking to reveal itself most naturally" (Goldman-Eisler 1968: 9). We have, therefore, tried to avoid contrived experimental situations which inhibit spontaneity of speech. Second, our methodology is based on the use of an audio frequency spectrometer and level recorder which yield a graphic record of the acoustic energy in terms of amplitude over time, from which all temporal responses can be measured directly. We believe this to be the most precise and objective measure of pause time available at this point in pausological research.

Our first study (O'Connell – Kowal – Hörmann 1969) derived from our reflections on the work of Goldman-Eisler (1968) and Maclay and Osgood

(1959). The research involved both readings and spontaneous stories based on the readings by German-speaking subjects. In the middle of the paragraph occurred either an ordinary event or an unusual one (accomplished by a simple exchange of subject and object). Our summary there best states our conclusions:

> The most important experimental finding was that both number and length of unfilled pauses are more frequent throughout the unusual stories as compared with the usual ones. In the readings, the effect was limited to the critical sentence and the pauses immediately thereafter. The evidence supports the view of the authors that the role of semantic context has been underestimated in psycholinguistic research to date. (1969: 50)

The study was done with German adults. A replication of the basic design was extended to German adolescents and American adults and adolescents (O'Connell – Kowal 1972a). The generality of the effects across two languages and two age brackets was confirmed.

In a brief excursion into glossolalic speech, Bryant and O'Connell (1971) found that glossolalic and English samples of speech from the same subjects were similar in syllables per second rate, but that the glossolalic syllables per pause rate was appreciably higher (18 > 10) than the English rate. O'Connell – Kowal 1972b also reviewed a number of measurement problems in psycholinguistic pause and rate research.

More recently, Kowal, O'Connell, O'Brien, and Bryant (1975) have performed a number of experiments. Their principal findings were: that the number of unfilled pauses in both readings and spontaneous stories based on the readings decreased as proficiency with a foreign language increased; that an analogous decrease in the use of unfilled pauses occurred from second to fourth grade; and that the corresponding decrease in both length and number of unfilled pauses with increasing age underwent a dramatic reversal in the case of poetry readings by well-educated adults. This last result was ascribed to the utilization of unfilled pauses by the well-educated adults for the purpose of rhetorical interpretation.

Kowal, O'Connell, and Sabin (1975) studied story telling in boys and girls at seven age levels in response to a set of cartoon pictures. Increased speech rate with age was due to a decrease in both length and frequency of unfilled pauses. Parenthetical remarks increased with age, whereas repeats decreased. Location of unfilled pauses was stable over age (81% before function words). We hypothesized that cognitive ability is reflected by the length of unfilled pauses, whereas linguistic skill is reflected in their frequency.

O'Connell 1977 presented a critique of pausological research that depends on one or another inadequate empirical definition of the sentence. O'Connell 1980 reviewed and criticized cross-linguistic studies of temporal dimensions of speech.

In addition to our research, recent studies have been conducted by our associates using the same basic methodology. The research of Clemmer (1980) originated in Brown's hypothesis (1973) that schizophrenic speech is linguistically normal and cognitively abnormal. Clemmer's design was essentially a replication of O'Connell – Kowal 1972a with some change in materials and the use of schizophrenic vs. normal subjects. For a number of response measures, support was found for the O'Connell and Kowal results regarding semantic determination of pauses as manifested in the reading and retelling of unusual passages. Insofar as the pausological correlates of linguistic factors showed very few differences between normal and schizophrenic subjects, Brown's thesis was also supported.

Szawara and O'Connell (1977) undertook a study to test whether there is a relationship between pause rate and spontaneity (or preparedness) in the delivery of homilies (sermons). The samples were taken from two groups of homilies: those taped for radio broadcast and those delivered to a congregation in church. As was expected, the more spontaneous homilies (those delivered in church) exhibited significantly longer pause duration, higher percentage of pause time, and slower speech rate than the less spontaneous homilies (those taped for radio broadcast).

A sociolinguistic study by Bassett, O'Connell, and Monahan (1977) partially replicated Kowal – O'Connell – Sabin 1975 with kindergarten and second grade children from high, medium, and low social classes. The results showed a significant difference in the frequency and length of unfilled pauses relative to social class at the kindergarten level. The low social group used much longer, but fewer silent pauses than the other groups. These differences, however, had been neutralized by second grade, presumably by the leveling factors of formal schooling. A similar study by Bassett and O'Connell (1978) investigated second-grade Guatemalan children. Urban children of high socioeconomic status used significantly shorter silent pauses and slower articulation rate than children of low status. A rural group fell between the two urban groups on these measures.

Funkhouser and O'Connell (1978) recorded readings of three well known modern poems: by the authors themselves, by university English professors and by educated adults. A rhetorical or expressive use of both more frequent and longer silent pauses by the authors was generally confirmed. Both speech rate and articulation rate of the authors were dramatically slower than those of the control groups.

Sabin, Clemmer, O'Connell, and Kowal (1979) have summarized a considerable amount of data on developmental aspects of pausology from previous research.

In stories told by native speakers of Spanish and English, de Johnson, O'Connell, and Sabin (1979) found faster articulation and speech rates in the

Spanish speakers. A high rate of parenthetical remarks in the Spanish appeared to be functionally equivalent to the high rate of filled pauses in the English.

Finally, Clemmer, O'Connell, and Loui (1979) compared readings of a passage from St. Paul by church lectors, beginning drama students, and advanced drama students. The readings by the advanced drama students were judged by raters to be the best and were characterized by faster articulation and speech rates and fewer silent pauses, but also by a greater number of *longer* silent pauses.

8 Summary and conclusions

It is very easy to record the archival literature for each successive year with a few essential details, an occasional smattering of critique or commentary, an incidental notation of historical relationship and still end up with something faintly resembling a telephone directory. And of course, we can always blame the lack of intelligibility on the intrinsic defects of the research. We must confess to having done something of that nature up until now.

What we have to say now can be blamed on no one other than the authors. It is now incumbent upon us somehow to distill whatever historical lessons can be garnered for the scientific community from a review of the literature in the area of pausology.

8.1 *Multidetermination*. We would like to return to this concept, introduced early in the article and referred to several times in its course, because it sums up in many respects our views on the history – and the future – of pausology. Most of the research that has been done has proceeded with the implicit assumption that some simple determinants of unfilled pauses and/or other hesitation phenomena can be experimentally isolated so that other determinants are not operative at the same time. But human speech is an extremely complex process in which nearly any conceivable independent variable is inextricably confounded with a number of others. This is not to say, however, that separate determinants do not exist or are not effective in determining in part fashion the complex resultant behavior. There are, for example, cognitive and affective determinants of unfilled pauses; but they can be kept constant in their mutual interaction upon one another in only the most trivialized human behavior. It is far more advisable scientifically to investigate speech with what Brunswik used to call representative design, i.e., in a realistic setting where it is allowed some normal scope, than to trivialize it.

Most of the studies we have reviewed have failed in one way or another to take multidetermination into account. One way this failing can enter into the design or interpretation of experiments is for the experimenter to fail to realize that there are options for subjects. Much of the early work on the relationship between anxiety and hesitation phenomena failed in this respect. It was assumed that there was a single, determinate manner in which anxiety would affect hesitations. Common sense should have led us to suspect, of course, that, as with nearly all very complex higher human processes, some people would talk faster, some slower, some coherently, some incoherently, some correctly, some incorrectly – all under the same influence of an anxiety inducing situation. In other words, the other side of the coin of multidetermination is individual differences or personal style. People differ in their reactions to complex situational stimuli in sophisticated ways, and even the same subject reacts differently from occasion to occasion.

This has been an inordinately long discourse on multidetermination, but the naive or careless neglect of such considerations has vitiated a great deal of pausological research.

8.2 *Methodological defects*. Some of the flaws in pausological research are quite understandable. The analysis of speech data requires great meticulousness. The 'shortcut' of using only a few subjects or subjective methods is a strong temptation. But the matter of subjective judgment of the location and frequency of unfilled pauses has been so widespread, even in more recent research, as to be embarrassing. Although the study of these subjective estimates is a legitimate perceptual investigation in its own right, those who used such measures have typically been professedly interested in the psychological importance of objective unfilled pauses and have assumed that subjective judgment was a good enough measure of them. This was clearly the case with Maclay and Osgood (1959). The same criticism must be made of the use of a stop watch or of other hand operated timing devices that obviously depend on the experimenter's perceptual processes.

Perhaps we should be even more explicit: The perceptual processes which enter into the experimenter's (or neutral judge's) estimates of time intervals in speech are profoundly affected by his own native (and/or foreign) language habits. It is not simply a matter of not having a measuring instrument with sufficiently fine discrimination; it is a systematically biased instrument which perceives some unfilled pauses that physically do not exist and misses some that are longer than the ones it does register.

8.3 *Ahistoricity*. The trend may indeed be no worse in pausological than in other research, but the general lack of historical perspective must nonetheless be noted as deplorable. Testament to this short-sightedness is the fact that none of the reviews to date have had thorough historical coverage. Indeed we are not satisfied with the coverage of our own presentation. But the individual research projects in the area of pausology have more often than not neglected past studies and started relatively from scratch on each occasion.

Hence, we find the phenomenon of recurrent rediscovery of generalizable or lawful behavior involving speech rate, unfilled pauses, and other hesitation phenomena.

The upshot of all this is a plethora of descriptive studies, so much so that we could very well say that the descriptive phase of the science has been adequately covered for the present. Nonetheless, we have already mentioned some methodological defects that force us to have reservations about the adequacy of this coverage from a methodological point of view. The descriptive studies have been limited almost entirely to oral reading and speech production in contrived, artificial situations. Situations which provide even minimal ecological validity have been neglected. Hence more descriptive studies are still needed in naturalistic situations, specifically, in dialogue and multilogue in which within-speaker pauses provide an as yet largely untapped source of data.

In addition, descriptive normative coverage does not imply an adequate taxonomy. This latter category poses a very real problem, not unrelated to methodological and measurement problems, and raises the further problem of implicit theories and assumptions. The taxonomy of pausology has become, largely because of the ahistorical development of the field, a major problem. One finds it hard to know what is intended by such terms as *hesitation, pause, juncture,* or *speech disturbance* in a given study. Frequently enough far reaching theoretical implications are antecedently built into the taxonomy so that the study is biased in favor of one interpretation or another from the very beginning. And more often than not, the theoretical bias is not even recognized by the researcher to be such, but is instead presented erroneously as an operationalized rubric with complete objectivity built into it. Suffice it to say that such a procedure is always either very naive or rather lacking in intellectual integrity.

One final note regarding the ahistorical conduct of pausology concerns the quality of research. Not only have the methodological background and normative data available from history been neglected, but it seems that many of the earlier studies, e.g., Cattell 1886 or Beer 1910, were – in consideration of the methodological tools at their disposal – considerably better research than more recent studies.

8.4 *Theory*. We have found few encouraging landmarks in our review of pausological research, due largely to the theoretical sterility of the field. What little theory has been developed has been rather low level, preliminary, or prototheoretical. Despite the criticism of Boomer (1970) and others (many of which we concur in), we find Goldman-Eisler's theoretical orientation one of the most promising, and quite obviously one of the most provocative and heuristic. On the one hand, we find the more typical dependence on linguistics (e.g., Boomer 1965) and the recommendation thereof (e.g., Fillenbaum 1971) inappropriate, and indeed a probable dead end for pausological theory. The very term *paralinguistic* embodies the isolationism and imperialism of linguistics with regard to pausological phenomena. There is no genuinely logical reason for the term, but it reflects an inveterate abstractionism within linguistics during the Chomsky era and an inability of that discipline to cope with pausological phenomena in an integrative fashion. It should be noted here, however, that the more recent trend within linguistics to move in the direction of a realistic sociolinguistics (e.g., Labov 1972a and b; Hawkins 1973) is much more promising for the future of pausological theory and its integration with other research traditions. On the other hand, we do not feel that the theoretical orientation of Jaffe and Feldstein (1970) shows real promise; they seem to lose in a welter of mathematics any kind of comprehensive view of the psychological function of pauses in dialogue or monologue. Duncan and Fiske (1979) can be similarly faulted.

Finally, some specific oversimplification must be excised from pausological theory. The either-or of proximal-distal perspective must be changed to a both-and. It is obvious that the complexity of speech behavior demands such a revision. Referring an unfilled pause forward or backward to one word (or phrase or clause) as its unique determinant is naive. This consideration brings us to the closely related problem of the unit of decoding and/or encoding. There is no category that can be identified as the unit, and pausologists must be cautious of this red herring. In this regard, we concur with Rochester:

> Finally, it may be that the research for *units* of encoding has itself been the most serious stumbling block to a view of multileveled decision-making by the speaker. Derived from probabilistic models of verbal behavior, the notion of units seems to require a stringently sequential process in which segregated groups of elements have stronger or weaker associations to each other. If the speaker makes a simultaneous lexical-structural decision, what is the "unit?" Perhaps it is wise to leave the search for units to engage in a pursuit of processes or operations which can and often do occur. (1973: 78)

We have emphasized (perhaps overemphasized) the experimental psycholinguistic aspects of pausological theory to the neglect of clinically oriented pausology. The lack of a consistent, coherent theory in the clinical research is, however, no less evident, and certainly no less important.

8.5 *Some perspectives.* We have mentioned in the course of this article a number of landmarks that have influenced subsequent research, some of them not too felicitously (e.g., Maclay – Osgood 1959). There are also some phases of the research endeavor which should be considered a *Zeitgeist* of the past. These would include preoccupation with the collection of normative data, characterization of oral reading, the pausological correlates of normal and pathological personality, the use of meaningless stimulation materials (e.g., numbers, nonsense syllables, isolated words, isolated sentences, and atypical, fabricated paragraphs), simulation of affect, and overdependence on linguistics. Obviously, some of these preoccupations or emphases were deleterious to worthwhile research from the very beginning.

On the other hand, some of the perspectives already to be found in research are to be commended and encouraged. The sociolinguistic trend has already introduced a preoccupation with more representative designs, naturalistic observation, realistic complex situations, dialectology, and socio-economic levels. Broen's (1971) study of the shift in the relationship of mothers to their children in speech interaction as the children grow older seems to us a promising lead.

In the spring of 1978, an interdisciplinary workshop was held in Kassel, Germany, under the title "Pausological implications of speech production". The proceedings of that conference have been published as *Temporal variables in speech. Studies in honour of Frieda Goldman-Eisler* (Dechert – Raupach 1980). That such a conference was even conceivable, that it attracted scholars from at least ten different countries, and that it could serve as an occasion to honor Frieda Goldman-Eisler for her pioneering work in the field of pausology, all bode well for pausological research.

Two more publications remain to be mentioned. The recent appearance of nine studies in a volume entitled *Of speech and time: Temporal speech patterns in interpersonal contexts*, edited by Siegman and Feldstein (1979) bodes well for the future of pausology. In it, veterans in pausological research, including Goldman-Eisler, join with newcomers to the field to present an impressive array of new ideas, hypotheses, procedures, and applications. The inclusion of the concept *interpersonal contexts* as part of the title reflects a refreshing new thrust toward integration within pausological research. The final entry in our own bibliography is itself *A selected bibliography on temporal variables in speech* (Appel – Dechert – Raupach 1980) published in English by a group of scholars at the University of Kassel.

It is to be hoped that the future of pausology will be with sociolinguistics rather than traditional psycholinguistics. The trivialization typical of many of the traditional experiments must go. Developmental studies show great promise. Naturalistic observation can be used in areas such as poetry, rhetoric, and drama. Finally, the cross-cultural and cross-linguistic applications of pausology (quite plausibly useful in the teaching of foreign language) have hardly been touched. In short, we feel pausology has a moderately unimpressive past and a promising future.

Note

1. The authors wish to express their gratitude for the support of the Deutsche Forschungsgemeinschaft and the help of colleagues and secretarial staff at both St. Louis University and the University of Kansas.

References

Aaronson, Doris
1973 "A refreshing monograph on the pause that refreshes: *Rhythms of dialogue* by J. Jaffe and S. Feldstein", *Journal of psycholinguistic research* 2: 369-374.

Agnello, Joseph C.
1963 *A study of intra- and inter-phrasal pauses and their relationship to rate of speech*, unpublished doctoral dissertation, Ohio State University.

Allen, George D.
1973 "Segmental timing control in speech production", *Journal of phonetics* 1: 219-237.

Appel, Gabriela – Hans W. Dechert – Manfred Raupach
1980 *A selected bibliography on temporal variables in speech* (Tübingen: Gunter Narr Verlag).

Arlow, Jacob A.
1961 "Silence and the theory of technique", *Journal of the American Psychoanalytic Association* 9: 44-55.

Aronson, Harriet – Walter Weintraub
1972 "Personal adaptation as reflected in verbal behavior", *Studies in dyadic communication*, edited by Aron Wolfe Siegman and Benjamin Pope (New York: Pergamon Press), 265-279.

Baker, Eldon E.
1964 "An experimental study of speech disturbance for the measurement of stage fright in the basic speech course", *Southern speech journal* 29: 232-243.

Baker, Sidney J.
1948 "Speech disturbances: a case for wider view of paraphasias", *Psychiatry* 11: 359-366.

Ball, Peter
1975 "Listeners' responses to filled pauses in relation to floor apportionment", *British journal of social and clinical psychology* 14: 423-424.

Barik, Henri C.
1968 "On defining juncture pauses: a note of Boomer's 'Hesitation and grammatical encoding'", *Language and speech* 11: 156-159.
1970 "Some findings on simultaneous interpretation", *Proceedings of the 78th annual convention of the American Psychological Association* (Washington, D.C.: American Psychological Association), 11-12.
1973 "Simultaneous interpretation: temporal and quantitative data", *Language and speech* 16: 237-270.
1975 "Simultaneous interpretation: qualitative and linguistic data", *Language and speech* 18: 272-297.
1977 "Cross-linguistic study of temporal characteristics of different types of speech materials", *Language and speech* 20: 116-126.

Bassett, Mary R. – Daniel C. O'Connell
1978 "Pausological aspects of Guatemalan children's narratives", *Bulletin of the Psychonomic Society* 12: 387-389.
Bassett, Mary R. – Daniel C. O'Connell – William J. Monahan
1977 "Pausological aspects of children's narratives", *Bulletin of the Psychonomic Society* 9: 166-168.
Beardsley, R. Brock – Carol M. Eastman
1971 "Markers, pauses and code switching in bilingual Tanzanian speech", *General linguistics* 11: 17-27.
Beattie, Geoffrey
1977 "The dynamics of interruption and the filled pause", *British journal of social and clinical psychology* 16: 283-284.
1978a "Floor apportionment and gaze in conversational dyads", *British journal of social and clinical psychology* 17: 7-15.
1978b "Sequential temporal patterns of speech and gaze in dialogue", *Semiotica* 23: 29-52.
1979 "Contextual constraints on the floor-apportionment function of gaze in dyadic conversation", *British journal of social and clinical psychology* 18: 391-392.
1980 "The role of language production processes in the organization of behaviour in face-to-face interaction", *Language production*, edited by Brian Butterworth (New York: Academic Press), 69-107.
Beattie, Geoffrey – J.R. Bradbury
1979 "An experimental investigation of the modifiability of the temporal structure of spontaneous speech", *Journal of psycholinguistic research* 8: 225-248.
Beer, Max
1910 "Die Abhängigkeit der Lesezeit von psychologischen und sprachlichen Faktoren", *Zeitschrift für Psychologie* 56: 264-298.
Bernstein, Basil
1962 "Linguistic codes, hesitation phenomena and intelligence", *Language and speech* 5: 31-46.
Birren, J.E. (ed.)
1959 *Handbook of aging and the individual* (Chicago: University of Chicago Press).
Black, John W.
1950 "The effect of room characteristics upon vocal intensity and rate", *Journal of the Acoustical Society of America* 22: 174-176.
Black, John W. – Oscar Tosi – Sadanand Singh – Yukio Takefuta
1966 "A study of pauses in oral reading of one's native language and English", *Language and speech* 9: 237-241.
Blankenship, Jane – Christian Kay
1964 "Hesitation phenomena in English speech: a study in distribution", *Word* 20: 360-372.
Bloomfield, Leonard
1933 *Language* (New York: Holt).
Blumenthal, Richard L.
1964 "The effects of level of health, premorbid history, and interpersonal stress upon the speech disruption of chronic schizophrenics", *Journal of nervous and mental disease* 139: 313-323.

Boguslawski, Marie
1975 *An investigation of the relationship between speech rate, preferred listening rate of speech and the perception of time*, unpublished doctoral dissertation, New York University, New York.
Bolinger, Dwight L. – Louis J. Gerstman
1957 "Disjuncture as a cue to constructs", *Word* 13: 246-255.
Böll, Heinrich
1958 *Doktor Murkes gesammeltes Schweigen* (Köln: Kiepenheuer und Witsch).
Boomer, Donald S.
1963 "Speech disturbances and body movement in interviews", *Journal of nervous and mental disease* 136: 263-266.
1965 "Hesitation and grammatical encoding", *Language and speech* 8: 148-158.
1970 "Review of *Psycholinguistics: Experiments in spontaneous speech* by F. Goldman-Eisler", *Lingua* 25: 152-164.
Boomer, Donald S. – Allen T. Dittman
1962 "Hesitation pauses and juncture pauses in speech", *Language and speech* 63: 215-220.
1964 "Speech rate, filled pause, and body movement in interviews", *Journal of nervous and mental disorders* 139: 324-327.
Boomer, Donald S. – D. Wells Goodrich
1961 "Speech disturbance and judged anxiety", *Journal of consulting psychology* 25: 160-164.
Bordone-Sacerdote, C. – G.G. Sacerdote
1976 "Distribution of pauses as a characteristic of individual voices", *Acustica* 34: 245-247.
Brady, Paul T.
1965 "A technique for investigating on-off patterns of speech", *Bell systems technical journal* 44: 1-22.
1968 "A statistical analysis of on-off patterns in 16 conversations", *Bell systems technical journal* 47: 73-91.
1969 "A model for generating on-off speech patterns in two-way conversation", *Bell systems technical journal* 48: 2445-2472.
Braehler, E. – H. Zenz
1975 "Artifacts in the registration and interpretation of speech-process variables", *Language and speech* 18: 166-179.
Braud, William G. – Stephen W. Holborn
1966 "Temporal context effects with two judgmental languages", *Psychonomic science* 6: 151-152.
Breskin, Stephen – Louis J. Gerstman – Joseph Jaffe
1971 "Methods for quantifying on-off speech patterns under delayed auditory feedback", *Journal of psycholinguistic research* 1: 89-98.
Breskin, Stephen – Joseph Jaffe
1970 "On the use of parametric statistical techniques to assess the on-off characteristics of speech", *Journal of psychology* 75: 41-44.
Brigance, William N.
1926 "How fast do we talk?", *Quarterly journal of speech education* 12: 337-342.
Broen, Patricia
1971 "A discussion of the linguistic environment of the young, language learning child", paper presented at the American Speech and Hearing Convention, Chicago, Illinois.

Broen, Patricia A. – Gerald M. Siegel
1972 "Variations in normal speech disfluencies", *Language and speech* 15: 219-231.
Brown, Eric – Murray S. Miron
1971 "Lexical and syntactic predictors of the distribution of pause time in reading", *Journal of verbal learning and verbal behavior* 10: 658-667.
Brown, Roger
1973 "Schizophrenia, language, and reality", *American psychologist* 5: 395-403.
Brubaker, R.S.
1972 "Rate and pause characteristics of oral reading", *Journal of psycholinguistic research* 1: 141-147.
Bruneau, Thomas J.
1973 "Communicative silences: forms and functions", *Journal of communication* 23: 17-46.
Bryant, Ernest – Daniel C. O'Connell
1971 "A phonemic analysis of nine samples of glossolalic speech", *Psychonomic science* 22: 81-83.
Butterworth, Brian
1973 "The science of silence", *New society* 26: 771-773.
1975 "Hesitation and semantic planning in speech", *Journal of psycholinguistic research* 1: 75-87.
1978 "Maxims for studying conversations", *Semiotica* 24: 317-339.
Butterworth, Brian – Geoffrey Beattie
1978 "Gesture and silence as indicators of planning in speech", *Recent advances in the psychology of language*, edited by R.N. Campbell and P.T. Smith (New York: Plenum), 347-360.
Butterworth, Brian – R.R. Hine – K.D. Brady
1977 "Speech and interaction in sound-only communication channels", *Semiotica* 20: 81-99.
Cantril, Hadley – Gordon W. Allport
1935 *The psychology of radio* (New York: Harper and Brothers).
Caraway, Kay E.
1965 *Measurements of speaking rates and oral reading rates for boys in grades four through twelve*, unpublished master's thesis, University of Kansas.
Carver, Ronald P.
1970 "Effect of 'chunked' typography on reading rate comprehension", *Journal of applied psychology* 54: 288-296.
Cassotta, Louis – Stanley Feldstein – Joseph Jaffe
1964 "AVTA: a device for automatic vocal transaction analysis", *Journal of the experimental analysis of behavior* 7: 99-104.
Cassotta, Louis – Joseph Jaffe – Stanley Feldstein – R. Moses
1964 "Operating manual: automatic vocal transaction analyzer", *Research bulletin No. 1* (New York: The William Alanson White Institute).
Cattell, James McKeen
1885 "Über die Zeit der Erkennung and Benennung von Schriftzeichen, Bildern und Farben", *Philosophische Studien* 2: 635-650.
1886 "The time it takes to see and name objects", *Mind* 11: 63-65.
Chapple, Eliot D.
1940 "Measuring human relations: an introduction to the study of the interaction of individuals", *Genetic psychology monographs* 22: 3-147.

1942 "The measurement of interpersonal behavior", *Transactions of the New York Academy of Science* 4: 222-223.

1949 "The Interaction Chronograph: its evolution and present application", *Personnel* 25: 295-307.

Chapple, Eliot D. – Erich Lindemann

1942 "Clinical implications of measurements of interaction rates in psychiatric interviews", *Applied anthropology* 1: 1-11.

Clark, Herbert H.

1971 "The importance of linguistics for the study of speech hesitations", *The perception of language* , edited by David L. Horton and James J. Jenkins (Columbus, Ohio: Charles E. Merrill), 69-78.

Clark, Herbert H. – Eve V. Clark

1977 *Psychology and language. An introduction to psycholinguistics* (New York: Harcourt Brace Jovanovich).

Clay, Marie M. – Robert H. Imlach

1971 "Juncture, pitch, and stress as reading behavior variables", *Journal of verbal learning and verbal behavior* 10: 133-139.

Clemmer, Edward J.

1980 "Psycholinguistic aspects of pauses and temporal patterns in schizophrenic speech", *Journal of psycholinguistic research* 9: 161-185.

Clemmer, Edward J. – Daniel C. O'Connell – Wayne Loui

1979 "Rhetorical pauses in oral reading", *Language and speech* 22: 397-405.

Cook, Mark

1968 "Speech disturbance and length of utterance", *Psychonomic science* 10: 125-126.

1969a "Anxiety, speech disturbances and speech rate", *British journal of social and clinical psychology* 8: 13-21.

1969b "Transition probabilities and the incidence of filled pauses", *Psychonomic science* 16: 191-192.

1971 "The incidence of filled pauses in relation to part of speech", *Language and speech* 14: 135-139.

Cook, Mark – Mansur G. Lalljee

1970 "The interpretation of pauses by the listener", *British journal of social and clinical psychology* 9: 375-376.

1972 "Verbal substitutes for visual signals in interaction", *Semiotica* 6: 212-221.

Cook, Mark – Jacqueline Smith – Mansur G. Lalljee

1974 "Filled pauses and syntactic complexity", *Language and speech* 17: 11-16.

Cotton, Jack C.

1936 "Syllabic rate: a new concept in the study of speech rate variation", *Speech monographs* 3: 112-117.

Cowan, J. Milton – Bernard Bloch

1948 "An experimental study of pause in English grammar", *American speech* 23: 89-99.

Crystal, David – Randolph Quirk

1964 *Systems of prosodic and paralinguistic features in English* (= *Janua Linguarum, series minor*, 39) (The Hague: Mouton).

Cukras, Grace-Ann Gorga

1973 *A clinical study of the prosodic elements of intensity and pauses related to reading comprehension at the intermediate-grade level*, unpublished doctoral dissertation, Fordham University.

Dale, Philip H.
1974 "Hesitations in maternal speech", *Language and speech* 17: 174-181.
Darley, Frederic L.
1940 *A normative study of oral reading rate*, unpublished master's thesis, State University of Iowa.
Dechert, Hans-Wilhelm – Manfred Raupach (eds)
1980 *Temporal variables in speech. Studies in honour of Frieda Goldman-Eisler* (= *Janua Linguarum, series major*, 86) (The Hague: Mouton).
Deese, James
1978 "Thought into speech", *American scientist* 66: 314-321.
Deich, Ruth F.
1971 "Reading time and error rates for normal and retarded readers", *Perceptual and motor skills* 32: 689-690.
DeVito, Joseph A.
1971 *Psycholinguistics* (Indianapolis: The Bobbs-Merrill Co.).
Dickerson, Wayne B.
1971 *Hesitation phenomena in the spontaneous speech of non-native speakers of English*, unpublished doctoral dissertation, University of Illinois at Urbana-Champaign.
Dillon, George L.
1976 "Clause, pause, and punctuation in poetry", *Linguistics* 169: 5-20.
Drommel, R.
1974 "Ein Überlick über die bisherigen Arbeiten zur Sprechpause", *Phonetica* 30: 221-238.
1974-75 "La función de las pausas de oclusión en español – un experimento psicoacústico", *Revista de filología española* 57: 289-303.
Duez, Danièle
1976 "Étude du debut et des pauses d'un discours politique", *Bulletin de l'Institut Phonétique de Grenoble* 5: 39-53.
Duncan, Starkey, Jr.
1969 "Nonverbal communication", *Psychological bulletin* 72: 118-137.
Duncan, Starkey, Jr. – Donald W. Fiske
1979 "Dynamic patterning in conversation", *American scientist* 67: 90-98.
Duncan, Starkey, Jr. – Laura N. Rice – John M. Butler
1968 "Therapists' paralanguage in peak and poor psychotherapy hours", *Journal of abnormal psychology* 73: 566-570.
Eagan, Sr. Ruth
1975 "An investigation into the relationship of the pausing phenomena in oral reading and reading comprehension", *Alberta journal of educational research* 21: 278-288.
Engel, Dorothea
1977 *Textexperimente mit Aphatikern* (Tübingen: TBL Verlag Gunter Narr).
Erdmann, Benno – Raymond Dodge
1898 *Psychologische Untersuchungen über das Lesen auf experimenteller Grundlage* (Halle a.d.S.: Max Niemeyer).
Essen, Otto von
1949 "Sprechtempo als Ausdruck psychischen Geschehens ", *Zeitschrift für Phonetik* 3: 317-341.

Fairbanks, Grant – Newman Guttman – Murray S. Miron
1957 "Effect of time compression upon the comprehension of connected speech", *Journal of speech and learning disorders* 22: 10-19.

Fairbanks, Grant – LeMar W. Hoaglin
1940 "An experimental study of the durational characteristics of the voice during the expression of emotion", *Speech monographs* 7: 85-90.

Feldman, Sandor S.
1959 *Mannerisms of speech and gestures in everyday life* (New York: International Universities Press).

Feldstein, Stanley
1962 "The relationship of interpersonal involvement and affectiveness of content to the verbal communication of schizophrenic patients", *Journal of abnormal and social psychology* 64: 39-45.
1968 "Interpersonal influence in conversational interaction", *Psychological reports* 22: 826-828.
1976 "Rate estimates of sound-silence sequences in speech", *Journal of the Acoustic society of America* 60, supplement No. 1: 46 (abstract).

Feldstein, Stanley – Marcia S. Brenner – Joseph Jaffe
1963 "The effect of subject sex, verbal interaction and topical focus on speech disruption", *Language and speech* 6: 229-239.

Feldstein, Stanley – Joseph Jaffe
1962a "A note about speech disturbances and vocabulary diversity", *Journal of communication* 12: 166-170.
1962b "The relationship of speech disruption to the experience of anger", *Journal of consulting psychology* 26: 505-509.
1963a "An IBM 650 program written in SOAP for the computation of speech disturbances per time, speaker, and group", *Behavioral science* 8: 86-87 (abstract).
1963b "Schizophrenic speech fluency: a partial replication and an hypothesis", *Psychological reports* 13: 775-780.

Feldstein, Stanley – Joseph Jaffe – Louis Cassotta
1967 "The effect of mutual visual access upon conversational time patterns", *American psychologist* 23: 594 (abstract).

Feldstein, Stanley – Carol Rogalski – Joseph Jaffe
1966 "Predictability and disruption of spontaneous speech", *Language and speech* 9: 137-152.

Fillenbaum, Samuel
1970 "Syntactic locus as a determinant of judged pause duration", *Perception and psychophysics* 9: 219-221.
1971 "Psycholinguistics", *Annual review of psychology* 22: 251-308.

Fliess, Robert
1949 "Silence and verbalization: a supplement to the theory of the 'analytic rule'", *International journal of psychoanalysis* 30: 21-30.

Fónagy, I.
1960 "Die Redepausen in der Dichtung", *Phonetica* 5: 169-203.

Fónagy, I. – K. Magdics
1960 "Speech of utterance in phrases of different lengths", *Language and speech* 3: 179-192.

Fodor, J.A. – T.G. Bever – M.F. Garrett
1974 *The psychology of language: an introduction to psycholinguistics and generative grammar* (New York: McGraw-Hill).
Ford, Boyce L.
1970 *Children's imitation of sentences which vary in pause and intonational pattern*, unpublished doctoral dissertation, Cornell University.
Foulke, Emerson (ed.)
1971 *Proceedings of the Second Louisville Conference on Rate and/or Frequency-Controlled Speech: October 22-24, 1969* (Louisville: University of Louisville).
Franke, Phyllis E.
1939 *A preliminary study validating the measurement of oral reading rate in words per minute*, unpublished master's thesis, University of Iowa.
Freedman, Norbert
1972 "The analysis of movement behavior during the clinical interview", *Studies in dyadic communication*, edited by Aron W. Siegman and Benjamin Pope (New York: Pergamon Press), 153-175.
Fröschels, Emil
1920 "Untersuchungen über das Sprechtempo", *Monatsschrift für Ohrenheilkunde und Laryngo-Rhinologie* 54: 867-871.
Funkhouser, Linda – Daniel C. O'Connell
1978 "Temporal aspects of poetry readings by authors and adults", *Bulletin of the Psychonomic Society* 12: 390-392.
Gerver, D. – G. Dineley
1972 "ASPA: automatic speech-pause analyzer", *Behavior research methods and instruments* 4: 265-270.
Gilbert, Harvey R.
1975 "Speech characteristics of miners with black lung disease (pneumoconiosis)", *Journal of communication disorders* 8: 129-140.
Gilbert, John H. – Kenneth W. Burk
1969 "Rate alterations in oral reading", *Language and speech* 12: 192-201.
Glukhov, A.A.
1975 "Statistical analysis of speech pauses for Romance and Germanic languages", *Soviet physics* (= *Acoustics* 21:) 71-72.
Goldman-Eisler, Frieda
1952 "Individual differences between interviewers and their effects on interviewees' conversational behavior", *Journal of mental science* 98: 660-671.
1954 "A study of individual differences and of interaction in the behavior of some aspects of language in interviews", *Journal of mental science* 100: 177-197.
1955 "Speech-breathing activity – a measure of tension and affect during interviews", *British journal of psychology* 46: 53-63.
1956a "The determinants of the rate of speech output and their mutual relations", *Journal of psychosomatic research* 1: 137-143.
1956b "Speech-breathing activity and content in psychiatric interviews", *British journal of medical psychology* 29: 35-48.
1957 "Speech production and language statistics", *Nature* 28: 1497.
1958a "The predictability of words in context and length of pauses in speech", *Language and speech* 1: 226-231.
1958b "Speech analysis and mental processes", *Language and speech* 1: 59-75.

1958c "Speech production and the predictability of words in context", *Quarterly journal of experimental psychology* 10: 96–106.
1961a "A comparative study of two hesitation phenomena", *Language and speech* 4: 18–26.
1961b " The continuity of speech utterance, its determinants and its significance", *Language and speech* 4: 220–231.
1961c "The distribution of pause durations in speech", *Language and speech* 4: 232–237.
1961d "Hesitation and information in speech", *Information theory*, edited by Colin Cherry (London: Butterworth), 162–174.
1961e "The significance of changes in the rate of articulation", *Language and speech* 4: 171–174.
1962 "Speech and thought", *Discovery* 23: 36.
1964a "Discussion and further comments", *New directions in the study of language*, edited by Eric H. Lenneberg (Cambridge, Mass.: The M.I.T. Press), 109–130.
1964b "Hesitation, information and levels of speech production", *Disorders of language*, edited by A. Reuck and M. O'Connor (London: J. and A. Churchill), 96–114.
1967 "Sequential temporal patterns and cognitive processes in speech", *Language and speech* 10: 122–132.
1968 *Psycholinguistics: experiments in spontaneous speech* (London: Academic Press).
1972a "Pauses, clauses, sentences", *Language and speech* 15: 103–113.
1972b "Segmentation of input in simultaneous translation", *Journal of psycholinguistic research* 1: 127–140.
1973 "La mesure des pauses: un outil pour l'étude des processes cognitifs dans la production verbale", *Bulletin de psychologie* 26: 383–390.

Goldman-Eisler, Frieda – Michèle Cohen
1974 "An experimental study of interference between receptive and productive processes relating to simultaneous translation", *Language and speech* 17: 1–10.
1975 "An experimental study of interference between receptive and productive processes involving speech", *Linguistics* 151: 5–16.

Goldman-Eisler, Frieda – R. Mendoza
1965 "Automatic pause-time recording, counting, and totalising equipment" (Springfield, Virginia: National Technical Information Center).

Goldman-Eisler, Frieda – Andrew Skarbek – Alan Henderson
1965a "Cognitive and neurochemical determination of sentence structure", *Language and speech* 8: 86–94.
1965b "The effect of chlorpromazine on speech behavior", *Psychopharmacologia* 7: 220–229.
1966 "Breath rate and the selective action of chlorpromazine on speech behavior", *Psychopharmacologia* 8: 415–427.
1967 "The effect of chlorpromazine on the control of speech-breathing mechanisms", *Journal of verbal learning and verbal behavior* 6: 73–77.

Gould, John D.
1978a "An experimental study of writing, dictating and speaking", *Attention and performance VII*, edited by J. Requin (Hillsdale, N.J.; Lawrence Erlbaum Associates), 299–319.

1978b "How experts dictate", *Journal of experimental psychology: Human perception and performance* 4: 648-661.

Gould, John D. – Stephen J. Boies

1978a "How authors think about their writing, dictating, and speaking", *Human factors* 20: 495-505.

1978b "Writing, dictating, and speaking letters", *Science* 201: 1145-1147.

Graham, Jean Ann – Simon Heywood

1975 "The effects of elimination of hand gestures and of verbal codability on speech performance", *European journal of social psychology* 5: 189-195.

Greenson, Ralph R.

1967 *The technique and practice of psychoanalysis* (New York: International Universities Press).

Griffith, Helen

1929 "Time patterns in prose: a study in prose rhythm based upon voice records", *Psychological monographs* 39 (3, whole no. 179).

Grobe, Robert P. – Timothy J. Pettibone – David W. Martin

1973 "Effects of lecturer pace on noise level in a university classroom", *Journal of educational research* 67: 73-75.

Grosjean, François

1979 "A study of timing in a manual and a spoken language: American Sign Language and English", *Journal of psycholinguistic research* 8: 379-405.

1980 "Temporal variables within and between languages", *Toward a cross-linguistic assessment of speech production*, edited by Hans-Wilhelm Dechert and Manfred Raupach (Frankfurt a.M.: Peter Lang), 39-53.

Grosjean, François – Maryann Collins

1979 "Breathing, pausing and reading", *Phonetica* 36: 98-114.

Grosjean, François – Alain Deschamps

1972 "Analyse des variables temporelles du français spontané", *Phonetica* 26: 129-156.

1973 "Analyse des variables temporelles du français spontané. II. Comparaison du français oral dans la description avec l'anglais (description) et avec le français (interview radiophonique)", *Phonetica* 28: 191-226.

1975 "Analyse contrastive des variables temporelles de l'anglais et du français: vitesse de parole et variables composantes, phénomènes d'hésitation", *Phonetica* 31: 144-184.

Grosjean, François – Lysiane Grosjean – Harlan Lane

1979 "The patterns of silence: performance structures in sentence production", *Cognitive psychology* 11: 58-81.

Grosjean, François – Harlan Lane

1974 "Effects of two temporal variables on the listener's perception of reading rate", *Journal of experimental psychology* 102: 893-896.

1976 "How the listener integrates the components of speaking rate", *Journal of experimental psychology: Human perception and performance* 2: 538-543.

1977 "Pauses and syntax in American Sign Language", *Cognition* 5: 101-117.

Gülich, Elisabeth

1970 *Makrosyntax der Gliederungssignale im gesprochenen Französisch* (München: Fink).

Gustafson, H.W.
1969 "Model for the analysis of talkspurt and silence durations in conversational interaction", *Proceedings of the 77th Annual Convention of the American Psychological Association* (Washington, D.C.: American Psychological Association), 43–44.
Hahn, Elise
1949 "An analysis of the delivery of the speech of first grade children", *Quarterly journal of speech* 35: 338-343.
Hanley, T.D. – J.C. Snidecor
1967 "Some acoustic similarities among languages", *Phonetica* 17: 141-148.
Hanley, T.D. – J.C. Snidecor – R.L. Ringel
1966 "Some acoustic differences among languages", *Phonetica* 14: 97-107.
Hannah, Elaine P. – Leo Engler
1967 "Juncture phenomena and the segmentation of a linguistic corpus", *Language and speech* 10: 228-233.
Hänni, Rolf
1974 "Auswirkungen der Störung von Sprechpausen", *Bericht über den 28. Kongress der Deutschen Gesellschaft für Psychologie in Saarbrücken, 1972.* Band 1: *Wissenschaftstheorie und Psycholinguistik* (Göttingen: Hogrefe).
Harris, Katherine S. – Jarvis Bastian – Alvin M. Liberman
1961 "Mimicry and the perception of a phonemic contrast induced by silent interval: electromyographic and acoustic measures", *Journal of the Acoustical Society of America* 33: 842 (abstract).
Hawkins, Peter R.
1971 "The syntactic location of hesitation pauses", *Language and speech* 14: 277-288.
1973 "The influence of sex, social class and pause-location in the hesitation phenomena of seven-year-old children", *Class, codes and control*, edited by Basil Bernstein (London: Routledge and Kegan Paul), 235-250.
Hegedüs, Lajos
1953 "On the problem of the pauses of speech", *Acta Linguistica Academiae Scientiarum Hungaricae* 3: 1-36.
1957 "Sprechtempoanalysen im Ungarischen", *Zeitschrift für Phonetik* 10: 8-20.
Helfrich, Hede
1975 "Hesitation phenomena in spontaneous speech", *Sophia Linguistica. Working papers in linguistics* 1: 4-16.
Helfrich, Hede – Gisela Dahme
1974 "Sind Verzögerungsphänomene beim spontanen Sprechen Indikatoren persönlichkeitsspezifischer Angstverarbeitung?" *Zeitschrift für Sozialpsychologie* 5: 55–65.
Henderson, Alan I.
1974 "Time patterns in spontaneous speech – cognitive stride or random walk? A reply to Jaffe, et al.", *Language and speech* 17: 119-125.
Henderson, Alan – Frieda Goldman-Eisler – Andrew Skarbek
1965a "The common value of pausing time in spontaneous speech", *Quarterly journal of experimental psychology* 17: 343-345.
1956b "Temporal patterns of cognitive activity and breath control in speech", *Language and speech* 8: 236-242.
1966 "Sequential temporal patterns in spontaneous speech", *Language and speech* 9: 207-216.

Henze, Reinhold

1953 "Experimentelle Untersuchungen zur Phänomenologie der Sprechgeschwindigkeit", *Zeitschrift für experimentelle und angewandte Psychologie* 1: 214-243.

Herriot, Peter

1970 *An introduction to the psychology of language* (London: Methuen).

Hockett, Charles F.

1958 *A course in modern linguistics* (New York: Macmillan).

Hörmann, Hans

1971 *Psycholinguistics: an introduction to research and theory* (New York: Springer-Verlag).

Houston, Susan H.

1972 *A survey of psycholinguistics* (= *Janua Linguarum, series minor*, 98) (The Hague: Mouton).

Howell, Richard W. – Harold J. Vetter

1968 "High and low frequency nouns as sources of hesitation in the production of speech", *Psychonomic science* 12: 157-158.

1969 "Hesitation in the production of speech", *Journal of general psychology* 81: 261-276.

1976 *Language in behavior* (New York: Human Sciences Press).

Hunt, Sonja M.

1971 "Spontaneous speech effects in hypnosis", *International journal of clinical and experimental hypnosis* 19: 225-233.

Hutton, Charles L., Jr.

1954 *A psychophysical study of speech rate*, unpublished doctoral dissertation, University of Illinois at Urbana-Champaign.

Jaffe, Joseph

1961 "Dyadic analysis of two psychotherapeutic interviews", *Comparative psycholinguistic analysis of two psychotherapeutic interviews*, edited by L.A. Gottschalk (New York: International Universities Press), 73-90, 162-173.

1968 "Computer assessment of dyadic interaction rules from chronographic data", *Research in psychotherapy 3*, edited by J. Shlien (Washington, D.C.: American Psychological Association), 260-276.

1970 "Linked probabilistic finite automata: a model for the temporal interaction of speakers", *Mathematical biosciences* 7: 191-204.

Jaffe, Joseph – Stephen Breskin

1970a "Further consequences of a Markov model of speech rhythms", *Computers and biomedical research* 3: 174-177.

1970b "Prediction of an individual speech pattern from dyadic interaction", *Perceptual and motor skills* 30: 363-368.

1970c "Temporal patterns of speech and sample size", *Journal of speech and hearing research* 13: 667-668.

Jaffe, Joseph – Stephen Breskin – Louis J. Gerstman

1972 "Random generation of apparent speech rhythms", *Language and speech* 15: 68-71.

Jaffe, Joseph – Louis Cassotta – Stanley Feldstein

1964 "Markovian model of time patterns of speech", *Science* 144: 884-886.

Jaffe, Joseph – Stanley Feldstein

1970 *Rhythms of dialogue* (New York: Academic Press).

Jaffe, Joseph – Stanley Feldstein – Louis Cassotta
1967a "Markovian models of dialogic time patterns", *Nature* 216: 93-94.
1967b "A stochastic model of speaker switching in natural dialogue", *Research in verbal behavior and some neurophysiological implications*, edited by Kurt Salzinger and Suzanne Salzinger (New York: Academic Press), 281-294.
Jaffe, Joseph – D.A. Norman
1964 "A simulation of the time patterns of dialogue", Scientific report no. C S.-4, Center for Cognitive Studies, Harvard University.
Jensen, Paul J. – Kenneth F. Ruder – Wayne D. Harrington
1972 "Pause adjustment mechanism and measurement system (PAMMS)", *Behavioral research methods and instrumentation* 4: 403-312.
Johnson, Teresa H. de – Daniel C. O'Connell – Edward J. Sabin
1979 "Temporal analysis of English and Spanish narratives", *Bulletin of the Psychonomic Society* 13: 347-350.
Johnson, Wendell
1961 "Measurements of oral reading and speaking rate and disfluency of adult male and female stutterers and nonstutterers", *Journal of speech and hearing disorders*, monograph supplement 7: 1-20.
Jones, Pauline A.
1974 "Elaborated speech and hesitation phenomena", *Language and speech* 17: 199-203.
Jones, Pauline A. – William B. McMillan
1973 "Speech characteristics as a function of social class and situational factors", *Child development* 44: 117-121.
Kanfer, Frederick H.
1959 "Verbal rate, content, and adjustment ratings in experimentally structured interviews", *Journal of abnormal and social psychology* 58: 305-311.
1960 "Verbal rate, eyeblink, and content in structured psychiatric interviews", *Journal of abnormal and social psychology* 61: 341-347.
Karger, Johanna
1951 *Psychologische Ursachen von Sprechpausen*, unpublished doctoral dissertation, Universität Wien.
Kasl, Stanislav V. – George F. Mahl
1956 "A simple device for obtaining certain verbal activity measures during interviews", *Journal of abnormal and social psychology* 53: 388-390.
1958 "Experimentally induced anxiety and speech disturbances", *American psychologist* 13: 349 (abstract).
1965 "The relationship of disturbances and hesitations in spontaneous speech to anxiety", *Journal of personality and social psychology* 1: 425-433.
Keilhacker, Martin
1940 "Sprechweise und Persönlichkeit", *Zeitschrift für angewandte Psychologie und Charakterkunde* 59: 215-241.
Kelly, J.C. – M.D. Steer
1949 "Revised concept of rate", *Journal of speech and hearing disorders* 14: 222-226.
Kleist, Heinrich von
undated "Über die allmähliche Verfertigung der Gedanken beim Reden, an R[ühle] v[on] L[ilienstern]", in: Kleist, Heinrich von, *Sämtliche Werke*, edited by K.F. Reinking (Wiesbaden: R. Löwit), 975-980.

Kools, Joseph A. – Joan D. Berryman
1971 "Differences in disfluency behavior between male and female non-stuttering children", *Journal of speech and hearing research* 14: 125-130.
Kowal, Sabine H. – Daniel C. O'Connell – Eileen A. O'Brien – Ernest T. Bryant
1975 "Temporal aspects of reading and speaking: three experiments", *American journal of psychology* 88: 549-569.
Kowal, Sabine H. – Daniel C. O'Connell – Edward J. Sabin
1975 "Development of temporal patterning of vocal hesitation in spontaneous narratives", *Journal of psycholinguistic research* 3: 196-206.
Kramer, Ernest
1963 "Judgment of personal characteristics and emotions from nonverbal properties of speech", *Psychological bulletin* 60: 408-420.
Krause, Merton S.
1961 "Anxiety in verbal behavior: an intercorrelational study", *Journal of consulting psychology* 25: 272.
Krause, Merton S. – Marc Pilisuk
1961 "Anxiety in verbal behavior: a validation study", *Journal of consulting psychology* 25: 414-419.
Künzel, Hermann
1974 "Eine experimentelle Untersuchung zur Pausenperzeption", *Arbeitsbericht Nr.* 2, Institut für Phonetik, Universität Kiel.
LaBelle, Joseph L.
1973 "Sentence comprehension in two age groups of children as related to pause position or the absence of pauses", *Journal of speech and hearing research* 16: 231-237.
Labov, William
1972a *Language in the Inner City: Studies in the Black Vernacular* (Philadelphia: University of Pennsylvania Press).
1972b *Sociolinguistic patterns* (Philadelphia: University of Pennsylvania Press).
Laffal, Julius
1965 "Pauses in the speech of a schizophrenic patient", *Journal of general psychology* 73: 299-305.
Lalljee, Mansur G. – Mark Cook
1969 "An experimental investigation of the function of filled pauses in speech", *Lcnguage and speech* 12: 24-28.
1973 "Uncertainty in first encounters", *Journal of personality and social psychology* 26: 137-141.
Lane, Harlan – François Grosjean
1973 "Perception of reading rate by speakers and listeners", *Journal of experimental psychology* 97: 141-147.
Lane, Harlan – François Grosjean – J. Le Berre – E. Lewin
1973 "Exploring some properties of foreign-language utterances that control their comprehension", *Linguistics* 112: 15-22.
Lass, Norman J.
1970 "The significance of intra-and intersentence pause times in perceptual judgments of oral reading rate", *Journal of speech and hearing research* 13: 777-784.
Lass, Norman J. – Julia D. Clegg
1973 "Comparative study of temporal characteristics of picture-elicited and topic-elicited speech", *Perceptual and motor skills* 36: 995-998.

Lass, Norman J. – Jodelle F. Deem
1972 "Temporal patterns of speech rate alterations", *Proceedings of the Seventh International Congress of Phonetic Sciences* 7: 922-928.
Lass, Norman J. – Dennis R. Lutz
1973 "Temporal patterns in a repetitive oral reading task", *Acta Symbolica* 4: 39-50.
1975 "The consistency of temporal speech characteristics in a repetitive oral reading task", *Language and speech* 18: 227-235.
Lass, Norman J. – Douglas Noll
1970 "A comparative study of rate characteristics in cleft palate and noncleft palate speakers", *Cleft palate journal* 7: 275-283.
Lass, Norman J. – Marcia D. Puffenberger
1971 "A comparative study of rate evaluations of experienced and inexperienced listeners", *Quarterly journal of speech* 57: 89-93.
Lass, Norman J. – J.C. Sandusky
1971 " A study of the relationship of diadochokinetic rate, speaking rate and reading rate", *Today's speech* 19: 49-54.
Lay, Clarry H. – Allan Paivio
1969 "The effects of task difficulty and anxiety on hesitations in speech", *Canadian journal of behavioral science* 1: 25-37.
Leeson, Richard
1970 "The exploitation of pauses and hesitation phenomena in second language teaching: some possible lines of exploration", *Audiovisual language journal* 8: 19-22.
1975 *Fluency and language teaching* (London: Longman).
Leitner, Margaret A.
1962 *A study of the effects of intraphrase rate and pause time on information gain and speaker image*, unpublished doctoral dissertation, University of Wisconsin.
Lennard, H.L. – A. Bernstein
1960 *The anatomy of psychotherapy* (New York: Columbia University Press).
Lenneberg, Eric H.
1967 *Biological foundations of language* (New York: John Wiley and Sons).
Levin, Harry – Irene Silverman
1965 "Hesitation phenomena in children's speech", *Language and speech* 8: 67-85.
Levin, Harry – Irene Silverman – Boyce Ford
1967 "Hesitations in children's speech during explanation and description", *Journal of verbal learning and verbal behavior* 6: 560-564.
Liberman, Alvin – Katherine S. Harris – Peter Eimas – Leigh Lisker – Jarvis Bastian
1961 "An effect of learning on speech perception: the discrimination of durations of silence with and without phonemic significance", *Language and speech* 4: 175-195.
Lieberman, P.
1965 "On the acoustic basis of the perception of intonation by linguists", *Word* 21: 40-54.
Liles, Betty Zoe
1973 *The effect of pause time on auditory comprehension of aphasic subjects*, unpublished doctoral dissertation, University of Minnesota.

Lindsley, James R.
1975 "Producing simple utterances: How far ahead do we plan?" *Cognitive psychology* 7: 1-19.
Little, LeRoy
1963 *The syntax of vocalized pauses in spontaneous cultivated speech*, unpublished doctoral dissertation, George Peabody College for Teachers.
Livant, William P.
1963 "Antogonistic functions of verbal pauses: filled and unfilled pauses in the solution of additions", *Language and speech* 6: 1-4.
Lorenz, Maria
1953 "Language behavior in manic patients", *Archives of neurology and psychiatry* 69: 14-26.
Lote, Georges
1911 "Le silence et la ponctuation dans l'alexandrin français", *Revue de phonétique* 1: 114-137, 233-259.
Lounsbury, Floyd G.
1954 "Transitional probability, linguistic structure, and systems of habit-family hierarchies", *Journal of abnormal and social psychology* 49, supplement, edited by Charles E. Osgood and Thomas A. Sebeok, 93-101.
Lucci, Vincent
1973 "Étude phonostylistique du rythme et de la variabilité de la longueur en français parlé et français lu", *Bulletin de l'Institut de Phonétique de Grenoble* 2: 139-161.
1974 "Rythme et longueur de message parlé. La conversation", *Bulletin de l'Institut de Phonétique de Grenoble* 3: 139-152.
Lumley, F.H.
1933 "Rates of speech in radio speaking", *Quarterly journal of speech* 19: 393-403.
Maclay, Howard – Charles Osgood
1959 "Hesitation phenomena in spontaneous English speech", *Word* 15: 19-44.
MacWhinney, Brian – Harry Osser
1977 "Verbal planning functions in children's speech", *Child development* 48: 978-985.
Mahl, George F.
1956a "Disturbances and silences in the patient's speech in psychotherapy", *Journal of abnormal and social psychology* 43: 1-16.
1956b "Normal disturbances in spontaneous speech: general quantitative aspects", *American psychologist* 11: 390 (abstract).
1958 "On the use of 'ah' in spontaneous speech: quantitative, developmental, characterological, situational, and linguistic aspects", *American psychologist* 13: 349 (abstract).
1959 "Measuring the patient's anxiety during interviews from 'expressive' aspects of his speech", *Transactions of the New York Academy of Sciences* 21: 249-257.
1961 "Measures of two expressive aspects of a patient's speech in two psychotherapeutic interviews", *Comparative psycholinguistic analysis of two psychotherapeutic interviews*, edited by L.A. Gottschalk (New York: International Universities Press), 91-114, 174-188.

1963 "The lexical and linguistic levels in the expression of the emotions", *Expression of the emotions in Man*, edited by Peter H. Knapp (New York: International Universities Press), 77-105.

1972 "People talking when they can't hear their voices", *Studies in dyadic communication*, edited by Aron W. Siegman and Benjamin Pope (New York: Pergamon Press), 211-264.

Mahl, George F. – Gene Schulze

1964 "Psychological research in the extralinguistic area", *Approaches to semiotics*, edited by T.A. Sebeok, A.S. Hayes and M.C. Bateson (The Hague: Mouton), 51-143.

Marbe, Karl

1908 "Über die Verwendung rußender Flammen in der Psychologie und deren Grenzgebieten", *Zeitschrift für Psychologie* 49: 206-217.

Marshall, Robert C. – Walter L. Cullinan

1971 "Effects of reward schedule changes on children's speech fluency", *Language and speech* 14: 341-357.

Martin, James G.

1967 "Hesitations in the speaker's production and listener's reproduction of utterances", *Journal of verbal learning and verbal behavior* 6: 903-909.

1968 "Two psychological mechanisms specified by hesitation in spontaneous speech", *Proceedings of the 76th Annual Convention of the American Psychological Association* (Washington, D.C.: American Psychological Association), 17-18.

1970 "On judging pauses in spontaneous speech", *Journal of verbal learning and verbal behavior* 9: 75-78.

1971 "Some acoustic and grammatical features of spontaneous speech", *The perception of language*, edited by David L. Horton and James J. Jenkins (Columbus, Ohio: Charles E. Merrill), 47-68.

Martin, James G. – Winifred Strange

1968a "Determinants of hesitations in spontaneous speech", *Journal of experimental psychology* 76: 474-479.

1968b "The perception of hesitation in spontaneous speech", *Perception and psychophysics* 3: 427-438.

Martin, Richard R. – Samuel K. Haroldson – Patricia Kuhl

1972 "Disfluencies in child-child and child-mother speaking situations", *Journal of speech and hearing research* 15: 743-752.

Matarazzo, Joseph D. – Harrie F. Hess – George Saslow

1962 "Frequency and duration characteristics of speech and silence behavior during interviews", *Journal of clinical psychology* 18: 416-426.

Matarazzo, Joseph D. – George Saslow – Ruth G. Matarazzo

1956 "The Interaction Chronograph as an instrument for objective measurement of interaction patterns during interviews", *Journal of psychology* 41: 347-367.

Matarazzo, Joseph D. – M. Weitman – George Saslow – Arthur N. Wiens

1963 "Interview influence on duration of interviewee speech", *Journal of verbal learning and verbal behavior* 1: 451-458.

Matarazzo, Joseph D. – Arthur N. Wiens

1967 "Interviewer influence on durations of interviewee silence", *Journal of experimental research in personality* 2: 56-69.

Matarazzo, Joseph D. – Arthur N. Wiens – Russell H. Jackson – Thomas S. Manaugh
1970a "Interviewee speech behavior under conditions of endogenously-present and exogenously-induced motivational states", *Journal of clinical psychology* 19: 141-148.
1970b "Interviewee speech behavior under different content conditions", *Journal of applied psychology* 54: 15-26.
Matarazzo, Joseph D. – Arthur N. Wiens – George Saslow
1965 "Studies in interview speech behavior", *Research in behavior modification: new developments and implications*, edited by L. Krasner and L.P. Ullman (New York: Holt), 179-210.
Matarazzo, Joseph D. – Arthur N. Wiens – George Saslow – B.V. Allen – M. Weitman
1964 "Interviewer mm-hmm and interviewee speech durations", *Psychotherapy: theory, research and practice* 1: 109-114.
Matarazzo, Joseph D. – Arthur N. Wiens – George Saslow – Richard M. Dunham – Robert D. Voas
1964 "Speech durations of astronaut and ground communicator", *Science* 143: 148-150.
Matarazzo, Ruth G. – Joseph D. Matarazzo – George Saslow – Jeanne S. Phillips
1958 "Psychological test and organismic correlates of interview interaction patterns", *Journal of abnormal and social psychology* 56: 329-338.
Matsuhashi, Ann – Charles Cooper
1978 "A video time-monitored observational study: the transcribing behavior and composing processes of a competent high school writer", paper presented at the American Educational Research Association, Toronto, Ontario.
Meerloo, Joost A.M.
1952 "Free association, silence and the multiple function of speech", *Psychiatric quarterly* 26: 21-32.
Mehrabian, Albert
1972 *Nonverbal communication* (Chicago: Aldine-Atherton).
Meinhold, Gottfried
1967 "Quantität und Häufigkeit von Pausen in gelesenen deutschen Texten im Zusammenhang mit dem Sprechtempo", *Wissenschaftliche Zeitschrift der Friedrich-Schiller-Universität Jena* 1: 107-111.
Meyerson, Marion D.
1976 "The effects of aging on communication", *Journal of gerontology* 31: 29-38.
Minifie, Fred D.
1963 *An analysis of the durational aspects of connected speech samples by means of an electronic speech duration analyzer*, unpublished doctoral dissertation, University of Iowa.
Miron, Murray S. – Eric Brown
1971 "The comprehension of rate-incremented aural coding", *Journal of psycholinguistic research* 1: 65-76.
Mishler, Elliot G. – Nancy E. Waxler
1970 "Functions of hesitations in the speech of normal families and families of schizophrenic patients", *Language and speech* 13: 102-117.
Murray, David C.
1971 "Talk, silence, and anxiety", *Psychological bulletin* 75: 244-260.

Mysak, Edward D. – T.D. Hanley
1958 "Aging processes in speech: pitch and duration characteristics", *Journal of gerontology* 13: 309-313.
1959 "Vocal aging", *Geriatrics*: 652–656.
Natale, Michael
1975 "Social desirability as related to convergence of temporal speech patterns", *Perceptual and motor skills* 40: 827-830.
Navas, Ricardo
1962 "Pausa, base verbal y grado cero", *Revista de filología española* 45: 273-284.
Newman, Stanley – Vera G. Mather
1938 "Analysis of spoken language of patients with affective disorders", *American journal of psychiatry* 94: 913-942.
Niepold, W.
1970 "Sprache und soziale Schicht" (privately published).
Norwine, A.C. – O.J. Murphy
1938 "Characteristic time intervals in telephonic conversation", *Bell systems technical journal* 17: 281-291.
O'Connell, Daniel C.
1977 "One of many units: the sentence", *Sentence production: developments in research and theory*, edited by Sheldon Rosenberg (Hillsdale, N.J.: Lawrence Erlbaum Associates), 307-313.
1980 "Cross-linguistic investigations of some temporal dimensions of speech", *Toward a cross-linguistic assessment of speech production*, edited by Hans-Wilhelm Dechert and Manfred Raupach (Frankfurt a.M.: Peter Lang), 23-38.
O'Connell, Daniel C. – Sabine H. Kowal
1972a "Cross-linguistic pause and rate phenomena in adults and adolescents", *Journal of psycholinguistic research* 1: 155-164.
1972b "Problems of measurement in psycholinguistic pause and rate research", *Proceedings* and *Abstract guide, XXth International Congress of Psychology* (Tokyo: Science Council of Japan), 348 and 386, respectively.
O'Connell, Daniel C. – Sabine H. Kowal – Hans Hörmann
1969 "Semantic determinants of pauses", *Psychologische Forschung* 33: 50–67.
Olson, Willard C. – Viola Schubart Koetzle
1936 "Amount and rate of talking of young children", *Journal of experimental education* 5: 175-179.
Orr, David B.
1968 "Time compressed speech – a perspective", *Journal of communication* 18: 288-292.
Osser, Harry – Frederick Peng
1964 "A cross cultural study of speech rate", *Language and speech* 7: 120-125.
Paivio, Allan
1963 "Audience influence, social isolation, and speech", *Journal of abnormal and social psychology* 67: 247-253.
Panek, David M. – Barclay Martin
1959 "The relationship between GSR and speech disturbances in psychotherapy", *Journal of abnormal and social psychology* 58: 402–405.
Parmenter, C.E. – S.N. Treviño
1935 "The length of the sounds of a Middle Westerner", *American speech* 10: 129-133.

Phillips, Jeanne S. – Ruth Matarazzo – Joseph D. Matarazzo – George Saslow – Frederick H. Kanfer

1961 "Relationships between descriptive content and interaction behavior in interviews", *Journal of consulting psychology* 25: 260-266.

Pike, Kenneth L.

1945 *The intonation of American English. University of Michigan Publications, Linguistics, Volume I* (Ann Arbor: University of Michigan).

1967 *Language in relation to a unified theory of the structure of human behavior* (The Hague: Mouton).

Pope, Benjamin – Aron W. Siegman

1962 "The effect of therapist verbal activity level and specificity on patient productivity and speech disturbances in the initial interview", *Journal of consulting psychology* 26: 489.

1964 "An intercorrelational study of some indices of verbal fluency", *Psychological reports* 15: 303-310.

1972 "Relationship and verbal behavior in the initial interview", *Studies in dyadic communication* (New York: Pergamon Press), 69-87.

Preston, Joan M. – R.C. Gardner

1967 "Dimensions of oral and written language fluency", *Journal of verbal learning and verbal behavior* 6: 936-945.

Publication manual of the American Psychological Association

1974 2nd ed. (Washington, D.C.: American Psychological Association).

Pürschel, Heiner

1975 *Pause und Kadenz: Interferenzerscheinungen bei der englischen Intonation deutscher Sprecher* (Tübingen: Max Niemeyer Verlag).

Quintilian

1958 *The Institutio Oratoria*, translated by H.E. Burler, vol. 4 (Cambridge: Harvard University Press).

Quinting, Gerd

1971 *Hesitation phenomena in adult aphasic and normal speech* (= *Janua Linguarum, series minor*, 126) (The Hague: Mouton).

Raffler-Engel, Walburga von – C.K. Sigelman

1971 "Rhythm, narration, description in the speech of black and white children", *Language sciences* 18: 9-14.

Ragsdale, J. Donald

1969 "Influences of sex, situation, and category differences on nonfluencies", *Central states speech journal* 20: 310-311.

1976 "Relationships between hesitation phenomena, anxiety, and self-control in a normal communication situation", *Language and speech* 19: 257-265.

Ramsay, R.W.

1968 "Speech patterns and personality", *Language and speech* 11: 54-63.

Ramsay, R.W. – L.N. Law

1966 "The measurement of duration of speech", *Language and speech* 9: 96-102.

Reich, Ben – Chris Sharma

1970 "A new device for speech pause analysis", *Journal of the Audio Engineering Society* 18: 68.

Reynolds, Allan – Allan Paivio

1968 "Cognitive and emotional determinants of speech", *Canadian journal of psychology* 22: 164-275.

Rieffert, J.B.

1932 "Sprechtypen", *Bericht über den XII. Kongreß der Deutschen Gesellschaft für Psychologie* (Jena: Verlag von Gustav Fischer), 409–412.

Rochester, S.R.

1973 "The significance of pauses in spontaneous speech", *Journal of psycholinguistic research* 2: 51-81.

1975-76 "Defining the silent pause in speech", *Journal of the Ontario Speech and Hearing Association* 8: 1–4.

Rochester, S.R. – Judith Gill

1973 "Production of complex sentences in monologues and dialogues", *Journal of verbal learning and verbal behavior* 12: 203-210.

Rochester, S.R. – Sharon Thurston – Judith Rupp

1977 "Hesitations as clues to failures in coherence: a study of the thought-disordered speaker", *Sentence production: developments in research and theory*, edited by Sheldon Rosenberg (Hillsdale, N.J.: Lawrence Erlbaum Associates), 65-87.

Rosenberg, Sheldon

1977 "Semantic constraints on sentence production: an experimental approach", *Sentence production: developments in research and theory*, edited by Sheldon Rosenberg (Hillsdale, N.J.: Lawrence Erlbaum Associates), 195-228.

Rowe, Mary Budd

1974 "Pausing phenomena: influence on the quality of instruction", *Journal of psycholinguistic research* 3: 203-224.

Ruder, Kenneth F.

1973 "Duration of silent interval as a perceptual cue of speech pauses", *Perceptual and motor skills* 36: 47-57.

Ruder, Kenneth F. – Paul J. Jensen

1972 "Fluent and hesitation pauses as a function of syntactic complexity", *Journal of speech and hearing research* 15: 49–60.

Ruesch, Jürgen – A. Rodney Prestwood

1949 "Anxiety: its initiation, communication and interpersonal management", *Archives of neurology and psychiatry* 62: 527-550.

Sabin, Edward J. – Edward J. Clemmer – Daniel C. O'Connell – Sabine Kowal

1979 "A pausological approach to speech development", *Of speech and time: temporal speech patterns in interpersonal contexts*, edited by Aron W. Siegman and Stanley Feldstein (Hillsdale, N.J.: Lawrence Erlbaum Associates), 35-55.

Saint-Bonnet, Monique – Jean-Louis Boe

1977 "Les pauses et les groupes rythmiques: leur durée et distribution en fonction de la vitesse d'élocution", *Journées d'étude sur la parole* 8: 337-343.

Samarin, William J.

1964 "The language of silence", *Practical anthropology* 11: 115-119.

Sansbury, David Lee

1969 *Silence as a variable in counseling interviews*, unpublished doctoral dissertation, Ohio State University.

Saslow, George – Joseph D. Matarazzo

1959 "A technique for studying changes in interview behavior", *Research in psychotherapy*, edited by E.A. Rubenstein and M.B. Parloff (Washington, D.C: American Psychological Association), 125-159.

Saslow, George – Joseph D. Matarazzo – S.B Guze
1955 "The stability of Interaction Chronograph patterns in psychiatric interviews", *Journal of consulting psychology* 19: 417–430.
Scherer, Klaus R. – Harvey London – Jared Wolf
1973 "The voice of confidence: paralinguistic cues and guidance evaluation", *Journal of research in personality* 7: 31–44.
Schulze, Gene – George F. Mahl – Jules D. Holzberg
1959 "A comparison of speech disturbance levels of paranoid schizophrenics and control subjects prior to and during exposure to an erotic stimulus", *American psychologist* 14: 403 (abstract).
Schulze, Gene – George F. Mahl – Edward J. Murray
1960 "Speech disturbances and content analysis categories as indices of underlying emotional states of patients in psychotherapy", *American psychologist* 15: 405 (abstract).
Schveiger, Paul
1973 "Review of *Hesitation phenomena in adult aphasic and normal speech* by G. Quinting", *Linguistics* 115: 120-126.
Schwartz, Joseph – Joseph Jaffe
1968 "Markovian prediction of sequential temporal patterns in spontaneous speech", *Language and speech* 11: 27-30.
Semiloff-Zelasko, Holly
1975 "Perception of speech style and rate in English", *Journal of the Acoustical Society of America* 58: 557 (abstract).
Sheerin, John B.
1944 "Monotonous preaching", *Homiletic and pastoral review* 44: 481–486.
Sheridan, Thomas
1787 *Courses of lecture on elocution* (London: J. Dodsley, Pall Mall).
Shipp, Thomas – Harry Hollien
1972 "Speech frequency and duration measures as a function of chronologic age", *Journal of the Acoustical Society of America* 51: 111 (abstract).
Shoen, Richard Lawrence
1975 *A developmental study of student speech fluency in responses to questions on cognitive levels*, unpublished doctoral dissertation, University of Massachusetts, Amherst, Massachusetts.
Siegman, Aron W. – Stanley Feldstein (eds)
1979 *Of speech and time: temporal speech patterns in interpersonal contexts* (Hillsdale, N.J.: Lawrence Erlbaum Associates).
Siegman, Aron W. – Benjamin Pope
1965 "Effects of question specificity and anxiety producing messages on verbal fluency in the initial interview", *Journal of personality and social psychology* 2: 522-530.
1972 "The effects of ambiguity and anxiety on interviewee verbal behavior", *Studies in dyadic communication*, edited by Aron Siegman and Benjamin Pope (New York: Pergamon Press), 29–68.
Silverman, Ellen-Marie
1971 "Generality of disfluency data collected from preschoolers", *Journal of speech and hearing research* 14: 84-91.
Silverman, Gerald
1973 "Redundancy, repetition and pausing in schizophrenic speech", *British journal of psychiatry* 122: 407–413.

Simkins, Lawrence
1963 "Modification of pausing behavior", *Journal of verbal learning and verbal behavior* 2: 462-469.

Snell, Ada L.F.
1918 *Contributions to rhetorical theory*, edited by Fred N. Scott, volume 8: *Pause: a study of its nature and its rhythmical function in verse, especially blank verse* (Ann Arbor, Michigan: The Ann Arbor Press).

Snidecor, J.C.
1943 "A comparative study of the pitch and duration characteristics of impromptu speaking and oral reading", *Speech monographs* 10: 50-56.

Spreen, Otfried – Robert S. Wachal
1973 "Psycholinguistic analysis of aphasic language: theoretical formulations and procedures", *Language and speech* 16: 130-146.

Steer, Angela B.
1974 "Sex differences, extraversion and neuroticism in relation to speech rate during the expression of emotion", *Language and speech* 17: 80-86.

Suci, George J.
1967 "The validity of pause as an index of units in language", *Journal of verbal learning and verbal behavior* 6: 26-32.

Szawara, Jill – Daniel C. O'Connell
1977 "Temporal reflections of spontaneity in homilies", *Bulletin of the Psychonomic Society* 9: 360-362.

Tannenbaum, Percy H. – Frederick Williams – Carolyn S. Hillier
1965 "Word predictability in the environments of hesitations", *Journal of verbal learning and verbal behavior* 4: 134-140.

Tannenbaum, Percy H. – Frederick Williams – Barbara S. Wood
1967 "Hesitation phenomena and related encoding characteristics in speech and typewriting", *Language and speech* 10: 203-215.

Taylor, Insup
1969 "Content and structure in sentence production", *Journal of verbal learning and verbal behavior* 8: 170-175.

Tindall, Ralph H. – Francis P. Robinson
1947 "The use of silence as a technique in counseling", *Journal of clinical psychology* 3: 136-141.

Toman, Walter
1953 "Pause analysis as a short interviewing technique", *Journal of consulting psychology* 17: 1-7.

Tosi, Oscar
1965 *A method for acoustic segmentation of continuous sound into pauses and signals and measurement of segment durations*, unpublished doctoral dissertation, Ohio State University.
1974a "Duration and measurement of pauses in speech", *Phonetic Papers*, edited by the Phonetic Society of Japan.
1974b "Pausometry: measurement of low levels of acoustic energy", *World papers in phonetics* (Tokyo: Phonetic Society of Japan), 129-144.

Tosi, Oscar – Brad Lashbrook
1970 "Pauses and circadian rhythm", *Journal of the Acoustic Society of America* 47: 67 (abstract).
1974 "Pauses and circadian rhythm", *Phonetic papers*, edited by the Phonetic Society of Japan.

Tosi, Oscar – Marsha A. Rockey – Roland Fischer
1968 "Quantitative measurement of time contraction induced by psilocybin", *Arzneimittel-Forschung* 18: 535-537.
Verzeano, Marcel – Jacob E. Finesinger
1949 "An automatic analyzer for the study of speech in interaction and in free association", *Science* 110: 45-46.
Wagoner, Lovisa C.
1925 "Speech as an indication of temperamental traits", *Quarterly journal of speech education* 11: 237-242.
Waldhorn, Herbert F.
1959 "The silent patient", *Journal of the American Psychoanalytic Association* 7: 548-560.
Walker, John
1811 *Elements of elocution* (Philadelphia: Ferrett and Walton).
Wallin, J.E.W.
1901 "Researches in the rhythm of speech", *Studies from the Yale Psychological Laboratory* 9: 1-142.
Webb, James T.
1969 "Subject speech rates as a function of interviewer behavior", *Language and speech* 12: 54-67.
Webb, Ralph – Frederick Williams – Fred D. Minifie
1967 "Effects of verbal decision behavior upon respiration during speech production", *Journal of speech and hearing research* 10: 49-56.
Weintraub, Walter – H. Aronson
1967 "The application of verbal behavior analysis to the study of psychological defense mechanisms. IV: Speech pattern associated with depressive behavior", *Journal of nervous and mental disease* 144: 22-28.
Weisman, Avery D.
1955 "Silence and psychotherapy", *Psychiatry* 18: 241-260.
Whalen, Suzanne
1976 "The suprasentential and the unstructured interview", *Psychological reports* 38: 155-162.
Wiens, Arthur N. – Thomas S. Manuagh – Jospeh D. Matarazzo
1976 "Speech and silence behavior of bilinguals conversing in each of two languages", *Linguistics* 152: 79-93.
Wiens, Arthur N. – Joseph D. Matarazzo – George Saslow
1965 "The interaction recorder: an electronic punched paper tape unit for recording speech behavior during interviews", *Journal of clinical psychology* 21: 142-145.
Wilkes, A.L.
1972 "Reading pauses during serial list learning with fixed or randomly changing groups", *Journal of experimental psychology* 94: 206-209.
Wilkes, A.L. – R.A. Kennedy
1969 "Relationship between pausing and retrieval latency in sentences of varying grammatical form", *Journal of experimental psychology* 79: 241-245.
1970 "The relative accessibility of list items within different pause-defined groups", *Journal of verbal learning and verbal behavior* 9: 197-201.
Wilkinson, Andrew
1971 *The foundations of language: talking and reading in young children* (London: Oxford University Press).

Williams, Frederick
1970 "Psychological correlates of speech characteristics: on sounding disadvantaged", *Journal of speech and hearing research* 13: 472–488.
Wingate, Marcel E.
1976 *Stuttering: theory and treatment* (New York: Wiley).
Wode, Henning
1968 "Pause und Pausenstelle im Deutschen", *Acta Linguistica Hafniensia* 11: 147–169.
Wolff, Dale Roland
1966 *The effects of stress on speech characteristics and perceived emotions of repressers and sensitizers*, unpublished doctoral dissertation, Washington University, St. Louis.
Woolbert, Charles H.
1920 "Effects of various modes of public reading", *Journal of applied psychology* 4: 162–185.
Wyckoff, W.L.
1973 "The effect of stimulus variation on learning from lecture", *Journal of experimental education* 41: 85–90.
Yairi, Ehud – Noel F. Clifton, Jr.
1972 "Disfluent speech behavior of preschool children, high school seniors, and geriatric persons", *Journal of speech and hearing research* 15: 714–719.
Zeligs, Meyer A.
1961 "The psychology of silence: its role in transference, countertransference and the psychoanalytic process", *Journal of the American Psychoanalytic Association* 9: 7–43.
Zimbardo, Philip G. – George F. Mahl – James W. Barnard
1963 "The measurement of speech disturbance in anxious children", *Journal of speech and hearing disorders* 28: 362–370.
Zuk, G.H.
1965 "On silence and babbling in family psychotherapy with schizophrenics", *Confinia Psychiatrica* 8: 49–56.

Bei Fragen zur Produktsicherheit wenden Sie sich bitte an:
If you have any questions regarding product safety,
please contact:

Walter de Gruyter GmbH
Genthiner Straße 13
10785 Berlin
productsafety@degruyterbrill.com